ZAGAT
2013

San Diego
City Guide

EDITORS
Seth Combs, Wendy Lemlin, David Nelson, Rebekah
Sagor and Julie Alvin

Published and distributed by
Zagat Survey, LLC
76 Ninth Avenue
New York, NY 10011
T: 212.977.6000
E: feedback@zagat.com
plus.google.com/local

ACKNOWLEDGMENTS

We're grateful to our local editors, Seth Combs, a freelance writer who has covered San Diego nightlife for *San Diego CityBeat* ("Shot on Scene") and *Riviera Magazine*; Wendy Lemlin, a writer who has lived in all four corners of the country but has been thrilled to call San Diego home since 2004; David Nelson, who has covered San Diego's Restaurant Row since 1980 as a columnist for the *Los Angeles Times, Westways* and *San Diego Magazine*; and Rebekah Sager, a San Diego–based culture and lifestyle writer and contributor to FOX News Latino; as well as contributors Chantal Gordon, Brandon Hernández and Maribeth Mellin. We also sincerely thank the thousands of people who participated in this survey – this guide is really "theirs."

We also thank Katie Carroll (editor), Chris Connolly, Gillian Flynn, Miles Sager and Jamie Selzer, as well as the following members of our staff: Aynsley Karps (editor), Brian Albert, Sean Beachell, Maryanne Bertollo, Reni Chin, Larry Cohn, John Deiner, Nicole Diaz, Kelly Dobkin, Jeff Freier, Alison Gainor, Curt Gathje, Matthew Hamm, Justin Hartung, Marc Henson, Ryutaro Ishikane, Natalie Lebert, Mike Liao, Vivian Ma, James Mulcahy, Polina Paley, Amanda Spurlock, Chris Walsh, Jacqueline Wasilczyk, Sharon Yates, Anna Zappia and Kyle Zolner.

ABOUT ZAGAT

In 1979, we asked friends to rate and review restaurants purely for fun. The term "user-generated content" had yet to be coined. That hobby grew into Zagat Survey; 34 years later, we have loyal surveyors around the globe and our content now includes nightlife, shopping, tourist attractions, golf and more. Along the way, we evolved from being a print publisher to a digital content provider. We also produce marketing tools for a wide range of corporate clients, and you can find us on Google+ and just about any other social media network.

Our reviews are based on public opinion surveys. The ratings reflect the average scores given by the survey participants who voted on each establishment. The text is based on quotes from, or paraphrasings of, the surveyors' comments. Phone numbers, addresses and other factual data were correct to the best of our knowledge when published in this guide.

JOIN IN

To improve our guides, we solicit your comments – positive or negative; it's vital that we hear your opinions. Just contact us at **nina-tim@zagat.com.** We also invite you to share your opinions at plus.google.com/local.

© 2012 Zagat Survey, LLC
ISBN-13: 978-1-60478-532-6
ISBN-10: 1-60478-532-2
Printed in the
United States of America

Contents

Ratings & Symbols

Name	Symbols		Cuisine	Zagat Ratings			
				FOOD	DECOR	SERVICE	COST

Area, Address & Contact

Tim & Nina's ◗ *Pizza*   ▽ 23 | 9 | 13 | $15

Gaslamp Quarter | 1000 Fifth Ave. (Market St.) | 619-555-1234 | www.zagat.com

Review, surveyor comments in quotes

"Peripatetic pizza purveyors" T & N have wandered back to San Diego, and acolytes are "thrilled" that the "smells of their pungent pies" – featuring "weird but wonderful" toppings like "mounds of offal" and Gorgonzola – once again fill the Gaslamp Quarter; still, critics cite a setting that "evokes a haunted boiler room" and service that "needs lots of help."

Ratings

On the Zagat 0 to 30 scale, covering key aspects of each category (e.g. Food, Decor, Service for Dining):

26 – 30   extraordinary to perfection
21 – 25   very good to excellent
16 – 20   good to very good
11 – 15   fair to good
0 – 10   poor to fair
▽   low response | less reliable

Cost

Dining: The price of dinner with a drink and tip. For unrated newcomers or write-ins, the price range is indicated as I ($25 and below); M ($26–$40); E ($41–$65); VE ($66 or above)

Sites & Attractions: High-season adult admission: $0 (free); I ($10 and below); M ($11–$25); E ($26–$40); VE ($41 or above)

All other costs are indicated as I (inexpensive); M (moderate); E (expensive); VE (very expensive); based on surveyor estimates.

Symbols

◗   dining: serves after 11 PM; shopping: usually open past 7 PM
Ⓢ   closed on Sunday
Ⓜ   closed on Monday
⊄   no credit cards accepted

About This Survey

- 11,658 surveyors
- Covering 624 restaurants, 190 nightspots, 316 shops and 29 sites and attractions
- Winners: **DINING: Sushi Ota** (Food), **Anthony's Fish Grotto** (Popularity); **NIGHTLIFE: Noble Experiment** (Atmosphere, Decor, Service), **Belly Up Tavern** (Popularity); **SHOPPING: Jerome's Furniture** (Popularity), **99 Ranch** (Popularity, Food and Wine); **ATTRACTIONS: San Diego Zoo** (Popularity, Appeal, Facilities, Service).

ON THE MENU: Japanese cuisine reigns supreme as **Sushi Ota** secures the area's highest Food score and recent additions like **Gaijin, Underbelly** and **Katsuya by Starck** pay tribute to the noodle house and the robata grill. Meanwhile, celeb chef Brian Malarkey expands his empire with newcomers **Gabardine, Gingham** and **Herringbone,** and diners continue to seek out local, seasonal and sustainable fare – newcomers like **Carnitas' Snack Shack** and **Table 926** fit the bill, as do trusted favorites like **Market** and **George's California Modern.**

RAISE A GROWLER: San Diego is to craft beer what Napa Valley is to wine, with connoisseurs countrywide coming to take tours and sample the suds at **Green Flash, Stone** and **Port** breweries (see Shopping: Food & Wine). Nightlife newcomers **Barleymash** and **Uptown Tavern** keep these labels on tap, as do favorites like **Blind Lady Ale House** and **Monkey Paw,** which brew their own too.

SHAKEN AND STIRRED: Recent entries like **The Propagandist** and **Seven Grand** signify a craft cocktail trend, while high scorers like **Prohibition, Vin de Syrah** and **Noble Experiment** – which won the Nightlife Survey's top honors for Atmosphere, Decor and Service – feature cleverly hidden entrances befitting the modern speakeasy. Other notable nightlife arrivals include **American Comedy Co.,** which attracts nationally known stand-ups acts, and **Block No. 16 Union & Spirits,** which challenges **Fluxx** and **Voyeur** for best Las Vegas imitation.

HOT SHOPS: San Diegans compete with Angelenos for SoCal style honors, turning to chic boutiques like La Jolla's **Pomegranate** or the new Solana Beach branch of **Gerhard,** as well as standbys like **Frock You** and **Hunt & Gather** for vintage looks. Active locals stock up on workout wear at high-scorers **Lululemon** and **Movin Shoes Running Center,** while surfers favor custom boards from **Bessell Surfboards** and lessons at **PB Surf Shop,** and skateboard buffs shop at new arrival **Adrenalina.**

SEE THE SIGHTS: The **San Diego Zoo** ranks as the city's most lauded attraction, winning top honors for Popularity, Appeal, Facilities and Service. The **Japanese Friendship Garden** in Balboa Park is undergoing a nine-acre expansion that includes plans for a traditional teahouse and a 300-seat pavilion. Visitors to the **Maritime Museum** can head to the nearby Spanish Landing build-site of the full-sized replica of Juan Rodriguez Cabrillo's famous *San Salvador* ship.

San Diego, CA   Seth Combs, David Nelson and Rebekah Sager
January 15, 2013

DINING

Most Popular

This list is plotted on the map at the back of this book.

1	Anthony's Fish | *Seafood*	**11**	333 Pacific | *Seafood/Steak*
2	Brigantine Seafood | *Seafood*	**12**	Burger Lounge | *Burgers*
3	Phil's BBQ | *BBQ*	**13**	Bertrand at Mister A's | *Amer.*
4	George's | *Californian*	**14**	Marine Room | *Eclectic/French*
5	94th Aero | *Amer./Steak*	**15**	Hodad's | *Burgers*
6	D.Z. Akin's | *Deli*	**16**	A.R. Valentien | *Calif.*
7	Donovan's Steak | *Steak*	**17**	Cucina Urbana | *Italian*
8	Broken Yolk Cafe | *American*	**18**	Arrivederci | *Italian*
9	Fish Market | *Seafood*	**19**	Mille Fleurs* | *French*
10	3rd Corner | *Californian*	**20**	Prado at Balboa Park | *Calif.*

MOST POPULAR CHAINS

1	In-N-Out | *Burgers*	**6**	Claim Jumper | *American*
2	Filippi's Pizza Grotto | *Italian*	**7**	Buca di Beppo | *Italian*
3	Outback Steakhse. | *Steak*	**8**	Ruth's Chris | *Steak*
4	Cheesecake Factory | *American*	**9**	BJ's | *Pub Food*
5	P.F. Chang's* | *Chinese*	**10**	Sammy's Woodfired | *Pizza*

Top Food

29 Sushi Ota | *Japanese*	Truluck's | *Seafood/Steak*
	Godfather | *Italian*
28 Tao | *Asian/Vegetarian*	George's | *Californian*
Market Rest. | *Californian*	Lefty's | *Pizza*
Tapenade | *French*	Bronx Pizza | *Pizza*
	Addison | *French*
27 Pamplemousse | *Amer./French*	
Vincent's | *French*	26 Dumpling Inn | *Chinese*
Ruth's Chris | *Steak*	Las Cuato Milpas | *Mexican*
Carnitas' | *Amer./Eclectic*	Tender Greens | *American*
Snooze | *American*	Costa Brava | *Spanish*
Donovan's Steak| *Steak*	In-N-Out | *Burgers*
West Steak | *Seafood/Steak*	Island Prime/C Level |
Blue Water Seafood | *Seafood*	*Seafood/Steak*
Mille Fleurs | *French*	Phil's BBQ | *BBQ*
Bertrand at Mister A's | *Amer.*	Farm House Café | *French*
Wine Vault | *Eclectic*	Bread & Cie | *Bakery*

BY CUISINE

AMERICAN (NEW)

27	Pamplemousse
	Carnitas'
	Snooze
25	Tractor Room
	Kitchen 1540

AMERICAN (TRAD.)

27	Bertrand at Mister A's
26	Bread & Cie
25	Original Pancake House
	Prepkitchen
	Cheesecake Factory

Excludes places with low votes; * indicates a tie with restaurant above

CALIFORNIAN

28 Market Rest.
27 George's
26 Paon
   Nine-Ten
   A.R. Valentien

FRENCH

28 Tapenade
27 Pamplemousse
   Vincent's
   Mille Fleurs
   Addison

ITALIAN

27 Godfather
26 Cucina Urbana
   Trattoria I Trulli
   Arrivederci
   Piatti

JAPANESE

29 Sushi Ota
26 Harney Sushi

   Nobu
25 Hane Sushi
   Sushi on the Rock

MEXICAN

26 Las Cuatro Milpas
   El Agave
   Chipotle
25 El Zarape
   Costa Azul Coronado

SEAFOOD

27 West Steak
   Blue Water Seafood
   Truluck's
26 Island Prime/C Level
   Point Loma Seafoods

STEAK

27 Ruth's Chris
   Donovan's Steak
   West Steak
   Truluck's
26 Island Prime/C Level

BY SPECIAL FEATURE

BREAKFAST/BRUNCH

27 Snooze
26 Farm House
   Mission
25 D.Z. Akin's
   Hash House

CHILD-FRIENDLY

25 Original Pancake House
24 BJ's
   Boomerangs Burgers
23 Sammy's Woodfired
20 Corvette Diner

HOTEL DINING

27 Addison (Grand Del Mar)
26 Nine-Ten (Grande Colonial)
   A.R. Valentien (Lodge/Torrey)
   Nobu (Hard Rock)
25 Roy's (Marriott Hotel/Marina)

NEWCOMERS (RATED)

27 Carnitas'
   Snooze
25 Slater's 50/50
24 Wang's North Park
23 Underbelly

OPEN LATE

26 Costa Brava
   In-N-Out

   Basic Urban
   URBN
   Harney Sushi

OUTDOOR DINING

26 Indigo Grill
   El Agave
   Mission
25 de'Medici
   La Bastide

QUIET CONVERSATION

28 Market Rest.
   Tapenade
27 Pamplemousse
   Vincent's
   Addison

ROMANTIC

28 Tapenade
27 Pamplemousse
   Vincent's
   Mille Fleurs
26 Paon

SINGLES SCENES

26 Farm House
   Fleming's
   Cucina Urbana
   Indigo Grill*
   Basic Urban

TRENDY

28 Tao
Market Rest.
Tapenade
26 Farm House
Cucina Urbana

VISITORS ON EXPENSE ACCOUNT

28 Market Rest.
Tapenade

27 Pamplemousse
Ruth's Chris
Donovan's Steak

WINNING WINE LISTS

28 Market Rest.
Tapenade
27 Pamplemousse
Vincent's
Mille Fleurs

BY LOCATION

BANKERS HILL

27 Bertrand at Mister A's
26 Cucina Urbana
25 Hane Sushi
Karen Krasne's Desserts
24 Bankers Hill

CORONADO

25 Costa Azul Coronado
Burger Lounge
24 1500 Ocean
Alexander's Pizza
Peohe's

DEL MAR/SOLANA BEACH

28 Market Rest.
27 Pamplemousse
Ruth's Chris
26 Del Mar Rendezvous
25 Del Mar Pizza
Kitchen 1540*

DOWNTOWN

27 Ruth's Chris
26 Hodad's
25 Roy's
Crab Hut
Morton's

GASLAMP QUARTER

27 Donovan's Steak
26 Fleming's Prime Steak
Rei do Gado
Nobu
Georges on Fifth

HILLCREST

27 Snooze
Bronx Pizza
26 Bread & Cie
Chipotle
Arrivederci

KEARNY MESA

27 Godfather
26 Dumpling Inn
In-N-Out
China Max
Bud's Louisiana Café

LA JOLLA

28 Tapenade
27 George's
26 Chipotle
Nine-Ten
Piatti

LITTLE ITALY

26 Indigo Grill
25 Extraordinary Desserts
Bencotto
Buon Appetito
Davanti Enoteca

NORTH PARK

27 Carnitas'
Lefty's
26 URBN
Urban Solace
Mission

PACIFIC BEACH

29 Sushi Ota
26 Costa Brava
In-N-Out
Chipotle
Rocky's Crown Pub

RANCHO BERNARDO/ RANCHO SANTA FE

27 Mille Fleurs
26 In-N-Out
25 Brett's BBQ
24 Bernard'O
Delicias

Top Decor

28 Bertrand at Mister A's	Truluck's
27 Marine Room	Mille Fleurs
Island Prime/C Level	Bali Hai
Stone World	Corvette Diner
George's	25 West Steak
JRDN	Wang's North Park
Prado at Balboa Park	Lei Lounge
Addison	Il Fornaio
26 Peohe's	Lou & Mickey's
Eddie V's	Burlap
Snooze	Casa de Pico
A.R. Valentien	Tractor Room
Hacienda de Vega*	Jake's Del Mar
Craft & Commerce	Anthology
Cucina Urbana	Donovan's Steak

OUTDOORS

A.R. Valentien	1500 Ocean
Bleu Bohème	Flavor Del Mar
Brockton Villa	George's (Ocean Terr.)
Busalacchi's A Modo Mio	Island Prime/C Level
Cafe Chloe	Pacifica Del Mar
Candelas on the Bay	333 Pacific

ROMANCE

Addison	Grant Grill
A.R. Valentien	Hexagone
Bernard'O	Kitchen 1540
Bertrand at Mister A's	Marine Room
Delicias	Mille Fleurs
George's (Calif. Modern)	Paon

ROOMS

Addison	Pamplemousse
Donovan's Steak	Paon
1500 Ocean	Po Pazzo
Grant Grill	Prado at Balboa Park
Mille Fleurs	Sally's Seafood
Morton's	Veladora

VIEWS

Brockton Villa	Marine Room
Eddie V's	Mistral
1500 Ocean	Pacifica Del Mar
Flavor Del Mar	Shores
George's (Calif. Modern)	South Beach B&G
JRDN	Steakhouse at Azul La Jolla

Top Service

Best Buys

In order of Bang for the Buck rating.

1. In-N-Out
2. Las Cuatro Milpas
3. Kono's Café
4. Rubio's
5. Lucha Libre
6. Five Guys
7. Habit Burger Grill
8. Babycakes
9. Pho T Cali
10. El Zarape
11. Chipotle
12. Bronx Pizza
13. Boudin Bakery
14. Cheese Shop
15. Del Mar Pizza
16. Big Kitchen
17. Hodad's
18. Chicken Pie Diner
19. Pizzeria Luigi
20. Bread & Cie

OTHER GOOD VALUES

Andre's Cuban & Puerto Rican
Big Kitchen
Blue Water Seafood
Boomerangs Burgers
Brazen BBQ
Brett's BBQ
Bud's Louisiana Café
Carnitas'
Crest Cafe
Dumpling Inn

Fidel's Little Mexico
Lefty's
Lorna's Italian Kitchen
Mama Testa
Original Pancake House
Rocky's Crown Pub
Slater's 50/50
Snooze
Tartine
Woodstock's Pizza

Dining Special Features

Listings cover the best in each category and include names, locations and Food ratings. Multi-location restaurants' features may vary by branch. These lists include low-vote places that do not qualify for top lists.

BREAKFAST

(See also Hotel Dining)

NEW Snooze | **Hillcrest**	27
Mission | **multi.**	26
D.Z. Akin's | **Grantville**	25
Hash House | **Hillcrest**	25
Shades Oceanfront | **Ocean Bch**	25
Fig Tree | **multi.**	25
Kono's Café | **Pacific Bch**	23
Broken Yolk | **Pacific Bch**	23
Harry's Coffee | **La Jolla**	23
Mimi's Cafe | **Mission Valley**	22
Hob Nob Hill | **Bankers Hill**	22
Ruby's Diner | **Carlsbad**	21

BRUNCH

Farm House | **University Hts**	26
Urban Solace | **North Pk**	26
Hash House | **Hillcrest**	25
Kitchen 4140 | **Morena District**	25
JRDN | **Pacific Bch**	24
Terra Amer. | **E San Diego**	24
Humphrey's | **Shelter Is**	24
NEW Veladora | **Rancho Santa Fe**	–

BUSINESS DINING

Primavera | **Coronado**	28
Tapenade | **La Jolla**	28
Vivace | **Carlsbad**	27
Pamplemousse | **Solana Bch**	27
Vincent's | **Escondido**	27
Ruth's Chris | **multi.**	27
Donovan's Stk. | **multi.**	27
Mistral | **Coronado**	27
Mille Fleurs | **Rancho Santa Fe**	27
Bertrand | **Bankers Hill**	27
George's Cal./Ocean | **La Jolla**	27
Fleming's | **Golden Triangle**	26
Nine-Ten | **La Jolla**	26
A.R. Valentien | **La Jolla**	26
Marine Rm. | **La Jolla**	26
WineSellar | **Sorrento Mesa**	26

Nobu | **Gaslamp Qtr**	26
Roy's | **Golden Triangle**	25
Kitchen 1540 | **Del Mar**	25
Morton's | **Downtown**	25
Oceanaire | **Gaslamp Qtr**	25
333 Pacific | **Oceanside**	25
Arterra | **Del Mar**	24
Bice | **Gaslamp Qtr**	24
Top/Market | **Downtown**	24
Hexagone | **Bankers Hill**	24
Roppongi | **La Jolla**	24
Delicias | **Rancho Santa Fe**	24
Cafe Japengo | **Golden Triangle**	24
Candelas | **Gaslamp Qtr**	24
Dobson's | **Downtown**	24
Donovan's Prime | **Gaslamp Qtr**	24
Blue Point | **Gaslamp Qtr**	23
NEW Veladora | **Rancho Santa Fe**	–

CELEBRITY CHEFS

Olivier Bioteau
Farm House | **University Hts**	26

Joe Busalacchi
Busalacchi's | **Hillcrest**	23

Jean-Michel Diot
Tapenade | **La Jolla**	28

Trey Foshee
George's Cal./Ocean | **La Jolla**	27

Vincent Grumel
Vincent's | **Escondido**	27

Bernard Guillas
Marine Rm. | **La Jolla**	26

Jeff Jackson
A.R. Valentien | **La Jolla**	26

Jason Knibb
Nine-Ten | **La Jolla**	26

Brian Malarkey
Searsucker | **Gaslamp Qtr**	24
Burlap | **Del Mar**	22
NEW Gingham | **La Mesa**	21

NEW Gabardine | **Pt Loma** 21
NEW Herringbone | **La Jolla** –

Nobu Matsuhisa
Nobu | **Gaslamp Qtr** 26

Paul McCabe
Delicias | **Rancho Santa Fe** 24

Mark Pelliccia
25 Forty Bistro | **Old Town** 23

Patrick Ponsaty
Mistral | **Coronado** 27

Wolfgang Puck
Jai | **La Jolla** 22

Brian Redzikowski
Flavor Del Mar | **Del Mar** 22

Carl Schroeder
Market | **Del Mar** 28
Bankers Hill | **Bankers Hill** 24

Jeffrey Strauss
Pamplemousse | **Solana Bch** 27

Martin Woesle
Mille Fleurs | **Rancho Santa Fe** 27

Su Mei Yu
Saffron | **Mission Hills** 24

Rama | **Gaslamp Qtr** 25
Cafe Chloe | **E Vill** 25
Roppongi | **La Jolla** 24
Peohe's | **Coronado** 24
Prado | **Balboa Pk** 24
Grant Grill | **Downtown** 24
Monsoon | **Gaslamp Qtr** 24
Bombay | **Hillcrest** 24
Candelas | **Gaslamp Qtr** 24
Sally's Seafood | **Downtown** 24
Ortega's | **Hillcrest** 23
Jsix | **E Vill** 23
Baleen | **Mission Bay** 23
Stone World | **Escondido** 23
Coronado Boathse. | **Coronado** 23
Masala | **Gaslamp Qtr** 23
Lei Lounge | **University Hts** 22
Vagabond | **South Pk** 21
Saltbox | **Downtown** 21
Po Pazzo | **Little Italy** 20
Hard Rock Cafe | **Gaslamp Qtr** 20
NEW Herringbone | **La Jolla** –
NEW Veladora | **Rancho Santa Fe** –

CHILD-FRIENDLY

(Alternatives to the usual fast-food places; * children's menu available)

Original Pancake* | **multi.** 25
BJ's* | **multi.** 24
Boomerangs* | **Clairemont** 24
Sammy's Pizza* | **multi.** 23
Corvette Diner* | **Pt Loma** 20

DRAMATIC INTERIORS

Market | **Del Mar** 28
Vivace | **Carlsbad** 27
Donovan's Stk. | **Golden Triangle** 27
Mille Fleurs | **Rancho Santa Fe** 27
Addison | **Carmel Valley** 27
Paon | **Carlsbad** 26
A.R. Valentien | **La Jolla** 26
Maitre D' | **La Jolla** 26
Nobu | **Gaslamp Qtr** 26
Tractor Rm. | **Hillcrest** 25
Karen Krasne's | **Little Italy** 25
Cowboy Star | **E Vill** 25

ENTERTAINMENT

(Call for days and times of performances)

Salvatore's | **Downtown** 25
Grant Grill | **Downtown** 24
Humphrey's | **Shelter Is** 24
Cafe Sevilla | **Gaslamp Qtr** 23
Croce's | **Gaslamp Qtr** 22
Anthology | **Downtown** 22
Hard Rock Cafe | **Gaslamp Qtr** 20
Dick's/Resort | **Gaslamp Qtr** 18

GREEN/LOCAL/ORGANIC

Market | **Del Mar** 28
Tender Greens | **multi.** 26
Urban Solace | **North Pk** 26
Prepkitchen | **multi.** 25
Burger Lounge | **multi.** 25
Jyoti-Bihanga | **Normal Heights** 24
Wild Note Cafe | **Solana Bch** 24
Ritual Tavern | **North Pk** 24
Zinc Cafe | **Solana Bch** 23

DINING

SPECIAL FEATURES

Solamar

Jsix | **E Vill** 23

St. James Ramada Hotel

Brian's | **Gaslamp Qtr** 23

Tower 23 Hotel

JRDN | **Pacific Bch** 24

U.S. Grant Hotel

Grant Grill | **Downtown** 24

Wyndham Stes.

333 Pacific | **Oceanside** 25

LATE DINING

(Weekday closing hour)

Costa Brava | 12 AM | **Pacific Bch** 26
In-N-Out | 1 AM | **multi.** 26
Basic Urban | 2 AM | **E Vill** 26
URBN | varies | **North Pk** 26
Harney Sushi | 12 AM | **multi.** 26
South Beach B&G | 2 AM | 26
Ocean Bch

El Zarape | 2 AM | **University Hts** 25
Turf Supper | 1 AM | **Golden Hill** 25
NEW Slater's 50/50 | 2 AM | 25
Pt Loma

Woodstock's | varies | **multi.** 25
Saska's | 12 AM | **Mission Bch** 25
Saigon/Fifth | 12 AM | **Hillcrest** 25
Etna Rest. | 2 AM | **E San Diego** 25
Chocolat Bistro/Crem. | 25
12 AM | **Gaslamp Qtr**

Habit Burger | 12 AM | 24
Carmel Mountain Ranch

BJ's | 12 AM | **multi.** 24
Neighborhood | 12 AM | **E Vill** 24
Nicky Rottens | 2 AM | **multi.** 24
Brian's | 24 hrs. | **Gaslamp Qtr** 23
NEW Brooklyn Girl | 12 AM | 23
Mission Hills

3rd Corner | 1 AM | **multi.** 23
Ortega's | 12 AM | **Hillcrest** 23
Alchemy | 12 AM | **South Pk** 23
Crest Cafe | 12 AM | **Hillcrest** 23
Red Fox Steakhouse | 12 AM | 23
North Pk

NEW Underbelly | 12 AM | 23
Little Italy

Bully's | 12 AM | **Del Mar** 23

NEW Cremolose | 12 AM | 23
Gaslamp Qtr

Studio Diner | 24 hrs. | 22
Kearny Mesa

Funky Garcia's | 2 AM | 22
Gaslamp Qtr

Fred's Mex. | varies | **multi.** 22
Bully's East | 12:15 AM | 22
Mission Valley

Rockin' Baja | 12 AM | **multi.** 22
Yard Hse. | varies | **Downtown** 22
Croce's | 12 AM | **Gaslamp Qtr** 22
Pink Noodle | varies | **Hillcrest** 22
Joe's Crab | 12 AM | **multi.** 22
Lei Lounge | 1 AM | **University Hts** 22
Baja Betty's | varies | **Hillcrest** 21
Nick's | 1 AM | **multi.** 21
West Coast Tav. | 2 AM | 21
North Pk

Analog Bar | 12 AM | **Gaslamp Qtr** 21
Gordon Biersch | 12:30 AM | 21
Mission Valley

Alfonso's | 2 AM | **La Jolla** 20
El Take It Easy | 12 AM | **North Pk** 20
City Deli/Bakery | 12 AM | 20
Hillcrest

East Lake/Vill./North Tav. | 20
varies | **multi.**

NEW Gaijin Noodle/Sake | 20
1 AM | **Gaslamp Qtr**

Glass Door | 12:30 AM | **Little Italy** 20
Gossip Grill | 1:30 AM | **Hillcrest** 20
Spot | 1 AM | **La Jolla** 20
Jose's Courtrm. | 12:30 AM | 19
La Jolla

Dick's/Resort | 12 AM | 18
Gaslamp Qtr

MEET FOR A DRINK

Tapenade | **La Jolla** 28
Vivace | **Carlsbad** 27
Pamplemousse | **Solana Bch** 27
Ruth's Chris | **multi.** 27
Donovan's Stk. | **Golden Triangle** 27
West Steak | **Carlsbad** 27
Mille Fleurs | **Rancho Santa Fe** 27
Bertrand | **Bankers Hill** 27
Truluck's | **Golden Triangle** 27

George's Cal./Ocean | **La Jolla** 27
Addison | **Carmel Valley** 27
Cucina Urbana | **Bankers Hill** 26
Paon | **Carlsbad** 26
El Agave | **Old Town** 26
Marine Rm. | **La Jolla** 26
URBN | **North Pk** 26
Roy's | **Golden Triangle** 25
Tractor Rm. | **Hillcrest** 25
Morton's | **Downtown** 25
Davanti Enoteca | **Little Italy** 25
Cowboy Star | **E Vill** 25
Saska's | **Mission Bch** 25
Cafe Chloe | **E Vill** 25
333 Pacific | **Oceanside** 25
Bleu Bohème | **Kensington** 24
Bankers Hill | **Bankers Hill** 24
Bice | **Gaslamp Qtr** 24
Hexagone | **Bankers Hill** 24
Roppongi | **La Jolla** 24
Searsucker | **Gaslamp Qtr** 24
Delicias | **Rancho Santa Fe** 24
JRDN | **Pacific Bch** 24
Grant Grill | **Downtown** 24
Steakhouse/Azul | **La Jolla** 24
Cafe Japengo | **Golden Triangle** 24
Vigilucci's | **Carlsbad** 24
Humphrey's | **Shelter Is** 24
Greystone | **Gaslamp Qtr** 24
Candelas | **Gaslamp Qtr** 24
Dobson's | **Downtown** 24
Neighborhood | **E Vill** 24
Sally's Seafood | **Downtown** 24
Donovan's Prime | **Gaslamp Qtr** 24
Ritual Tavern | **North Pk** 24
Sessions Public | **Pt Loma** 24
Nicky Rottens | **Gaslamp Qtr** 24
3rd Corner | **Ocean Bch** 23
Ortega's | **Hillcrest** 23
Jake's Del Mar | **Del Mar** 23
Blue Point | **Gaslamp Qtr** 23
Alchemy | **South Pk** 23
RA Sushi | **Downtown** 23
Craft/Commerce | **Little Italy** 23
Red Fox Steakhouse | **North Pk** 23
Avenue 5 | **Bankers Hill** 23

Bully's | **Del Mar** 23
Karl Strauss | **multi.** 23
Jayne's | **North Pk** 23
Busalacchi's | **Hillcrest** 23
Riviera Supper | **La Mesa** 23
Whisknladle | **La Jolla** 23
Masala | **Gaslamp Qtr** 23
Funky Garcia's | **Gaslamp Qtr** 22
Red Tracton's | **Solana Bch** 22
Burlap | **Del Mar** 22
Jimmy's Tavern | **Shelter Is** 22
Bully's East | **Mission Valley** 22
Croce's | **Gaslamp Qtr** 22
Anthology | **Downtown** 22
Flavor Del Mar | **Del Mar** 22
Lei Lounge | **University Hts** 22
Casa de Reyes | **Old Town** 21
Poseidon | **Del Mar** 21
Saltbox | **Downtown** 21
Alfonso's | **La Jolla** 20
East Lake/Vill./North Tav. | **E Vill** 20
Glass Door | **Little Italy** 20
Green Flash | **Pacific Bch** 20
Currant | **Downtown** 19
McP's Irish | **Coronado** 19
Dick's/Resort | **Gaslamp Qtr** 18

MICROBREWERIES

Pizza Port | **multi.** 25
Karl Strauss | **multi.** 23
Coronado Brew | **Coronado** 21
Gordon Biersch | **Mission Valley** 21

NEWCOMERS

Carnitas' | **North Pk** 27
Snooze | **Hillcrest** 27
Slater's 50/50 | **Pt Loma** 25
Wang's North Park | **North Pk** 24
Brooklyn Girl | **Mission Hills** 23
Underbelly | **Little Italy** 23
Table 926 | **Pacific Bch** 23
Cremolose | **Gaslamp Qtr** 23
Katsuya | **Downtown** 22
Gingham | **La Mesa** 21
Gabardine | **Pt Loma** 21
Gaijin Noodle/Sake | **Gaslamp Qtr** 20
Herringbone | **La Jolla** -

DINING

SPECIAL FEATURES

Mia Francesca | **Del Mar** ⊐

Veladora | **Rancho Santa Fe** ⊐

OUTDOOR DINING

Puerto La Boca | **Little Italy** 27

Solare | **Pt Loma** 27

George's Cal./Ocean | **La Jolla** 27

Island Prime | **Harbor Island** 26

Indigo Grill | **Little Italy** 26

El Agave | **Old Town** 26

Trattoria Fantastica | **Little Italy** 26

A.R. Valentien | **La Jolla** 26

Mission | **E Vill** 26

de'Medici | **Gaslamp Qtr** 25

La Bastide | **Scripps Ranch** 25

Buon Appetito | **Little Italy** 25

Kitchen 4140 | **Morena District** 25

Pacifica Del Mar | **Del Mar** 25

Kensington Grill | **Kensington** 25

Cafe Chloe | **E Vill** 25

333 Pacific | **Oceanside** 25

Bleu Bohème | **Kensington** 24

Lou/Mickey's | **Gaslamp Qtr** 24

1500 Ocean | **Coronado** 24

La Pizzeria | **Hillcrest** 24

Roppongi | **La Jolla** 24

Delicias | **Rancho Santa Fe** 24

Osteria Panevino | **Gaslamp Qtr** 24

Prado | **Balboa Pk** 24

Il Fornaio | **multi.** 24

Sally's Seafood | **Downtown** 24

Nicky Rottens | **Gaslamp Qtr** 24

Brockton Villa | **La Jolla** 23

Stone World | **Escondido** 23

Jayne's | **North Pk** 23

Busalacchi's | **Hillcrest** 23

La Taverna | **La Jolla** 22

Barbarella | **La Jolla** 22

Flavor Del Mar | **Del Mar** 22

Lei Lounge | **University Hts** 22

Candelas/Bay | **Coronado** 21

Poseidon | **Del Mar** 21

NEW Veladora | **Rancho Santa Fe** ⊐

PEOPLE-WATCHING

Tapenade | **La Jolla** 28

Pamplemousse | **Solana Bch** 27

Donovan's Stk. | **Golden Triangle** 27

Mille Fleurs | **Rancho Santa Fe** 27

Bertrand | **Bankers Hill** 27

George's Cal./Ocean | **La Jolla** 27

Cucina Urbana | **Bankers Hill** 26

Indigo Grill | **Little Italy** 26

Trattoria Fantastica | **Little Italy** 26

Hodad's | **Ocean Bch** 26

A.R. Valentien | **La Jolla** 26

Marine Rm. | **La Jolla** 26

Nobu | **Gaslamp Qtr** 26

Roy's | **Golden Triangle** 25

Tractor Rm. | **Hillcrest** 25

Taka | **Gaslamp Qtr** 25

Bencotto | **Little Italy** 25

Turf Supper | **Golden Hill** 25

Buon Appetito | **Little Italy** 25

Morton's | **Downtown** 25

Cowboy Star | **E Vill** 25

Oceanaire | **Gaslamp Qtr** 25

Saigon/Fifth | **Hillcrest** 25

Bice | **Gaslamp Qtr** 24

Roppongi | **La Jolla** 24

Searsucker | **Gaslamp Qtr** 24

Grant Grill | **Downtown** 24

Cafe Japengo | **Golden Triangle** 24

Dobson's | **Downtown** 24

Neighborhood | **E Vill** 24

Ritual Tavern | **North Pk** 24

Blue Point | **Gaslamp Qtr** 23

Alchemy | **South Pk** 23

Craft/Commerce | **Little Italy** 23

Jayne's | **North Pk** 23

Busalacchi's | **Hillcrest** 23

Riviera Supper | **La Mesa** 23

Burlap | **Del Mar** 22

Croce's | **Gaslamp Qtr** 22

Anthology | **Downtown** 22

Flavor Del Mar | **Del Mar** 22

Lei Lounge | **University Hts** 22

Baja Betty's | **Hillcrest** 21

Vagabond | **South Pk** 21

West Coast Tav. | **North Pk** 21

East Lake/Vill./North Tav. | **E Vill** 20

Currant | **Downtown** 19

McP's Irish | **Coronado** 19

Dick's/Resort | **Gaslamp Qtr** 18

POWER SCENES

Tapenade | **La Jolla** 20

Pamplemousse | **Solana Bch** 27

Ruth's Chris | **multi.** 27

Donovan's Stk. | **Golden Triangle** 27

Mille Fleurs | **Rancho Santa Fe** 27

Bertrand | **Bankers Hill** 27

Truluck's | **Golden Triangle** 27

George's Cal./Ocean | **La Jolla** 27

Fleming's | **Golden Triangle** 26

Cucina Urbana | **Bankers Hill** 26

A.R. Valentien | **La Jolla** 26

Marine Rm. | **La Jolla** 26

Nobu | **Gaslamp Qtr** 26

Roy's | **Golden Triangle** 25

Eddie V's | **La Jolla** 25

Bencotto | **Little Italy** 25

Morton's | **Downtown** 25

333 Pacific | **Oceanside** 25

Bice | **Gaslamp Qtr** 24

Top/Market | **Downtown** 24

Delicias | **Rancho Santa Fe** 24

Cafe Japengo | **Golden Triangle** 24

Vigilucci's | **Carlsbad** 24

Dobson's | **Downtown** 24

Donovan's Prime | **Gaslamp Qtr** 24

Blue Point | **Gaslamp Qtr** 23

Manhattan | **La Jolla** 23

Jai | **La Jolla** 22

Burlap | **Del Mar** 22

PRIVATE ROOMS

(Restaurants charge less at off
times; call for capacity)

Tapenade | **La Jolla** 28

Vivace | **Carlsbad** 27

Pamplemousse | **Solana Bch** 27

Ruth's Chris | **Del Mar** 27

Donovan's Stk. | **Golden Triangle** 27

Mille Fleurs | **Rancho Santa Fe** 27

Bertrand | **Bankers Hill** 27

George's Cal./Ocean | **La Jolla** 27

Addison | **Carmel Valley** 27

Fleming's | **multi.** 26

Nine-Ten | **La Jolla** 26

A.R. Valentien | **La Jolla** 26

WineSellar | **Sorrento Mesa** 26

Roy's | **Golden Triangle** 25

Morton's | **Downtown** 25

Pacifica Del Mar | **Del Mar** 25

Oceanaire | **Gaslamp Qtr** 25

Rama | **Gaslamp Qtr** 25

Salvatore's | **Downtown** 25

Arterra | **Del Mar** 24

Lou/Mickey's | **Gaslamp Qtr** 24

Bernard'O | **Rancho Bernardo** 24

Roppongi | **La Jolla** 24

Delicias | **Rancho Santa Fe** 24

Emerald Chinese | **Kearny Mesa** 24

Candelas | **Gaslamp Qtr** 24

Jasmine | **Kearny Mesa** 24

Ortega's | **Hillcrest** 23

Stone World | **Escondido** 23

Anthology | **Downtown** 22

NEW Veladora | **Rancho Santa Fe** –

PRIX FIXE MENUS

(Call for prices and times)

Market | **Del Mar** 28

Tapenade | **La Jolla** 28

Mille Fleurs | **Rancho Santa Fe** 27

George's Cal./Ocean | **La Jolla** 27

Addison | **Carmel Valley** 27

Nine-Ten | **La Jolla** 26

WineSellar | **Sorrento Mesa** 26

Blue Point | **Gaslamp Qtr** 23

QUICK BITES

Tender Greens | **Pt Loma** 26

Bread & Cie | **Hillcrest** 10

Basic Urban | **E Vill** 26

URBN | **North Pk** 26

Girard Gourmet | **La Jolla** 25

Woodstock's | **multi.** 25

Pizza Port | **multi.** 25

Prepkitchen | **La Jolla** 25

Jyoti-Bihanga | **Normal Heights** 24

Opera Café | **Serra Mesa** 24

Boomerangs | **Clairemont** 24

Cheese Shop | **Gaslamp Qtr** 24

Emerald Chinese | **Kearny Mesa** 24

Neighborhood | **E Vill**	24
Saffron | **Mission Hills**	24
Lucha Libre | **Mission Hills**	23
Come On In | **multi.**	23
Zinc Cafe | **Solana Bch**	23
Islands | **multi.**	23
Funky Garcia's | **Gaslamp Qtr**	22
Pei Wei | **multi.**	21
Dick's/Resort | **Gaslamp Qtr**	18

QUIET CONVERSATION

Primavera | **Coronado**	28
Market | **Del Mar**	28
Tapenade | **La Jolla**	28
Vivace | **Carlsbad**	27
Pamplemousse | **Solana Bch**	27
Vincent's | **Escondido**	27
Ruth's Chris | **Del Mar**	27
Mistral | **Coronado**	27
Mille Fleurs | **Rancho Santa Fe**	27
George's Cal./Ocean | **La Jolla**	27
Addison | **Carmel Valley**	27
Nine-Ten | **La Jolla**	26
Maitre D' | **La Jolla**	26
WineSellar | **Sorrento Mesa**	26
Morton's | **Downtown**	25
Caffe Bella | **Pacific Bch**	25
Cafe Chloe | **E Vill**	25
Saigon/Fifth | **Hillcrest**	25
Salvatore's | **Downtown**	25
Bice | **Gaslamp Qtr**	24
Hexagone | **Bankers Hill**	24
Palm | **Downtown**	24
Grant Grill | **Downtown**	24
Andiamo | **Tierrasanta**	24
Shores | **La Jolla**	24
Au Revoir | **Hillcrest**	24
Antica Trattoria | **La Mesa**	23
3rd Corner | **Ocean Bch**	23
Kous Kous | **Hillcrest**	23
Jsix | **E Vill**	23
Red Door | **Mission Hills**	23
Avenue 5 | **Bankers Hill**	23
Jayne's | **North Pk**	23
Busalacchi's | **Hillcrest**	23

Whisknladle | **La Jolla**	23
Zenbu Sushi | **La Jolla**	22
Barolo | **University City**	22
Cody's La Jolla | **La Jolla**	22
Lotus Thai | **multi.**	22
La Taverna | **La Jolla**	22
Olivetto | **Mission Hills**	21
Saltbox | **Downtown**	21
Glass Door | **Little Italy**	20
Cosmopolitan Rest. | **Old Town**	20
Currant | **Downtown**	19
NEW Veladora | **Rancho Santa Fe**	–

RAW BARS

Pacifica Del Mar | **Del Mar**	25
Fish Market | **multi.**	25
Oceanaire | **Gaslamp Qtr**	25
333 Pacific | **Oceanside**	25
Top/Market | **Downtown**	24
Brigantine | **multi.**	24
King's Fish | **multi.**	24
Blue Point | **Gaslamp Qtr**	23
Tin Fish | **Pt Loma**	22
Crab Catcher | **La Jolla**	22
Harbor House | **Downtown**	21

ROMANTIC PLACES

Trattoria/Vecchio | **Del Mar**	28
Primavera | **Coronado**	28
Market | **Del Mar**	28
Tapenade | **La Jolla**	28
Vivace | **Carlsbad**	27
Pamplemousse | **Solana Bch**	27
Vincent's | **Escondido**	27
Mistral | **Coronado**	27
Mille Fleurs | **Rancho Santa Fe**	27
Bertrand | **Bankers Hill**	27
George's Cal./Ocean | **La Jolla**	27
Addison | **Carmel Valley**	27
Paon | **Carlsbad**	26
Trattoria I Trulli | **Encinitas**	26
Nine-Ten | **La Jolla**	26
A.R. Valentien | **La Jolla**	26
Marine Rm. | **La Jolla**	26
Maitre D' | **La Jolla**	26
WineSellar | **Sorrento Mesa**	26
Kitchen 1540 | **Del Mar**	25

Rama	**Gaslamp Qtr**	25
Cafe Chloe	**E Vill**	25
Saigon/Fifth	**Hillcrest**	25
Salvatore's	**Downtown**	25
Bleu Bohème	**Kensington**	24
Bernard'O	**Rancho Bernardo**	24
Hexagone	**Bankers Hill**	24
Delicias	**Rancho Santa Fe**	24
Grant Grill	**Downtown**	24
Steakhouse/Azul	**La Jolla**	24
Vigilucci's	**Carlsbad**	24
Monsoon	**Gaslamp Qtr**	24
Au Revoir	**Hillcrest**	24
Candelas	**Gaslamp Qtr**	24
Sally's Seafood	**Downtown**	24
Sapori	**Coronado**	24
Kous Kous	**Hillcrest**	23
Ortega's	**Hillcrest**	23
Manhattan	**La Jolla**	23
Red Door	**Mission Hills**	23
Jayne's	**North Pk**	23
Busalacchi's	**Hillcrest**	23
Old Trieste	**Bay Pk**	23
Whisknladle	**La Jolla**	23
La Taverna	**La Jolla**	22
Olivetto	**Mission Hills**	21
Candelas/Bay	**Coronado**	21
Glass Door	**Little Italy**	20
NEW Veladora	**Rancho Santa Fe**	-

SINGLES SCENES

Farm House	**University Hts**	26
Fleming's	**multi.**	26
Cucina Urbana	**Bankers Hill**	26
Indigo Grill	**Little Italy**	26
Basic Urban	**E Vill**	26
URBN	**North Pk**	26
Roy's	**Golden Triangle**	25
Tractor Rm.	**Hillcrest**	25
Turf Supper	**Golden Hill**	25
Cowboy Star	**E Vill**	25
Saska's	**Mission Bch**	25
Bankers Hill	**Bankers Hill**	24
Searsucker	**Gaslamp Qtr**	24
JRDN	**Pacific Bch**	24
Vigilucci's	**Carlsbad**	24

Neighborhood	**E Vill**	24
Ritual Tavern	**North Pk**	24
Nicky Rottens	**Gaslamp Qtr**	24
Ortega's	**Hillcrest**	23
Jsix	**E Vill**	23
Alchemy	**South Pk**	23
RA Sushi	**Downtown**	23
Craft/Commerce	**Little Italy**	23
Red Fox Steakhouse	**North Pk**	23
Bully's	**Del Mar**	23
Karl Strauss	**multi.**	23
Jayne's	**North Pk**	23
Riviera Supper	**La Mesa**	23
Funky Garcia's	**Gaslamp Qtr**	22
Burlap	**Del Mar**	22
Jimmy's Tavern	**Shelter Is**	22
Bully's East	**Mission Valley**	22
Yard Hse.	**Downtown**	22
Anthology	**Downtown**	22
Lei Lounge	**University Hts**	22
Baja Betty's	**Hillcrest**	21
Nick's	**Ocean Bch**	21
West Coast Tav.	**North Pk**	21
El Take It Easy	**North Pk**	20
East Lake/Vill./North Tav.	**E Vill**	20
Green Flash	**Pacific Bch**	20

SPECIAL OCCASIONS

Tapenade	**La Jolla**	28
Vivace	**Carlsbad**	27
Pamplemousse	**Solana Bch**	27
Vincent's	**Escondido**	27
Ruth's Chris	**multi.**	27
Donovan's Stk.	**Golden Triangle**	27
Mistral	**Coronado**	27
Mille Fleurs	**Rancho Santa Fe**	27
Bertrand	**Bankers Hill**	27
Solare	**Pt Loma**	27
Truluck's	**Golden Triangle**	27
George's Cal./Ocean	**La Jolla**	27
Paon	**Carlsbad**	26
A.R. Valentien	**La Jolla**	26
WineSellar	**Sorrento Mesa**	26
Nobu	**Gaslamp Qtr**	26
Roy's	**Golden Triangle**	25
Eddie V's	**La Jolla**	25

DINING

SPECIAL FEATURES

Kitchen 1540 | **Del Mar**	25
Morton's | **Downtown**	25
Cowboy Star | **E Vill**	25
333 Pacific | **Oceanside**	25
Arterra | **Del Mar**	24
Bice | **Gaslamp Qtr**	24
Top/Market | **Downtown**	24
Roppongi | **La Jolla**	24
Vigilucci's | **Carlsbad**	24
Donovan's Prime | **Gaslamp Qtr**	24
Manhattan | **La Jolla**	23
Busalacchi's | **Hillcrest**	23
Burlap | **Del Mar**	22
Anthology | **Downtown**	22
Flavor Del Mar | **Del Mar**	22

THEME RESTAURANTS

Benihana | **multi.**	25
Peohe's | **Coronado**	24
Corvette Diner | **Pt Loma**	20
Hard Rock Cafe | **Gaslamp Qtr**	20

TRENDY

Tao | **Normal Heights**	28
Market | **Del Mar**	28
Farm House | **University Hts**	26
Cucina Urbana | **Bankers Hill**	26
Indigo Grill | **Little Italy**	26
Paon | **Carlsbad**	26
Basic Urban | **E Vill**	26
URBN | **North Pk**	26
Urban Solace | **North Pk**	26
Roy's | **Golden Triangle**	25
Tractor Rm. | **Hillcrest**	25
Eddie V's | **La Jolla**	25
Bencotto | **Little Italy**	25
Rama | **Gaslamp Qtr**	25
Cafe Chloe | **E Vill**	25
333 Pacific | **Oceanside**	25
Chocolat Bistro/Crem. | **multi.**	25
Bleu Bohème | **Kensington**	24
Bankers Hill | **Bankers Hill**	24
BO-beau | **Ocean Bch**	24
Roppongi | **La Jolla**	24
Searsucker | **Gaslamp Qtr**	24
Delicias | **Rancho Santa Fe**	24

JRDN | **Pacific Bch**	24
Cafe Japengo | **Golden Triangle**	24
Neighborhood | **E Vill**	24
Donovan's Prime | **Gaslamp Qtr**	24
Ritual Tavern | **North Pk**	24
Sessions Public | **Pt Loma**	24
Mama Testa | **Hillcrest**	23
Ortega's | **Hillcrest**	23
Spice & Rice | **La Jolla**	23
Alchemy | **South Pk**	23
Craft/Commerce | **Little Italy**	23
Avenue 5 | **Bankers Hill**	23
Jayne's | **North Pk**	23
Busalacchi's | **Hillcrest**	23
Riviera Supper | **La Mesa**	23
Whisknladle | **La Jolla**	23
Burlap | **Del Mar**	22
Anthology | **Downtown**	22
Linkery | **North Pk**	22
Flavor Del Mar | **Del Mar**	22
Lei Lounge | **University Hts**	22
Baja Betty's | **Hillcrest**	21
Vagabond | **South Pk**	21
West Coast Tav. | **North Pk**	21
Saltbox | **Downtown**	21
East Lake/Vill./North Tav. | **E Vill**	20

VIEWS

Mistral | **Coronado**	27
Bertrand | **Bankers Hill**	27
George's Cal./Ocean | **La Jolla**	27
Marine Rm. | **La Jolla**	26
South Beach B&G | **Ocean Bch**	26
Eddie V's | **La Jolla**	25
Shades Oceanfront | **Ocean Bch**	25
Pacifica Del Mar | **Del Mar**	25
333 Pacific | **Oceanside**	25
1500 Ocean | **Coronado**	24
Brigantine | **Pt Loma**	24
JRDN | **Pacific Bch**	24
Steakhouse/Azul | **La Jolla**	24
Shores | **La Jolla**	24
Sally's Seafood | **Downtown**	24
Anthony's | **multi.**	24
Kono's Café | **Pacific Bch**	23
Sbicca | **Del Mar**	23

Baleen | **Mission Bay** 23
Brockton Villa | **La Jolla** 23
Crab Catcher | **La Jolla** 22
Tom Ham's | **Harbor Island** 22
Flavor Del Mar | **Del Mar** 22
Ruby's Diner | **Oceanside** 21
Nick's | **Ocean Bch** 21
Candelas/Bay | **Coronado** 21
Poseidon | **Del Mar** 21
Green Flash | **Pacific Bch** 20

VISITORS ON EXPENSE ACCOUNT

Market | **Del Mar** 28
Tapenade | **La Jolla** 28
Vivace | **Carlsbad** 27
Pamplemousse | **Solana Bch** 27
Ruth's Chris | **multi.** 27
Donovan's Stk. | **Golden Triangle** 27
West Steak | **Carlsbad** 27
Mille Fleurs | **Rancho Santa Fe** 27
Bertrand | **Bankers Hill** 27
Truluck's | **Golden Triangle** 27
George's Cal./Ocean | **La Jolla** 27
Addison | **Carmel Valley** 27
Island Prime | **Harbor Island** 26
Paon | **Carlsbad** 26
Nine-Ten | **La Jolla** 26
A.R. Valentien | **La Jolla** 26
Marine Rm. | **La Jolla** 26
Maitre D' | **La Jolla** 26
WineSellar | **Sorrento Mesa** 26
Nobu | **Gaslamp Qtr** 26
Roy's | **Golden Triangle** 25
Eddie V's | **La Jolla** 25
Kitchen 1540 | **Del Mar** 25
Morton's | **Downtown** 25
Cowboy Star | **E Vill** 25
Salvatore's | **Downtown** 25
333 Pacific | **Oceanside** 25
1500 Ocean | **Coronado** 24
Bice | **Gaslamp Qtr** 24
Top/Market | **Downtown** 24
Roppongi | **La Jolla** 24
Searsucker | **Gaslamp Qtr** 24
Palm | **Downtown** 24
Delicias | **Rancho Santa Fe** 24

JRDN | **Pacific Bch** 24
Grant Grill | **Downtown** 24
Steakhouse/Azul | **La Jolla** 24
Cafe Japengo | **Golden Triangle** 24
Vigilucci's | **Carlsbad** 24
Candelas | **Gaslamp Qtr** 24
Dobson's | **Downtown** 24
Sally's Seafood | **Downtown** 24
Donovan's Prime | **Gaslamp Qtr** 24
Jake's Del Mar | **Del Mar** 23
Blue Point | **Gaslamp Qtr** 23
Jsix | **E Vill** 23
RA Sushi | **Downtown** 23
McCormick/Schmick | **E Vill** 23
Busalacchi's | **Hillcrest** 23
Zenbu Sushi | **La Jolla** 22
Red Tracton's | **Solana Bch** 22
Burlap | **Del Mar** 22
Crab Catcher | **La Jolla** 22
Acqua Al 2 | **Gaslamp Qtr** 22
Anthology | **Downtown** 22
Flavor Del Mar | **Del Mar** 22
Red Pearl | **Gaslamp Qtr** 21
Po Pazzo | **Little Italy** 20
Glass Door | **Little Italy** 20
NEW Veladora | **Rancho Santa Fe** —

WATERSIDE

Marine Rm. | **La Jolla** 26
Eddie V's | **La Jolla** 25
Shades Oceanfront | **Ocean Bch** 25
Fish Market | **Downtown** 25
1500 Ocean | **Coronado** 24
Peohe's | **Coronado** 24
JRDN | **Pacific Bch** 24
Il Fornaio | **multi.** 24
Shores | **La Jolla** 24
Sally's Seafood | **Downtown** 24
Anthony's | **Downtown** 24
Kono's Café | **Pacific Bch** 23
Jake's Del Mar | **Del Mar** 23
Brockton Villa | **La Jolla** 23
Bali Hai | **Shelter Is** 23
Coronado Boathse. | **Coronado** 23
Cody's La Jolla | **La Jolla** 22
Crab Catcher | **La Jolla** 22

Harbor House | **Downtown**	21	Kitchen 1540 | **Del Mar**	25
Poseidon | **Del Mar**	21	Morton's | **Downtown**	25
Green Flash | **Pacific Bch**	20	Cowboy Star | **E Vill**	25

WINE BARS

		Oceanaire | **Gaslamp Qtr**	25
Pappalecco | **Hillcrest**	27	Cafe Chloe | **E Vill**	25
Fleming's | **Gaslamp Qtr**	26	Arterra | **Del Mar**	24
Davanti Enoteca | **multi.**	25	Roppongi | **La Jolla**	24
Chocolat Bistro/Crem. | **Hillcrest**	25	Grant Grill | **Downtown**	24
		Greystone | **Gaslamp Qtr**	24
Red Door | **Mission Hills**	23	Shores | **La Jolla**	24
Villa Capri | **Poway**	23	Donovan's Prime | **Gaslamp Qtr**	24
Olivetto | **Mission Hills**	21	3rd Corner | **Ocean Bch**	23

WINNING WINE LISTS

		Jsix | **E Vill**	23
		Whisknladle | **La Jolla**	23
Market | **Del Mar**	28	Zenbu Sushi | **La Jolla**	22
Tapenade | **La Jolla**	28	NEW Veladora | **Rancho Santa Fe**	–
Vivace | **Carlsbad**	27

WORTH A TRIP

Pamplemousse | **Solana Bch**	27	Carlsbad	
Vincent's | **Escondido**	27	West Steak	27
Ruth's Chris | **multi.**	27	Paon	26
Donovan's Stk. | **Golden Triangle**	27	Coronado	
West Steak | **Carlsbad**	27	Primavera	28
Mistral | **Coronado**	27	Del Mar	
Mille Fleurs | **Rancho Santa Fe**	27	Market	28
Bertrand | **Bankers Hill**	27	Arterra	24
Truluck's | **Golden Triangle**	27	Escondido	
George's Cal./Ocean | **La Jolla**	27	Vincent's	27
Addison | **Carmel Valley**	27	Stone World	23
Fleming's | **Golden Triangle**	26	Oceanside	
Cucina Urbana | **Bankers Hill**	26	333 Pacific	25
Paon | **Carlsbad**	26	Rancho Santa Fe	
Nine-Ten | **La Jolla**	26	Mille Fleurs	27
Piatti | **La Jolla**	26	NEW Veladora	–
A.R. Valentien | **La Jolla**	26	Solana Beach	
Marine Rm. | **La Jolla**	26	Pamplemousse	27
WineSellar | **Sorrento Mesa**	26	Red Tracton's	22
Roy's | **Golden Triangle**	25

Dining Cuisines

Includes names, locations and Food ratings. These lists include low-vote places that do not qualify for top lists.

AFGHAN

Khyber Pass | **Hillcrest** 25

AMERICAN

Pamplemousse | **Solana Bch** 27
NEW Carnitas' | **North Pk** 27
NEW Snooze | **Hillcrest** 27
Bertrand | **Bankers Hill** 27
Smoking Goat | **North Pk** 27
Tender Greens | **multi.** 26
Bread & Cie | **Hillcrest** 26
Urban Solace | **North Pk** 26
Tractor Rm. | **Hillcrest** 25
Hash House | **Hillcrest** 25
Kitchen 1540 | **Del Mar** 25
Kitchen 4140 | **Morena District** 25
Shades Oceanfront | **Ocean Bch** 25
Original Pancake | **multi.** 25
Cowboy Star | **E Vill** 25
Prepkitchen | **multi.** 25
Big Kitchen | **South Pk** 25
Cheesecake Factory | **multi.** 25
Kensington Grill | **Kensington** 25
Amaya | **Carmel Valley** 25
Rhino Cafe/Grill | **Coronado** 25
Arterra | **Del Mar** 24
Bankers Hill | **Bankers Hill** 24
Searsucker | **Gaslamp Qtr** 24
Terra Amer. | **E San Diego** 24
Cafe on Park | **Hillcrest** 24
Tony Roma's | **Pacific Bch** 24
Cheese Shop | **Gaslamp Qtr** 24
Neighborhood | **E Vill** 24
Claim Jumper | **multi.** 24
Ritual Tavern | **North Pk** 24
Nicky Rottens | **multi.** 24
NEW Brooklyn Girl | **Mission Hills** 23
Kono's Café | **Pacific Bch** 23
Cafe 222 | **Downtown** 23
Chicken Pie | **Poway** 23
Parkhouse | **University Hts** 23
San Diego Chicken | **North Pk** 23

Crest Cafe | **Hillcrest** 23
Red Door | **Mission Hills** 23
Harry's B&G | **Golden Triangle** 23
Sbicca | **Del Mar** 23
Broken Yolk | **multi.** 23
Craft/Commerce | **Little Italy** 23
Come On In | **multi.** 23
Avenue 5 | **Bankers Hill** 23
Ricky's | **Mission Valley** 23
Karl Strauss | **multi.** 23
Harry's Coffee | **La Jolla** 23
Islands | **multi.** 23
Grill/Torrey Pines | **La Jolla** 23
Richard Walker's | **Downtown** 23
Cody's La Jolla | **La Jolla** 22
Forever Fondue | **La Jolla** 22
Burlap | **Del Mar** 22
Beach Grass | **Solana Bch** 22
Jimmy's Tavern | **Shelter Is** 22
94th Aero | **Kearny Mesa** 22
Yard Hse. | **Downtown** 22
Croce's | **Gaslamp Qtr** 22
Mimi's Cafe | **multi.** 22
Americana | **Del Mar** 22
Hob Nob Hill | **Bankers Hill** 22
Ruby's Diner | **multi.** 21
NEW Gingham | **La Mesa** 21
Nick's | **multi.** 21
West Coast Tav. | **North Pk** 21
Saltbox | **Downtown** 21
Gordon Biersch | **Mission Valley** 21
Union Kitchen | **Encinitas** 21
Corvette Diner | **Pt Loma** 20
East Lake/Vill./North Tav. | **multi.** 20
Glass Door | **Little Italy** 20
Gossip Grill | **Hillcrest** 20
Hard Rock Cafe | **Gaslamp Qtr** 20
Spot | **La Jolla** 20
Cosmopolitan Rest. | **Old Town** 20
Dick's/Resort | **Gaslamp Qtr** 18
Maryjane's | **Gaslamp Qtr** 17

ARGENTINEAN

Puerto La Boca | **Little Italy** — 27

ASIAN

Tao | **Normal Heights** — 28
Mission | **multi.** — 26
Roy's | **multi.** — 25
Sally's Seafood | **Downtown** — 24
Jai | **La Jolla** — 22
Burlap | **Del Mar** — 22
Red Pearl | **Gaslamp Qtr** — 21
Pei Wei | **multi.** — 21

BAKERIES

Bread & Cie | **Hillcrest** — 26
Babycakes | **Hillcrest** — 25
Boudin Bakery | **multi.** — 22

BARBECUE

Phil's BBQ | **multi.** — 26
Brett's BBQ | **multi.** — 25
Coops BBQ | **Lemon Grove** — 24
Tony Roma's | **Pacific Bch** — 24
Brazen BBQ | **Hillcrest** — 23
Abbey's Real TX | **Mira Mesa** — 22

BELGIAN

Girard Gourmet | **La Jolla** — 25

BRAZILIAN

Rei do Gado | **Gaslamp Qtr** — 26

BURGERS

In-N-Out | **multi.** — 26
Hodad's | **multi.** — 26
Rocky's Crown | **Pacific Bch** — 26
NEW Slater's 50/50 |
  Pt Loma — 25
Burger Lounge | **multi.** — 25
Habit Burger | **multi.** — 24
Crazee Burger | **Old Town** — 24
Boomerangs | **Clairemont** — 24
Neighborhood | **E Vill** — 24
Nicky Rottens | **Gaslamp Qtr** — 24
Counter | **multi.** — 23
Islands | **multi.** — 23
Five Guys | **multi.** — 23
Fatburger | **multi.** — 21

CAJUN

Crab Hut | **multi.** — 25

CALIFORNIAN

Market | **Del Mar** — 28
George's Cal./Ocean | **La Jolla** — 27
Paon | **Carlsbad** — 26
Nine-Ten | **La Jolla** — 26
A.R. Valentien | **La Jolla** — 26
Café 21 | **North Pk** — 25
Fig Tree | **multi.** — 25
Pacifica Breeze | **Del Mar** — 24
1500 Ocean | **Coronado** — 24
Bernard'O | **Rancho Bernardo** — 24
Adams Ave. | **University Hts** — 24
Delicias | **Rancho Santa Fe** — 24
Wild Note Cafe | **Solana Bch** — 24
JRDN | **Pacific Bch** — 24
Prado | **Balboa Pk** — 24
Grant Grill | **Downtown** — 24
Cottage | **La Jolla** — 24
Humphrey's | **Shelter Is** — 24
Shores | **La Jolla** — 24
Dobson's | **Downtown** — 24
3rd Corner | **multi.** — 23
Belle Fleur | **Carlsbad** — 23
Jake's Del Mar | **Del Mar** — 23
Jsix | **E Vill** — 23
Sheerwater | **Coronado** — 23
NEW Table 926 | **Pacific Bch** — 23
Brockton Villa | **La Jolla** — 23
Zodiac/Neiman Marcus |
  Mission Valley — 23
Whisknladle | **La Jolla** — 23
Tom Ham's | **Harbor Island** — 22
Anthology | **Downtown** — 22
Rimel's Rotisserie | **multi.** — 22
Flavor Del Mar | **Del Mar** — 22
Poseidon | **Del Mar** — 21
Currant | **Downtown** — 19
NEW Herringbone | **La Jolla** — ▬
NEW Veladora | **Rancho Santa Fe** — ▬

CHINESE

(* dim sum specialist)
Dumpling Inn* | **Kearny Mesa** — 26
Del Mar Rendezvous | **Del Mar** — 26

China Max* | **Kearny Mesa** 26

Spicy City | **Kearny Mesa** 26

P.F. Chang's | **multi.** 24

NEW Wang's North Park | **North Pk** 24

Emerald Chinese* | **Kearny Mesa** 24

Jasmine* | **Kearny Mesa** 24

Mandarin Hse. | **multi.** 22

Todai | **Mission Valley** 19

CONTINENTAL

Dobson's | **Downtown** 24

CREOLE

Bud's Louisiana | **Kearny Mesa** 26

CUBAN

Andre's | **Morena District** 22

DELIS

D.Z. Akin's | **Grantville** 25

Girard Gourmet | **La Jolla** 25

Cheese Shop | **Gaslamp Qtr** 24

Milton's | **Del Mar** 21

City Deli/Bakery | **Hillcrest** 20

Elijah's | **La Jolla** 18

DESSERT

Michele Coulon | **La Jolla** 26

Karen Krasne's | **multi.** 25

Ghirardelli's Soda | **Gaslamp Qtr** 25

Cheesecake Factory | **multi.** 25

Chocolat Bistro/Crem. | **multi.** 25

Opera Café | **Serra Mesa** 24

Cafe Zucchero | **Little Italy** 23

NEW Cremolose | **Gaslamp Qtr** 23

DINER

Mission | **multi.** 26

Big Kitchen | **South Pk** 25

Brian's | **Gaslamp Qtr** 23

Eggery | **Pacific Bch** 23

Crest Cafe | **Hillcrest** 23

Ricky's | **Mission Valley** 23

Harry's Coffee | **La Jolla** 23

Studio Diner | **Kearny Mesa** 22

Mimi's Cafe | **multi.** 22

Ruby's Diner | **multi.** 21

Corvette Diner | **Pt Loma** 20

Maryjane's | **Gaslamp Qtr** 17

ECLECTIC

NEW Carnitas' | **North Pk** 27

Wine Vault | **Mission Hills** 27

Nine-Ten | **La Jolla** 26

Marine Rm. | **La Jolla** 26

Cafe on Park | **Hillcrest** 24

Luc's Bistro | **Poway** 24

Sessions Public | **Pt Loma** 24

Parkhouse | **University Hts** 23

Alchemy | **South Pk** 23

Zodiac/Neiman Marcus | **Mission Valley** 23

Stone World | **Escondido** 23

Linkery | **North Pk** 22

Lei Lounge | **University Hts** 22

Vagabond | **South Pk** 21

Analog Bar | **Gaslamp Qtr** 21

ETHIOPIAN

Muzita Abyssinian | **University Hts** 26

EUROPEAN

Tartine | **Coronado** 26

Come On In | **multi.** 23

FONDUE

Melting Pot | **multi.** 24

Forever Fondue | **La Jolla** 22

FRENCH

Tapenade | **La Jolla** 28

Pamplemousse | **Solana Bch** 27

Vincent's | **Escondido** 27

Mistral | **Coronado** 27

Mille Fleurs | **Rancho Santa Fe** 27

Addison | **Carmel Valley** 27

Smoking Goat | **North Pk** 27

Farm House | **University Hts** 26

Marine Rm. | **La Jolla** 26

Maitre D' | **La Jolla** 26

WineSellar | **Sorrento Mesa** 26

La Bastide | **Scripps Ranch** 25

French Gourmet | **Pacific Bch** 25

Cafe Chloe | **E Vill** 25

Bleu Bohème | **Kensington** 24

DINING

CUISINES

Bernard'O | **Rancho Bernardo**	24
BO-beau | **Ocean Bch**	24
Hexagone | **Bankers Hill**	24
Opera Café | **Serra Mesa**	24
Au Revoir | **Hillcrest**	24
French Mkt. | **Rancho Bernardo**	23
Whisknladle | **La Jolla**	23

GASTROPUB

Neighborhood | Amer. | **E Vill**	24
Sessions Public | Eclectic | **Pt Loma**	24
Craft/Commerce | Amer. | **Little Italy**	23
Jayne's | Continental | **North Pk**	23
Analog Bar | Eclectic | **Gaslamp Qtr**	21

GERMAN

Kaiserhof | **Ocean Bch**	23

GREEK

Cafe Athena | **Pacific Bch**	25
Yanni's Bistro | **Poway**	24
Alborz Rest. | **Del Mar**	23
Athens Market | **multi.**	22

HAWAIIAN

Roy's | **multi.**	25
Bali Hai | **Shelter Is**	23
Aloha Sushi | **La Jolla**	21

ICE CREAM PARLORS

Ghirardelli's Soda | **Gaslamp Qtr**	25

INDIAN

Ashoka the Great | **Mira Mesa**	24
Monsoon | **Gaslamp Qtr**	24
Bombay | **Hillcrest**	24
Masala | **Gaslamp Qtr**	23
Royal India | **Gaslamp Qtr**	22

IRISH

Field | **Gaslamp Qtr**	23

ITALIAN

(N=Northern)

Trattoria/Vecchio | **Del Mar**	28
Primavera | N | **Coronado**	28

Vivace | **Carlsbad**	27
Pappalecco | **Hillcrest**	27
Jack/Giulio's | **Old Town**	27
Solare | **Pt Loma**	27
Godfather | **Kearny Mesa**	27
Island Pasta | **Coronado**	26
Cucina Urbana | **Bankers Hill**	26
Trattoria I Trulli | **Encinitas**	26
Trattoria Fantastica | **Little Italy**	26
Arrivederci | **multi.**	26
Piatti | **La Jolla**	26
de'Medici | **Gaslamp Qtr**	25
Baci | **Morena District**	25
Venetian | N | **Pt Loma**	25
Bencotto | **Little Italy**	25
Buon Appetito | **Little Italy**	25
Enoteca Adriano | **Pacific Bch**	25
Davanti Enoteca | **multi.**	25
Mona Lisa | **Little Italy**	25
Caffe Bella | N | **Pacific Bch**	25
Filippi's | **multi.**	25
Osteria Romantica | **La Jolla**	25
Etna Rest. | **E San Diego**	25
Salvatore's | **Downtown**	25
Chocolat Bistro/Crem. | **multi.**	25
Bice | **Gaslamp Qtr**	24
Yanni's Bistro | **Poway**	24
Osteria Panevino | **Gaslamp Qtr**	24
Vigilucci's | **multi.**	24
Andiamo | N | **Tierrasanta**	24
Il Fornaio | **multi.**	24
Lorna's Italian | **University City**	24
Pizza Nova | **multi.**	24
Sapori | **Coronado**	24
Via Italia | N | **Encinitas**	24
Antica Trattoria | **La Mesa**	23
25 Forty Bistro | **Old Town**	23
Manhattan | **La Jolla**	23
Harry's B&G | **Golden Triangle**	23
Cafe Zucchero | **Little Italy**	23
Villa Capri | **multi.**	23
Busalacchi's | **Hillcrest**	23
NEW Cremolose | **Gaslamp Qtr**	23
Old Trieste | **Bay Pk**	23
Barolo | **University City**	22
Operacaffe | **Gaslamp Qtr**	22

Romano's	**multi.**	22
Acqua Al 2	N	**Gaslamp Qtr**	22
Buca di Beppo	**multi.**	22
Old Spaghetti	**Gaslamp Qtr**	22
La Taverna	N	**La Jolla**	22
Barbarella	**La Jolla**	22
Leucadia Pizzeria	**Golden Triangle**	22
Old Venice	**Pt Loma**	22
Cicciotti's	**Cardiff-by-the-Sea**	21
Olivetto	**Mission Hills**	21
Po Pazzo	**Little Italy**	20
NEW Mia Francesca	**Del Mar**	–

JAPANESE
(* sushi specialist)

Sushi Ota*	**Pacific Bch**	29
Harney Sushi*	**multi.**	26
Nobu*	**Gaslamp Qtr**	26
Hane Sushi*	**Bankers Hill**	25
Taka*	**Gaslamp Qtr**	25
Sushi/Rock*	**La Jolla**	25
Benihana	**multi.**	25
Tajima	**Kearny Mesa**	25
P.F. Chang's	**Golden Triangle**	24
Roppongi*	**La Jolla**	24
Azuki Sushi*	**Bankers Hill**	24
Cafe Japengo*	**Golden Triangle**	24
RA Sushi*	**Downtown**	23
NEW Underbelly	**Little Italy**	23
Zenbu Sushi*	**multi.**	22
NEW Katsuya	**Downtown**	22
Aloha Sushi	**La Jolla**	21
NEW Gaijin Noodle/Sake	**Gaslamp Qtr**	20
Todai*	**Mission Valley**	19

JEWISH

D.Z. Akin's	**Grantville**	25
Elijah's	**La Jolla**	18

KOREAN
(* barbecue specialist)

Buga Korean BBQ*	**Clairemont**	25
Convoy Tofu	**Kearny Mesa**	24

MEDITERRANEAN

Aladdin Hillcrest	**Hillcrest**	24

MEXICAN

Las Cuatro Milpas	**Barrio Logan**	26
El Agave	**Old Town**	26
Chipotle	**multi.**	26
South Beach B&G	**Ocean Bch**	26
El Zarape	**multi.**	25
Costa Azul	**Coronado**	25
El Vitral	**E Vill**	25
Los Arcos	**Chula Vista**	25
Rubio's	**multi.**	25
Casa De Pico	**La Mesa**	24
El Indio	**Mission Hills**	24
Fidel's Little Mex.	**Solana Bch**	24
Ponce's	**Kensington**	24
Miguel's Cocina	**multi.**	24
Candelas	**Gaslamp Qtr**	24
Barrio Star	**Bankers Hill**	24
Mama Testa	**Hillcrest**	23
Hacienda/Vega	**Escondido**	23
Ortega's	**Hillcrest**	23
Cafe Coyote	**Old Town**	23
El Callejon	**Encinitas**	23
Casa Guadalajara	**Old Town**	23
Lucha Libre	**Mission Hills**	23
Wahoo's	**multi.**	23
Jimmy Carter's	**Hillcrest**	22
Funky Garcia's	**Gaslamp Qtr**	22
Old Town Mex.	**Old Town**	22
Fred's Mex.	**multi.**	22
Rockin' Baja	**multi.**	22
Baja Fresh	**multi.**	22
Acapulco	**Old Town**	22
Baja Betty's	**Hillcrest**	21
El Torito	**multi.**	21
Casa de Reyes	**Old Town**	21
Candelas/Bay	**Coronado**	21
Alfonso's	**La Jolla**	20
El Take It Easy	**North Pk**	20
Cosmopolitan Rest.	**Old Town**	20
Jose's Courtrm.	**La Jolla**	19

MIDDLE EASTERN

Café 21	**multi.**	25
Aladdin Café	**Clairemont**	25
Ali Baba	**El Cajon**	22

DINING

CUISINES

MOROCCAN

Kous Kous | **Hillcrest** 23

NOODLE SHOPS

Dumpling Inn | **Kearny Mesa** 26
Saffron | **Mission Hills** 24
NEW Underbelly | **Little Italy** 23

NUEVO LATINO

Mission | **multi.** 26

PACIFIC NORTHWEST

Indigo Grill | **Little Italy** 26

PACIFIC RIM

Cafe Japengo | **Golden Triangle** 24

PAN-LATIN

Isabel's Cantina | **Pacific Bch** 25

PERSIAN

Bandar | **Gaslamp Qtr** 24
Alborz Rest. | **Del Mar** 23

PIZZA

Lefty's | **multi.** 27
Bronx Pizza | **Hillcrest** 27
Basic Urban | **E Vill** 26
URBN | **North Pk** 26
Blue Ribbon | **Encinitas** 25
Del Mar Pizza | **Del Mar** 25
Woodstock's | **multi.** 25
Pizza Port | **multi.** 25
Filippi's | **multi.** 25
La Pizzeria | **Hillcrest** 24
Alexander's Pizza | **Coronado** 24
Pizzeria Luigi | **Golden Hill** 24
Local Habit | **Hillcrest** 24
Pizza Nova | **multi.** 24
Sammy's Pizza | **multi.** 23
Calif. Pizza | **multi.** 23
Leucadia Pizzeria | 22
   Golden Triangle

POLYNESIAN

Peohe's | **Coronado** 24
Bali Hai | **Shelter Is** 23

PUB FOOD

BJ's | **multi.** 24
Field | **Gaslamp Qtr** 23

Coronado Brew | **Coronado** 21
Gordon Biersch | **Mission Valley** 21
East Lake/Vill./North Tav. | **multi.** 20
McP's Irish | **Coronado** 19

PUERTO RICAN

Andre's | **Morena District** 22

SANDWICHES

(See also Delis)
Pappalecco | **Little Italy** 27
Tartine | **Coronado** 26
Karen Krasne's | **Little Italy** 25
Local Habit | **Hillcrest** 24
Cheese Shop | **Gaslamp Qtr** 24
Islands | **multi.** 23
Boudin Bakery | **multi.** 22

SEAFOOD

Donovan's Stk. | **Golden Triangle** 27
West Steak | **Carlsbad** 27
Blue Water | **India St** 27
Sea Rocket | **North Pk** 27
Truluck's | **Golden Triangle** 27
Island Prime | **Harbor Island** 26
Point Loma Seafoods | **Pt Loma** 26
Georges on Fifth | **Gaslamp Qtr** 26
Fishery | **Pacific Bch** 26
South Beach B&G | **Ocean Bch** 26
de'Medici | **Gaslamp Qtr** 25
Eddie V's | **La Jolla** 25
Crab Hut | **multi.** 25
El Pescador | **La Jolla** 25
Pacifica Del Mar | **Del Mar** 25
Saska's | **Mission Bch** 25
Fish Market | **multi.** 25
Bay Park Fish | **Bay Pk** 25
Los Arcos | **Chula Vista** 25
Oceanaire | **Gaslamp Qtr** 25
333 Pacific | **Oceanside** 25
Top/Market | **Downtown** 24
Brigantine | **multi.** 24
Steakhouse/Azul | **La Jolla** 24
Vigilucci's | **multi.** 24
Humphrey's | **Shelter Is** 24
Emerald Chinese | **Kearny Mesa** 24
Jasmine | **Kearny Mesa** 24

Share your reviews on plus.google.com/local

Sally's Seafood | **Downtown**	24
Donovan's Prime | **Gaslamp Qtr**	24
King's Fish | **multi.**	24
Anthony's | **multi.**	24
Jake's Del Mar | **Del Mar**	22
Blue Point | **Gaslamp Qtr**	23
Adam's/Albie's | **Mission Valley**	23
Jsix | **E Vill**	23
McCormick/Schmick | **E Vill**	23
Wahoo's | **multi.**	23
Red Fox Steakhouse | **North Pk**	23
Baleen | **Mission Bay**	23
Coronado Boathse. | **Coronado**	23
World Famous | **Pacific Bch**	23
Tin Fish | **multi.**	22
Boathouse | **Harbor Island**	22
Red Tracton's | **Solana Bch**	22
Crab Catcher | **La Jolla**	22
Bully's East | **Mission Valley**	22
94th Aero | **Kearny Mesa**	22
Tom Ham's | **Harbor Island**	22
Joe's Crab | **multi.**	22
Harbor House | **Downtown**	21
Nick's | **multi.**	21
Green Flash | **Pacific Bch**	20
Cosmopolitan Rest. | **Old Town**	20
Escape Fish | **Gaslamp Qtr**	19

SMALL PLATES

(See also Spanish tapas specialist)

Dumpling Inn | Chinese | **Kearny Mesa**	26
Harney Sushi | Japanese | **multi.**	26
Taka | Japanese | **Gaslamp Qtr**	25
Cafe Chloe | French | **E Vill**	25
Sessions Public | Eclectic | **Pt Loma**	24
3rd Corner | Cal. | **multi.**	23
Alchemy | Eclectic | **South Pk**	23
RA Sushi | Japanese | **Downtown**	23
Harry's B&G | Italian | **Golden Triangle**	23
Craft/Commerce | Amer. | **Little Italy**	23
Lei Lounge | Eclectic | **University Hts**	22

Saltbox | Amer. | **Downtown**	21
El Take It Easy | Cal. | **North Pk**	20

SOUTHERN

Luc's Bistro | **Poway**	24

SPANISH

(* tapas specialist)

Costa Brava* | **Pacific Bch**	26
Cafe Sevilla | **Gaslamp Qtr**	23

STEAKHOUSES

Ruth's Chris | **multi.**	27
Donovan's Stk. | **multi.**	27
West Steak | **Carlsbad**	27
Truluck's | **Golden Triangle**	27
Island Prime | **Harbor Island**	26
Fleming's | **multi.**	26
Georges on Fifth | **Gaslamp Qtr**	26
Butcher Shop | **Kearny Mesa**	25
Eddie V's | **La Jolla**	25
Turf Supper | **Golden Hill**	25
Morton's | **Downtown**	25
Cowboy Star | **E Vill**	25
Saska's | **Mission Bch**	25
333 Pacific | **Oceanside**	25
Palm | **Downtown**	24
Outback | **multi.**	24
Steakhouse/Azul | **La Jolla**	24
Vigilucci's | **multi.**	24
Greystone | **Gaslamp Qtr**	24
Argyle Steak | **Carlsbad**	24
Adam's/Albie's | **Mission Valley**	23
Red Fox Steakhouse | **North Pk**	23
Baleen | **Mission Bay**	23
Bully's | **Del Mar**	23
Coronado Boathse. | **Coronado**	23
Riviera Supper | **La Mesa**	23
Boathouse | **Harbor Island**	22
Red Tracton's | **Solana Bch**	22
Bully's East | **Mission Valley**	22
94th Aero | **Kearny Mesa**	22
Gaslamp/La Jolla Strip | **multi.**	21
Po Pazzo | **Little Italy**	20

DINING

CUISINES

THAI

Original Sab-E-Lee | **Linda Vista**	27
Amarin | **Hillcrest**	26
Rama | **Gaslamp Qtr**	25
Celadon | **Hillcrest**	24
Royal Thai | **Gaslamp Qtr**	24
Saffron | **Mission Hills**	24
Spice & Rice | **La Jolla**	23
Antique Thai | **Midway District**	23
Lotus Thai | **multi.**	22
Pink Noodle | **Hillcrest**	22

VEGETARIAN

Tao | **Normal Heights**	28
Jyoti-Bihanga | **Normal Heights**	24
Loving Hut* | **multi.**	23
Zinc Cafe | **Solana Bch**	23

VIETNAMESE

Le Bambou | **Del Mar**	25
Phuong Trang | **Kearny Mesa**	25
Saigon/Fifth | **Hillcrest**	25
P.F. Chang's | **Golden Triangle**	24
Pho T Cali | **Clairemont**	24

Share your reviews on plus.google.com/local

Dining Locations

Includes names, cuisines and Food ratings. These lists include low-vote places that do not qualify for top lists.

BALBOA PARK

Prado	*Cal.*	24

BANKERS HILL

Bertrand	*Amer.*	27
Cucina Urbana	*Italian*	26
Hane Sushi	*Japanese*	25
Karen Krasne's	*Dessert*	25
Bankers Hill	*Amer.*	24
Hexagone	*French*	24
Azuki Sushi	*Japanese*	24
Barrio Star	*Mex.*	24
Avenue 5	*Amer.*	23
Mandarin Hse.	*Chinese*	22
Hob Nob Hill	*Amer.*	22

BARRIO LOGAN

Las Cuatro Milpas	*Mex.*	26

BAY PARK

Bay Park Fish	*Seafood*	25
Old Trieste	*Italian*	23

BONITA

El Torito	*Mex.*	21

CARDIFF-BY-THE-SEA

Zenbu Sushi	*Japanese*	22
Rimel's Rotisserie	*Cal.*	22
Cicciotti's	*Italian*	21

CARMEL HEIGHTS

Villa Capri	*Italian*	23

CARMEL MOUNTAIN RANCH

Habit Burger	*Burgers*	24
Claim Jumper	*Amer.*	24
Wahoo's	*Mex./Seafood*	23
Karl Strauss	*Amer.*	23
Islands	*Amer.*	23
Calif. Pizza	*Pizza*	23
Athens Market	*Greek*	22

CARMEL VALLEY

Addison	*French*	27
Amaya	*Amer.*	25
Villa Capri	*Italian*	23

CLAIREMONT

Aladdin Café	*Mideast.*	25
Buga Korean BBQ	*Korean*	25
Outback	*Steak*	24
Boomerangs	*Burgers*	24
Pho T Cali	*Viet.*	24
Islands	*Amer.*	23

COASTAL TOWNS

Trattoria/Vecchio	*Italian*	28
Market	*Cal.*	28
Pamplemousse	*Amer./French*	27
Ruth's Chris	*Steak*	27
Trattoria I Trulli	*Italian*	26
Chipotle	*Mex.*	26
Del Mar Rendezvous	*Chinese*	26
Blue Ribbon	*Pizza*	25
Brett's BBQ	*BBQ*	25
Del Mar Pizza	*Pizza*	25
Kitchen 1540	*Amer.*	25
Original Pancake	*Amer.*	25
Davanti Enoteca	*Italian*	25
Pacifica Del Mar	*Seafood*	25
Pizza Port	*Pizza*	25
Le Bambou	*Viet.*	25
Prepkitchen	*Amer.*	25
Fish Market	*Seafood*	25
Arterra	*Amer.*	24
Pacifica Breeze	*Cal.*	24
Habit Burger	*Burgers*	24
Brigantine	*Seafood*	24
Wild Note Cafe	*Cal.*	24
Fidel's Little Mex.	*Mex.*	24
Vigilucci's	*Italian*	24
Il Fornaio	*Italian*	24
Pizza Nova	*Italian*	24
Via Italia	*Italian*	24
3rd Corner	*Cal.*	23
Sammy's Pizza	*Pizza*	23
Jake's Del Mar	*Cal./Seafood*	23
El Callejon	*Mex.*	23
Sbicca	*Amer.*	23

Wahoo's	*Mex./Seafood*	23
Alborz Rest.	*Greek/Persian*	23
Counter	*Burgers*	23
Bully's	*Steak*	23
Zinc Cafe	*Veg.*	23
Islands	*Amer.*	23
Five Guys	*Burgers*	23
Calif. Pizza	*Pizza*	23
Red Tracton's	*Seafood/Steak*	22
Burlap	*Amer.*	22
Beach Grass	*Amer.*	22
Flavor Del Mar	*Cal.*	22
Americana	*Amer.*	22
Pei Wei	*Asian*	21
Milton's	*Deli*	21
Poseidon	*Cal.*	21
Union Kitchen	*Amer.*	21
NEW Mia Francesca	*Italian*	-

COLLEGE EAST

Chipotle	*Mex.*	26
Rubio's	*Mex.*	25

CORONADO

Primavera	*Italian*	28
Mistral	*French*	27
Island Pasta	*Italian*	26
Tartine	*Euro.*	26
Costa Azul	*Mex.*	25
Burger Lounge	*Burgers*	25
Rhino Cafe/Grill	*Amer.*	25
1500 Ocean	*Cal.*	24
Alexander's Pizza	*Pizza*	24
Peohe's	*Polynesian*	24
Brigantine	*Seafood*	24
Vigilucci's	*Seafood/Steak*	24
Miguel's Cocina	*Mex.*	24
Il Fornaio	*Italian*	24
Sapori	*Italian*	24
Nicky Rottens	*Amer.*	24
Sheerwater	*Cal.*	23
Five Guys	*Burgers*	23
Coronado Boathse.	*Seafood/Steak*	23
Coronado Brew	*Pub*	21
Candelas/Bay	*Mex.*	21
McP's Irish	*Pub*	19

Ruth's Chris	*Steak*	27
Hodad's	*Burgers*	26
Roy's	*Hawaiian*	25
Crab Hut	*CajunSeafood*	25
Morton's	*Steak*	25
Fish Market	*Seafood*	25
Salvatore's	*Italian*	25
Top/Market	*Seafood*	24
Palm	*Steak*	24
Grant Grill	*Cal.*	24
Dobson's	*Cal./Continental*	24
Sally's Seafood	*Asian/Seafood*	24
Anthony's	*Seafood*	24
Cafe 222	*Amer.*	23
Sammy's Pizza	*Pizza*	23
RA Sushi	*Japanese*	23
Counter	*Burgers*	23
Karl Strauss	*Amer.*	23
Richard Walker's	*Amer.*	23
Athens Market	*Greek*	22
Yard Hse.	*Amer.*	22
Baja Fresh	*Mex.*	22
Buca di Beppo	*Italian*	22
Anthology	*Cal.*	22
NEW Katsuya	*Japanese*	22
Joe's Crab	*Seafood*	22
Harbor House	*Seafood*	21
Saltbox	*Amer.*	21
Currant	*Cal.*	19

EAST COUNTY

Casa De Pico	*Mex.*	24
Brigantine	*Seafood*	24
Outback	*Steak*	24
BJ's	*Pub*	24
Claim Jumper	*Amer.*	24
Anthony's	*Seafood*	24
Antica Trattoria	*Italian*	23
Sammy's Pizza	*Pizza*	23
Riviera Supper	*Steak*	23
NEW Gingham	*Amer.*	21

EAST SAN DIEGO

Woodstock's	*Pizza*	25
Etna Rest.	*Italian*	25
Terra Amer.	*Amer.*	24

EAST VILLAGE

Basic Urban | *Pizza*	26
Mission | *Asian/Nuevo Latino*	26
El Vitral | *Mex.*	25
Cowboy Star | *Amer. Steak*	25
Cafe Chloe | *French*	25
Neighborhood | *Gastropub*	24
Jsix | *Cal./Seafood*	23
Broken Yolk | *Amer.*	23
McCormick/Schmick | *Seafood/Steak*	23
Lotus Thai | *Thai*	22
East Lake/Vill./North Tav. | *Amer.*	20

EL CAJON

In-N-Out | *Burgers*	26
Arrivederci | *Italian*	26
Outback | *Steak*	24
Ali Baba | *Mideast.*	22

GASLAMP QUARTER

Donovan's Stk. | *Steak*	27
Fleming's | *Steak*	26
Rei do Gado | *Brazilian*	26
Nobu | *Japanese*	26
Georges on Fifth | *Seafood/Steak*	26
de'Medici | *Italian*	25
Taka | *Japanese*	25
Café 21 | *Cal./Mideast.*	25
Ghirardelli's Soda | *Dessert/Ice Cream*	25
Oceanaire | *Seafood*	25
Rama | *Thai*	25
Burger Lounge | *Burgers*	25
Chocolat Bistro/Crem. | *Dessert/Italian*	25
Lou/Mickey's | *Seafood/Steak*	24
Bandar | *Persian*	24
Bice | *Italian*	24
Searsucker | *Amer.*	24
Melting Pot | *Fondue*	24
Osteria Panevino | *Italian*	24
Cheese Shop | *Deli*	24
Royal Thai | *Thai*	24
Greystone | *Steak*	24
Monsoon | *Indian*	24
Candelas | *Mex.*	24

Donovan's Prime | *Seafood*	24
Nicky Rottens | *Amer.*	24
Brian's | *Diner*	23
Blue Point | *Seafood*	23
Cafe Sevilla | *Spanish*	23
Field | *Irish*	23
NEW Cremolose | *Dessert/Italian*	23
Masala | *Indian*	23
Tin Fish | *Seafood*	22
Funky Garcia's | *Mex.*	22
Fred's Mex. | *Mex.*	22
Operacaffe | *Italian*	22
Rockin' Baja | *Mex.*	22
Acqua Al 2 | *Italian*	22
Croce's | *Amer.*	22
Old Spaghetti | *Italian*	22
Royal India | *Indian*	22
Red Pearl | *Asian*	21
Gaslamp/La Jolla Strip | *Steak*	21
Analog Bar | *Eclectic*	21
NEW Gaijin Noodle/Sake | *Japanese*	20
Hard Rock Cafe | *Amer.*	20
Escape Fish | *Seafood*	19
Dick's/Resort | *Amer.*	18
Maryjane's | *Diner*	17

GOLDEN HILL

Turf Supper | *Steak*	25
Pizzeria Luigi | *Pizza*	24

GOLDEN TRIANGLE

Donovan's Stk. | *Steak*	27
Truluck's | *Seafood/Steak*	27
Fleming's | *Steak*	26
Roy's | *Hawaiian*	25
Rubio's | *Mex.*	25
P.F. Chang's | *Chinese*	24
Melting Pot | *Fondue*	24
Cafe Japengo | *Pac. Rim*	24
Sammy's Pizza | *Pizza*	23
Harry's B&G | *Amer./Italian*	23
Leucadia Pizzeria | *Pizza*	22

GRANTVILLE

D.Z. Akin's | *Deli*	25

DINING

LOCATIONS

GROSSMONT

Chipotle | *Mex.* 26

HARBOR ISLAND

Island Prime | *Seafood/Steak* 26
Boathouse | *Seafood/Steak* 22
Tom Ham's | *Cal./Seafood* 22

HILLCREST

Pappalecco | *Sandwiches* 27
NEW Snooze | *Amer.* 27
Bronx Pizza | *Pizza* 27
Bread & Cie | *Bakery* 26
Chipotle | *Mex.* 26
Arrivederci | *Italian* 26
Amarin | *Thai* 26
Tractor Rm. | *Amer.* 25
Hash House | *Amer.* 25
Khyber Pass | *Afghan* 25
Babycakes | *Bakery* 25
Fig Tree | *Cal.* 25
Burger Lounge | *Burgers* 25
Saigon/Fifth | *Viet.* 25
Chocolat Bistro/Crem. | *Dessert/Italian* 25
Aladdin Hillcrest | *Med.* 24
La Pizzeria | *Pizza* 24
Celadon | *Thai* 24
Local Habit | *Pizza/Sandwiches* 24
Cafe on Park | *Amer.* 24
Bombay | *Indian* 24
Au Revoir | *French* 24
Mama Testa | *Mex.* 23
Kous Kous | *Moroccan* 23
Ortega's | *Mex.* 23
Crest Cafe | *Diner* 23
Brazen BBQ | *BBQ* 23
Busalacchi's | *Italian* 23
Five Guys | *Burgers* 23
Jimmy Carter's | *Mex.* 22
Lotus Thai | *Thai* 22
Pink Noodle | *Thai* 22
Baja Betty's | *Mex.* 21
City Deli/Bakery | *Deli* 20
Gossip Grill | *Amer.* 20

IMPERIAL BEACH

Tin Fish | *Seafood* 22

INDIA STREET

Blue Water | *Seafood* 27

KEARNY MESA

Godfather | *Italian* 27
Dumpling Inn | *Chinese* 26
In-N-Out | *Burgers* 26
China Max | *Chinese* 26
Bud's Louisiana | *Creole* 26
Spicy City | *Chinese* 26
Butcher Shop | *Steak* 25
Crab Hut | *Cajun/Seafood* 25
Original Pancake | *Amer.* 25
Tajima | *Japanese* 25
Filippi's | *Italian* 25
Phuong Trang | *Viet.* 25
Rubio's | *Mex.* 25
Convoy Tofu | *Korean* 24
Emerald Chinese | *Chinese* 24
Jasmine | *Chinese/Seafood* 24
Studio Diner | *Diner* 22
94th Aero | *Amer./Steak* 22

KENSINGTON

Kensington Grill | *Amer.* 25
Burger Lounge | *Burgers* 25
Bleu Bohème | *French* 24
Ponce's | *Mex.* 24

LA JOLLA

Tapenade | *French* 28
George's Cal./Ocean | *Cal.* 27
Michele Coulon | *Dessert* 26
Chipotle | *Mex.* 26
Nine-Ten | *Cal./Eclectic* 26
Piatti | *Italian* 26
A.R. Valentien | *Cal.* 26
Marine Rm. | *Eclectic/French* 26
Maitre D' | *French* 26
Eddie V's | *Seafood/Steak* 25
Sushi/Rock | *Japanese* 25
El Pescador | *Seafood* 25
Girard Gourmet | *Belgian/Deli* 25
Prepkitchen | *Amer.* 25
Osteria Romantica | *Italian* 25
Burger Lounge | *Burgers* 25
Roppongi | *Asian* 24

BJ's	*Pub*	24
Steakhouse/Azul	*Steak*	24
Cottage	*Cal.*	24
Shores	*Cal.*	24
Sammy's Pizza	*Pizza*	23
Spice & Rice	*Thai*	23
Manhattan	*Italian*	23
Wahoo's	*Mex./Seafood*	23
Come On In	*Amer./Euro.*	23
Brockton Villa	*Cal.*	23
Karl Strauss	*Amer.*	23
Harry's Coffee	*Diner*	23
Islands	*Amer.*	23
Grill/Torrey Pines	*Amer.*	23
Calif. Pizza	*Pizza*	23
Whisknladle	*Cal./French*	23
Jai	*Asian*	22
Zenbu Sushi	*Japanese*	22
Cody's La Jolla	*Amer.*	22
Forever Fondue	*Fondue*	22
Crab Catcher	*Seafood*	22
Mandarin Hse.	*Chinese*	22
La Taverna	*Italian*	22
Rimel's Rotisserie	*Cal.*	22
Barbarella	*Italian*	22
Aloha Sushi	*Hawaiian/Japanese*	21
Alfonso's	*Mex.*	20
Spot	*Amer.*	20
Jose's Courtrm.	*Mex.*	19
Elijah's	*Deli*	18
NEW Herringbone	*Cal.*	-

LEMON GROVE

Coops BBQ | *BBQ* 24

LINDA VISTA

Original Sab-E-Lee | *Thai* 27

LITTLE ITALY

Pappalecco	*Sandwiches*	27
Puerto La Boca	*Argent.*	27
Indigo Grill	*Pac. NW*	26
Trattoria Fantastica	*Italian*	26
Karen Krasne's	*Sandwiches*	25
Bencotto	*Italian*	25
Buon Appetito	*Italian*	25
Davanti Enoteca	*Italian*	25

Mona Lisa	*Italian*	25
Filippi's	*Italian*	25
Prepkitchen	*Amer.*	25
Burger Lounge	*Burgers*	25
Craft/Commerce	*Amer.*	23
NEW Underbelly	*Japanese*	23
Cafe Zucchero	*Italian*	23
Po Pazzo	*Italian/Steak*	20
Glass Door	*Amer.*	20

MIDWAY DISTRICT

Antique Thai | *Thai* 23

MIRA MESA

In-N-Out	*Burgers*	26
Chipotle	*Mex.*	26
Ashoka the Great	*Indian*	24
Loving Hut	*Vegan*	23
Islands	*Amer.*	23
Buca di Beppo	*Italian*	22
Mimi's Cafe	*American/French*	22
Abbey's Real TX	*BBQ*	22
El Torito	*Mex.*	21

MISSION BAY/ MISSION BEACH

Mission	*Asian/Nuevo Latino*	26
Saska's	*Seafood/Steak*	25
Rubio's	*Mex.*	25
Baleen	*Seafood/Steak*	23

MISSION HILLS

Wine Vault	*Eclectic*	27
Lefty's	*Pizza*	27
El Indio	*Mex.*	24
Saffron	*Thai*	24
NEW Brooklyn Girl	*Amer.*	23
Red Door	*Amer.*	23
Lucha Libre	*Mex.*	23
Olivetto	*Italian*	21

MISSION VALLEY

In-N-Out	*Burgers*	26
Chipotle	*Mex.*	26
Benihana	*Japanese*	25
Filippi's	*Italian*	25
Cheesecake Factory	*Amer.*	25
Rubio's	*Mex.*	25

P.F. Chang's	*Chinese*	24
Habit Burger	*Burgers*	24
Outback	*Steak*	24
King's Fish	*Seafood*	24
Sammy's Pizza	*Pizza*	23
Adam's/Albie's	*Seafood/Steak*	23
Wahoo's	*Mex./Seafood*	23
Ricky's	*Amer.*	23
Zodiac/Neiman Marcus	*Cal./Eclectic*	23
Islands	*Amer.*	23
Calif. Pizza	*Pizza*	23
Boudin Bakery	*Bakery*	22
Bully's East	*Seafood/Steak*	22
Mimi's Cafe	*American/French*	22
Joe's Crab	*Seafood*	22
Ruby's Diner	*Diner*	21
Pei Wei	*Asian*	21
Gordon Biersch	*Pub Food*	21
Todai	*Chinese/Japanese*	19

MORENA DISTRICT

Baci	*Italian*	25
Kitchen 4140	*Amer.*	25
Andre's	*Cuban/Puerto Rican*	22

NORMAL HEIGHTS

Tao	*Asian/Veg.*	28
El Zarape	*Mex.*	25
Jyoti-Bihanga	*Veg.*	24

NORTH COUNTY

Vivace	*Italian*	27
Vincent's	*French*	27
West Steak	*Seafood/Steak*	27
Mille Fleurs	*French*	27
In-N-Out	*Burgers*	26
Paon	*Cal.*	26
Brett's BBQ	*BBQ*	25
Benihana	*Japanese*	25
Pizza Port	*Pizza*	25
Filippi's	*Italian*	25
P.F. Chang's	*Chinese*	24
Bernard'O	*Cal./French*	24
Brigantine	*Seafood*	24
Delicias	*Cal.*	24
Vigilucci's	*Italian/Seafood/Steak*	24

Miguel's Cocina	*Mex.*	24
Claim Jumper	*Amer.*	24
Argyle Steak	*Steak*	24
King's Fish	*Seafood*	24
Belle Fleur	*Cal.*	23
Sammy's Pizza	*Pizza*	23
Hacienda/Vega	*Mex.*	23
French Mkt.	*French*	23
Broken Yolk	*Amer.*	23
Villa Capri	*Italian*	23
Karl Strauss	*Amer.*	23
Islands	*Amer.*	23
Stone World	*Eclectic*	23
Five Guys	*Burgers*	23
Romano's	*Italian*	22
Buca di Beppo	*Italian*	22
Ruby's Diner	*Diner*	21
Pei Wei	*Asian*	21
Fatburger	*Burgers*	21
East Lake/Vill./North Tav.	*Amer.*	20
NEW Veladora	*Cal.*	-

NORTH PARK

NEW Carnitas'	*Amer./Eclectic*	27
Sea Rocket	*Seafood*	27
Lefty's	*Pizza*	27
Smoking Goat	*French*	27
URBN	*Pizza*	26
Urban Solace	*Amer.*	26
Mission	*Asian/Nuevo Latino*	26
Café 21	*Cal./Mideast.*	25
Pizzeria Luigi	*Pizza*	24
Crazee Burger	*Burgers*	24
NEW Wang's North Park	*Chinese*	24
Ritual Tavern	*Amer.*	24
San Diego Chicken	*Amer.*	23
Loving Hut	*Vegan*	23
Red Fox Steakhouse	*Seafood/Steak*	23
Jayne's	*Gastropub*	23
Linkery	*Eclectic*	22
West Coast Tav.	*Amer.*	21
El Take It Easy	*Mex.*	20

OCEAN BEACH

Hodad's	*Burgers*	26
South Beach B&G	*Mex./Seafood*	26

Share your reviews on plus.google.com/local

Shades Oceanfront	*Amer.*	25
Pizza Port	*Pizza*	25
BO-beau	*French*	24
3rd Corner	*Cal.*	23
Kaiserhof	*German*	23
Wahoo's	*Mex./Seafood*	23
Nick's	*American*	21

OCEANSIDE

Harney Sushi	*Japanese*	26
333 Pacific	*Seafood/Steak*	25
Outback	*Steak*	24
Tin Fish	*Seafood*	22
Romano's	*Italian*	22
Mimi's Cafe	*American/French*	22
Joe's Crab	*Seafood*	22
Ruby's Diner	*Diner*	21

OLD TOWN

Jack/Giulio's	*Italian*	27
El Agave	*Mex.*	26
Harney Sushi	*Japanese*	26
Crazee Burger	*Burgers*	24
Miguel's Cocina	*Mex.*	24
25 Forty Bistro	*Italian*	23
Cafe Coyote	*Mex.*	23
Casa Guadalajara	*Mex.*	23
Old Town Mex.	*Mex.*	22
Fred's Mex.	*Mex.*	22
Rockin' Baja	*Mex.*	22
Acapulco	*Mex.*	22
Casa de Reyes	*Mex.*	21
Cosmopolitan Rest.	*Amer./Mex.*	20

PACIFIC BEACH

Sushi Ota	*Japanese*	29
Costa Brava	*Spanish*	26
In-N-Out	*Burgers*	26
Chipotle	*Mex.*	26
Rocky's Crown	*Burgers*	26
Fishery	*Seafood*	26
Isabel's Cantina	*Pan-Latin*	25
Cafe Athena	*Greek*	25
French Gourmet	*French*	25
Enoteca Adriano	*Italian*	25
Woodstock's	*Pizza*	25

Caffe Bella	*Italian*	25
Filippi's	*Italian*	25
Fig Tree	*Cal.*	25
Rubio's	*Mex.*	25
JRDN	*Cal.*	24
Tony Roma's	*BBQ*	24
Eggery	*Diner*	23
Kono's Café	*Amer.*	23
Broken Yolk	*Amer.*	23
NEW Table 926	*Cal.*	23
Five Guys	*Burgers*	23
World Famous	*Seafood*	23
Fred's Mex.	*Mex.*	22
Joe's Crab	*Seafood*	22
Fatburger	*Burgers*	21
Nick's	*American*	21
Green Flash	*Seafood*	20

POINT LOMA

Solare	*Italian*	27
Tender Greens	*Amer.*	26
Point Loma Seafoods	*Seafood*	26
Venetian	*Italian*	25
NEW Slater's 50/50	*Burgers*	25
Brigantine	*Seafood*	24
Miguel's Cocina	*Mex.*	24
Pizza Nova	*Italian*	24
Sessions Public	*Eclectic*	24
Sammy's Pizza	*Pizza*	23
Five Guys	*Burgers*	23
Tin Fish	*Seafood*	22
Baja Fresh	*Mex.*	22
Old Venice	*Italian*	22
NEW Gabardine	*Seafood*	21
Corvette Diner	*Diner*	20

POWAY

In-N-Out	*Burgers*	26
Chipotle	*Mex.*	26
Original Pancake	*Amer.*	25
Filippi's	*Italian*	25
Yanni's Bistro	*Greek/Italian*	24
Brigantine	*Seafood*	24
Outback	*Steak*	24
Luc's Bistro	*Eclectic/Southern*	24
Chicken Pie	*Amer.*	23
Villa Capri	*Italian*	23

SAN MARCOS

Phil's BBQ | *BBQ* — 26
Pizza Nova | *Italian* — 24
Sammy's Pizza | *Pizza* — 23
Broken Yolk | *Amer.* — 23
Five Guys | *Burgers* — 23
Pei Wei | *Asian* — 21

SANTEE

Phil's BBQ | *BBQ* — 26
Mimi's Cafe | *American/French* — 22

SCRIPPS RANCH

La Bastide | *French* — 25
Filippi's | *Italian* — 25
Sammy's Pizza | *Pizza* — 23

SERRA MESA

Opera Café | *French* — 24

SHELTER ISLAND

Humphrey's | *Cal./Seafood* — 24
Bali Hai | *Hawaiian/Polynesian* — 23
Jimmy's Tavern | *Amer.* — 22

SORRENTO MESA

WineSellar | *French* — 26
Come On In | *Amer./Euro.* — 23
Karl Strauss | *Amer.* — 23

SOUTH BAY

In-N-Out | *Burgers* — 26
Filippi's | *Italian* — 25
Los Arcos | *Mex./Seafood* — 25
Cheesecake Factory | *Amer.* — 25
P.F. Chang's | *Chinese* — 24
Outback | *Steak* — 24
BJ's | *Pub Food* — 24
Miguel's Cocina | *Mex.* — 24

King's Fish | *Seafood* — 24
Broken Yolk | *Amer.* — 23
Villa Capri | *Italian* — 23
Islands | *Amer.* — 23
Calif. Pizza | *Pizza* — 23
Romano's | *Italian* — 22
East Lake/Vill./North Tav. | *Amer.* — 20

SOUTHCREST

Five Guys | *Burgers* — 23

SOUTH PARK

Big Kitchen | *Diner* — 25
Alchemy | *Eclectic* — 23
Vagabond | *Eclectic* — 21

SPORTS ARENA

In-N-Out | *Burgers* — 26
Phil's BBQ | *BBQ* — 26
Chipotle | *Mex.* — 26

TIERRASANTA

Andiamo | *Italian* — 24

UNIVERSITY CITY

Tender Greens | *Amer.* — 26
Lorna's Italian | *Italian* — 24
Five Guys | *Burgers* — 23
Boudin Bakery | *Bakery* — 22
Barolo | *Italian* — 22

UNIVERSITY HEIGHTS

Farm House | *French* — 26
Muzita Abyssinian | *Ethiopian* — 26
El Zarape | *Mex.* — 25
Adams Ave. | *Cal.* — 24
Parkhouse | *Amer./Eclectic* — 23
Lei Lounge | *Eclectic* — 22
Gaslamp/La Jolla Strip | *Steak* — 21

Dining

Ratings & Symbols

Food, Decor & **Service** are rated on a 30-point scale.

Cost reflects the price of dinner with a drink and tip; lunch is usually 25% to 30% less. For unrated newcomers, the price range is as follows:

⌐I $25 and below	E $41 to $65
M $26 to $40	VE $66 or above
● serves after 11 PM	M closed on Monday
Ø closed on Sunday	

Abbey'sReal Texas BBQ *BBQ*   `22` `16` `20` `$19`
Mira Mesa | 6904 Miramar Rd. (bet. Commerce & Production Aves.) | 858-566-2333 | www.abbeystexasbbq.com

It's "Texas style!" say fans of the "excellent, messy" Lone Star–inspired barbecue at this "local" Mira Mesa joint, which a few pardners call "the best" in these here parts; it's a simple "hole-in-the-wall", but the "casual" atmosphere, mild prices and cheerful counter service make it "great for lunch or dinner."

Acapulco *Mexican*   `22` `21` `22` `$26`
Old Town | 2467 Juan St. (Harney St.) | 619-291-0878 | www.acapulcorestaurants.com

This Old Town outpost of an "above-average chain" pleases south-of-the-border fans with its "surprisingly good" midpriced Mexican fare washed down by margaritas and such; "great" staffers tend to the "lively" crowd as they dine in "bright" environs or on a pleasant outdoor patio – "the best place to sit" – and enjoy occasional live music.

Acqua Al 2 *Italian*   `22` `19` `21` `$42`
Gaslamp Quarter | 322 Fifth Ave. (K St.) | 619-230-0382 | www.acquaal2.com

Make "a quick trip to Florence" at this "authentic" Italian Gaslamp spot that pays tribute to a ristorante of the same name located just "down the way from the Duomo", with dishes like its signature "must-have" blueberry steak; though it's "expensive", the "prompt" service and a "cozy, rustic, romantic" setting make it "ideal for a first date."

Adams Avenue Grill *Californian*   `24` `19` `22` `$32`
University Heights | 2201 Adams Ave. (Mississippi St.) | 619-298-8440 | www.adamsavenuegrill.com

"Terrific" salads, "innovative" entrees and "always-interesting" specials from "passionate" chef-owner Tom Kleitis make up the "reasonable" menu at this "casual" University Heights Californian; the "homey" space can get "a little crowded", but the "caring" staff helps make it "the kind of place every neighborhood should have."

	FOOD	DECOR	SERVICE	COST

Adam's Steak 'n' Eggs *American* | 23 | 17 | 22 | $26 |

Mission Valley | 1201 Hotel Circle S. (Fashion Valley Rd.) | 619-291-1103

Albie's Beef Inn *Seafood/Steak*

Mission Valley | 1201 Hotel Circle S. (Fashion Valley Rd.) | 619-291-1103
www.albiesbeefinn.com

Side by side in Mission Valley's Hotel Circle, Adam's serves "old-fashioned breakfast at its best" enhanced by "cheap prices", "snappy" waitresses and an "unironic retro" coffee-shop setting; meanwhile, Albie's "good-value" steakhouse fare competes for attention with "throwback", "noir-movie-set" surrounds featuring paintings of "scantily clad women" and a "place-to-be" piano bar.

Addison ⌧Ⓜ *French* | 27 | 27 | 27 | $130 |

Carmel Valley | Grand Del Mar | 5200 Grand Del Mar Way (Meadows Del Mar) | 858-314-1900 | www.addisondelmar.com

"First class in every respect", this "extravagant" New French draws seekers of "ethereal flavors" to Carmel Valley's "ultraposh" Grand Del Mar resort, where chef William Bradley's "superior" prix fixe dinners (with "astounding" wine pairings) rank among "SoCal's best"; the food is matched by "opulent villa" surroundings where you're "treated like royalty" by a "formal but warm" staff that earns the No. 1 score for Service in San Diego – though you may have to "pawn the family jewels to afford it."

Aladdin Café *Mideastern* | 25 | 20 | 23 | $23 |

Clairemont | 5420 Clairemont Mesa Blvd. (Doliva Dr.) | 858-573-0000 | www.aladdincafe.com

"Excellent" Middle Eastern eats – think "tangy" hummus, "smoky" baba ghanoush and "sinful" baklava – draw diners to this "casual" Clairemont Mesa place with a simple "strip-mall" setting; there's often a "busy lunch rush", but "warm, welcoming staffers and "moderate" prices make it "worth the effort."

Aladdin Hillcrest Cafe *Mediterranean* | 24 | 21 | 23 | $24 |
(aka Aladdin Restaurant)

Hillcrest | 3900 Vermont St. (Cleveland Ave.) | 619-574-1111 | www.aladdinsd.com

"Known for its wonderful aromas and flavors" this "affordable" eatery in Hillcrest's happening Uptown District serves some of "the best Mediterranean food" in the area, like "deliciously garlicky" hummus and meze appetizers that are "little dishes of heaven"; the "hospitable" owner often personally "dotes on customers" in a "relaxed" setting that includes an outdoor patio.

Alborz Restaurant *Greek/Persian* | 23 | 19 | 20 | $25 |

Del Mar | 2672 Del Mar Heights Rd. (Mango Dr.) | 858-792-2233 | www.alborzinc.com

"Hearty" portions of "tasty", "authentic" Persian and Greek fare are served by an "attentive" crew at this affordable Del Mar spot, making it a "great place to feed an empty stomach"; "atmosphere is lacking" in the red and white space but live music and belly dancers add some pizzazz.

Alchemy ● *Eclectic*   23 | 20 | 23 | $31

South Park | 1503 30th St. (Beech St.) | 619-255-0616 |
www.alchemysandiego.com

"Inventive" chef Ricardo Heredia turns "locally sourced" ingredients
into an Eclectic small plates "tour of the world", bringing "touches
of adventure" to this "reasonably priced" South Park "up and comer";
"superb" cocktails are served by "friendly" bartenders while "on-
the-ball" waiters tend to the spare but "nice-looking" dining area,
whose striking centerpiece is a large twisted-metal treeform.

Alexander's Pizza   *Pizza*   24 | 19 | 22 | $24

Coronado | 849 Orange Ave. (9th St.) | 619-435-5747 |
www.alexanderspizza.com

"Try the Greek pizza" or any number of "inventive" creations at this
Coronado pie peddler, a "great local place" that may be "more expensive than some" but is still easy on the wallet; though takeout
and delivery are a big slice of its business, plenty of folks dine in so
they can take advantage of happy-hour specials, sidewalk seating
and competent cashiers.

Alfonso's of La Jolla ● *Mexican*   20 | 18 | 20 | $34

La Jolla | 1251 Prospect St. (Roslyn Ln.) | 858-454-2232 |
www.alfonsosoflajolla.com

"Enormous portions" (think "plate-sized" burritos) washed down by
"fabulous" margaritas have made this midpriced Mexican mainstay
a La Jolla "classic" despite some claims that it's "pedestrian" and
"overpriced"; the decor "needs updating" too, but a "festive" feel
and an "accommodating" staff keep it a "crowd-pleaser."

Ali Baba   *Mideastern*   22 | 19 | 21 | $22

El Cajon | 421 E. Main St. (Avocado Ave.) | 619-442-3622 |
www.alibabahalal.com

"Excellent" Middle Eastern fare at wallet-friendly prices – including
"huge" kebabs, "wonderful" breads and elaborate salads – is the draw
at this "family-run" meeting place for El Cajon's Iraqi-Chaldean
community; it may not look like much from the outside, but the interior is decorated with draped fabrics and tented booths.

Aloha Sushi   *Hawaiian/Japanese*   21 | 11 | 21 | $21

La Jolla | 7731 Fay Ave. (bet. Kline & Silverado Sts.) |
858-551-5000 | www.alohasushilounge.com

"Plenty good" Hawaiian-meets-Japanese cuisine makes up the "reasonable" menu at this La Jolla hybrid, where "quality" sushi in creative
incarnations is served alongside a pupu platter of Pacific palate-
pleasers; staffers are "inviting", and the same goes for the cabana
seating and outdoor patio.

Amarin Thai   *Thai*   26 | 23 | 23 | $21

Hillcrest | 3843 Richmond St. (University Ave.) | 619-296-6056 |
www.amarinthaisandiego.com

Hillcresters "highly recommend" this Thai "jewel" for "rich, tasty"
curries, "super-spicy" seasonings and "slightly unique takes on clas-

sics", all at an "uncommon value"; "accommodating" staffers that "always aim to please" and "quaint" surrounds in a "traditional" style add to the "special treat."

Amaya *American*　25 | 24 | 26 | $57

Carmel Valley | Grand Del Mar | 5300 Grand Del Mar Ct. (Carmel County Rd.) | 858-314-2727 | www.thegranddelmar.com
"Generally excellent" American cuisine with a Mediterranean bent and "friendly yet respectful" service bring guests to this special-occasion spot in the posh Grand Del Mar resort; there are "wonderful" views from the terrace, and a "warm", "sumptuous" interior outfitted with "well-spaced" tables provides diners "a sense of privacy" – perhaps a "beautiful place to propose?"

Americana *American*　22 | 19 | 20 | $29

Del Mar | 1454 Camino Del Mar (15th St.) | 858-794-6838 | www.americanarestaurant.com
"Sinful" pancakes, "healthy" egg dishes and coffee "master-pieces" make breakfast the "meal of choice" at this midpriced Del Mar American, where guests enjoy a "charming" interior full of "energy" and "unbeatable" beach views from sidewalk seats; some say the "surfer-style" service "suffers" when it's "crowded" so just "be prepared for a leisurely meal" and "enjoy the parade of people strolling by."

Analog Bar ●Ⓜ *Eclectic*　21 | 23 | 20 | $22

Gaslamp Quarter | 801 Fifth Ave. (F St.) | 619-233-1183 | www.analogbar.com
Rock fans "love the atmosphere" at this "very cool" Gaslamp Eclectic, where "clever", affordable fare is "a step up from the typical", but much of the appeal lies in the funky, faux-recording-studio-styled space bedecked with LPs; service is "quick", and live DJs make it a "great place" to take an "old-school music head" for a drink at the long bar.

Andiamo Ristorante Italiano *Italian*　24 | 21 | 23 | $36

Tierrasanta | Gateway Shopping Ctr. | 5950 Santo Rd. (Portobelo Dr.) | 858-277-3501 | www.andiamo-ristorante.com
"You probably don't know this place exists" unless you live in Tierrasanta, but "neighborhood" regulars relish this "upscale" Italian "tucked in a strip mall" for its "reasonable" prices and "creative de-livery of traditional ingredients"; with "super-friendly" servers and a "lovely" outdoor patio, you may easily "forget Little Italy."

Andre's Cuban &
Puerto Rican *Cuban/Puerto Rican*　22 | 15 | 19 | $23

Morena District | 1235 Morena Blvd. (bet. Naples & Savannah Sts.) | 619-275-4114 | www.andresrestaurantsd.com
"Save the airfare to Havana" at this "affordable" Morena District "find", where "warm, comforting" Cuban and Puerto Rican fare "se-duces your senses" and leads some converts to dub it the "most authentic" – if "one of the only" – of its kind in the area; service is a bit "relaxed" and decor "spartan", but it remains "a hit" nonetheless.

	FOOD	DECOR	SERVICE	COST

Anthology ● *Californian* | 22 | 25 | 21 | $47 |

Downtown | 1337 India St. (bet. A & Ash Sts.) | 619 595 0300 |
www.anthologysd.com

Guests who "come for the music" and other "great entertainment" are "pleasantly surprised" by the "well-prepared" if "pricey" Californian cuisine at this "New York–class" boîte Downtown; an "attentive" staff patrols the "sleek", modern space, which has several levels, each offering "exceptional" views of the elevated stage.

Anthony's Fish Grotto *Seafood* | 24 | 20 | 22 | $31 |

Downtown | 1360 N. Harbor Dr. (Ash St.) | 619-232-5103
La Mesa | 9530 Murray Dr. (Water St.) | 619-463-0368

Anthony's Fishette *Seafood*

Downtown | 1360 N. Harbor Dr. (Ash St.) | 619-232-5103
www.gofishanthonys.com

"Around for decades", these "classic" midpriced seafooders, voted Most Popular in San Diego, still turn out "famous" chowder and other "delicious" daily catches for "tourists and locals" alike; service is "family-friendly", and though critics call these La Mesa and Downtown spots fairly "dated", they're won over by the "completely unpretentious" feel and "fresh ocean breezes" at the latter locale's more "casual" Fishette adjunct.

Antica Trattoria *Italian* | 23 | 19 | 22 | $38 |

La Mesa | 5654 Lake Murray Blvd. (Cowles Mountain Blvd.) |
619-463-9919 | www.anticatrattoria.com

Offering "a taste of Sicily" in a La Mesa strip mall, this "little neighborhood gem" dishes up "freshly made" pastas and "excellent" entrees at a "great value"; a "charming" staff presides over the "cozy", "intimate" interior decorated with trompe l'oeil murals of Italy, which complement the "authentic" food.

Antique Thai Cuisine *Thai* | 23 | 21 | 22 | $34 |

Midway District | 3373 Rosecrans St. (Midway Dr.) | 619-222-0689 |
www.antiquethaicuisine.com

"Don't be fooled" by the strip-mall location (or somewhat "hidden" entrance) of this Midway Thai – its dishes are "delicious, plentiful and, best of all, inexpensive"; what's more, the candlelit setting, decorated with native artwork, is "cozy and warm" and tended to by "attentive, unobtrusive" staffers who are always "quick to recognize regulars."

Argyle Steakhouse ⓜ *Steak* | 24 | 22 | 22 | $50 |

Carlsbad | Park Hyatt Aviara Resort | 7447 Batiquitos Dr. (Kingfisher Ln.) |
760-603-6908 | www.argylesteakhouse.com

"Glorious" patio views of Batiquitos Lagoon and the 18th hole make this steakhouse in the golf club at Carlsbad's Park Hyatt Aviara Resort a "delightful lunch spot", with "tasty" chops and "to-die-for" desserts that may not be "imaginative" but still place it "consistently above" typical golf course cuisine; it's certainly "expensive" so patrons save it for "a special occasion."

FOOD | DECOR | SERVICE | COST

Arrivederci *Italian* | 26 | 20 | 23 | $32

El Cajon | 2963 Jamacha Rd. (Campo Rd.) | 619-660-8200
Hillcrest | 3845 Fourth Ave. (bet. Robinson & University Aves.) |
619-299-6282
www.arrivederciristorante.com

"Awesome, authentic" Italian fare, like "must-try" minestrone,
"amazingly light" gnocchi and "top-prize" tiramisu, makes guests
feel "really at home" at these Hillcrest and El Cajon eateries; hand
in hand with the "homey" fare is a "casual", "rustic" setting and
"straight-from-Italy" waiters who are "always charming", even
when it's "crowded."

Arterra *American* | 24 | 23 | 24 | $48

Del Mar | San Diego Marriott Del Mar | 11966 El Camino Real
(Valley Centre Dr.) | 858-369-6032 | www.arterrarestaurant.com

An "exception" to the "hotel-restaurants-are-bastions-of-bland"
rule, this "imaginative" American in the Marriott Del Mar remains
"surprisingly excellent" despite a "revolving band of chefs", offering
an "ever-changing" menu of "farm-fresh" meals served with a hint of
"whimsy"; "superb" service, a "beautiful, dark, open" space and a
"hopping" bar scene help make it "a cut above" – though guests
should "bring an extra arm and leg" as payment.

A.R. Valentien *Californian* | 26 | 26 | 26 | $67

La Jolla | Lodge at Torrey Pines | 11480 N. Torrey Pines Rd. (Callan Rd.) |
858-777-6635 | www.arvalentien.com

Chef Jeff Jackson "works wonders" with the "freshest" of "farm-to-
table" ingredients to create a "constantly changing" menu of "incomparable" Cal cuisine at this "unique destination" in La Jolla's
Lodge at Torrey Pines; "impeccable" service that's "gracious yet unobtrusive" and a "beautiful, Craftsman-style" setting with "majestic"
golf-course views make it a "gift to San Diego" – albeit a "pricey" one.

Ashoka the Great *Indian* | 24 | 21 | 23 | $24

Mira Mesa | 9474 Black Mountain Rd. (Miramar Rd.) | 858-695-9749 |
www.ashokasd.com

"One of the better" options in Mira Mesa's Little India, this subcon-
tinental spot offers tandooris, "fresh breads" and "don't-miss" on-
ion bhaji served by "kind" staffers in simple surrounds; a mostly
"working crowd" appreciates the "great" bargain lunch buffet, and
the BYO option contributes to an affordable dinner.

Athens Market Café *Greek* | 22 | 19 | 22 | $25

Carmel Mountain Ranch | Carmel Mountain Plaza |
11640 Carmel Mountain Rd. (Rancho Carmel Dr.) | 858-675-2225 |
www.athensmarketcafe.com

Athens Market Taverna ⌰ *Greek*

Downtown | 109 W. F St. (1st Ave.) | 619-234-1955 |
www.athensmarkettaverna.com

For "a taste of Greece", the "not-to-be-missed" lamb chops, "light,
fluffy" pastitsio and other "authentic", "reasonably priced" treats do
the trick at these "family-run" faves in Carmel Mountain Ranch and

Downtown; there's "nothing fancy" about the spaces but "ultimate hostess" and proprietor Mary Pappas makes you feel like "a guest" in her home regardless; P.S. scores do not reflect a recent renovation to the Downtown branch.

Au Revoir French Bistro *French*

24 | 21 | 23 | $34

Hillcrest | 420 Robinson Ave. (4th Ave.) | 619-268-2400 | www.aurevoirbistrohillcrest.net

"Even my French friends" lavish "rave reviews" reports one surveyor about the "superb" fare at this bistro in "the middle of all Hillcrest has to offer"; add in a "good value" and "wonderful" native staffers who tend to "cute, romantic" surrounds, and don't be surprised if you too "fall in love with the place."

Avenue 5 *American*

23 | 21 | 23 | $41

Bankers Hill | 2760 Fifth Ave. (Olive St.) | 619-542-0394 | www.avenue5restaurant.com

After sourcing "fresh" produce from local purveyors, chef/co-owner Colin MacLaggan and his team whip up "creative", "well-prepared" American fare at this Bankers Hill bistro also known for "nicely poured" cocktails and "affordable" wines; the "pretty", "spacious" setting, featuring "coveted" window tables, is managed with aplomb by an "enthusiastic", "unpretentious" staff that helps get diners to events at the Old Globe or Balboa Park on time.

Azuki Sushi Lounge *Japanese*

24 | 21 | 23 | $37

Bankers Hill | 2321 Fifth Ave. (bet. Juniper & Kalmia Sts.) | 619-238-4760 | www.azukisushi.com

"Memorable meals" take place at this "tiny" Bankers Hill lounge, where "creative" midpriced sushi "of the freshest quality" and a sake selection that's among the "nicest in town" are served in a spare, "modern" environment; it's also a natural choice for those in a rush to catch the curtain at nearby Old Globe thanks to "friendly, effective" service.

Babycakes *Bakery*

25 | 21 | 23 | $14

Hillcrest | 3766 Fifth Ave. (Robinson Ave.) | 619-296-4173 | www.babycakessandiego.com

Sure, there's a limited sandwiches-and-salads menu but most guests are "holding out for dessert" at this affordable Hillcrest bakery/bar that specializes in "amazing cupcakes in inventive flavors" (think tres leches and PB&J) washed down with equally quirky cocktails; staffers are "always friendly", and there's "character, character, character" to spare here, especially during the "awesome" Sunday 'Church' party offering DJs and drink deals.

Baci ☒ *Italian*

25 | 22 | 24 | $48

Morena District | 1955 W. Morena Blvd. (Ashton St.) | 619-275-2094 | www.sandiegobaci.com

"Outstanding Italian" that "Tony Soprano would love" is the hallmark of this Morena District "landmark", which has been serving "to-drool-for" fare that's worth the "occasional splurge" since 1979; "well-trained" waiters in "black tie" have "been there for ages" too, and though a few say the "traditional" decor looks a little "long in the tooth", most praise its "old-world charm."

Baja Betty's ◐ *Mexican* 21 | 22 | 23 | $21

Hillcrest | 1421 University Ave. (Richmond St.) | 619-269-8510 | www.bajabetty.com

"Where else can you have this much fun with your clothes on?" ask "lively" patrons of this "loud, fun, gay" Hillcrest "party" spot, where "gringo"-style Mexican meals are "better than average" and "cheap" to boot; the real draw, though, is the "campy, festive" feel fueled by "margaritas galore" and "fierce", "flamboyant" servers.

Baja Fresh Mexican Grill *Mexican* 22 | 18 | 20 | $18

Downtown | 145 Broadway (Broadway Circle) | 619-702-2252
Point Loma | 3369 Rosecrans St. (Midway Dr.) | 619-222-3399
www.bajafresh.com

"Fast" and "fresh" are the watchwords of this California-born taqueria with Downtown and Point Loma outposts dispensing Mexican fare that's "tasty for the price you pay"; counter service is "nice" if perfunctory, there's a "to-die-for" salsa bar and though decor is pure "fast-food"-style, overall it's still "not bad for a chain."

Baleen *Seafood/Steak* 23 | 24 | 23 | $50

Mission Bay | Paradise Point Resort & Spa | 1404 Vacation Rd. (Ingraham St.) | 858-490-6363 | www.paradisepoint.com

"Stunning" views of Mission Bay might be the "absolute best part" of this "special-occasion" destination "tucked in" the Paradise Point Resort, also offering "wonderful", "expensive" steak and seafood plus "expertly crafted" cocktails; service can swing from "attentive" to "somewhat slow" in the "French colonial/ Caribbean-inspired" room, so "don't be in a rush" and just "watch the romance unfold" around you.

Bali Hai *Hawaiian/Polynesian* 23 | 26 | 23 | $37

Shelter Island | 2230 Shelter Island Dr. (Rosecrans St.) | 619-222-1181 | www.balihairestaurant.com

"A romantic throwback to the '50s", this Shelter Island "survivor" of the era's "tiki bars of yore" has undergone an "impressive remodel" that "stands up" to the "million-dollar bayside setting" much beloved by "tourists"; "terrific" staffers ferry an "updated menu" that lends Hawaiian-Polynesian chow a "California accent", while the "potent" mai tais soften tabs some deem "too pricey"; P.S. Sunday's champagne brunch is popular.

Bandar *Persian* 24 | 23 | 23 | $32

Gaslamp Quarter | 845 Fourth Ave. (E St.) | 619-238-0101 | www.bandarrestaurant.com

Enjoy "wonderful, healthy Persian food" at this "great-value" Gaslamp find, known for a "tried-and-true" menu of "easy-to-love" dishes both "unfamiliar" and classic in "extremely generous" portions; guests seated in the "upscale" dining room or "year-round" outdoor patio feel "welcomed and comfortable" thanks to a "spot-on" staff.

	FOOD	DECOR	SERVICE	COST

Bankers Hill *American*

| | 24 | 24 | 24 | $37 |

Bankers Hill | 2202 Fourth Ave. (Ivy St.) | 619 231 0222 | www.bankershillsd.com

"See-and-be-seen" clients crowd Bankers Hill's eponymous hot spot for "modernized" American "comfort fare" from chef Carl Schroeder (also of Market), served by "knowledgeable" staffers at "reasonable" prices; the "simple, open" space has an "unfinished edge" and "sexy" vibe, and though a few complain it's "loud" most thrive on the "energy."

Barbarella *Italian*

| | 22 | 22 | 24 | $34 |

La Jolla | 2171 Avenida de la Playa (El Paseo Grande) | 858-454-7373 | www.barbarellarestaurant.com

It's "adorable and cozy" on an average night but this La Jolla Shores "labor of love" by proprietor Barbara Beltaire really "shines on Halloween and Valentine's Day" when they break out "must-see" decorations that "alone are worth the trip"; also appealing is the "casual, no-fuss" Italian fare served at "reasonable" prices by "intelligent", "engaging" staffers.

Barolo *Italian*

| | 22 | 19 | 21 | $35 |

University City | Renaissance Towne Ctr. | 8935 Towne Centre Dr. (Excalibur way) | 858-622-1202 | www.barolos.com

"Italian home cooking" is *molto buono* at this "neighborhood" trattoria "tucked away" in a University City strip mall, where "hearty", "authentic" fare is offered alongside more creative dishes like "signature" pear ravioli; service is "inconsistent" but "friendly", and "quaint yet inviting" decor plus prices that "won't eat into your mortgage payment" add to the appeal.

Barrio Star *Mexican*

| | 24 | 22 | 21 | $26 |

Bankers Hill | 2706 Fifth Ave. (Nutmeg St.) | 619-501-7827 | www.isabelscantina.com

Proprietor Isabel Cruz "has done it again" with this "real-deal" Bankers Hill "sister restaurant" to her eponymous cantina, using "fresh ingredients" and a "unique blending of flavors" to craft "refreshing" Mexican dishes; margaritas are "made to perfection" by a "friendly" staff, and the Dia de los Muertos decor adds interest.

Basic Urban Kitchen & Bar ● *Pizza*

| | 26 | 23 | 21 | $24 |

East Village | 410 10th Ave. (J St.) | 619-531-8869 | www.barbasic.com

"Cracker-thin, crispy crust" pizza, a "wide" beer selection and "reasonable" prices bring a "casual" crowd to this "post-work or pre-Padres" place in East Village; "chill" staffers tend the "garagey", "modern-loft" space that turns "clubby" on weekends, and "great" art openings and music events add appeal.

Bay Park Fish Co. *Seafood*

| | 25 | 16 | 21 | $22 |

Bay Park | 4121 Ashton St. (Morena Blvd.) | 619-276-3474 | www.bayparkfishco.com

"Friendly, efficient" staffers "share their passion for fresh fish" at this "reasonably priced" Bay Park seafood "shack" and market, where "heavenly" entrees – like the "vaunted" tacos – are "simply pre-pared" and "catches of the day" are available at the counter; the "urban-industrial" decor may be a bit "bare-bones" but some love its "informal", "unaffected" feel.

Beach Grass Cafe *American*

22 | 17 | 20 | $20

Solana Beach | 159 S. Hwy. 101 (Plaza St.) | 858-509-0632 | www.beachgrasscafe.com

For "something fresh and unique" this Solana Beach cafe is a "wel-come break" from the usual, serving an "intriguing menu" of "solid" American fare (especially popular for breakfast) at value pricing; an airy if simple setting and "decent" enough service seal the deal for what fans call "funky and fun."

Belle Fleur *Californian*

23 | 23 | 23 | $40

Carlsbad | Carlsbad Premium Outlets | 5610 Paseo Del Norte (Car Country Dr.) | 760-603-1919 | www.bellefleur.com

Shoppers accessorize a day of designer discount hunting at Carlsbad Premium Outlets with a "relaxing" lunch or "excellent" Sunday buf-fet brunch complete with "flowing champagne" at this "pleasant" Californian cafe; it's "kinda fancy" for its mall-adjacent location, with prices to match the "upscale" setting and pleasing service.

Bencotto Ⓜ *Italian*

25 | 23 | 23 | $39

Little Italy | 750 W. Fir St. (bet. India St. & Kettner Blvd.) | 619-450-4786 | www.lovebencotto.com

"Bringing real Italian to Little Italy", Emilia Romagna–born chef Fabrizio Cavallini offers an "affordable" menu of "housemade every-thing" with a "cutting-edge" twist, served by staffers that reflect a "perfect balance" of "hard work, knowledge and attention to detail"; the "modern, sleek" setting attracts a "noisy", "hip" crowd, and it's "always busy, so get reservations."

Benihana *Japanese*

25 | 23 | 24 | $44

Mission Valley | 477 Camino Del Rio S. (Mission Center Rd.) | 619-298-4666

Carlsbad | 755 Raintree Dr. (Avenida Encinas) | 760-929-8311 www.benihana.com

Chefs "skilled in theatrics" are "entertaining for the whole family" at these Carlsbad and Mission Valley links of the Japanese steakhouse chain; some praise "surprisingly good" teppanyaki and a "super-fun" atmosphere, but others deem it "outdated" and "too spendy", suggesting you go "strictly for the show."

Bernard'O Ⓩ *Californian/French*

24 | 21 | 23 | $49

Rancho Bernardo | 12457 Rancho Bernardo Rd. (Pomerado Rd.) | 858-487-7171 | www.bernardorestaurant.com

This "delicious, elegant and expensive" French-Californian in upscale Rancho Bernardo has a "deeply loyal following" that favors it as a "special-occasion" destination thanks to a "spot-on" menu that's "refreshed with the season" and a "wonderful" wine list; "comfort-able" environs and "attentive but not intrusive" staffers will "trans-port you far away" from the "shopping-center" location.

Bertrand at Mister A's *American*

27 | 28 | 27 | $70

Bankers Hill | Fifth Avenue Financial Ctr. | 2550 Fifth Ave., 12th fl.
(Laurel St.) | 619-239-1377 | www.bertrandatmisteras.com

Bertrand Hug's "sensational" Bankers Hill American "screams special occasion" thanks to "simply breathtaking" bay and skyline views
and a setting that's "as elegant as you get" in these parts, earning it
the highest Decor score in the San Diego Restaurant Survey; an "apex
of fine dining", the French-inflected menu is ferried by "professional,
hospitable" staffers, and though tabs are "pricey", they seem "pro-
portional to the offerings."

Bice *Italian*

24 | 24 | 22 | $51

Gaslamp Quarter | 425 Island Ave. (4th Ave.) | 619-239-2423 |
www.bicesandiego.com

"*Molto Italiano*" fare takes a "nouvelle" turn at this Gaslamp link of
a Milan-based chain, where guests go "weak in the knees" for the
"legendary salumi" and "tempting" cheese bar; the "pro" staff and
"Euro-chic" decor match the clientele, just bring plenty of "lire" in
order to "dine stylishly" – or opt for the "terrific" daily happy hour.

Big Kitchen *Diner*

25 | 19 | 24 | $15

South Park | 3003 Grape St. (30th St.) | 619-234-5789 |
www.bigkitchencafe.com

"Honest, rich and wonderful" breakfast bites in "generous" portions –
think "hubcap-sized hot cakes" – have made this "legendary" South
Park diner a "community treasure"; a "warm, welcoming" staff
helmed by proprietor and "local celeb" Judy Forman tends to an
"eclectic" crowd in "hippie, homey" surrounds that lead fans to call
it the "grooviest" in SD – so "don't bring your conservative friends."

BJ's *Pub Food*

24 | 22 | 22 | $25

La Mesa | Grossmont Shopping Ctr. | 5500 Grossmont Center Dr.
(Center Dr.) | 619-589-7222 ◑
La Jolla | 8873 Villa La Jolla Dr. (Holiday Ct.) | 858-455-0662
Chula Vista | 555 Broadway (H St.) | 619-591-2490 ◑
www.bjsbrewhouse.com

"Standard" pub fare at this American brewhouse chain includes
"delicately crispy, light" pizza ("thumbs up" for a gluten-free option), "lots of fried things" and a variety of housemade beers, all at
"affordable" prices; the "casual", "sporty" setting makes it a "go-to"
for "group" dining, and staffers strike a "good balance" of "friendly
vs. overly familiar."

Bleu Bohème *French*

24 | 23 | 22 | $36

Kensington | 4090 Adams Ave. (Kensington Dr.) | 619-255-4167 |
www.bleuboheme.com

Francophiles even "drive across town" to dine at Ken Irvine's "charming" French bistro in Kensington, where "delicious, steaming bowls
of mussels" served "any way you like them" and other "approachable" items are "prepared with care and craft" and offered at decent
prices; staffers are "young but attentive", and the "romantic", "cozy
setting" helps "date"-night diners "get in the mood."

	FOOD	DECOR	SERVICE	COST

Blue Point Coastal Cuisine *Seafood* · 23 · 23 · 23 · $47

Gaslamp Quarter | 565 Fifth Ave. (Market St.) | 619-233-6623 |
www.cohnrestaurants.com

"One of the better bets" in the Gaslamp, this seafooder from the Cohn
"empire" (Indigo Grill, Island Prime, etc.) serves "dynamite" dishes in
"diverse" combos that leave guests in "love" despite "pre-recession
prices"; combining an "East Coast feel and West Coast hospitality",
the "clubby, masculine" space is tended by a "young, scrubbed"
staff that handles a "bustling" crowd with "humor and aplomb."

Blue Ribbon Artisan Pizzeria *Pizza* · 25 · 18 · 21 · $28

Encinitas | 897 S. Coast Hwy. 101 (H St.) | 760-634-7671 |
www.blueribbonpizzeria.com

Serving some of "the best pizza in North County", this "lively little
pizzeria" in Encinitas "shines like a beacon" thanks to a "healthy,
tasty" menu of wood-fired pies, "fresh" apps and "superior" wine
and craft beer offerings at reasonable prices; service is solid, and
though the quarters may be "small", fans still "love this place."

Blue Water Seafood *Seafood* · 27 · 15 · 20 · $21

India Street | 3667 India St. (bet. Chalmers & Washington Sts.) |
619-497-0914 | www.bluewaterseafoodsandiego.com

Fish doesn't get any "fresher" "unless you catch it yourself" say fans of
this "bang-for-the-buck" India Street restaurant/market's "delicious,
customizable seafood"; there's "no pretension – or ambiance", so
patrons can wait in the "long lines" "wearing drenched wet suits"
and dine on "paper plates with plastic utensils."

Boathouse *Seafood/Steak* · 22 · 22 · 22 · $44

Harbor Island | 2040 Harbor Island Dr. (Harbor Dr.) | 619-291-8011 |
www.boathouserestaurant.com

With its "marina decor" and "fantastic" views of the hundreds of
pleasure crafts moored below, this Harbor Island surf 'n' turfer becomes a "special-occasion" destination "when you get a table by the
harbor"; service varies, but "real-deal" specials like the Wednesday
whole lobster dinner are "particularly worth the price."

BO-beau Kitchen + Bar *French* · 24 · 24 · 23 · $39

Ocean Beach | 4996 W. Point Loma Blvd. (Bacon St.) | 619-224-2884 |
www.bobeaukitchen.com

"Great twists on classics" draw "dedicated foodies" to this "adventurous" French bistro in "offbeat" Ocean Beach from the Cohn Group
(Indigo Grill, Island Prime), where the likes of "to-die-for" signature
Brussels sprouts "not like mom's" and "amazing" moules come at
"reasonable prices"; staffers who are "flawlessly friendly" and a
"rustic", "countryside"-like setting complete the "welcoming" vibe.

Bombay *Indian* · 24 · 24 · 21 · $25

Hillcrest | 3960 Fifth Ave. (Washington St.) | 619-297-7777 |
www.monsoonrestaurant.com

"Staying true to its regional roots", this "exotic" Hillcrest Indian offers "nuclear-powered spice blends", "tangy" tandoori and "piping

hot" pakoras served by "educated" staffers who "kindly guide new-bies through the menu", the all-you-can-eat lunch buffet is an "exceptional value", while "Bollywood" videos and a "dramatic" waterfall add to the "festive" feel.

Boomerangs Burgers *Burgers*

| 24 | 19 | 20 | $21 |

Clairemont | 4577 Clairemont Dr. (Clairemont Mesa Blvd.) | 858-483-9500 | www.boomerangburgers.com

"Original" hamburger combos are crafted at this affordable Clairemont standby where there are over 30 sauces, a dozen types of cheese and "maybe too many" toppings (like grilled mango or fresh horseradish) to choose from; while the bites will "tickle your taste buds", the "laid-back" sports-bar setting and "spotty" service keep the atmosphere just "a step above the drive-ins."

Boudin Bakery & Cafe *Bakery*

| 22 | 18 | 20 | $13 |

Mission Valley | Fashion Valley Mall | 7007 Friars Rd. (Via De La Moda) | 619-683-3962

University City | UTC Shopping Ctr. | 4417 La Jolla Village Dr. (Genessee Ave.) | 858-453-1849
www.boudinbakery.com

"Delicious" bread made on the premises is "the star" at this affordable Mission Valley branch of the San Francisco–based bakery chain, serving soups, "flavorful, exotic" salads and "fresh" sandwiches; inside, it's basic but "pleasant", and the "friendly, accommodating" counter service staffers are "always smiling."

Brazen BBQ *BBQ*

| 23 | 20 | 22 | $21 |

Hillcrest | 441 Washington St. (Brant St.) | 619-816-1990 | www.brazenbbq.com

It's "slow-cooked heaven" at this Hillcrest barbecue joint, where "moist, smoky" ribs, "tangy" sauces and "delicious" cornbread are served in a "friendly, open" space decorated with rustic wood and industrial accents; "helpful, kind" servers man the cashiers, ringing up some "awesome" meals at not-so-brazen prices.

Bread & Cie *Bakery*

| 26 | 16 | 20 | $14 |

Hillcrest | 350 University Ave. (bet. 3rd & 4th Aves.) | 619-683-9322 | www.breadandciecatering.com

"Everyone knows" this Hillcrest bakery/cafe turns out some of "the best bread in San Diego", with "unbeatable quality" loaves served on their own or stuffed with "delectable" sandwich fixings and offered at "honest" prices; guests endure "madhouse" morning waits to order via "well-run" counter service and dig in amid "cute"-enough coffeehouse-style surrounds or on the outdoor patio.

Brett's BBQ *BBQ*

| 25 | 16 | 22 | $18 |

Encinitas | 1505 Encinitas Blvd. (El Camino Real) | 760-436-7427
Rancho Bernardo | 4S Commons Town Ctr. | 10550 Craftsman Way (Dove Canyon Rd.) | 858-487-7427
www.brettsbbq.com

Serving up "real-deal" BBQ at "reasonable prices" in Encinitas and Rancho Bernardo, this "carnivorous" duo peddles "fall-off-the-bone" ribs, "authentic, hickory-smoked" meats and "tangy" sauces that recall time spent "in Texas"; "friendly, helpful" staffers man the registers, and those who can't "overlook the warehouse atmosphere" say their "best advice" is to carry out.

Brian's 24 ● *Diner*   23 | 17 | 23 | $19

Gaslamp Quarter | St. James Ramada Hotel | 828 Sixth Ave. (bet. E & F Sts.) | 619-702-8410 | www.brians24.com

Offering "monster" portions of "excellent" breakfast and "solid" diner fare 24/7, this Gaslamp "comfort-food capital" is a "local hangout for many", from families and sports fans during the day (there's a big bar and several TVs) to those looking to get their "sober on" once the nightclubs close; though "service varies in quality", "reasonable prices" seal the deal.

Brigantine Seafood   *Seafood*   24 | 22 | 23 | $35

Del Mar | 3263 Camino Del Mar (Via De La Valle) | 858-481-1166
Coronado | 1333 Orange Ave. (Adella Ave.) | 619-435-4166
La Mesa | 9350 Fuerte Dr. (bet. Grossmont Blvd. & Severin Dr.) | 619-465-1935
Escondido | 421 W. Felicita Ave. (Centre City Pkwy.) | 760-743-4718
Point Loma | 2725 Shelter Island Dr. (Shafter St.) | 619-224-2871
Poway | 13445 Poway Rd. (Community Rd.) | 858-486-3066
www.brigantine.com

For "flavorful, simple" fare that "satisfies your seafood cravings" – think "favorite" fish tacos and "perfectly cooked" fillets – this "upscale chain" meets "high expectations", especially during the "vibrant", "affordable" happy hour; the "polite" staff is "speedy" even when there's a "huge crush" of customers, and though the "dust needs to be blown off" some locations, Del Mar is "newly renovated."

Brockton Villa   *Californian*   23 | 23 | 21 | $27

La Jolla | 1235 Coast Blvd. (Prospect St.) | 858-454-7393 | www.brocktonvilla.com

Though it's "worth going just for the location" on "awesome" La Jolla Cove, this "thoughtfully restored beach cottage" with a "breezy" patio overlooking the Pacific is "unmatched" for breakfast (especially the "to-die-for" French toast) and supplies "straightforward", mid-priced Californian fare through dinnertime; so even if service is "spotty" and parking is "impossible", it's "always busy."

Broken Yolk Cafe   *American*   23 | 18 | 22 | $17

East Village | 355 Sixth Ave. (J St.) | 619-338-9655
Carlsbad | 7670 El Camino Real (La Costa Ave.) | 760-943-8182
Pacific Beach | 1851 Garnet Ave. (bet. Kendall & Lamont Sts.) | 858-270-9655
San Marcos | 101 S. Las Posas Rd. (Grand Ave.) | 760-471-9655
Chula Vista | Village Walk Mall | 884 Eastlake Pkwy. (Miller Dr.) | 619-216-1144
www.thebrokenyolkcafe.com

"Lots of food for a reasonable price" explains why this local chain of breakfast and lunch specialists (open till 3 PM) is "über-crowded on weekends" with diners filling up on "tasty, typical American" fare in "obscene" portions; it's a favorite of those hoping to "cure their hangovers", and the "young, happy and full-of-energy" servers fit with the "busy, noisy" feel.

Bronx Pizza 🍽 Pizza
27 | 13 | 20 | $12

Hillcrest | 111 Washington St. (1st Ave.) | 619-291-3341 | www.bronxpizza.com

"New York-style" pizzas are served with East Coast "attitude" to match at this "legendary" Hillcrest pizzeria where "gruff" counter service is forgiven with a bite of the "soft, crunchy, oily, garlicky" pies offered in a "staggering" array of combos; tabs are "cheap" (cash only), and even the "nondescript" decor of vinyl booths and stark lighting doesn't prevent "lines out the door."

NEW Brooklyn Girl ◑ American
▽ 23 | 25 | 23 | $32

Mission Hills | 4033 Goldfinch St. (Fort Stockton Dr.) | 619-296-4600 | www.brooklyngirleatery.com

With "SoHo"-style decor and a "great vibe", this "real gem" in Mission Hills is "more like a NY or SF spot", with a "multigenerational crowd" lending a "lively" milieu; early adopters say it's already "running on all cylinders", giving competitors "a run for their money" with an "unbeatable" American menu of "interesting" family-style entrees, "quite good" desserts and "best-deal" bar bites.

Buca di Beppo Italian
22 | 22 | 22 | $31

Downtown | 705 Sixth Ave. (G St.) | 619-233-7272
Mira Mesa | 10749 Westview Pkwy. (Mira Mesa Blvd.) | 858-536-2822
Carlsbad | 1921 Calle Barcelona (Woodfern Ln.) | 760-479-2533
www.bucadibeppo.com

"Mountains of food" draw "the big eaters in the family" to these "standard" Italian chain links, where "homestyle" shared plates "bring back memories of mama's cooking"; some say it's "nothing memorable" and that "flash-from-the-past" decor can be "hokey", but "reasonable" prices and "super-friendly" staffers make it "perfect for group parties."

Bud's Louisiana Café 🖾 Creole
26 | 18 | 24 | $22

Kearny Mesa | 4320 Viewridge Ave. (bet. Balboa Ave. & Ridgehaven Ct.) | 858-573-2837 | www.budscafe.com

Chef-owner Bud Deslatte brings "a taste of the South to the West Coast" with his "Cajunlicious" and Creole New Orleans fare, peddling "real-deal" gumbo, po' boys and jambalaya "with a genuine smile"; the Kearny Mesa industrial park location is "accommodating for a crowd", and though decor is "adequate" but "certainly not fancy", low prices match the basic digs.

Buga Korean Barbecue Korean
▽ 25 | 19 | 22 | $31

Clairemont | 5580 Clairemont Mesa Blvd. (Jacob Dekema Frwy.) | 858-560-1010 | www.bugabbq.com

Serving "deliciously marinated meat" cooked over "a sizzling fire right at your table", this Clairemont spot is "100% Korean" from "the staff to virtually all of the patrons", though there's also "superb" sushi on the menu; while some find it "a little too expensive" for the motel-adjacent location, the "terrific-value" lunch specials make up for that.

Bully's Del Mar ● *Steak* | 23 | 17 | 21 | $32 |
Del Mar | 1404 Camino Del Mar (15th St.) | 858-755-1660 | www.bullysdelmar.com

"A staple after the races", this "standby" steakhouse near the Del Mar track attracts "old-timers" and "singles" hoping to "glimpse a jockey", "get a buzz on" with "retro cocktails" and devour "classic" prime rib ferried by "old-pro" staffers; while some enjoy the "glow of dark wood and cushy leather booths", others find the "throwback" decor "past its prime" and suggest "spending your winnings elsewhere."

Bully's East ● *Seafood/Steak* | 22 | 18 | 21 | $36 |
Mission Valley | 2401 S. Camino Del Rio (Texas St.) | 619-291-2665 | www.bullyseastsd.com

Though "drinking men" say this "old-school" Mission Valley "mainstay" is "primarily a bar", diners maintain that the "classic" American surf 'n' turf fare, "specialty" prime rib and "nothing-but-value" specials make it more than a "meet market"; with "up-to-par" service and "dated" decor that takes on the "pleasant" feel of "grandpa's study", it "survives quite nicely on longtime customers" and others who enjoy the "unpretentious" atmosphere.

Buon Appetito *Italian* | 25 | 20 | 22 | $35 |
Little Italy | 1609 India St. (Cedar St.) | 619-238-9880 | www.buonappetito.signonsandiego.com

"Ample, thoroughly enjoyable" Italian fare and "well-matched wines" served by "engaging" expat staffers make this "moderately priced" Little Italy trattoria a "pleasant surprise" – "cheek kisses" included; folks are "clawing to get in" the "quaint, cozy" spot, so wait at their "comforting, friendly" wine bar next door.

Burger Lounge *Burgers* | 25 | 19 | 22 | $16 |
Coronado | 922 Orange Ave. (9th St.) | 619-435-6835
Gaslamp Quarter | 528 Fifth Ave. (Island Ave.) | 619-955-5727
Hillcrest | 406 University Ave. (4th Ave.) | 619-487-1183
Kensington | 4116 Adams Ave. (Kensington Dr.) | 619-584-2929
La Jolla | 1101 Wall St. (Herschel Ave.) | 858-456-0196
Little Italy | 1608 India St. (Cedar St.) | 619-237-7878
www.burgerlounge.com

"Now that's an outstanding burger" declare enthusiasts of this chain peddling "juicy, flavorful, lip-smacking" grass-fed beef patties and other "fresh, healthy" versions like organic quinoa, free-range turkey and wild salmon via "efficient" counter service; the "plain", playful spaces are "always crowded and noisy" with "youthful" clientele, leading to a plea for "more locations!"

Burlap *American* | 22 | 25 | 21 | $44 |
Del Mar | Del Mar Highlands Town Ctr. | 12995 El Camino Real (Del Mar Heights Rd.) | 858-369-5700 | www.burlapeats.com

"All the current buzz seems well deserved" say fans of celeb chef Brian Malarkey's "East-meets–Old West" eatery in Del Mar, where "mouthwatering" New American fusion fare with "in-your-face" flavors and "unique" cocktails are ferried by staffers who "do a great job considering the crowd"; the "stunning" Asian-influenced decor "changes character from day to night" when it becomes "quite the meat market" for a "trendy" crew that doesn't mind "unbearable" noise and "over-the-top" prices.

Busalacchi's A Modo Mio *Italian*　　23 | 22 | 21 | $35

Hillcrest | 3707 Fifth Ave. (Pennsylvania Ave.) | 619-298-0119 | www.busalacchis.com

Chef-owner Joe Busalacchi brings "fantastic tastes" from his native Sicily to the "well-presented", "reasonably priced" Italian menu at this Hillcrest "class act", leaving guests "very satisfied" but "not overstuffed"; service provides "everything you need", whether seated in the contemporary dining room or "under the stars" on the "romantic" outdoor patio.

Butcher Shop *Steak*　　25 | 21 | 24 | $43

Kearny Mesa | 5255 Kearny Villa Rd. (Complex Dr.) | 858-565-2272 | www.butchershop.signonsandiego.com

"If you like steak", this chophouse in Kearny Mesa is "the place to go", offering a standard, if "nothing innovative", beef-centric menu of American fare at upscale prices; service is solid, and the clubby, "old-timey" interior (it's been around since 1985) is reminiscent of the Rat Pack era, making it "popular with the older crowd."

Cafe Athena *Greek*　　25 | 20 | 22 | $23

Pacific Beach | 1846 Garnet Ave. (Lamont St.) | 858-274-1140 | www.cafeathena.com

"Absolutely reliable" Greek fare, including "plenty" of "satisfying, tasty" vegetarian dishes, all at a "great value" contributes to the "well-earned longevity" of this Pacific Beach Hellenic "hidden" in a neighborhood shopping center; some say the "standard" decor is "nothing special", but "friendly" service rounds out the "satisfying package."

Cafe Chloe *French*　　25 | 23 | 22 | $32

East Village | 721 Ninth Ave. (G St.) | 619-232-3242 | www.cafechloe.com

"Oh-so-French", this "hip little bistro" with "wonderful Parisian ambiance" and "appealing intimacy" draws "top chefs" and "the pretty people now inhabiting East Village" for "joie de vivre"–affirming meals and "killer" wines; staffers are "attentive but not fawning", and though some call costs "inflated", others deem the experience "priceless."

Cafe Coyote *Mexican*　　23 | 22 | 22 | $24

Old Town | 2461 San Diego Ave. (Conde St.) | 619-291-4695 | www.cafecoyoteoldtown.com

"Authentic, savory and so dang tasty" entrees on "freshly made" tortillas (there are women patting *masa* outside) and "mouthwatering" margaritas are served by a "quick" staff at this moderately priced Old Town Mexican; those who call it a "tourist trap" wonder "what the hype is all about", but for others, the "festive" decor and "blaring" mariachi music make it the "place for a fiesta."

| | FOOD | DECOR | SERVICE | COST |

Cafe Japengo *Pacific Rim*

24 | 23 | 23 | $46

Golden Triangle | Hyatt Regency La Jolla at Aventine |
8960 University Center Ln. (Lebon Dr.) | 858-450-3355 |
www.cafejapengo.com

"Garden of Eden" for sushi fans and San Diego "singles", this "pricey"
Golden Triangle "meet market" tempts a "too-cool" clientele with "flavorful" rolls and "exotic" Pacific Rim flavors, plus the city's "best eye
candy"; also "attractive" are the "good-looking" staffers (which
a few find a bit "snobby") and "seductive", "Asian-inspired" decor.

Cafe on Park *American*

24 | 18 | 21 | $21

Hillcrest | 3831 Park Blvd. (University Ave.) | 619-293-7275 |
www.cafeonpark.com

"Belly-busting" omelets and "platter-sized" pancakes make mornings
"quite an event" at this "inexpensive" American in a "neat little pocket"
of Hillcrest; staffers are "harried but friendly", and the "warehouse-
trendy" decor and "raucous" full bar ("cool to see at breakfast")
draw "long" lines on weekends so "come early" – it closes at 2 PM.

Cafe Sevilla *Spanish*

23 | 23 | 22 | $32

Gaslamp Quarter | 353 Fifth Ave. (J St.) | 619-233-5979 |
www.cafesevilla.com

"Tip-top for tasty tapas" and "great sangria", this "fun" Gaslamp
Spanish is "the place to be" on weekends thanks to a "club atmosphere", live music and flamenco performances, but "you better
have reservations"; it has a "just-like-Madrid" feel and solid service,
but "bring *muchos pesos*" because "those little dishes sure add up."

Café 21 *Californian/Mideastern*

25 | 21 | 24 | $23

Gaslamp Quarter | 750 Fifth Ave. (F St.) | 619-795-0721
North Park | 2736 Adams Ave. (Idaho St.) | 619-640-2121 Ⓜ
www.cafe-21.com

"Fresh ingredients" and "full flavors" make up the "well-priced"
Californian–Middle Eastern meals at this Gaslamp–North Park duo,
where "star" Azerbaijani owners helm a "friendly" staff that may "take
a little time" but it's "only because they're making food from scratch";
a "pleasant" vibe and "interesting" decor help make it a "standout."

Cafe 222 *American*

23 | 17 | 21 | $18

Downtown | 222 Island Ave. (2nd Ave.) | 619-236-9902 |
www.cafe222.com

This "funky", breakfast-and-lunch-only Downtown American serves
"eclectic offerings and twists on old favorites" (think peanut butter-
and-banana French toast) in a "quirky, modern" setting of bright walls
and cutlery chandeliers; a few find it "a little expensive" for eggs and
grouse about "long" waits, but others laud the "hardworking" servers and "never miss a chance" to dine here.

Cafe Zucchero *Italian*

23 | 21 | 20 | $27

Little Italy | 1731 India St. (Date St.) | 619-531-1731 |
www.cafezucchero.com

The "reasonably priced" Italian fare is "consistently good" at this
Little Italy ristorante, but make sure to "leave room" for a "mouth-

watering" treat from the "entire counter of tempting desserts", a "wonderful way to end the meal", especially when enjoyed on the "quiet, romantic" outdoor patio; "comfortable" environs and a "carefree" atmosphere help make up for what some describe as "disinterested" service.

Caffe Bella Italia *Italian*   ▽ 25 | 22 | 25 | $31

Pacific Beach | 1525 Garnet Ave. (Haines St.) | 858-273-1224 | www.caffebellaitalia.com

"Spectacular" wood-fired pizzas, "deliciously fresh" antipasti and "to-die-for" desserts will "always leave you satisfied" at this "slightly upscale but not too pricey" Pacific Beach Italian; the atmosphere is "cozy and intimate", and expat staffers that are "the cutest this side of the equator" will make you a "regular customer."

California Pizza Kitchen *Pizza*   23 | 19 | 21 | $23

Carmel Mountain Ranch | Carmel Mountain Plaza | 11602 Carmel Mountain Rd. (Rancho Carmel Dr.) | 858-675-4424
Solana Beach | Beachwalk Plaza | 437 S. Coast Hwy. 101 (Dahlia) | 858-793-0999
La Jolla | 3363 Nobel Dr. (San Diego Frwy.) | 858-457-4222
Mission Valley | Fashion Valley Mall | 7007 Friars Rd. (Fashion Valley Rd.) | 619-298-4078
Chula Vista | Otay Ranch Town Ctr. | 2015 Birch Rd. (Eastlake Pkwy.) | 619-591-4630
www.cpk.com

"Pretty darn good for a chain", these popular spots "elevate" everyday pizza with "designer flavors" and "tasty twists on traditional" pies offered alongside "satisfying", "internationally inspired" pastas and salads at "reasonable" prices; while some find the digs "nondescript", the operation is "well run" by a "sociable" staff that'll "get you in and out", and parents appreciate the "kid-friendly" atmosphere.

Candelas *Mexican*   24 | 22 | 23 | $49

Gaslamp Quarter | 416 Third Ave. (J St.) | 619-702-4455 | www.candelas-sd.com

In a city "teeming" with cantinas, this Gaslamp "gem" is "deliciously different from the norm", offering "elegant", "lovingly prepared" "nouvelle Mexican" served by "knowledgeable" waiters "in white jackets"; the "romantic", "candlelit" decor is decidedly "upscale" and so are prices that "might take a bite out of your wallet."

Candelas on the Bay *Mexican*   21 | 23 | 22 | $38

Coronado | Ferry Landing Mktpl. | 1201 First St. (bet. B & C Aves.) | 619-435-4900 | www.candelas-coronado.com

"Romance and top-quality food collide" at this Coronado sibling of the Gaslamp "gem", offering "fresh, sophisticated" Mexican "palate-pleasers" and an "engaging" setting "exceeded only by the view" of "San Diego's skyline reflected in the water"; the staffers are "courteous and professional", if occasionally "sluggish" to some, and though a few find the tabs "inflated", many still give their "compliments to the chef."

	FOOD	DECOR	SERVICE	COST

NEW Carnitas' Snack Shack *American/Eclectic*

27 | 17 | 22 | $15

North Park | 2632 University Ave. (Oregon St.) | 619-294-7675 | www.carnitassnackshack.com

Named for chef/co-owner Hanis Cavin's pet pig (whose likeness adorns the roof), this North Park American-Eclectic peddles porcine pleasures such as "stacked-high" sandwiches and "yummy" pork belly at reasonable prices; though there "can be a wait", the counter service is "friendly" and there's "limited" seating on a pleasant patio.

Casa De Pico *Mexican*

24 | 25 | 23 | $23

La Mesa | Grossmont Shopping Ctr. | 5500 Grossmont Center Dr. (Murray Dr.) | 619-463-3267 | www.casadepico.com

With "wandering mariachis", staffers dressed in "full traditional uniform" and "hacienda" decor, this Grossmont Center Mexican has a "festive" feel that gets a boost from "birdbath-sized margaritas"; some dismiss it as "gringo" fare, but many others find it "delicious", "affordable" and "perfect for a party, happy hour or girls' night out."

Casa de Reyes *Mexican*

∇ 21 | 20 | 20 | $23

Old Town | Fiesta de Reyes | 2754 Calhoun St. (bet. Mason & Wallace Sts.) | 619-220-5040 | www.fiestadereyes.com

You'll "feel like you're south of the border" at this Old Town Mexican, where "*delicioso*" dishes and "reasonable" prices keep it "crowded"; the spacious patio and "authentic" interior are tended by "quick" servers who will "make sure your experience is a success."

Casa Guadalajara *Mexican*

23 | 24 | 23 | $22

Old Town | 4105 Taylor St. (Juan St.) | 619-295-5111 | www.casaguadalajara.com

If you're "too shy to brave the real thing in Tijuana", fans recommend this Old Town spot for "always reliable" "Baja-Mex" and "never-ending" margaritas at "affordable" prices; "efficient" staffers "move crowds in and out fast", and the "vibrant", "tourist"-filled setting is "especially festive" on the "colorful, umbrella-filled patio."

Celadon *Thai*

24 | 24 | 21 | $27

Hillcrest | 3671 Fifth Ave. (bet. Anderson Pl. & Pennsylvania Ave.) | 619-297-8424 | www.celadonrestaurant.com

Fans deem this Hillcrest "favorite" a "step above the other Thai joints", citing an "exciting menu" of "creatively prepared", "well-presented" fare; opinions vary on the service ("helpful" vs. "unconcerned"), but fans tout the "grown-up" look of its "new location", with a "clean, modern, hip" style that says "upscale – without the price."

Cheesecake Factory *American*

25 | 23 | 23 | $29

Mission Valley | Fashion Valley Mall | 7067 Friars Rd. (Ulric St.) | 619-683-2800
Chula Vista | Otay Ranch Town Ctr. | 2015 Birch Rd. (Eastlake Pkwy.) | 619-421-2500
www.thecheesecakefactory.com

"Humongous lines accompany humongous portions" at these "cheap-for-what-you-get" American chain links in Mission Valley and Chula

Vista, serving a "too-gigantic" menu of "insane" cheesecakes and
entrees "extravagantly high in calories", which fans call the "best
mass-produced meals anywhere"; the "huge space" is tended by staff
ers that are "always helpful" but can be "a tad slow due to crowds."

Cheese Shop *Deli* | 24 | 16 | 21 | $13 |

Gaslamp Quarter | Horton Grand Hotel | 311 Island Ave. (bet. 3rd &
4th Aves.) | 619-232-2303 | www.cheeseshopdeli.com

Patrons support this deli's move from Fourth Avenue quarters into
the "historic" Horton Grand Hotel, where a "low-key, local" crowd
gathers for "popular", "freshly made" sandwiches at lunchtime and
"good breakfast basics" at "decent" prices; whether it's "eat-in or
takeout", the "quirky" staff maintains a "good turnaround time."

Chicken Pie Diner *American* | 23 | 16 | 23 | $14 |

Poway | 14727 Pomerado Rd. (Colony Dr.) | 858-748-2445 |
www.chickenpiediner.com

Guests in pursuit of "home cooking like the old days" order "piping
hot" mashed potatoes, pot pies "you think your grandmother made"
and other slices of Americana at this "cheap" Poway spot; waitresses
are "old-school" and so is the '50s "diner"-style decor that some
say "needs updating."

China Max *Chinese* | 26 | 17 | 20 | $26 |

Kearny Mesa | 4698 Convoy St. (Engineer Rd.) | 858-650-3333 |
www.chinamaxsandiego.com

Fans say you can expect an "excellent" meal at this "always reliable"
Chinese on Kearny Mesa's Asian Restaurant Row, praised for "authentic" Cantonese cuisine and "quite tasty" dim sum that's "made
to order – not on carts"; it's "more expensive than most", and while
some complain the service "lacks warmth", it is "efficient" and the
setting is "pleasant and clean."

Chipotle *Mexican* | 26 | 20 | 23 | $14 |

Encinitas | 268 N. El Camino Real (Mountain Vista Dr.) |
760-635-3863
College East | 5842 Hardy St. (College Ave.) | 619-265-2778
Grossmont | 8005 Fletcher Pkwy. (Baltimore Dr.) | La Mesa |
619-589-2250
Hillcrest | 734 University Ave. (Cabrillo Frwy.) | 619-209-3888
La Jolla | 8657 Villa La Jolla Dr. (Nobel Dr.) | 858-554-1866
Mira Mesa | 8250 Mira Mesa Blvd. (Camino Ruiz) | 858-586-2147
Mission Valley | 1025 Camino de la Reina (Auto Circle) | 619-491-0481
Pacific Beach | 1504 Garnet Ave. (Haines St.) | 858-274-3093
Poway | 13495 Poway Rd. (Midland Rd.) | 858-748-9200
Sports Arena | 3680 Rosecrans St. (Sports Arena Blvd.) | 619-222-0508
www.chipotle.com
Additional locations throughout the San Diego area

"Amazing" Mexican fare, including fully customizable burritos, tacos
and salads, comes "fresh, tasty, fast" at these links in the affordable
national chain; the "contemporary" decor is "pleasant", and some
call the service "the best I've seen in a fast-food restaurant" – plus,
"you can actually see the food being made."

	FOOD	DECOR	SERVICE	COST

Chocolat Bistro *Dessert/Italian* | 25 | 21 | 21 | $19 |

Hillcrest | 3896 Fifth Ave. (University Ave.) | 619-574-8500 |
www.chocolat-hillcrest.com

Chocolat Cremerie ◗ *Dessert/Italian*

Gaslamp Quarter | 509 Fifth Ave. (Island Ave.) | 619-238-9400 |
www.chocolatsandiego.com

Sweet teeth are "delighted" by these "not-to-be-missed" Italian cafes
in Gaslamp and Hillcrest, where "light dinners" of "distinctive" savory fare are complemented by "sublime" gelato, "luscious" crêpes
and "silky smooth" coffee that "wow" diners; some say it's "too expensive", but "polite" service and a "chic" interior full of "sparkles
and cowhide" elevate the experience.

Cicciotti's *Italian* | 21 | 20 | 24 | $30 |

Cardiff-by-the-Sea | 1933 San Elijo Ave. (Birmingham Dr.) |
760-634-2335 | www.cicciottiscardiff.com

"Friendly" chef-owner Gaetano Cicciotti will "enjoy your company"
at his moderately priced Cardiff Italian, which is "worth a stop" for
the "uniformly good" menu of "thin-crust" pizzas, "hit-out-of-the-
park" specials and other "solid" fare according to fans; a casual
crowd enjoys "looking out at the sea" for a "beautiful view at sunset"
and live music provides entertainment.

City Delicatessen & Bakery ◗ *Deli* | 20 | 17 | 21 | $18 |

Hillcrest | 535 University Ave. (6th Ave.) | 619-295-2747 |
www.citydeli.com

For an "NY-style deli without the attitude", this "reasonable" Hillcrest
spot is a "worthwhile" option for "solid if unspectacular" pastrami
sandwiches, matzo ball soup and breakfast spreads; staffers are
"accommodating" and the "plain-Jane" setting is enhanced by personal jukeboxes and jars of complimentary pickles.

Claim Jumper *American* | 24 | 22 | 23 | $32 |

Carmel Mountain Ranch | 12384 Carmel Mountain Rd.
(Rancho Carmel Dr.) | 858-485-8370
La Mesa | Grossmont Shopping Ctr. | 5500 Grossmont Center Dr.
(Center Dr.) | 619-469-3927
Carlsbad | 5958 Avenida Encinas (Palomar Airport Rd.) | 760-431-0889
www.claimjumper.com

Unless you were "born with a hollow leg", wags predict "you'll never
make it to dessert" at this fairly priced American chain famed for
"huge" portions of "reasonably good" fare in lodgelike surroundings;
some say it "makes up in quantity what it lacks in quality", while others insist it's "not bad for a chain."

Cody's La Jolla *American*   ▽ | 22 | 22 | 20 | $25 |

La Jolla | 8030 Girard Ave. (Coast Blvd.) | 858-459-0040 |
www.codyslajolla.com

The American "comfort food" is "consistent" and "moderately priced"
at this La Jolla "brunch spot", but some say the "view is what you
come for", with a "relaxing" patio outside the "very cute beach cottage" offering "wonderful" Pacific vistas and "people-watching"; a

"young" staff "tries hard to please" the "endless stream of tourists" that squeezes in before the 3 PM close.

Come On In Café *American/European*   23 | 16 | 20 | $18

La Jolla | UCSD Torrey Pines Center S. | 10280 N. Torrey Pines Rd. (Genesse Ave.) | 858-657-9166 🏧
La Jolla | 1030 Torrey Pines Rd. (Herschel Ave.) | 858-551-1063
La Jolla | Rebecca & John Moores UCSD Cancer Ctr. |
3855 Health Sciences Dr. (Voigt Dr.) | 858-550-9643 🏧
Sorrento Mesa | 10068 Pacific Heights Blvd. (Barnes Canyon Rd.) |
858-638-0088 🏧
Sorrento Mesa | 10184 Telesis Ct. (Lusk Blvd.) | 858-558-8964 🏧
Sorrento Mesa | Gen Probe | 10210 Genetic Center Dr. (Mira Mesa Blvd.) |
858-731-5990 🏧
www.comeonincafe.com

For a "quick, inexpensive" meal, diners head to this La Jolla–born chain of American-European "neighborhood cafes", where the "fresh, tasty" soups and salads, "moist, chocolaty" desserts and "wonderful" breakfasts are "surprisingly upscale"; the "informal" spaces fill up during the "lunch rush" but "efficient" staffers keep crowds moving.

Convoy Tofu House *Korean*   24 | 16 | 20 | $14

Kearny Mesa | 4229 Convoy St. (Othello Ave.) | 858-573-2511 |
www.convoytofuhousemenu.info

Have it "hot, hot and hotter" at this affordable spot on Convoy Street's Asian Restaurant Row, where guests enjoy solid Korean "without having to drive up to LA" and fans fawn over "the best spicy tofu soup" in Kearny Mesa; some say the no-frills spot could use "more attention to detail", but others declare it a "favorite."

Coops BBQ Ⓜ *BBQ*   ▽ 24 | 14 | 21 | $15

Lemon Grove | 2625 Lemon Grove Ave. (Cypress Ave.) | 619-589-0478 |
www.coopsbbq.com

Even those "born in Texas" vouch for the "smoky" ribs, "melt-in-your-mouth" brisket and "perfect" sauce at this Lone Star State–style BBQ joint in Lemon Grove, where "great" prices and portions mean there's "so much food to take home"; "patient, quick" staff tends the "not-fancy" space and serves up meals with a side of "Southern hospitality."

Coronado Boathouse 1887 *Seafood/Steak*   23 | 22 | 23 | $42

Coronado | 1701 Strand Way (Silver Strand Blvd.) | 619-435-0155 |
www.coronado-boathouse.com

Built in 1887, this "lovely restored boathouse" that initially served the Hotel Del Coronado now caters to a "touristy" crowd, offering "standard" surf 'n' turf fare amid "cutesy nautical decor"; though some deem dishes "lackluster" and "overpriced", others praise "deliciously fresh" seafood and "great" steaks ferried by "engaging" waiters.

Coronado Brewing Company *Pub Food*   21 | 20 | 22 | $25

Coronado | 170 Orange Ave. (2nd St.) | 619-437-4452 |
www.coronadobrewingcompany.com

A "respite from upscale, expensive dinners" common on Coronado, this "casual" microbrewery and restaurant serves "fabulous" house made beers and "basic" pub fare at "reasonable" prices; a "come-as-you-are" crowd of families and service people from the nearby naval bases is tended by "knowledgeable" staffers in a "sports bar-like" setting that gets "loud and busy."

Corvette Diner *Diner*

| 20 | 26 | 23 | $22 |

Point Loma | Liberty Station | 2965 Historic Decatur Rd. (Barnett Ave.) | 619-542-1476 | www.dinecrg.com

"Fifties-fabulous" decor "transports" guests to another era at this memorabilia-jammed funhouse in Point Loma, where a "gorgeous" antique Corvette anchors the "retro" setting and "sassy waitresses sporting blue beehives" roller-skate around and pelt patrons with "straws and Bazooka gum"; "typical diner food" is offered at "reasonable prices" but all is secondary to the "raucous", "nostalgic" setting.

Cosmopolitan Restaurant *American/Mexican*

| ▽ 20 | 23 | 18 | $30 |

Old Town | Cosmopolitan | 2660 Calhoun St. (Mason St.) | 619-297-1874 | www.sdcosmo.com

"Painstakingly restored" to reflect its 19th-century roots, this "historic" hotel restaurant in Old Town State Park "accurately" represents its "Victorian-era" heritage in "even the smallest detail", from the antique furnishings to the waiters' outfits; though some find the Mexican-American fare "just ok for the price", and the service "down-to-earth" but "slow", for many it's still a "refreshing" venue.

Costa Azul Coronado *Mexican*

| 25 | 25 | 26 | $41 |

Coronado | 1031 Orange Ave. (C Ave.) | 619-435-3525 | www.costaazulcoronado.com

"After a day at the beach", families and locals flock to this "casual" Coronado eatery for "great" Mexican food from a midpriced menu that's "varied" enough "to please everyone"; staffers are "nice" and special props go to "friendly" bartenders pouring "strong" drinks.

Costa Brava ❶ *Spanish*

| 26 | 23 | 25 | $35 |

Pacific Beach | 1653 Garnet Ave. (Jewell St.) | 858-273-1218 | www.costabravasd.com

Reminiscent of a "neighborhood bar in Barcelona", this kinda "pricey" Pacific Beach tapas spot serves "authentic" small plates and "tantalizing" sangria in a "surprisingly quaint, romantic" setting that becomes more "lively" during evening flamenco performances; "professional" staffers tend to the crowd, which includes "lots of native Spaniards" who come to "feel at home."

The Cottage *Californian*

| 24 | 22 | 23 | $26 |

La Jolla | 7702 Fay Ave. (Kline St.) | 858-454-8409 | www.cottagelajolla.com

A "bustling, fast-paced favorite", this "charming" La Jolla Californian turns out "consistently delicious" daytime fare (and dinner in summer), including especially "amazing" breakfast offerings, all ferried by "efficient" staffers; prices are generally "reasonable" and though some ~~~ay "long lines" render it "too crowded to even approach on sunny ~~~ekends", those who make it inside declare it a "definite must."

	FOOD	DECOR	SERVICE	COST

The Counter *Burgers* | 23 | 17 | 21 | $19 |

Del Mar | Del Mar Highlands Town Ctr. | 12867 El Camino Real (Townsgate Dr.) | 858-481-9821
NEW **Downtown** | 695 Sixth Ave. (G St.) | 619-810-1850
www.thecounterburger.com

The "build-your-own" burger concept is "taken to a higher level" at these no-frills Downtown and Del Mar chain links that "offer more combinations than you thought possible", with "lots of toppings, premium and ordinary", plus your choice of patty, sauce and bun; luckily servers are on hand to "make great suggestions", and fans "highly recommend" it overall.

Cowboy Star Ⓜ *American/Steak* | 25 | 24 | 25 | $48 |

East Village | 640 10th Ave. (bet. G & Market Sts.) | 619-450-5880 | www.thecowboystar.com

At the "frontier" of American fare, this "pricey" but "ultrafine" East Village chophouse offers "premier cuts of beef" that are trimmed and cooked "to perfection" and can be accompanied by "inventive alternatives" such as offal and wild game; staffers are "attentive but not intrusive", and the white-linens-meets–"Wild West" decor and adjoining butcher shop make it a "welcome break" from its more "traditional" competitors.

Crab Catcher *Seafood* | 22 | 22 | 21 | $43 |

La Jolla | Coast Walk | 1298 Prospect St. (bet. Cave St. & Ivanhoe Ave.) | 858-454-9587 | www.crabcatcher.com

For those "trying to impress" a date or "out-of-town guest", the "spectacular" view at this "perennial favorite" seafood spot will do the trick – the "appealing" outdoor patio seems to "hang over a cliff" on La Jolla Cove; "timely" staffers proffer "well-prepared" entrees, oysters and sushi that some find "on the expensive side", while diners "enjoy the sunset."

Crab Hut *Cajun/Seafood* | 25 | 20 | 22 | $26 |

Downtown | 1007 Fifth Ave. (B'way) | 619-234-0628
Kearny Mesa | 4646 Convoy St. (Opportunity Rd.) | 858-565-1678
www.crabhutrestaurant.com

Cajun seafood comes "casual" at these midpriced Downtown and Kearny Mesa fish joints, where diners are advised to "wear their grubbies" to tuck into the "messy, sloppy goodness" of crab legs, lobster, clams and mussels; "great" staffers tend to the nautical-themed room where the tables are stocked with rolls of paper towels.

Craft & Commerce *New American* | 23 | 26 | 21 | $26 |

Little Italy | 675 W. Beech St. (Kettner Blvd.) | 619-269-2202 | www.craft-commerce.com

"You can't help but feel cool" upon entering this "dark, packed" Little Italy gastropub, where the "clever" decor eschews a "cookie-cutter" formula and matches the "unique" midpriced menu of "quality, farm-fresh" New American food and "artisan" cocktails "crafted with care"; the attention to "details" and "super-friendly" service reflect the "passion" of the management and staff.

Crazee Burger *Burgers* | 24 | 16 | 19 | $16 |

North Park | 4201 30th St. (Howard Ave.) | 619-282-6044
Old Town | 2415 San Diego Ave. (Conde St.) | 619-269-3333
www.crazeeburger.com

"Feel like a true caveman" at these affordable Old Town and North Park burger joints, where "wild beasts" like boar, kangaroo and antelope are made into "delicious patties", topped with gourmet fixings and served with "outstanding" fries; decor is "hole-in-the-wall" and there's "no service to speak of" since patrons order at the counter, but the "exotic" eats keep 'em coming nonetheless.

🆕 Cremolose ● *Dessert/Italian* | ∇ 23 | 23 | 21 | $21 |

Gaslamp Quarter | 840 Fifth Ave. (bet. E & F Sts.) | 619-233-9900 | www.cremolosesd.com

While this affordable Gaslamp Italian cafe serves pizza and pasta, it's the "yummy" gelato, "signature" *cremolose* (a cold, creamy treat) and "wonderful" pastries that are the star; the Euro-style space features an embossed tin ceiling and full bar, but you can also BYO.

Crest Cafe ● *Diner* | 23 | 17 | 21 | $18 |

Hillcrest | 425 Robinson Ave. (bet. 4th & 5th Aves.) | 619-295-2510 | www.crestcafe.net

The affordable "comfort food" "always delights" at this "eclectic" diner in the Hillcrest "gayborhood", where "Mexican-inspired" breakfasts, "superb" burgers and "heavenly" salads come in "huge" portions at "reasonable" prices; "fast" staffers work the "greasy-spoon" setting, whether ferrying morning meals or "late-night" snacks.

Croce's ● *American* | 22 | 22 | 22 | $39 |

Gaslamp Quarter | 802 Fifth Ave. (F St.) | 619-233-4355 | www.croces.com
Operated by the widow of "musical legend" Jim Croce, this "pricey-but-worth-it" Gaslamp eatery is "full of his memorabilia" and plays the singer-songwriter's hits "on a loop" when there's no "live jazz" on hand; still, it's not "all about the entertainment" here, as owner Ingrid also pays attention to the "well-prepared" New American menu, and ensures that staffers are "approachable" and "attentive."

Cucina Urbana *Italian* | 26 | 26 | 25 | $37 |

Bankers Hill | 505 Laurel St. (5th Ave.) | 619-239-2222 | www.urbankitchengroup.com

"Unlike anything else in San Diego", this "swinging" Bankers Hill Italian by restaurateur Tracy Borkum is "where the cool people go" for "reliable, innovative" entrees and "amazing" bottles that sell at retail (plus corkage fee) from an on-site wine shop; it's "unusually kind on the wallet" given the "rustic, sexy, California-cool" decor and "upbeat", "personal" service.

Currant *Californian* | 19 | 21 | 19 | $34 |

Downtown | Sofia Hotel | 140 W. Broadway (bet. 1st Ave. & Front St.) | 619-702-6309 | www.currantrestaurant.com

"Nostalgic" bistro decor and a "European" feel lend considerable "character" to this midpriced Californian brasserie on the ground floor of Downtown's boutiquey Sofia Hotel; while some quip that "continents drift faster" than the "spotty" staffers and find the fare merely "decent", absinthe service and a "bargain" happy hour help make it "worthwhile."

Davanti Enoteca *Italian*   25 | 23 | 24 | $32

NEW **Del Mar** | Del Mar Highlands Town Ctr. | 12955 El Camino Real (bet. Del Mar Heights Rd. & Townsgate Dr.) | 858-519-5060 | www.davantidelmar.com
Little Italy | 1655 India St. (Date St.) | 619-237-9606 | www.davantisandiego.com

"Fabulous, fabulous, fabulous" Italian fare comes "out of nowhere" to garner praise as some of the "best" in town at these "cool" Chicago imports in Little Italy and Del Mar, with almost "too many" small and large plates to choose from on their "excellent" midpriced menus; service earns solid scores, as do "large", attractive interiors and "awesome" outdoor patios.

Delicias ⚅ *Californian*   24 | 23 | 24 | $51

Rancho Santa Fe | 6106 Paseo Delicias (La Granada) | 858-756-8000 | www.deliciasrestaurant.com

"The name says it all" gush fans of this "old friend" in "the heart of historic Rancho Santa Fe", where new chef Paul McCabe "breathes life" into the "pricey" Californian menu with "luscious, satisfying" starters and entrees; "charming", "conscientious" staffers tend to an "elegant, upscale" room adorned with a working fireplace and "incredible floral arrangements" that make it a "special-occasion haunt."

Del Mar Pizza *Pizza*   25 | 17 | 21 | $14

Del Mar | 211 15th St. (Stratford Ct.) | 858-481-8088 | www.delmarpizza.net

Fans swear the "best pizza ever" comes from this petite pie parlor in downtown Del Mar, where "nice guys" who "know what they're doing" dish up "greasy but good" subs, pastas and salads to complement the main event; it's inexpensive and casual, with a "fun vibe" that makes it a "hangout for local teens" who don't mind minimal decor.

Del Mar Rendezvous *Chinese*   26 | 22 | 25 | $32

Del Mar | Del Mar Plaza | 1555 Camino Del Mar (15th St.) | 858-755-2639 | www.delmarrendezvous.com

"Delicately flavored" with a "focus on fresh ingredients", the "upscale Chinese" at this Del Mar Plaza eatery is "consistently yummy" and "priced very fairly" – especially on half-price wine nights; "full" gluten-free and vegetarian menus, "charming, personable" staffers and a "comfortable" setting adorned with Asian art also help make it a "favorite" of many.

de'Medici *Italian*   25 | 24 | 24 | $44

Gaslamp Quarter | 815 Fifth Ave. (F St.) | 619-702-7228 | www.demedicisandiego.com

Regulars return "for seconds" at this "upscale" Gaslamp Italian, where the "broad" menu of "traditional" dishes and seafood entrees is "spot-on" and "informative" servers prepare Caesar salad and steak Diane tableside; though a few find it "overpriced" and call the decor "outdated", most say it's "elegant but not overdone."

Dick's Last Resort ❶ *American*   18 | 19 | 19 | $25

Gaslamp Quarter | 345 Fourth Ave. (J St.) | 619-231-9100 | www.dickslastresort.com
You need to "know what you're in for" at this Gaslamp branch of the national American chain, where some deem the staff's "abrasive" shtick "offensive" but most say it's part of the "charm, or anti-charm"; it's a "good place to let your hair down", but some critics dismiss it as a "last resort for food."

Dobson's ☒ *Californian/Continental*   24 | 22 | 24 | $43

Downtown | Spreckels Bldg. | 956 Broadway Circle (B'way) | 619-231-6771 | www.dobsonsrestaurant.com
Diners return "time and time again" to this "venerable" Downtown "classic" for "solid", if "pricey", Californian-Continental fare (mussel bisque is "worth a detour") and the hospitality of "seasoned host" Paul Dobson, who makes guests feel "special and at home"; the "clubby" setting is "charming" and the "business set" does "important deals" at the bar, making it a "high-powered hobnob spot."

Donovan's Prime Seafood ☒ *Seafood*   24 | 23 | 22 | $52

Gaslamp Quarter | Trellis Bldg. | 333 Fifth Ave. (bet. J & K Sts.) | 619-906-4850 | www.donovansprimeseafood.com
From the team behind Donovan's Steak & Chop House, this upmarket Gaslamp seafood spot "maintains high standards" set by its sibling, with "top-notch" fare prepared "with finesse" and "prompt, helpful" service; the sleek digs with an "NYC feeling" are ideal for a "date night" or going "out with friends"; P.S. a post-Survey chef change may not be reflected in the Food score.

Donovan's Steak & Chop House *Steak*   27 | 25 | 26 | $68

Gaslamp Quarter | 570 K St. (6th Ave.) | 619-237-9700
Golden Triangle | 4340 La Jolla Village Dr. (Genesee Ave.) | 858-450-6666 ☒
www.donovanssteakhouse.com
Beef eaters boast "you'll never have a better steak" than at these Golden Triangle and Gaslamp "temples of red meat" where a "superb" team proffers "generous" plates of "tender", "top-quality" cuts "with all the fixin's" and "smooth" martinis at "through-the-roof" prices; the "dark, clubby" decor pleases, though "noisy, upscale crowds" make an "intimate dinner" unlikely.

Dumpling Inn Ⓜ *Chinese*   26 | 10 | 16 | $18

Kearny Mesa | 4619 Convoy St. (Dagget St.) | 858-268-9638 | www.dumplinginn.menutoeat.com
Aficionados advise "arrive early to beat the crowds" at this "wonderful, tiny" Kearny Mesa Chinese for some of the "best traditional dumplings in San Diego" and other cheap chow that's "so good, nothing compares"; it looks like a "hole-in-the-wall" and "brusque, hands-off" staffers are "always on the run", but fans promise your patience will be "rewarded" with "awesome" eats.

	FOOD	DECOR	SERVICE	COST

D.Z. Akin's *Deli* | 25 | 16 | 22 | $20 |

Grantville | 6930 Alvarado Rd. (70th St.) | 619-265-0218 |
www.dzakinsdeli.com

For a "pastrami fix", fans tout this affordable Jewish deli in Grantville,
whose "overstuffed" sandwiches, "delish" matzo ball soup and "homemade" pickles are the "closest thing in these parts" to an "NY"-style
nosh; "fast" staffers scoot around the "kitschy" space serving the
"enormous crowds" seated in "vintage Formica booths" or standing in
line at the "enticing" bakery counter.

East Lake Tavern + Bowl *American* | 20 | 22 | 21 | $22 |

Chula Vista | Design District | 881 Showroom Pl. (Fenton St.) |
619-565-2695 | www.bowlelt.com

East Village Tavern + Bowl ◑ *American*

East Village | 930 Market St. (9th Ave.) | 619-677-2695 |
www.bowlevt.com

North County Tavern + Bowl ◑ *American*

Escondido | 200 E. Via Rancho Pkwy. (Havocado Hwy.) |
760-690-2300 | www.bowlnct.com

A "new take on the old classic", this bowling alley–and–sports bar
trio eschews the usual "inedible snack food" and dingy decor in favor of "unique, fresh" pub fare and a "cool, trendy" setting that make
it the "hippest" of its kind; "friendly" staffers take orders over the
"clash of pins" and "loud, beer-soaked conversation", and though
some find it a bit "expensive" for what it is, for many it's a "great way
to spend an evening or afternoon."

Eddie V's *Seafood/Steak* | 25 | 26 | 25 | $58 |

La Jolla | 1270 Prospect St. (Ivanhoe Ave.) | 858-459-5500 |
www.eddiev.com

"Sweeping vistas of the Pacific" draw diners to this "pricey" La Jolla
Cove surf 'n' turfer, but fans insist the "ultraprime" steaks, "off-the-
charts" seafood and "hefty cocktails" are "worth a return visit on
their own"; "upbeat" staffers impress many with their "courtesy and
professionalism" while tending a "happening" crowd in the "classy-
chic" dining room and on the rooftop patio.

The Eggery *Diner* ∇ | 23 | 18 | 22 | $19 |

Pacific Beach | 4150 Mission Blvd. (Pacific Beach Dr.) | 858-274-3122 |
www.theeggery.com

"Eggs a zillion ways" are the focus of this Pacific Beach diner, though
it serves other "fresh" breakfast and lunch staples, like pancakes,
salads and sandwiches too; "friendly" service, affordable prices and
a country-style setting complete the picture.

El Agave Tequileria *Mexican* | 26 | 23 | 23 | $39 |

Old Town | 2304 San Diego Ave. (Old Town Ave.) | 619-220-0692 |
www.elagave.com

Amigos aver "you'll thank your stars you're in a border town" after
a forkful of the "rich, subtle, flavorful" moles and "sophisticated,
complex" entrees at this "high-end" Old Town Mexican located above
a liquor store; an "astounding" selection of tequilas "adorns every

square inch" of the "dimly lit" space, and while a few grouse about "slow" service, others praise the staff as "friendly and attentive."

El Callejon *Mexican*   23 | 20 | 22 | $25

Encinitas | 345 S. Coast Hwy. 101 (Encinitas Blvd.) | 760-634-2793 | www.el-callejon.com

It's "worth exploring" this colorful Encinitas cantina's broad menu, which "extends beyond the usual fare" and offers the "genuine flavors of Mexico" at affordable prices, backed by what many say are the "best margaritas in town"; service gets solid marks, though a few say it can vary "from spotty to excellent."

Elijah's *Deli*   18 | 14 | 19 | $21

La Jolla | 8861 Villa La Jolla Dr. (Holiday Ct.) | 858-455-1461 | www.elijahsrestaurant.com

Pastrami sandwiches in "generous portions", "first-rate" challah French toast and "worthwhile breakfast specials" "comfort the locals" at this La Jolla Jewish deli, but some critics sniff that the nosh is "nothing to write home about", service "borders on serve yourself" and the digs look "rundown"; still, many appreciate the "casual, unpretentious" vibe and "decent" prices.

El Indio Mexican Restaurant *Mexican*   24 | 14 | 20 | $15

Mission Hills | 3695 India St. (Winder St.) | 619-299-0333 | www.el-indio.com

Open since 1940, this Mission Hills "institution" stays put thanks to its "authentic" Mexican food and "bargain prices", serving "the best" chips, "well-seasoned" meats and "homemade" tortillas "cafeteriastyle"; there's "something charming about it" despite "long" lines and "no atmosphere", and those craving "fresh air" can hit the outdoor seats across the street.

El Pescador Fish Market *Seafood*   ∇ 25 | 10 | 20 | $22

La Jolla | 627 Pearl St. (bet. Cuvier St. & Draper Ave.) | 858-456-2526 | www.elpescadorfishmarket.com

"Don't be turned off" by the "modest" storefront or "cramped" seating – the seafood is "outstanding" at this La Jolla "hole-in-the-wall", where fin fare "caught by locals" is "as fresh as you can get" and "simply prepared"; while opinions split on the staff of "young" surfer dudes, service is "fast" and prices are "reasonable" for what you get.

El Take It Easy ◑ *Mexican*   20 | 21 | 19 | $24

North Park | 3926 30th St. (University Ave.) | 619-291-1859 | www.eltakeiteasy.com

"Super-crafty", "well-made" cocktails shine at this North Park spot, and complement an "eccentric" Mexican menu that's "reasonable" in price and "full of robust personality"; a "cool" storefront with a "calm, low-light" interior and "efficient" service make it an "awesome addition" to the neighborhood.

El Torito *Mexican*   21 | 21 | 21 | $25

Bonita | Westfield Plaza Bonita | 3030 Plaza Bonita Rd. (Bonita Mesa Rd.) | 619-470-3072

(continued)

El Torito

Mira Mesa | Mira Mesa Mall | 8223 Mira Mesa Blvd. (Reagan Rd.) | 858-566-5792
www.eltorito.com

"Super-good" burritos are the star on the menu of "Americanized", "semi-fast" Mexican fare at these local chain links in Bonita and Mira Mesa, where 2 PM happy hours and cheap taco Tuesdays keep the crowds coming; the colorful decor doesn't elicit any comments, while some find the service "hit-or-miss."

El Vitral *Mexican*

∇ 25 | 25 | 22 | $31

East Village | 815 J St. (8th Ave.) | 619-236-9420 | www.elvitralrestaurant.com

"Edgy" Mexican fare and dozens of tequilas combine with a "fantastic" view into Petco Park to make this "high-end" East Village cantina a "great spot before the game" – or during since you can "almost watch the Padres from the patio"; "enthusiastic" staffers tend a "cavernous", "breathtaking" space boasting high windows, a colorful bar and the "ultimate centerpiece", an open kitchen bedecked in "floor-to-ceiling stainless steel."

El Zarape *Mexican*

25 | 17 | 21 | $13

Normal Heights | 3201 Adams Ave. (32nd St.) | 619-578-2600 Ⓜ
University Heights | 4642 Park Blvd. (bet. Adams & Madison Aves.) | 619-692-1652 ◑
www.elzarape.biz

"More adventurous than traditional" Mexican, the "super-fresh" fare at this "cheap, casual" duo is "outstanding and inspired", with "addictive" seafood-stuffed tacos and burritos earning raves; filled with "high-quality folk art" and a "lively" crowd, the "capacious" Normal Heights location is a "nice step up" from its "closet-sized" University Heights sibling, and while some grouse about "slow" service, others praise the "friendly" staff.

Emerald Chinese
Seafood Restaurant *Chinese*

24 | 17 | 18 | $24

Kearny Mesa | Pacific Gateway Plaza | 3709 Convoy St. (Aero Dr.) | 858-565-6888 | www.emeraldrestaurant.com

"Fabulous" dim sum and an "enormous variety" of "unique" Chinese dishes make up the "affordable" menu at this "vast, Hong Kong–type establishment" in Kearny Mesa, where the "warehouse" setting suggests "they focus on the food" rather than ambiance; some praise the "helpful" cart-steering staffers, while others find them "difficult to communicate" with, and counsel "If you can't bring an interpreter, bring a boatload of patience", and you'll be "rewarded."

Enoteca Adriano *Italian*

∇ 25 | 21 | 23 | $30

Pacific Beach | 4864 Cass St. (bet. Beryl & Law Sts.) | 858-490-0085 | www.enotecaadriano.com

A "tiny place with a big personality", this "unique neighborhood Italian" in Pacific Beach is adored for "fresh, flavorful" fare prepared with the utmost love" and served at affordable prices in a "cozy" setting; the "hands-on" owner and "friendly" staffers will "ensure you're satisfied" and "looking forward to the next visit."

Escape Fish Bar *Seafood*

▽ 19 | 17 | 20 | $21

Gaslamp Quarter | 738 Fifth Ave. (bet. F & G Sts.) | 619-702-9200 | www.escapefishbar.com

"Fast and friendly" servers dish up Asian-Mexican–inspired seafood at this Gaslamp spot where "fresh", "local" fish is breaded in tempura flakes and accompanied by "incredibly complementary" Asian sauces and slaws in tacos and other entrees; some find it "a little pricey" and decor earns middling marks, but many are still willing to "recommend this place" to others.

Etna Restaurant ❶ *Italian*

25 | 19 | 23 | $20

East San Diego | Etna Restaurant | 4427 El Cajon Blvd. (Highland Ave.) | 619-280-1877 | www.etnapizza.com

Fans insist it's "worth a drive" to this affordable Italian in "out-of-the-way" East San Diego, especially if it's "ultralate" and you "don't want Taco Bell" – it's open until 2:30 AM on weekends, "unheard of for a sit-down spot" in these parts; surveyors "vouch" for "decent" counter service and "delicious" pizza and calzones "as big as your head", which come slathered with "tangy, classic marinara."

Farm House Café Ⓜ *French*

26 | 21 | 25 | $39

University Heights | 2121 Adams Ave. (Mississipi St.) | 619-269-9662 | www.farmhousecafesd.com

Put "farm-fresh California ingredients" in the hands of "talented" French chef Olivier Bioteau and expect "subtle", "stellar" results at this "neighborhood bistro" located "off the beaten path" in University Heights; "thoughtful" staffers make suggestions from a wine list "filled with European delights" in an "intimate, informal" setting, and most find the prices "reasonable" for the quality.

Fatburger *Burgers*

21 | 17 | 17 | $13

Escondido | 314 W. Valley Pkwy. (Escondido Blvd.) | 760-489-9999
Pacific Beach | 4516 Mission Blvd. (bet. Felspar St. & Garnet Ave.) | 858-581-1955
www.fatburger.com

A "cut above" your "standard fast-food fare", the Escondido and Pacific Beach links of this cheap hamburger chain offer "juicy" beef, turkey and veggie burgers topped with "amazing" extras like fried egg, chili and guacamole, and served with fat or skinny fries; "fast" service and "cool diner" decor are further pluses, and the nearby "benches along the shore" in PB offer a "great view while chowing down."

Fidel's Little Mexico *Mexican*

24 | 20 | 22 | $21

Solana Beach | Fidel's | 607 Valley Ave. (Genevieve St.) | 858-755-5292 | www.fidelslittlemexico.com

For "solid, well-prepared" Mex with "a touch of finesse", amigos head to this "huge, rambling casa" in Solana Beach, a circa-1961 "institution" serving affordable fare and "solid" margs in a "colorful" setting; while some complain it's "crowded and noisy", others "love the energy" and credit "attentive" staffers with keeping things moving.

The Field *Irish*

| 23 | 24 | 21 | $22 |

Gaslamp Quarter | 544 Fifth Ave. (bet. Island Ave. & Market St.) | 619-232-9840 | www.thefield.com

Brought over from Ireland and reassembled in the Gaslamp, this "dark, cozy" Irish pub is an "oasis" from the "put-on, chic clubs" nearby, offering "authentic, hearty" fare and beer from "friendly" staffers who know "how to pull a pint"; "can't-beat prices" further explain why it attracts a "constant crowd of revelers."

1500 Ocean Ⓜ *Californian*

| 24 | 24 | 24 | $65 |

Coronado | Hotel del Coronado | 1500 Orange Ave. (Glorietta Blvd.) | 619-522-8490 | www.dine1500ocean.com

The "imaginative", "outstanding" Californian cuisine "delights" at this dining room in the "iconic" Hotel Del Coronado, where guests enjoy "captivating" ocean views from the "warm, wood-paneled" interior or outdoor veranda; rounding out its charms is the "solicitous" staff that treats guests "like royalty" – for a "king's ransom."

Fig Tree Cafe *Californian*

| 25 | 22 | 24 | $20 |

Hillcrest | 416 University Ave. (4th Ave.) | 619-298-2010 | www.figtreecafehillcrest.com
Pacific Beach | 5119 Cass St. (Tourmaline St.) | 858-274-2233 | www.figtreecafepb.com

"Any breakfast lover" will adore these "reasonable" Californian cafes in Hillcrest and Pacific Beach, where "mouthwatering" French toast, "super-healthy" vegetarian options and "many farm-to-table" plates make guests "wish they were open" later than 3 PM; staffers are "on top of their game" amid "cute, quaint" environs, and PB's "shade-dappled" patio makes brunch feel like a "Saturday morning vacation."

Filippi's Pizza Grotto *Italian*

| 25 | 19 | 22 | $24 |

Kearny Mesa | 5353 Kearny Villa Rd. (Complex Dr.) | 858-279-7240
Little Italy | 1747 India St. (bet. Date & Fir Sts.) | 619-232-5095
Mission Valley | 10330 Friars Rd. (Riverdale St.) | 619-291-3511
Escondido | 114 W. Grand Ave. (B'way) | 760-747-2650
Pacific Beach | 962 Garnet Ave. (Cass St.) | 858-483-6222
Poway | 13000 Oak Knoll Dr. (Poway Rd.) | 858-748-1800
Scripps Ranch | 9969 Mira Mesa Blvd. (Hilbert St.) | 858-586-0888
Chula Vista | 82 Broadway (bet. Chula Vista & D Sts.) | 619-427-6650
www.realcheesepizza.com

"Ooey, gooey, cheesy" pizzas and "unbelievably huge" plates of "red-sauce" Italian taste like they came from "grandma's kitchen" at this chain, where "reasonable" prices and "friendly" service "make the meal complete"; "tucked behind" a specialty market, the original Little Italy location is an "institution", with "kitschy" decor of "checkered tablecloths" and "old Chianti bottles hanging from the ceiling."

	FOOD	DECOR	SERVICE	COST

The Fishery *Seafood*

26 | 19 | 22 | $35

Pacific Beach | 5040 Cass St. (bet. Loring & Opal Sts.) | 858-272-9985 | www.thefishery.com
"As if it flipped out of the net and onto your plate" cheer fans of the "first-rate seafood" "excellently prepared" at this "relaxed" Pacific Beach "gem"; some say it's "on the expensive side" for "eating in a fish market", but the staff is "responsive and helpful" and the "functional" setting "pleasant."

The Fish Market *Seafood*

25 | 22 | 22 | $35

Solana Beach | 640 Via de la Valle (Jimmy Durante Blvd.) | 858-755-2277
Downtown | 750 N. Harbor Dr. (B'way) | 619-232-3474
www.thefishmarket.com
For "fish so fresh it's still flopping", fin fans point to this Downtown "standby" (with a Solana Beach offshoot), where the "simply prepared" seafood is "fairly priced" (the upstairs Top of the Market is "more refined"); with "casual" service and a "fantastic bayfront setting" offering "unbelievable" views, patrons say "you can't get more California."

Five Guys *Burgers*

23 | 18 | 22 | $12

Encinitas | 130 N. El Camino Real (bet. Encinitas Blvd & Via Molena) | 760-436-0857
Coronado | NAS North Island, Bldg. 2017 (Callagan Hwy.) | 619-522-9604
Hillcrest | 670 University Ave. (7th Ave.) | 619-299-9105
Escondido | 1348 W. Valley Pkwy. (bet. Auto Pkwy. & 9th Ave.) | 760-740-8624
Pacific Beach | 1020 Garnet Ave. (Cass St.) | 858-272-2105
Point Loma | Liberty Station | 2445 Truxtun Rd. (Womble Rd.) | 619-223-1679
San Marcos | 151 S. Las Posas Dr. (Grand Ave.) | 760-736-8489
Southcrest | 2260 Callagan Hwy. (bet. Colton Ave. & 30th St.) | 619-236-8513
University City | 8650 Genesee Ave. (Esplanade Ct.) | 858-658-0778
www.fiveguys.com
"Customize your burger" at these hamburger chain links, where "fresh-as-they-get" patties are topped with "condiments galore" and served with hand-cut fries; it's "not good for your health" but "fair" prices are easy on the wallet, and many deem the food "the best I've had from a corporate chain."

Flavor Del Mar *Californian*

22 | 24 | 21 | $44

Del Mar | Del Mar Plaza | 1555 Camino Del Mar (15th St.) | 858-755-3663 | www.flavordelmar.com
"Go at lunch or at sunset" to enjoy the "wonderful" ocean vistas from the slick dining room or "happening" bar at this upmarket Del Mar Californian, where many go "for the view, but the food won't disappoint" either; "creative" chef Brian Redzikowski serves up the "usual hip stuff", and a "great staff" proffers an "excellent" wine list full of bottles "from around the globe."

	FOOD	DECOR	SERVICE	COST

Fleming's Prime Steakhouse & Wine Bar Steak

| 26 | 24 | 25 | $59 |

Gaslamp Quarter | 380 K St. (4th Ave.) | 619-237-1155
Golden Triangle | Aventine | 8970 University Center Ln. (Lebon Dr.) |
858-535-0078
www.flemingssteakhouse.com

"Always a winner" thanks to "top-notch" chops, "sophisticated" wine offerings and "excellent" service, these "well-worth-the-money" expense-account spots in Golden Triangle and Gaslamp inhabit the "upper tier of chain steakhouses"; the "elegant but comfortable" setting is characterized by "wood paneling, intimate booths, perfect lighting" and an "inviting" bar.

Forever Fondue Fondue

| 22 | 23 | 23 | $38 |

La Jolla | 909 Prospect St. (Fay Ave.) | 858-551-4509 |
www.foreverfonduesd.com

"Melted cheese to start and melted chocolate to finish" are the "highlights" of this DIY La Jolla fondue spot where guests dip "all kinds of delightful things" to create "decadent" meals; a few fume that it's "expensive for something you prepare yourself" amid "dated" surroundings, but "dim" lighting helps make it a "romantic" option for a "playful date."

Fred's Mexican Cafe Mexican

| 22 | 21 | 21 | $21 |

Gaslamp Quarter | 527 Fifth Ave. (bet. Island Ave. & Market St.) |
619-232-8226 ◑
Old Town | 2470 San Diego Ave. (Harney St.) | 619-858-8226 ◑
Pacific Beach | 1165 Garnet Ave. (Everts St.) | 858-483-8226
www.fredsmexicancafe.com

Though some say it's "more American than Mexican", that doesn't stop a "loud" crowd from downing "bowl-sized" margaritas and "big plates" of "decent" *comida* at this trio of "party" places; it may not be a "culinary experience", but affordable prices, "good-looking" staffers and "fiesta decor" complete a *picante* package.

French Gourmet French

| 25 | 19 | 24 | $32 |

Pacific Beach | 960 Turquoise St. (Cass St.) | 858-488-1725 |
www.thefrenchgourmet.com

"Recommended" by many for "French food without the pretense", this Pacific Beach bistro serves "well-prepared" fare at "decent" prices, but it's the "tremendous" pastries, "specialty" cakes and "fresh" breads from the on-site bakery that make it "extremely popular"; "eager-to-please" staffers and "cozy ambiance" don't hurt, either.

French Market Grille French

| 23 | 23 | 21 | $39 |

Rancho Bernardo | 15717 Bernardo Heights Pkwy. (Bermardo Rd.) |
858-485-8055 | www.frenchmarketgrille.com

"Proper, elegant" French fare and a "well-chosen" wine list attract North County residents and resort guests to this "nice neighborhood bistro" in a Rancho Bernardo shopping center; it's "pricey", but competent service and "traditional" decor complete with fireplace and garden room make it "one of the better dining experiences in the area."

	FOOD	DECOR	SERVICE	COST

Funky Garcia's ● *Mexican* ▽ 22 | 21 | 21 | $26

Gaslamp Quarter | 421 Market St. (bet. 4th & 5th Aves.) |
619-233-8659 | www.funkygarcias.com

While some "prefer to drink here as opposed to eating", others praise
the "tasty", affordable Mexican fare at this Gaslamp cantina, where
slashed prices and discounted drinks make it especially "cheap" on
Taco Tuesdays; though some complain that service is "slow at best",
"fun" music and a young, casual crowd make it a fiesta.

NEW Gabardine *Seafood* 21 | 20 | 20 | $35

Point Loma | 1005 Rosecrans St. (Talbot St.) | 619-398-9810 |
www.gabardineeats.com

Top Chef contestant Brian Malarkey adds to his empire with this
midpriced Shelter Island seafood spot, where guests recline in a
"comfortable" setting to sample from a "unique" menu that often
demonstrates the chef's "wonderful way with fish"; "not everything's a hit" and service can be "uneven", leading some to wonder
if it's got "more attitude than substance", but others report they've
"not been disappointed yet."

NEW Gaijin Noodle + ▽ 20 | 22 | 21 | $20
Sake House ●Ⓜ *Japanese*

Gaslamp Quarter | 627 Fourth Ave. (Market St.) | 619-238-0567 |
www.gaijinsd.com

Scenesters steer toward this Gaslamp Japanese, where cooks
churn out "specialty" noodles and yakitori from an open kitchen
amid Asian-inflected decor; they certainly keep things creative
with "sake snow cones and bacon s'mores" but some guests lament
"inconsistent" quality and "small" portions that can lead even petite
tabs to seem "overpriced."

Gaslamp Strip Club *Steak* 21 | 21 | 20 | $36

Gaslamp Quarter | 340 Fifth Ave. (K St.) | 619-231-3140 |
www.cohnrestaurants.com

La Jolla Strip Club Ⓩ *Steak*

University Heights | 4282 Esplanade Ct. (Genesee Ave.) |
858-450-1400 | www.lajollasteak.com

"Choose your meat and grill it yourself" at these midpriced Gaslamp
and Golden Triangle steakhouses, where groups gather to "drink
with friends" and work the communal barbecues ("what could go
wrong?"); to the "dismay" of some patrons, "strip" refers to the cut of
beef – the only nude women here are those featured in the Vargas
prints adorning the walls of the "fun but loud" space; P.S. 21-plus only.

George's California Modern *Californian* 27 | 27 | 26 | $51

La Jolla | 1250 Prospect St. (bet. Cave St. & Ivanhoe Ave.) | 858-454-4244

George's Ocean Terrace *Californian*

La Jolla | 1250 Prospect St. (bet. Cave St. & Ivanhoe Ave.) | 858-454-4244
www.georgesatthecove.com

With "fantastic" Californian fare from chef Trey Foshee, an "eclectic, extensive" wine list and a "one-of-a-kind" setting boasting "un-
surpassed" ocean views, it's no wonder proprietor George Hauer's

"tried-and-true performer" in La Jolla "endures with consistency"; the "accommodating" staff "operates like a well-oiled machine", plus the "relaxed" rooftop terrace offers a less "pricey" option for equally "enjoyable" meals.

Georges on Fifth *Seafood/Steak*   26 | 24 | 25 | $50

Gaslamp Quarter | 835 Fifth Ave. (bet. E & F Sts.) | 619-702-0444 | www.georgesonfifth.com

"Among the best in Gaslamp", this "traditional" surf 'n' turf spot (of no relation to La Jolla's George's California Modern) offers "cooked-to-perfection" steaks, "signature" crab cakes and an "excellent" wine list that almost stand up to "five-star pricing"; "upbeat" staffers "anticipate every desire" while the "relaxed" feel and "great" live piano round out a "very nice experience."

Ghirardelli's   25 | 21 | 20 | $15
Soda Fountain *Dessert/Ice Cream*

Gaslamp Quarter | 643 Fifth Ave. (G St.) | 619-234-2449 | www.ghirardelli.com

Maybe "it's for tourists" but this "traditional" Gaslamp ice-cream parlor by the famous San Francisco chocolatier still offers what fans call "the best sundaes in San Diego", with "incredibly rich" scoops and "decadent" toppings; some find it "expensive" for dessert, and the "cute, old-time" place is often "noisy and crowded", but those with a "sweet tooth" don't mind.

NEW Gingham *American*   21 | 21 | 20 | $32

La Mesa | 8384 La Mesa Blvd. (4th St.) | 619-797-1922 | www.ginghameats.com

This La Mesa American by celeb chef Brian Malarkey is a "treat", thanks to a "reasonably priced" menu of smokehouse BBQ and "gourmet" bites; while some say it's "still shaking out" the kinks, the spacious patio, "funky" urban-cowboy decor and "informal" feel help make it a "nice addition."

Girard Gourmet *Belgian/Deli*   25 | 14 | 21 | $20

La Jolla | 7837 Girard Ave. (Silverado St.) | 858-454-3325 | www.girardgourmet.com

Soups and sandwiches are "always delicious" and it "takes a lot of restraint" to resist the "wonderful selection" of baked goods at this affordable "little gem" of a Belgian deli on La Jolla's Girard Avenue; those who want to linger can grab a "pleasant outdoor table", but it's really "popular" for "takeout in a pinch", with regulars saying they "couldn't survive" without it.

Glass Door ◑ *American*   20 | 23 | 21 | $33

Little Italy | Porto Vista Hotel | 1835 Columbia St., 4th fl. (Fir St.) | 619-564-3755 | www.portovistasd.com

This "top-floor" New American eatery in the Porto Vista Hotel boasts "the only great ocean view in Little Italy" and a "trendy" look thanks to a "major face-lift" in 2012; though some think the fare can be "hit-or-miss", "solid" bartenders, "quick" service and "can't-beat" prices keep many coming back, even if only just "for drinks."

	FOOD	DECOR	SERVICE	COST

The Godfather *Italian*
27 | 23 | 26 | $36

Kearny Mesa | 7878 Clairemont Mesa Blvd. (Convoy St.) |
858-560-1747 | www.godfatherrestaurant.com
"Old-time Italian" just "like back East" is the MO at this "consistently
outstanding" strip-mall institution in Kearny Mesa, where rotating
dinner specials and "value" prices keep diners "coming back"; other
pluses include service that's "right-on-the-money" and "charming",
"traditionally decorated" surrounds.

Gordon Biersch ◗ *Pub Food*
21 | 21 | 20 | $31

Mission Valley | Mission Valley Ctr. | 5010 Mission Center Rd.
(Camino Del Rio) | 619-688-1120 | www.gordonbiersch.com
With a "great" list of craft ales and a "consistent" menu of "American
favorites", this Mission Valley brewpub is "always packed" with a
"lively" crowd; though some say the midpriced food is "uninspired"
and suggest they "stick to beer", the "friendly" staffers and "open,
airy" space are additional ingredients in its "recipe for success."

Gossip Grill ◗ *American*
20 | 21 | 23 | $24

Hillcrest | 1440 University Ave. (Normal St.) | 619-260-8023 |
www.thegossipgrill.com
It's "always a good time" at this Hillcrest bar and grill, where they
serve "good" American food but the "local lesbian population" comes
"mostly for alcohol consumption", aided by "friendly" bartenders
slinging "quirky" cocktails; events like Thigh High Thursdays and
Bang Bang Brunch offer "great" prices and keep it "bumping."

Grant Grill *Californian*
24 | 24 | 23 | $54

Downtown | U.S. Grant Hotel | 326 Broadway (3rd Ave.) |
619-744-2077 | www.grantgrill.com
"Top-notch in all respects", this "sophisticated" dining room in
Downtown's "classy" U.S. Grant Hotel offers "highly imaginative"
Californian cuisine à la carte or on a "wonderful" tasting menu;
though "pricey", it boasts "extremely attentive" service and an "elegant" atmosphere of "gorgeous, gilded-age decor" that delights old
guarders, theatergoers and business folk alike.

Green Flash *Seafood*
20 | 20 | 20 | $28

Pacific Beach | 701 Thomas Ave. (Ocean Blvd.) | 858-270-7715 |
www.greenflashrestaurant.com
Perched "right on the boardwalk in Pacific Beach", this "competitively
priced" beach bar may have a reputation for "solid but not inspiring"
seafood-centric fare and "harried" service, but it's "the location"
that makes it special; patrons watching "the bronzed and beautiful
pass by" get to take in an "incredible" view of "the sun sinking into
the Pacific" when they "might catch the elusive green flash."

Greystone the Steakhouse *Steak*
24 | 20 | 24 | $54

Gaslamp Quarter | 658 Fifth Ave. (G St.) | 619-232-0225 |
www.greystonesteakhouse.com
Lauded by its fans as "carnivore heaven", this "elegant" Gaslamp
steakhouse provides "fine dining as it should be" to an expense-

account crowd craving "tremendous" beef, "melt-in-your-mouth" seafood and a "superb" wine list; "professional" servers and "warm yet traditional" surrounds complete the "enjoyable" experience.

Grill at Torrey Pines *American*   23 | 22 | 22 | $37

La Jolla | Lodge at Torrey Pines | 11480 N. Torrey Pines Rd. (Callan Rd.) | 858-777-6645 | www.lodgetorreypines.com

An "easy alternative" to "posh" A.R. Valentien upstairs, this "class act" in the Lodge at Torrey Pines gets a hole in one with "always friendly" service and "top-notch" American fare (try the "to-die-for" burger) at prices more "reasonable" than its neighbor; the "clubby" room is appealing, but it's the "beautiful" setting "on the edge of a world-famous golf course" that really wows.

Habit Burger Grill *Burgers*   24 | 20 | 22 | $13

Carmel Mountain Ranch | 12002 Carmel Mountain Rd. (Conference Way.) | 858-485-9991 ◗

NEW Solana Beach | 909 Lomas Santa Fe Dr. (San Diego Frwy.) | 858-523-9697

Mission Valley | 845 Camino de la Reina (Auto Circle) | 619-299-9913 www.habitburger.com

"Tasty" burgers and "crispy" fries are "always fresh" and "prepared to your liking" at the local links of this Cali fast-food chain; "if you're on a budget, this is your place", and though decor is basic, there's "nice" outdoor seating.

Hacienda de Vega *Mexican*   23 | 26 | 21 | $30

Escondido | 2608 S. Escondido Blvd. (Citracado Pkwy.) | 760-738-9804 | www.haciendadevega.com

"Several tasty reasons" to visit this Mexican cantina in Escondido include a midpriced menu offering "great" house specialties, spice-spiked margaritas and "a number" of vegetarian options; adding to the list, the "beautiful" restored adobe ranch house provides a "charming" setting and "ample" outdoor seating in a "lovely" garden.

Hane Sushi Ⓜ *Japanese*   25 | 20 | 22 | $49

Bankers Hill | 2760 Fifth Ave. (Olive St.) | 619-260-1411

Serving the same "delicate, flavorful, exotic and lovely" fare as top-ranked sibling Sushi Ota but in a "much more inviting" atmosphere, "master" Yukito Ota and Roger Nakanura's "heavenly" Bankers Hill Japanese is a "favorite" – despite costing "the contents of one's wallet"; adding to the "overall excellence", servers are "very steady" and bartenders make "fine guides" through the sake and cocktail lists.

Harbor House *Seafood*   21 | 22 | 21 | $38

Downtown | Seaport Vill. | 831 W. Harbor Dr. (Kettner Blvd.) | 619-232-1141 | www.harborhousesd.com

"You can watch the boats come in while you eat" at this seafooder "right on the harbor" in Seaport Village; while the views are "magnificent", they don't fully compensate for relatively "high" tabs considering the "acceptable but not great" fare and "polite but not enthused" service, so locals only come when escorting "out-of-town visitors."

	FOOD	DECOR	SERVICE	COST

Hard Rock Cafe *American* `20` `24` `21` `$29`

Gaslamp Quarter | 801 Fourth Ave. (F St.) | 619-615-7625 |
www.hardrock.com

Music mavens "can't miss" at this tourist-heavy Gaslamp eatery,
where the "rock memorabilia" decor draws solid scores and voters
vouch for "generous" drink pours and "not bad" – if "overpriced" –
American fare; though events and concerts are a big draw, others
say you'll be "heartily rewarded" by visiting during off hours, when
"upbeat" staffers might let you pick the tunes.

Harney Sushi ● *Japanese* `26` `22` `22` `$34`

Oceanside | 301 Mission Ave. (Cleveland St.) | 760-967-1820
Old Town | 3964 Harney St. (bet. Congress St. & San Diego Ave.) |
619-295-3272
www.harneysushi.com

Serving an "ingenious" menu of sushi in "innovative" varieties, this
"trendy" midpriced Old Town and Oceanside Japanese is a "winner";
"late nights are where it's at", though some say the "hot beats from
a DJ" are "way too loud" and the service is "spotty", making it "more
of a scene than a restaurant."

Harry's Bar & American Grill ✉ *American/Italian* `23` `22` `23` `$39`

Golden Triangle | Northern Trust | 4370 La Jolla Village Dr. (Executive Way) |
858-373-1252 | www.harrysbarandamericangrill.com

Offering "classy" Italian and American fare, this "power-lunch
spot" in the Golden Triangle draws expense-accounters who
"compete for space and mobile bandwidth at the bar" amid a
"clubby" setting tended by a "knowledgeable" staff; though
some voters say it's "a little pricey for what you get", the "free grub"
at happy hour helps.

Harry's Coffee Shop *Diner* `23` `16` `23` `$19`

La Jolla | 7545 Girard Ave. (bet. Pearl St. & Torrey Pines Rd.) |
858-454-7381 | www.harryscoffeeshop.com

Around "for years", this affordable La Jolla diner and "iconic
breakfast spot" is usually "packed" in the mornings with "families, college students and seniors" enjoying "large, indulgent
dishes" and "tasty coffee"; the "friendly, efficient" servers let
guests linger "without being hassled", and "simple decor" adds to
the "down-to-earth" vibe.

Hash House a Go Go *American* `25` `20` `22` `$26`

Hillcrest | 3628 Fifth Ave. (Brookes Ave.) | 619-298-4646 |
www.hashhouseagogo.com

Famed for portions "huge" "enough to feed your neighborhood",
this American kitchen in Hillcrest "is not simply quantity over
quality" – its fans say that the "incredible" country food makes it
"the undisputed champion of breakfast" at a "good value", plus
it serves an "excellent" dinner; the setting's "hip", the servers are
"nice" and, though lines can get "crazy", the consensus is it's "well
worth the wait."

	FOOD	DECOR	SERVICE	COST

NEW Herringbone *Californian*

— | — | — | E

La Jolla | 7837 Herschel Ave. (Silverado St.) | 858-459-0221 |
www.herringboneeats.com

The most dramatic of celeb chef Brian Malarkey's restaurant empire,
this restored 1930s-era warehouse in La Jolla village boasts original,
barrel-vaulted wooden ceilings and century-old olive trees growing
out of the floor; able staffers tend well-heeled but casual locals as
they sample the contemporary Californian fare.

Hexagone *French*

24 | 22 | 23 | $45

Bankers Hill | 495 Laurel St. (5th Ave.) | 619-236-0467 |
www.hexagonerestaurant.com

"Often superb" French fare is "authentic" at this "reasonably priced"
Bankers Hill bistro, which many call the "best pre-theater spot" thanks
to free transport to the nearby Old Globe; decor is "classy, not flashy"
and it's "quiet" enough to " have a conversation", though guests are
split on service – is it endearingly "unhurried" or just "slow"?

Hob Nob Hill *American*

22 | 17 | 23 | $21

Bankers Hill | 2271 First Ave. (Juniper St.) | 619-239-8176 |
www.hobnobhill.com

"Mom must be in the kitchen" at this Bankers Hill "fixture" (opened
in 1944), serving "old-fashioned" American "home cooking" at "unbeatable" prices in a "blast-from-the-past" setting; even the "waitresses are from a time gone by", and you might find yourself dining
with "retirees to your right and the mayor to your left."

Hodad's *Burgers*

26 | 20 | 21 | $15

Downtown | 945 Broadway (10th Ave.) | 619-234-6323
Ocean Beach | 5010 Newport Ave. (Bacon St.) | 619-224-4623
www.hodadies.com

Adored for its "life-changing" burgers "stacked high with fixin's" and
"kitschy", "off-the-wall" atmosphere, this affordable Ocean Beach
"icon" and its Downtown twin offer "laid-back" service to the "omni-
present" "surfers and wannabes" (and "tourists"); the "only draw-
back" is "out-the-door" lines during peak hours.

Humphrey's *Californian/Seafood*

24 | 24 | 24 | $44

Shelter Island | Humphrey's Half Moon Inn | 2241 Shelter Island Dr.
(Anchorage Ln.) | 619-224-3577 | www.humphreysrestaurant.com

"Hearty", seafood-focused Cal cuisine "exceeds expectations" at this
Shelter Island restaurant and performance venue tended by "attentive,
polished" servers; guests "stroll over" to the stage after enjoying the
"elegant, comfortable" setting and "spectacular" marina views –
"that's what you pay for" after all – though some suggest you "only
eat here" for the dinner/show package or "elegant" Sunday brunch.

Il Fornaio *Italian*

24 | 25 | 23 | $41

Del Mar | Del Mar Plaza | 1555 Camino Del Mar (15th St.) | 858-755-8876
Coronado | 1333 First St. (Marine Way) | 619-437-4911
www.ilfornaio.com

"Striking" views at this regional chain's Coronado and Del Mar locations make dining "like a mini-vacation", where guests "watch the

sunset year-round" while tucking into "to-die-for" bread baskets and "tasty, fresh" if occasionally "formulaic" Italian fare; "on-the-ball" staffers and a "buzzing" scene mitigate "fancy" prices.

Indigo Grill *Pacific NW*   26 | 24 | 24 | $37
Little Italy | 1536 India St. (Cedar St.) | 619-234-6802 | www.cohnrestaurants.com

Housed in a "funky", "rustic" space in Little Italy, chef Deborah Scott's "eclectic" kitchen delivers "innovative" Pacific Northwest fare with a "fiery" Southwestern flair; those who find it "too eccentric" are outweighed by fans of the "lumberjack" portions and "above-par" service who say prices are "very reasonable", making this "another Cohn restaurant that meets the test."

In-N-Out Burger ✪ *Burgers*   26 | 18 | 24 | $10
El Cajon | 1541 N. Magnolia Ave. (Bradley Ave.)
Kearny Mesa | 4375 Kearny Mesa Rd. (Armour St.)
Mira Mesa | 9410 Mira Mesa Blvd. (Westview Pkwy.)
Mission Valley | 2005 Camino Del Este (Camino Del Rio)
Carlsbad | 5950 Avenida Encinas (Palomar Airport Rd.)
Rancho Bernardo | 11880 Carmel Mountain Rd. (Rancho Carmel Dr.)
Pacific Beach | 2910 Damon Ave. (Mission Bay Dr.)
Poway | 12890 Gregg Ct. (Community Rd.)
Chula Vista | 1725 Eastlake Pkwy. (Dawn Crest Ln.)
Sports Arena | 3102 Sports Arena Blvd. (Rosecrans St.)
800-786-1000 | www.in-n-out.com
Additional locations throughout the San Diego area

Rated Most Popular chain and top Bang for the Buck in San Diego, this "classic-Cal" burger chain is "beloved" for "fresh-cut fries, fresh-cut produce and fresh beef" that all add up to "heaven on a bun" and can be complemented with grilled cheese, Neapolitan milkshakes and saucy "animal-style" patties from the "secret menu"; a "chipper" counter crew and "extra-clean" locations help offset "long waits" and a sometimes "slow drive-thru."

Isabel's Cantina *Pan-Latin*   25 | 21 | 20 | $23
Pacific Beach | 966 Felspar St. (Cass St.) | 858-272-8400 | www.isabelscantina.com

The "exotic, delicious" Asian and Pan-Latin fare is "definitely worth a try" at this fusion "gem" in Pacific Beach boasting one of the "best breakfasts in town"; "value" pricing and a "warm, comfortable" (if "noisy") wood-trimmed space make up for occasionally "quirky" service and "tough parking."

Island Pasta   ▽ 26 | 21 | 25 | $17
Coronado *Italian*
Coronado | 1202 Orange Ave. (Loma Ave.) | 619-435-4545 | www.islandpastacoronado.com

Occupying prime real estate on Coronado's upbeat Orange Avenue, this kid-friendly Italian serves "fresh" pastas and pizzas "for a low price" along with "many wines by the glass"; solid staffers tend to a simple dining room and sidewalk patio, which offers views of Hotel Del.

	FOOD	DECOR	SERVICE	COST

Island Prime/C Level Lounge *Seafood/Steak* 26 | 27 | 25 | $46
Harbor Island | 880 Harbor Island Dr. (Harbor Dr.) | 619-298-6802 |
www.cohnrestaurants.com

"Show off your hometown" at this Harbor Island waterfronter from
Cohn Restaurant Group, with "spectacular" skyline views ("what
more decor do you need?") and "well-crafted, flavorful" steak and
seafood dishes from chef Deborah Scott; whether in the "upscale"
Island Prime or "more casual, less costly" C-Level Lounge, the staff
lends a "pleasant" touch.

Islands *American* 23 | 22 | 23 | $20
Carmel Mountain Ranch | 12224 Carmel Mountain Rd. (Conference Way) |
858-485-8075
Clairemont | 7637 Balboa Ave. (Jacob Dekema Frwy.) | 858-569-8866
Encinitas | The Plaza Encinitas Ranch | 1588 Leucadia Blvd.
(Town Center Pl.) | 760-943-0271
La Jolla | 3351 Nobel Dr. (San Diego Frwy.) | 858-455-9945
Mira Mesa | 10669 Westview Pkwy. (Mira Mesa Blvd.) | 858-578-6500
Mission Valley | 2441 Fenton Pkwy. (Friars Rd.) | 619-640-2727
Carlsbad | 889 Palomar Airport Rd. (Paseo Del Norte) | 760-602-9898
Chula Vista | 2255 Otay Lakes Rd. (Eastlake Pkwy.) | 619-397-2643
www.islandsrestaurants.com

"Every day is summer" at this tropics-inspired chain, offering affordable American fare like "delicious" burgers with gourmet fixings,
"excellent" cheese fries and islands-style cocktails; though a minor-
ity of surveyors isn't thrilled with "fast-food quality" fare, most enjoy
the cheerful service and tiki-style setting.

Jack & Giulio's *Italian* ▽ 27 | 20 | 24 | $30
Old Town | 2391 San Diego Ave. (Arista St.) | 619-294-2074 |
www.jackandgiulios.com

Fans "have been coming here for years and have yet to be disappointed" by the "top-notch" pastas and "otherwordly" scampi at this
"old-school" Italian "joint" in tourist-heavy Old Town; service gets high
marks, but bills can border on "pricey" and some say the dining room
"needs an upgrade", so "be sure to sit outside" on warm evenings.

Jai by Wolfgang Puck Ⓜ *Asian* 22 | 22 | 21 | $49
La Jolla | La Jolla Playhouse Grounds | 2910 La Jolla Village Dr.
(Revelle College Dr.) | 858-638-7778 | www.wolfgangpuck.com

"Best for pre-show eating" thanks to its "convenient" location next to
the La Jolla Playhouse, this UTC entry from Wolfgang Puck features
a "creative", "well-prepared" Asian menu presented by an "efficient"
crew; a few find the fare "uneven" and "not up to the standards of
Spago", but a "cool", "contemporary" setting makes it "worth the
occasional splurge"; P.S. it's only open when there's a show running,
so call ahead.

Jake's Del Mar *Californian/Seafood* 23 | 25 | 23 | $45
Del Mar | 1660 Coast Blvd. (15th St.) | 858-755-2002 |
www.jakesdelmar.com

"You'll feel like the waves are going to break on your table" at this
somewhat pricey Del Mar seafoodery, offering "panoramic views"

from a dining room that sits "right on the beach"; the Californian fare may be secondary but it's still "spot on", and patrons appreciate the "such-a-steal" happy hour and "attentive" service.

Jasmine *Chinese/Seafood* `24` `15` `18` `$25`

Kearny Mesa | 4609 Convoy St. (Dagget St.) | 858-268-0888 | www.jasmineseafoodrestaurant.com

"A little bit of Hong Kong" in Kearny Mesa, this affordable dim sum destination features "tasty", "truly authentic" Chinese tidbits from "carts full of goodies" that circle the "cavernous, hangarlike" space; the "busy, noisy, chaotic" setting and service that some call "mediocre at best" mean you "can't be shy" when placing orders, and weekend guests should "plan on a wait."

Jayne's Gastropub 🗷Ⓜ *Gastropub* ▽ `23` `22` `22` `$37`

North Park | 4677 30th St. (Adams Ave.) | 619-563-1011 | www.jaynesgastropub.com

"One of North Park's up-and-coming spots", this gastropub "classes up the neighborhood" with "inventive, market-fresh" fare and leaves guests "pleasantly content" despite the borderline "pricey" tabs; "always-there" owners and a "small, intimate" setting with a "twinkle-lit" patio make it feel like a "home away from home."

Jimmy Carter's Mexican Café *Mexican* `22` `16` `20` `$19`

Hillcrest | 3172 Fifth Ave. (Spruce St.) | 619-295-2070 | www.jimmycartersmexicancafe.com

"No, it's not owned by the former president", but this "eclectic" Hillcrest cantina is still "popular" for breakfast, lunch and dinner with "flavorful", "inexpensive" Mexican eats ("stick to the basics"); "warm" service and a "cheery, multicolored" dining room with a "friendly feel" earn it a steady following of "neighborhood residents."

Jimmy's Famous
American Tavern *American* `22` `24` `23` `$27`

Shelter Island | Promenade at Point Loma | 4990 N. Harbor Dr. (Nimitz Blvd.) | 619-226-2103 | www.j-fat.com

Set "right on the water" in Shelter Island with "beautiful views" of the harbor, this "casual" American features "dynamite" sandwiches, "big" burgers and a "fine beer selection" presented by a "fast, friendly" staff; even if a few find it "pricey" for the genre, most guests leave "very satisfied."

Joe's Crab Shack ❶ *Seafood* `22` `20` `21` `$32`

Downtown | Rowing Club | 525 E. Harbor Dr. (Park Blvd.) | 619-233-7391
Mission Valley | Hazard Ctr. | 7610 Hazard Center Dr. (Frazee Rd.) | 619-574-8617
Oceanside | Cape Cod Vill. | 314 Harbor Dr. (Carmelo Dr.) | 760-722-1345
Pacific Beach | 4325 Ocean Blvd. (bet. Grand & Thomas Aves.) | 858-274-3474
www.joescrabshack.com

It's "kind of a fast-food joint", but lots of surveyors "still love these places" for their "casual", kid-friendly, fish-shack settings and large helpings of "simply prepared" seafood, even if critics call the offerings "formulaic"; modest tabs make up for sit-down service that some find just "ok."

Jose's Courtroom ● *Mexican* ▽ 19 | 18 | 21 | $22

La Jolla | 1037 Prospect St. (Herschel Ave.) | 858-454-7655 | www.joses.com

"Perfect for a post-beach margarita", this "casual, unpretentious" eatery and watering hole is "one of the more popping spots in La Jolla", offering "inexpensive" Mexican that's "solid, but nothing out of the ordinary" to a "noisy" crowd of "tourists" and regulars; "prompt" staffers tend to the "sports bar"–style space, which features multiple TVs, ocean views and live music.

JRDN *Californian* 24 | 27 | 23 | $45

Pacific Beach | Tower 23 Hotel | 723 Felspar St. (Mission Blvd.) | 858-270-5736 | www.jrdn.com

"See and be seen" at this "gorgeous, beachside" Californian located in the "stylish" Tower 23 Hotel on the Pacific Beach boardwalk, where a "slick", "stunning" setting complements the "sophisticated" menu; "it ain't cheap" and service toggles between "gracious" and "standoffish", but a "very glamorous" crowd still "leaves satisfied" – especially after the "stupendous, reasonable" brunch.

Jsix *Californian/Seafood* 23 | 22 | 22 | $50

East Village | Hotel Solamar | 616 J St. (6th Ave.) | 619-531-8744 | www.jsixrestaurant.com

Lauded as the "antidote to the hot dogs and fries surrounding Petco Park", this "expensive" seafood-centric Californian in the Gaslamp's Hotel Solamar prepares its mostly "stellar" menu "with flair", especially during the five-course "Chef's Mercy" menu; "likable" staffers tend to a "hip, young" crowd that fills the "attractive" rooftop bar and "luxurious" dining room decked out in "rich golds, blues and terra-cotta."

Jyoti-Bihanga ⊠ *Vegetarian* 24 | 16 | 20 | $17

Normal Heights | 3351 Adams Ave. (Felton St.) | 619-282-4116 | www.jyotibihanga.com

Meat-free folks "sigh with vegetarian pleasure" over the "adventurous", "delicious and surprisingly inexpensive" eats (try the "famous" Neatloaf) at this Normal Heights hideaway run by students of a spiritual master; "courteous, methodical" staffers and a "soothing" setting full of "positive energy" make it a place to "unwind", but "call in advance" as it closes for long stretches in April and August.

Kaiserhof Ⓜ *German* 23 | 19 | 22 | $29

Ocean Beach | 2253 Sunset Cliffs Blvd. (Lotus St.) | 619-224-0606 | www.kaiserhofrestaurant.com

"As German as it gets" in Southern California, this "authentic" Bavarian "gasthaus" in Ocean Beach satisfies those craving "crispy, tender" schnitzel and "yards of wursts" washed down with "liters of fine beer"; the "folk costume"–wearing waitresses are "brusque" but "efficient", and though some find the "old-fashioned" decor "leaves something to be desired", guests love the tented back garden.

	FOOD	DECOR	SERVICE	COST

Karen Krasne's
Extraordinary Desserts *Dessert*

| 25 | 21 | 19 | $18 |

Bankers Hill | 2929 Fifth Ave. (bet. Palm St. & Quince Dr.) | 619-294-2132

Extraordinary Desserts *Sandwiches*
(fka Karen Krasne's Little Italy)

Little Italy | 1430 Union St. (bet. Ash & Beech Sts.) | 619-294-7001

www.extraordinarydesserts.com

"Gorgeously decorated" cakes, "rich" pastries and "excellent" coffee are the hallmarks of this frequently "crowded" San Diego dessert duo; a menu of savory options plus table service and a "spacious" setting help the Little Italy location stand apart from the original Balboa Park shop, but fans are "never disappointed" at either one.

Karl Strauss
Brewing Company *American*

| 23 | 23 | 23 | $27 |

NEW Carmel Mountain Ranch | 10448 Reserve Dr. (F St.) | 858-376-2739

Downtown | 1157 Columbia St. (B St.) | 619-234-2739

La Jolla | 1044 Wall St. (Herschel Ave.) | 858-551-2739

Carlsbad | Grand Pacific Palisades Resort & Hotel | 5801 Armada Dr. (Palomar Airport Rd.) | 760-431-2739

Sorrento Mesa | 9675 Scranton Rd. (Mira Sorrento Pl.) | 858-587-2739

www.karlstrauss.com

"Bring an appetite" for "divine" craft ales to this local brewpub chain, which hangs its hat on an "excellent" selection of suds poured by a "knowledgeable, beer-geek staff" but also offers "large portions" of "borderline-gourmet" American fare; guests enjoy "fair" prices and "laid-back" surrounds that vary by location – the "lovely Japanese garden" at the Sorrento Mesa outpost is "Shangri-la in a parking lot."

NEW Katsuya by Starck *Japanese*

| ▽ 22 | 24 | 21 | $42 |

Downtown | 600 F St. (bet. 6th & 7th Aves.) | 619-814-2000 | www.sbe.com

"Only for the young and hip", this Downtown Japanese originally from Los Angeles features a "chic, trendy" Philippe Starck–designed interior and "fancy" sushi, robata and sake at somewhat "high" prices; though some say it lacks "oomph" and service can be spotty, crowds still congregate for the 'social hour' specials.

Kensington Grill *American*

| 25 | 23 | 24 | $37 |

Kensington | 4055 Adams Ave. (Terrace Dr.) | 619-281-4014 | www.kensingtongrill.com

"Off the beaten path" in "charming" Kensington, this "inviting" New American peddles a "refined but unpretentious" menu of "exciting updates to comfort-food classics", using "local, organic" ingredients and charging "reasonable" prices; "well-informed" staffers work "with grace and ease" to serve a "convivial" crowd that comes to the "cozy" spot when they want to "be spoiled, yet feel like they're home."

	FOOD	DECOR	SERVICE	COST

Khyber Pass *Afghan*
25 | 22 | 23 | $35

Hillcrest | 523 University Ave. (5th Ave.) | 619-294-7579 |
www.khyberpasssandiego.com

"They do wonders with kebabs" ("lamb is the star") at this "rare
Afghan entry" in Hillcrest famed for its "tasty", "authentic" cuisine
at "reasonable" prices; with a "pleasant, sincere" staff and "upscale", "sophisticated" surroundings, the consensus is it's a "true
find" in the area.

King's Fish House *Seafood*
24 | 21 | 22 | $34

Mission Valley | 825 Camino de la Reina (Mission Center Rd.) |
619-574-1230
Carlsbad | 5625 Paseo Del Norte (Palomar Airport Rd.) |
760-431-3474
Chula Vista | Otay Ranch Town Ctr. | 2015 Birch Rd. (Eastlake Pkwy.) |
619-591-1690
www.kingsfishhouse.com

"Darn good fish" is "simply prepared" at this "reliable", "kid-
friendly" seafood chain earning kudos for its "fresh oysters" and lobster specials; staffers are "gracious", and though the "informal",
"East Coast"–style interiors are "nothing fancy", guests delight in
the moderate bills.

Kitchen 1540 *American*
25 | 24 | 24 | $52

Del Mar | L'Auberge Del Mar | 1540 Camino Del Mar (15th St.) |
858-793-6460 | www.kitchen1540.com

"If your date isn't impressed here, get a new one" assert fans of
this "stellar" New American in the "fashionable" L'Auberge Del
Mar, where a well-heeled crowd coos over a "creative" menu in-
corporating "molecular gastronomy and local, seasonal ingredients"
served by a "professional" staff; the dining room is "elegant", but for
many, the real appeal lies in the "fantastic" outdoor cabanas hosting
a "happening" scene.

Kitchen 4140 *American*
∇ 25 | 24 | 23 | $23

Morena District | 4140 Morena Blvd. (Avati Dr.) | 858-483-4140 |
www.kitchen4140.com

"Definitely worth the drive off the beaten path", this "foodie's
paradiso" housed in a "modern", "dinerlike" Morena District space
serves a "slow-food" American menu made "all from scratch" using
"the best products" sourced from local "artisans" and its own "organic garden"; the "outstanding" meals "without fine-dining prices"
and a "cool" staff make it "a breath of fresh air."

Kono's Café ⊅ *American*
23 | 20 | 22 | $12

Pacific Beach | 704 Garnet Ave. (Mission Blvd.) | 858-483-1669

"Amazingly long lines" form at this "iconic" American in Pacific
Beach, where "surfers" and "tourists" alike clamor for "reliably
prepared" breakfast fare to "fill the hungriest belly" sold at "1950s
prices"; guests order via "timely" counter service and find "limited"
seating in the "very casual" dining area or deck "overlooking the
beach"; P.S. closes at 3 PM weekdays and 4 PM weekends.

| | | FOOD | DECOR | SERVICE | COST |

Kous Kous Moroccan Bistro *Moroccan* | 23 | 22 | 23 | $29 |

Hillcrest | Plaza on Fourth | 3940 Fourth Ave. (Washington St.) |
619-295-5560 | www.kouskousrestaurant.com

A go-to for "wonderfully priced" Moroccan, this Hillcrest "favorite"
offers "to-die-for" kebabs and tagines "bursting with flavor and
spices" prepped by a "personable" chef who, along with "charming"
staffers,"treats you like friends coming to a dinner party"; "romantic" rooms filled with "authentic" rugs and glass lamps create a
"magical atmosphere" that's "chic" yet "welcoming."

La Bastide Bistro *French* | 25 | 21 | 24 | $34 |

Scripps Ranch | 10006 Scripps Ranch Blvd. (Pomerado Rd.) |
858-577-0033 | www.labastidebistro.com

"Flavorful", "reasonably priced" French "classics" are paired with a
"short, but excellent" wine list at this "little bit of Provence" in Scripps
Ranch; the "suburban-shopping-mall" setting may be "unassuming"
but an "unpretentious" feel and "welcoming" servers make it a "gem"
for family dinners and work lunches.

La Pizzeria Arrivederci *Pizza* | ▽ 24 | 18 | 19 | $32 |

Hillcrest | 3789 Fourth Ave. (Robinson Ave.) | 619-542-0293 |
www.arrivederciristorante.com

"Fantastic, authentic" pizza "like you had in Sicily" and a "smatter-
ing" of "comforting, simple" Italian favorites come with "affordable"
wines at this Hillcrest sibling to the Arriverderci ristorantes; the
space is "tiny" but "charming", and though some say service isn't a
strong suit, a "friendly" staff with "cute smiles and entertaining accents" makes up for it.

Las Cuatro Milpas ⊠⊅ *Mexican* | 26 | 10 | 21 | $9 |

Barrio Logan | 1857 Logan Ave. (Cesar E. Chavez Pkwy.) | 619-234-4460

"Unless you have a Mexican grandmother", you've "gotta go" to this
"extremely cheap" Barrio Logan spot serving "salt-of-the-earth"
comfort food crafted with "handmade" tortillas since 1933; "faithful" fans happily "drive 20 miles" to join the "line of locals out the
door" and eat amid "picnic-table decor"; P.S. closes at 3 PM.

La Taverna ⊠ *Italian* | ▽ 22 | 19 | 21 | $41 |

La Jolla | 927 Silverado St. (Drury Ln.) | 858-454-0100 |
www.lataverna.com

"A tiny little spot", this "cozy, down-to-earth" eatery near La Jolla
Cove is known for its "large", "reasonably priced" portions of
"homestyle" Italiana; guests can escape the "intimate" interior for
"people-watching" on the terrace, while a "delightful, exuberant"
owner and "professional" staff complete the "high-value package."

Le Bambou Ⓜ *Vietnamese* | ▽ 25 | 18 | 25 | $23 |

Del Mar | 2634 Del Mar Heights Rd. (Mango Dr.) | 858-259-8138 |
www.lebamboudelmar.com

It's an "adventure" in Vietnamese cooking at this "wonderful neighborhood place" in Del Mar, where guests always "discover new delights" on the lengthy menu; the "strip-mall" setting and "minimal"

decor may "leave something to be desired", but most find the "personable" staff and prices that are "excellent given the quality" make it "all worthwhile."

Lefty's Chicago Pizzeria Ⓜ *Pizza*   27 | 15 | 21 | $17

Mission Hills | 4030 Goldfinch St. (bet. Fort Stockton Dr. & Washington St.) | 619-299-4030
North Park | 3448 30th St. (bet. Myrtle Ave. & Upas St.) | 619-295-1720
www.leftyspizza.com

"Hearty" deep-dish pizzas "dusted with cornmeal" and smeared with "divine" sauce bring a "taste of the Windy City" to this affordable North Park "dive" and larger Mission Hills offshoot, where the Midwestern menu also includes "authentic" Chicago dogs, Italian beef sandwiches and Pabst Blue Ribbon; service is "friendly", but "call ahead" or "be prepared to wait" since those signature pies have an hour-long bake time.

Lei Lounge ◗ *Eclectic*   22 | 25 | 21 | $29

University Heights | 4622 Park Blvd. (Madison Ave.) | 619-813-2272 | www.leilounge.com

It's "sophisticated, LA-style dining" at this University Heights Eclectic where "chill" digs, "gorgeous" fire pits and a "hip" crowd provide "good eye candy" – as do the "cute" servers; the cocktails are "top-notch" and the "fairly priced" Asian-influenced menu is generally "well prepared", though some say "drink here, flirt here, don't eat here."

Leucadia Pizzeria & Italian Restaurant *Pizza*   22 | 18 | 20 | $22

Golden Triangle | 7748 Regents Rd. (Arriba St.) | 858-597-2222 | www.leucadiapizza.com

Locals praise the "wide variety" of "consistently good" pizzas, "terrific" garlic bread and other Italian favorites at this affordable link in a local mini-chain, with take-out and eat-in options in the Golden Triangle; service scores are solid, and the patio is the place for a "sunset dinner."

The Linkery ◗ *Eclectic*   22 | 19 | 20 | $28

North Park | 3794 30th St. (Park Way) | 619-255-8778 | www.thelinkery.com

This "trendy" North Park "gastropub" remains at "the forefront of the farm-to-table movement" with "inventive" Eclectic dishes featuring "quality" "locally grown items", including "popular" housemade sausages, all complemented by "notable" local beers and offered at moderate prices; the "industrial" space has "wall-sized windows that open to the street", and guests either "love or hate" the mandatory 18% service charge, most likely depending on whether they receive "attentive" or "spotty" service.

Local Habit *Pizza/Sandwiches*   ▽ 24 | 20 | 22 | $23

Hillcrest | 3827 Fifth Ave. (Robinson Ave.) | 619-795-4770 | www.mylocalhabit.com

"Fantastic" pizzas, sandwiches and small plates – many available in gluten-free and vegan versions – showcase "local, organic, delicious" herbs, veggies and meats and complement the "amazing" craft beer selection at this "reasonable" Hillcrest hangout; "genuine, upbeat" servers rush about an "urban-hip" room that has "soaring" ceilings and windows overlooking the "always interesting" street scene.

Lorna's Italian Kitchen 🅼 *Italian* ▽ 24 | 14 | 20 | $33

University City | University Square Shopping Ctr. | 3945 Governor Dr. (Genesee Ave.) | 858-452-0661 | www.lornasitalian.com
"Enormous" portions of "reliable" "red-sauce Italian", "reasonable" prices and "friendly" staffers keep this University City eatery almost "always busy"; perhaps there's "no ambiance whatsoever" in the "1970s strip-mall" setting, but fans find it "great" for "lazy Friday night" takeout or delivery.

Los Arcos *Mexican/Seafood* ▽ 25 | 19 | 21 | $21

Chula Vista | 89 Bonita Rd. (Bonita Glen Dr.) | 619-934-3517 | www.losarcossd.com
"Authentic", affordable Mexican cooking featuring "quality" Pacific Coast seafood makes this Chula Vista branch of a south-of-the-border chain a "welcome" neighborhood asset; "fast" staffers tend to a "colorful" dining room adorned with wall-sized murals, and though some say the venue "loses something in translation" from its cousins, others call it "paradise."

Lotus Thai Cuisine *Thai* 22 | 21 | 22 | $23

East Village | 906 Market St. (9th St.) | 619-595-0115
Hillcrest | 3761 Sixth Ave. (Robinson Ave.) | 619-299-8272
www.lotusthaisd.com
Cooks "spice it up" at these East Village and Hillcrest Thai "gems", creating curry "with a bite" and "lots of healthy vegan options" at "reasonable" prices; service with "manners and a smile" and environs that are both "relaxing and hip" further up the favorable "quality-price ratio" for a "can't-be-beat" meal.

Lou & Mickey's *Seafood/Steak* 24 | 25 | 25 | $45

Gaslamp Quarter | 224 Fifth Ave. (K St.) | 619-237-4900 | www.louandmickeys.com
"Killer" steaks, "flavorful" seafood and "exotic" cocktails make this "slightly expensive" Gaslamp Quarter surf 'n' turfer a "top contender" in the area; "attentive service" and polished wood and leather decor lend a "gentlemen's-club feel", although the space takes on a decidedly more "lively" vibe when fans descend "after a Padres Game" at nearby Petco Park.

Loving Hut *Vegan* 23 | 17 | 21 | $15

Mira Mesa | 9928 Mira Mesa Blvd. (Scripps Ranch Blvd.) | 858-578-8885
North Park | 1905 El Cajon Blvd. (Florida St.) | 619-683-9490 🔡
www.lovinghut.us
A "mecca" for meat-free eaters, these affordable Mira Mesa and North Park vegans – bright, basic outposts of the international fast-food chain – serve a "massive menu" of "great-for-your-health" meals with an Asian bent; counter service is solid, but hours are limited, so call ahead.

	FOOD	DECOR	SERVICE	COST

Lucha Libre *Mexican*

23 | 23 | 20 | $12

Mission Hills | 1810 W. Washington St. (India St.) | 619-296-8226 | www.tacosmackdown.com

Though some say the "kitschy", "quirky" decor of "Mexican wrestling memorabilia everywhere" and "hilarious" old matches playing on TV make this Mission Hills spot "more of a novelty" than a dining destination, others rave about the "killer" salsa bar, "generous" tacos, "monster burritos" and "cheap prices"; it's "über-popular" so there's "always a line" but "quick" counter service mitigates waits.

Luc's Bistro Ⓜ *Eclectic/Southern*

▽ 24 | 20 | 23 | $22

Poway | Poway Crossings | 12642 Poway Rd. (Silver Lake Dr.) | 858-748-9330 | www.lucsbistro.com

"Out-of-this-world yummy" Southern soul food and other "delicious" "homestyle" Eclectic fare with "imaginative twists" await at this Poway "labor of love"; modest tabs, "professional" staffers and an "understated" vibe make it "the sort of place you want in your 'hood."

Maitre D' Ⓩ Ⓜ *French*

▽ 26 | 24 | 25 | $63

La Jolla | 5523 La Jolla Blvd. (Midway St.) | 858-456-2111 | www.maitredlj.com

"For old-style elegance" and "top-notch" fare, guests "dress up" and head to this "special-occasion" "favorite" in La Jolla, which serves "wonderful, traditional French" with a side of "glamour" – think "ice swans, lillies and tableside productions"; the "ornate" (some say "outdated") space is tended by a "master" staff, providing "fabulous" service that matches the "expensive" tabs.

Mama Testa *Mexican*

23 | 17 | 20 | $18

Hillcrest | 1417A University Ave. (Richmond St.) | 619-298-8226 | www.mamatestataqueria.com

"Amazing" street tacos and other Mexican "family recipes" get a "unique" kick from the "fantastic salsa bar" at this Hillcrest "price performer"; guests order via "fast" counter service and find a seat in a "festive" dining room full of "funky" knickknacks and "bright" colors.

Mandarin House *Chinese*

22 | 15 | 21 | $32

Bankers Hill | 2604 Fifth Ave. (Maple St.) | 619-232-1101
La Jolla | 6765 La Jolla Blvd. (bet. Bonair St. & Playa Del Norte) | 858-454-2555
www.mandarinhousesandiego.com

"Old-school" Chinese washed down with "tropical cocktails in tiki mugs" wavers between "addictive" and "ho-hum" at these '70s-era "standbys" in Bankers Hill and La Jolla, where the lunch prices especially are a "great deal"; service is "expedient", so even if the "dark" "outdated" spaces "harken back to the restaurants your grandparents went to", for most "that's not a bad thing."

Manhattan *Italian*

23 | 22 | 24 | $44

La Jolla | Empress Hotel | 7766 Fay Ave. (Silverado St.) | 858-459-0700 | www.manhattanoflajolla.com

"Long a standby", this East Coast–style Italian in La Jolla's Empress Hotel boasts an "old-school" feel, "insane" live jazz and "waiters in tuxes" offering "tableside" preparations; an "older crowd" dines on "well-prepared" entrees (try the "outrageous" veal chop) and "solid" pastas or orders in the lounge at happy hour to avoid the somewhat "expensive" tabs.

Marine Room *Eclectic/French*

26 | 27 | 26 | $66

La Jolla | 2000 Spindrift Dr. (Paseo Dorado) | 866-644-2351 | www.marineroom.com

Achieve the "quintessential Southern Californian" experience at this "seaside treasure" in La Jolla, where "waves splash against the windows" of the "sophisticated" dining room during high tide while guests feast on chef Bernard Guillas' "first-class" menu of French-Eclectic dishes "full of flavor and beautiful color"; "impeccable" service shines too, and though it's "as pricey as it gets", it's "well worth" it when "celebrating life's big moments."

Market Restaurant & Bar *Californian*

28 | 23 | 26 | $69

Del Mar | 3702 Via de la valle (El Camino Real) | 858-523-0007 | www.marketdelmar.com

"Everything is spectacular" on "genius" chef-owner Carl Schroeder's "irresistible" menu at this "expensive-but-worth-it" Del Mar "must", where "inventive" Californian dishes (plus sushi) drawing on "many cultures" pair with "unknown gems" from a "thoughtful" wine list; you may need to "borrow a Ferrari" to fit in, but most say the "super-relaxed" surrounds and "pro" servers who are "anxious to please" complete the "flawless" night.

Maryjane's Coffee Shop *Diner*

▽ 17 | 19 | 19 | $18

Gaslamp Quarter | Hard Rock Hotel San Diego | 207 Fifth Ave. (L St.) | 619-764-6950 | www.hardrockhotelsd.com

Guests love the "bright, fun" digs and "cool vibes" at this Hard Rock Hotel diner, "the spot" for "late-night" burgers and "hangover breakfasts" in the Gaslamp; some lament "nothing-special" eats and "slow" service, but bills are easygoing and revelers that come "after the club" leave here "happy . . . and even more drunk."

Masala *Indian*

▽ 23 | 21 | 23 | $32

Gaslamp Quarter | 314 Fifth Ave. (K St.) | 619-232-5050 | www.masalarestaurant.com

"As good as Bombay but with more room to breathe", this Gaslamp Indian is appreciated for both "very flavorful" and "reasonably spicy" fare and an "exciting" setting, with a dining room that looks like "the richest man in the world's" idea of "elegant"; even if some say the "friendly" service could use some "polishing", the "best-deal" lunch buffet "shouldn't be missed."

McCormick & Schmick's *Seafood/Steak*

23 | 22 | 20 | $47

East Village | Omni Hotel | 675 L St. (Tony Gwynn Dr.) | 619-645-6545 | www.mccormickandschmicks.com

"Consistent on all levels", this national chain outpost in East Village's Omni Hotel serves "reliable" seafood and steakhouse fare that's "delicious" if "without adventure" in a "slightly upscale" setting; guests compliment the "perky, playful" servers and a "bargain"

	FOOD	DECOR	SERVICE	COST

menu at the "happiest hour around", which tempers tabs some otherwise find a "bit overpriced."

McP's Irish Pub & Grill *Pub Food*

| 19 | 17 | 20 | $22 |

Coronado | 1107 Orange Ave. (C Ave.) | 619-435-5280 | www.mcpspub.com

"Ogle cute Navy pilots" and SEALS at this "dependable" Coronado Irish-American bar, where bartenders pour a "proper pint" and "flowing beer and greasy pub food" fuel the "active-duty" gents and a "chummy, loud" crowd of "twentysomethings" who make it "rowdy on weekends"; escape the noise on the "wonderful outside patio" and "watch the lively neighborhood" go by.

Melting Pot *Fondue*

| 24 | 23 | 23 | $52 |

Gaslamp Quarter | Gaslamp Plaza Stes. | 901 Fifth Ave. (E St.) | 619-234-5554
Golden Triangle | Aventine | 8980 University Center Ln. (Lebon Dr.) | 858-638-1700
www.meltingpot.com

"Everything is better with cheese and chocolate!" profess fans of the "absolutely delicious" fondues at these "pricey" Gaslamp and Golden Triangle chain links, where the "delightful" setting and "dark", "romantic" booths cater to both "groups of friends" and "significant others"; service is "welcoming" and "quick" but "prepare for a leisurely experience" nonetheless – "like three hours" – since "you're the one cooking."

NEW Mia Francesca *Italian*

| - | - | - | E |

Del Mar | Del Mar Highlands Town Ctr. | 12955 El Camino Real (bet. Carmel Country & Del Mar Heights Rds.) | 858-519-5055 | www.miafrancesca.com

North County foodies cheer this sophisticated yet casual Italian trattoria set beside sibling Davanti Enoteca in Del Mar's Highlands Town Center; expect an ever-changing menu of rustic fare at moderate prices, served in the airy interior or on the ample covered patio.

Michele Coulon Dessertier 🖾 *Dessert*

| ▽ 26 | 13 | 20 | $17 |

La Jolla | Sycamore Ct. | 7556 Fay Ave. (bet. Kline & Pearl Sts.) | 858-456-5098 | www.dessertier.com

With "melt-in-your-mouth" pastries and other "exquisite" desserts "made with real butter and fresh fruit", diners are apt to overlook the "limited" (but "fabulous") bistro menu and go straight for the sweets counter at this "premier" La Jolla bakery; guests take lunch or "afternoon tea" in the "charming" space, where staffers are "cheerful, attentive" and happy to place orders for special-occasion confections.

Miguelito's *Mexican*

| 24 | 22 | 23 | $26 |

Coronado | 1142 Adella Ave. (Orange Ave.) | 619-437-1379

Miguel's Cocina *Mexican*

Coronado | 1351 Orange Ave. (Adella Ave.) | 619-437-4237
NEW Carlsbad | 5980 Avenida Encinas (Palomar Airport Rd.) | 760-759-1843

(continued)

(continued)
Miguelito's

Rancho Bernardo | 4S Commons Town Ctr. | 10514 Craftsman Way (Rancho Bernardo Rd.) | 858-924-9200
Old Town | 2444 San Diego Ave. (Conde St.) | 619-298-9840
Point Loma | 2912 Shelter Island Dr. (Scott St.) | 619-224-2401
Chula Vista | East Lake Vill. | 970 Eastlake Pkwy. (Otay Lakes Rd.) | 619-656-2822
www.brigantine.com

Customers "kick back" at these "popular" "decently priced" cantinas offering "huge portions" of "authentic enough" Mexican fare – including chips with "addictive" cheese sauce – and "super" margaritas are "prepared with fresh juice"; "rockin'" servers and "great bartenders" tend to the "festive, loud" space, making sure amigos leave "happy and very full."

Mille Fleurs *French*   27 | 26 | 27 | $76

Rancho Santa Fe | Country Squire Courtyard | 6009 Paseo Delicias (La Granada) | 858-756-3085 | www.millefleurs.com

"Mon dieu!" exclaim "stylish" fans of chef Martin Woesle's "delightful" New French creations at this "epitome of culinary indulgence" in Rancho Santa Fe, where "extraordinary" service bolsters the "first-class" (a few say "stuffy") atmosphere in a Provençal "country-home" setting; there's also a "special" patio and "welcoming" piano bar, where those not up for "investment dining" can enjoy a more "accessible" menu.

Milton's *Deli*   21 | 17 | 20 | $23

Del Mar | Flower Hill Promenade | 2660 Via de la Valle (San Diego Frwy.) | 858-792-2225 | www.miltonsdeli.com

"Stick to the basics" instruct regulars of this Jewish delicatessen, where "obscenely large" portions of "very tasty" classics – think "mile-high" smoked meat sandwiches and "authentic" liverwurst – provide a "little bit of New York" in Del Mar, even if critics say it's "not on par" with the real thing and a touch "pricey" too; "attentive" staffers tend to both the take-out counter and a "not-fancy", "family-friendly" dining area.

Mimi's Cafe *American/French*   22 | 22 | 21 | $22

Mira Mesa | 10788 Westview Pkwy. (Mira Mesa Blvd.) | 858-566-6667
Mission Valley | 5180 Mission Ctr. Rd. (Camino De La Reina) | 619-491-0284
Oceanside | 2177 Vista Way (Jefferson St.) | 760-721-7170
Santee | 9812 Mission Gorge Rd. (Cuyamaca St.) | 619-562-2644
www.mimiscafe.com

"Decent food, prepared to order" from an extensive, "inexpensive" French-American menu makes the local links of this national chain a "reasonable choice for brunch" or dinner; the cottage-style settings are "cutesy to the max", and though some report "ill-equipped" staffers, on the whole most find them "friendly and attentive."

	FOOD	DECOR	SERVICE	COST

The Mission *Asian/Nuevo Latino*   26 | 19 | 22 | $17

East Village | 1250 J St. (13th St.) | 619-232-7662
Mission Beach | 3795 Mission Blvd. (San Jose Pl.) | 858-488-9060
North Park | 2801 University Ave. (28th St.) | 619-220-8992
www.themissionsd.com

"Carefully conceived and prepared" breakfasts and lunches feature an "interesting" "hippie international twist" at this Asian/Nuevo Latino trio, where prices are "reasonable" and portions will "last you all day"; service gets mixed marks ("fast" vs. "erratic") and decor could use some "sprucing up", but that doesn't prevent "long lines of hip, hungry twentysomethings."

Mistral *French*   ∇ 27 | 27 | 25 | $66

Coronado | Loews Coronado Bay Resort | 4000 Coronado Bay Rd. (Silver Strand Blvd.) | 619-424-4000 | www.dineatmistral.com

For "a meal you won't forget", surveyors recommend this upscale Loews Coronado dining room by chef Patrick Ponsaty, where "impeccable" staffers proffer a "varied" menu of "excellent" New French fare; the "masterpiece" meals are "enhanced" by "fantastic bay views", and wise guests take their "cleverly positioned" seats "early for the sunset view."

Mona Lisa *Italian*   25 | 18 | 23 | $20

Little Italy | 2061 India St. (Laurel St.) | 619-234-4893 | www.monalisalittleitaly.com

Stocking a "whole slew" of items for "cooking great Italian at home", this moderately priced Little Italy market and eatery has been catering to folks seeking "olive oils, sausages, pastas and cheese galore" since 1972; meanwhile, "sit-down" patrons enjoy "to-die-for" meat sauces and some of the "best" lasagna around in the back restaurant amid nostalgic, sepia-tinted portraits and red leather booths.

Monsoon *Indian*   ∇ 24 | 25 | 21 | $30

Gaslamp Quarter | 729 Fourth Ave. (bet. F & G Sts.) | 619-234-5555 | www.monsoonrestaurant.com

"Dramatic" surroundings complete with golden chandeliers and a "jaw-dropping" waterfall "set the mood for a memorable experience" at this Gaslamp Indian eatery delivering "delicious if not totally authentic" cuisine that will "stimulate your palate"; "educated" staffers kindly guide "newbies" through the "wide variety" of options, and though it's "not cheap", the lunch buffet is an "exceptional value."

Morton's The Steakhouse *Steak*   25 | 23 | 25 | $66

Downtown | The Harbor Club | 285 J St. (3rd Ave.) | 619-696-3369 | www.mortons.com

"True carnivores" tout this Downtown link of the "grand steakhouse" chain for its "bloody good" beef, "dreamy" soufflés and "superb" wines and cocktails at "expense-account" prices; "professional" servers tend the "dark, clubby, intimate" interior, and though some wonder what happened to the "coat-and-tie" dress code, it's still a "guaranteed pleaser."

	FOOD	DECOR	SERVICE	COST

Muzita Abyssinian Bistro *Ethiopian* | 26 | 21 | 22 | $28 |

University Heights | 4651 Park Blvd. (Spalding Pl.) | 619-546-7900 | www.muzita.com

"Mighty tasty" Ethiopan food draws "word-of-mouth" raves for this moderately priced University Heights bungalow, where "great" staffers show guests how to wrap "so delicious" meat and veggies in injera bread and eat it with their hands; decor earns solid scores despite a "cramped" outdoor patio, and patrons deem it "definitely worth a trip."

Neighborhood ◐ *Gastropub* | 24 | 24 | 20 | $23 |

East Village | 777 G St. (8th Ave.) | 619-446-0002 | www.neighborhoodsd.com

"Any self-respecting hipster knows" that this midpriced East Village gastropub is "the place to be", thanks to "local and unusual" craft beers and "gourmet" burgers crowned with "artisanal" toppings – they "don't believe in ketchup"; "knowledgeable" servers tend both the "clean, urban" dining area and Noble Experiment, the "secret", "speakeasy"-style bar in a back room.

Nick's at the Beach ◐ *American* | 21 | 20 | 22 | $27 |

Pacific Beach | 809 Thomas Ave. (Mission Blvd.) | 858-270-1730 | www.nicksatthebeach.com

Nick's at the Pier ◐ *American*

Ocean Beach | 5083 Santa Monica Ave. (bet. Abbott & Bacon Sts.) | 619-222-7437 | www.nicksatthepier.com

"Super-friendly" servers juggle "excellent fish dishes" plus burgers and bar food at these "reliable" Ocean Beach and Pacific Beach Americans, where "chill" patrons enjoy a menu fit for "different appetites and credit limits"; both "jumpin' joints" boast ocean views and ideal environs for "watching a game", and the PB location invites 21-plus peeps to "watch the sunset" from the rooftop bar while OB hosts them at a more upscale lounge.

Nicky Rottens ◐ *American* | 24 | 20 | 22 | $25 |

Coronado | 100 Orange Ave. (1st St.) | 619-537-0280
Gaslamp Quarter | 560 Fifth Ave. (Market St.) | 619-702-8068
www.nickyrottens.com

Fans cheer for "enormous", "outstanding" burgers, "sides that don't skimp" and games "on every channel" at this midpriced American tavern in Gaslamp (with a newer Coronado branch); it has a "sports-bar feel" of "dark-wood floors and rock music", and "cute" waitresses are "prompt" in tending the "packed" space – a bonus before a trip to nearby Petco Park.

Nine-Ten *Californian/Eclectic* | 26 | 22 | 24 | $61 |

La Jolla | Grande Colonial | 910 Prospect St. (Girard Ave.) | 858-964-5400 | www.nine-ten.com

"Talented young chef" Jason Knibb crafts "edgy", "inspiring" Cal-Eclectic dishes at this "delightful surprise" in La Jolla's Grande Colonial Hotel offering "splurge"-worthy à la carte and tasting menu dinners, as well as "bargain" bites at happy hour; "expert" wine service and "ap-

propriately attentive" treatment from the staff, plus a "contemporary" dining space with a "superb" terrace complete the offerings

94th Aero Squadron

22	22	22	$32

Restaurant *American/Steak*

Kearny Mesa | 8885 Balboa Ave. (Ponderossa Ave.) | 858-560-6771 |
www.94thaerosquadron.signonsandiego.com

Offering "predictable but always tasty" surf 'n' turf, a "great"
Sunday brunch and solid service, this Kearny Mesa "standby"
near Montgomery Field invites high-flying fans to dine then "walk
to their private plane and take off"; those who find the antiques-
packed interior "faded" can enjoy a "lovely landscaped outdoor area",
where they can watch jets disembark "with the wind in their hair."

Nobu *Japanese*

26	23	23	$67

Gaslamp Quarter | Hard Rock Hotel San Diego | 207 Fifth Ave. (L St.) |
619-814-4124 | www.noburestaurants.com

"Imaginative" sushi, "mouthwatering" sashimi and "fantastic"
Japanese fusion signatures like miso black cod headline at Nobu
Matsuhisa's "sleek", "sexy" outpost in the Gaslamp's Hard Rock
Hotel; it's "expensive", but with a "good-looking", "highly knowl-
edgeable" staff and "modern, arty" space, most don't mind don't
mind "opening their wallets."

Oceanaire Seafood Room *Seafood*

25	24	24	$61

Gaslamp Quarter | 400 J St. (4th Ave.) | 619-858-2277 |
www.theoceanaire.com

Join an "upscale", "high-energy" crowd for "super-fresh" fish at this
Gaslamp link of the "popular" seafood chain, where the "expansive"
menu includes "enormous" sides, "to-die-for" desserts and "sophisticated" wines; a "beautiful staircase" leads up to a "mahogany and
brass-wrapped" space styled like an "ocean liner" and captained by
"well-trained" servers who "go out of their way" to make your evening worth the "splurge."

The Old Spaghetti Factory *Italian*

22	22	22	$23

Gaslamp Quarter | 275 Fifth Ave. (K St.) | 619-233-4323 |
www.osf.com

A "great family restaurant", this Gaslamp chain link is a "go-to" say
fans cheering the "inexpensive but good" pasta and other Italian
"basics" served in "plentiful portions"; antique furnishings and plenty
of wood decorate the casual environs, which shares space with
Dussini Loft Bar, a cocktails and tapas spot.

Old Town Mexican Cafe *Mexican*

22	20	20	$25

Old Town | 2489 San Diego Ave. (Harney St.) | 619-297-4330 |
www.oldtownmexcafe.com

"Tourists and locals alike" just "can't get enough" of the burritos, enchiladas and "all things spicy" at this "slightly Americanized" Old
Town Mexican, where "skilled women" pat out "hand-pressed tortillas" and the "huge margaritas" deliver a "kick"; service can be uneven
("attentive" vs. "nonexistent") and the "colorful" decor is "nothing
exciting", but "fair" prices and a "festive" vibe keep it "crowded."

	FOOD	DECOR	SERVICE	COST

Old Trieste ⊠Ⓜ *Italian* ▽ 23 | 15 | 23 | $52

Bay Park | 2335 Morena Blvd. (bet. Kane & Lister Sts.) | 619-276-1841 | www.oldtriesterestaurant.com

"Longtime" fans wouldn't change a thing about this "throwback to old–New York Italian" in Bay Park where "multicourse, traditional" meals are served by tuxedoed waiters who "remember and pamper" regulars; perhaps the decor "looks like it hasn't changed in 40 years", but that may help account for the all-inclusive prices that are "less expensive than many"; P.S. jacket and tie encouraged

Old Venice *Italian* 22 | 23 | 19 | $27

Point Loma | 2910 Canon St. (Scott St.) | 619-222-5888 | www.oldvenicerestaurant.com

"Happy families" and "first dates" both enjoy this Italian "jewel" in Point Loma, where a "fairy-tale" garden lit with "hundreds of candles" and "twinkling lights" sets the scene for a "romantic, relaxing" evening, and guests can "catch jazz" by the fireplace in the "happening" bar; service can be "spotty" and reviews are mixed on the fare ("delicious" vs. "mediocre"), but moderate prices and a "lovely wine list" make it "always enjoyable."

Olivetto *Italian* ▽ 21 | 19 | 19 | $28

Mission Hills | 860 W. Washington St. (bet. Falcon & Goldfinch Sts.) | 619-220-8222 | www.olivettosd.com

"Flavorful" Italian plates "made with love and talent" bring folks to this well-priced Mission Hills "neighborhood restaurant" where "responsive" waiters make "great recommendations" from a "reasonably priced" menu; the "cozy" setting holds equal appeal as a "cocktail lounge" or "family dinner" spot.

Opera Café & Patisserie ⊠ *French* ▽ 24 | 17 | 19 | $17

Serra Mesa | 9254 Scranton Rd. (Mira Mesa Blvd.) | 858-458-9050 | www.operadesserts.com

"Fabulous" pastries are the big draw at this Serra Mesa French "delight", a "great place to meet" over croissants and "delicious, smooth" coffee or "inventive" sandwiches, crêpes and quiches; "reasonable prices" and "fast" counter service please "office" escapees, while "ladies of leisure" linger on the "lovely" patio until the 2:30 PM close.

Operacaffe *Italian* ▽ 22 | 20 | 21 | $30

Gaslamp Quarter | 835 Fourth Ave. (bet. E & F Sts.) | 619-234-6538 | www.operacaffe.com

"Genuine, homey" Italian fare "cooked with love" highlights the Tuscan heritage of chef-proprieter and husband-wife team Roberto Bernardoni and Patrizia Branchi at this midpriced Gaslamp eatery; the "sweet", "mellow" atmosphere is an "unexpected pleasure" amid more "glitzy" options, and service is "on point" too.

Original Pancake House *American* 25 | 17 | 22 | $17

Encinitas | 160 S. Rancho Santa Fe Rd. (Encinitas Blvd.) | 760-943-1939
Kearny Mesa | 3906 Convoy St. (bet. Ostrow St. & Othello Ave.) | 858-565-1740

(continued)
Original Pancake House
Poway | Target Shopping Ctr. | 14905 Pomerado Rd. (Twin Peaks Rd.) |
858-679-0186
www.originalpancakehouse.com
"Bring an appetite" for "comfy" breakfast food at these "carb heaven"
American chain links, serving "strong" coffee, "unbeatable" flapjacks
and "puffy" baked omelets; though some find it "overpriced" and lament the perpetual "lines to the parking lot" and minimal ambiance,
they still complain that it closes at 3 PM – people want "pancakes
for supper" too.

Original Sab-E-Lee Ⓜ🍴 *Thai*
∇ 27 | 8 | 19 | $12

Linda Vista | 2405 Ulric St. (bet. Eastman St. & Linda Vista Rd.) |
858-650-6868 | www.originalsab-e-lee.webs.com
Fans "love the curries" and other "delicious" dishes of Thailand's
northeastern Isaan region offered at this Linda Vista eatery, but
warn "be conservative when choosing spice level"; decor is definitely "hole-in-the-wall" and some guests are irked by the cash-only
and no-alcohol policies, but most still "wish they would build fran-
chises all over" anyhow.

Ortega's, a Mexican Bistro ● *Mexican*
23 | 21 | 22 | $28

Hillcrest | 141 University Ave. (3rd Ave.) | 619-692-4200 |
www.ortegasbistro.com
For "sophisticated Mexican" with a "Baja" bent, diners try this
Hillcrest cantina, where "homemade" tortillas, salsa "with some
kick" and "tableside" guac are all "divine", but the "killer" pomegranate margaritas "steal the show" – and "get you sloppy"; although it may be a "tad expensive" for the genre, service is usually
"on key" and the "tasteful" setting with "knotty pine floors and
walls" is "charming" too.

Osteria Panevino *Italian*
∇ 24 | 21 | 21 | $43

Gaslamp Quarter | 722 Fifth Ave. (G St.) | 619-595-7959 |
www.osteriapanevino.com
"Of the thousand places" in the Gaslamp, "locals know" to pick this
upmarket Italian for "delicious, uncomplicated" pastas and "creative"
entrees that are "a notch above" the usual; the brick-lined space is
"romantic", and though service can be "spotty", expat *camerieres*
will "share a laugh" and "make you feel at home."

Osteria Romantica *Italian*
∇ 25 | 21 | 25 | $35

La Jolla | 2151 Avenida de la Playa (Calle de la Plata) | 858-551-1221 |
www.osteriaromantica.com
"Wonderful" "affordable" Italian is paired with "food-friendly"
wines poured "to the top" by "gregarious" expat staffers at this La
Jolla Shores trattoria; nab a sidewalk table and "work on that tan" or
enjoy the "jovial" "cottage" setting inside – either way, fans find it's
"always a pleasure."

| | FOOD | DECOR | SERVICE | COST |

Outback Steakhouse *Steak*

| 24 | 21 | 23 | $34 |

Clairemont | 4196 Clairemont Mesa Blvd. (Clairemont Dr.) |
858-274-6283
La Mesa | Vons Shopping Ctr. | 5628 Lake Murray Blvd. (Baltimore Dr.) |
619-466-9795
El Cajon | 722 Jamacha Rd. (Washington Ave.) | 619-588-4332
Mission Valley | Mission Valley Mall | 1640 Camino Del Rio N.
(Mission Center Rd.) | 619-294-8998
Oceanside | 2485 Vista Way (El Camino Real) | 760-754-8825
Poway | 14701 Pomerado Rd. (Ted Williams Pkwy.) | 858-486-1563
Chula Vista | 2980 Plaza Bonita Rd. (Sweetwater Rd.) | 619-475-4329
www.outback.com

"Surprisingly good" cuts of beef and "addicting" bloomin' onions
draw diners to this Australian-themed steakhouse chain, where "accommodating" waiters are "quick to deliver" amid "excessive noise"
akin to an "active airport runway"; with lodge-y decor and a "kid-
friendly" feel, "you can always count on it" when you want a "reliable" meal "without feeling you've been fleeced."

Pacifica Breeze Cafe *Californian*

| ∇ 24 | 21 | 22 | $21 |

Del Mar | Del Mar Plaza | 1555 Camino Del Mar (15th St.) |
858-509-9147 | www.pacificadelmar.com

Take an "automatic vacation" at this "breezy" Californian cafe (downstairs from upscale sibling Pacifica Del Mar), where "locals" place
orders at the counter "cafeteria-style" and linger over "amazing"
breakfasts and "healthy, tasty" lunches on the "gorgeous" terrace,
often with "Fido" in tow; with "terrific" long-distance eyefuls of the
ocean, it's one of the "cheapest views" in town; P.S. closes at 4 PM.

Pacifica Del Mar *Seafood*

| 25 | 24 | 23 | $49 |

Del Mar | Del Mar Plaza | 1555 Camino Del Mar (15th St.) |
858-792-0476 | www.pacificadelmar.com

"Always a treat", this "pricey" Del Mar seafood "standard" offers
"polite" service from a "friendly" staff and "inventive" fare that
some say is almost as "extraordinary" as the distant ocean views;
"super" happy-hour prices and half-price wine nights bring a "very
pretty" crowd of "locals" to the "lively" Ocean Bar area, and the
'sunset' dinner deal draws early diners.

The Palm *Steak*

| 24 | 22 | 24 | $72 |

Downtown | 615 J St. (6th Ave.) | 619-702-6500 | www.thepalm.com

Downtown San Diego's branch of this "venerable" NYC-based chain is
a "classy way to dine" say fans touting the "mouthwatering, luscious"
steaks and "killer" wine list, all served in "clubby" "white-tablecloth"
environs; service that's "attentive without being intrusive" further
ensures it's an "ideal place for a business meal" – just don't be surprised by "over-the-top" prices.

Pamplemousse Grille *American/French*

| 27 | 22 | 26 | $71 |

Solana Beach | 514 Via de la Valle (I-5) | 858-792-9090 |
www.pgrille.com

Even those "not easily impressed" will be "blown away" by the
French–New American "masterpieces", "magisterial" wine list and

"sticker-shock prices" at this "class act" in a Solana Beach office complex; "bigger-than-life" chef-owner Jeffrey Strauss is a "great host", guiding "warm yet not intrusive" service in an "elegant, comfortable" space (decorated with "farm paintings") that attracts a "winning" crowd from the nearby racetrack.

Paon *Californian*   26 | 24 | 25 | $59

Carlsbad | 2975 Roosevelt St. (Carlsbad Village Dr.) | 760-729-7377 | www.paoncarlsbad.com

"Graze to your heart's delight" on "extraordinary", "elegantly prepared" French-inflected Cal cuisine from chef David Gallardo at this "pricey" Carlsbad restaurant; "impeccable" service plus a "stately" dining room with "buzz-worthy bar" and "fairyland" patio make for a "wonderful experience" all around.

Pappalecco *Sandwiches*   ▽ 27 | 22 | 24 | $12

Hillcrest | 3650 Fifth Ave. (Pennsylvania Ave.) | 619-906-5566
Little Italy | 1602 State St. (Cedar St.) | 619-238-4590
www.pappalecco.com

Surveyors find a "real Italian bar experience" at these affordable Little Italy and Hillcrest cafes serving "authentic" panini, bruschetta and salads, as well as Boot-inspired breakfasts; for dessert, the "cute" counter staffers pour macchiatos and scoop up some of "the best" housemade gelato in San Diego that guests can enjoy inside or out on the patio.

Parkhouse Eatery *American/Eclectic*   23 | 20 | 22 | $28

University Heights | 4574 Park Blvd. (Madison Ave.) | 619-295-7275 | www.parkhouseeatery.com

Lines are "out the door" at this "quaint little house turned restaurant" in University Heights, where "people who care" prepare American-Eclectic "comfort food with a twist" in the form of "lazy breakfasts" and "imaginative" dinners; though some call it a tad "overpriced" for what it offers, others are more than willing to pay for "professional" service "with a hint of humor" and a "delightful" outdoor patio.

Pei Wei   21 | 18 | 20 | $17
Asian Diner *Asian*

Encinitas | Plaza at Encinitas Ranch | 1560 Leucadia Blvd. (Garden View Rd.) | 760-635-2888
Mission Valley | 1025 Camino de la Reina (Mission Center Rd.) | 619-321-6670
Rancho Bernardo | 4S Commons Town Ctr. | 10562 Craftsman Way (Dove Canyon Rd.) | 858-207-2730
San Marcos | Grand Plaza | 113 S. Las Posas Rd. (Furniture Row) | 760-304-7010
www.peiwei.com

When you are "on a budget" and "want to grab quick bite", fans recommend this "P.F. Chang's offspring", which offers "reliable" Chinese in the style of its parent, dished up by "prompt" counter service staffers; "upscale fast-food" decor and "uneven" quality may irk some, but it remains a "guilty pleasure" for many.

Peohe's *Polynesian*

24 | 26 | 23 | $46

Coronado | Ferry Landing Mktpl. | 1201 First St. (bet. B & C Aves.) | 619-437-4474 | www.peohes.com

"Under-the-sea" decor and "giant" fish tanks bring a "little bit of Hawaii" to this "bayside" Coronado "classic", where "tasty" Polynesian cuisine matches the "tropical" setting and the "picturesque" views may even "outshine the food"; outdoor seating and "fast, courteous" staffers keep patrons pleased despite the somewhat "spendy" bills.

P.F. Chang's China Bistro *Chinese*

24 | 24 | 23 | $30

Golden Triangle | 4540 La Jolla Village Dr. (Executive Way) | 858-458-9007

Mission Valley | Fashion Valley Mall | 7077 Friars Rd. (Avenida Del Rio) | 619-260-8484

Carlsbad | Paseo Del Norte | 5621 Paseo Del Norte (Car Country Dr.) | 760-795-0595

Chula Vista | Otay Ranch Town Ctr. | 2015 Birch Rd. (Eastlake Pkwy.) | 619-421-2080

www.pfchangs.com

"Enthusiastic" servers proffer "familiar favorites" with "lots of flavor" at this "upscale Chinese" chain, where guests enjoy "delicious", if "Westernized", fare like lettuce wraps and a popular happy hour offers "value"; not everyone enjoys the "high-octane" atmosphere, nor the frequent "waits."

Phil's BBQ Ⓜ *BBQ*

26 | 20 | 22 | $22

San Marcos | 579 Grand Ave. (San Marcos Blvd.) | 760-759-1400
NEW Santee | 9816 Mission Gorge Rd. (Cuyamaca St.) | 619-449-7700
Sports Arena | 3750 Sports Arena Blvd. (Hancock St.) | 619-226-6333
www.philsbbq.net

"Wonderful aromas" of "scrumptious", "exceedingly tender" ribs and pulled pork draw lines "longer than Disneyland" to these "affordable" Sports Arena and San Marcos "benchmark BBQ" spots where an "eager-to-please" counter staff makes sure queues "move fast"; diners dig in at basic tables equipped with "plenty of paper towels" to mop up the "finger-lickin'" feast; P.S. a third branch is now open in Santee.

Pho T Cali *Vietnamese*

24 | 17 | 20 | $12

Clairemont | 7351 Clairemont Mesa Blvd. (Ruffner St.) | 858-565-6997 | www.photcalisd.com

"Man oh man" is the pho a hit at this "always good" Vietnamese amid Clairemont's many Asian markets and eateries; "well-priced", "authentic" spring rolls, curries and soups keep tables full during the lunch rush despite "fair" service and "not much" ambiance.

Phuong Trang *Vietnamese*

25 | 14 | 19 | $16

Kearny Mesa | 4170 Convoy St. (Othello Ave.) | 858-565-6750 | www.phuongtrangrestaurant.com

"Authentic", inexpensive Vietnamese fare is heaped out in "generous" portions at this Kearny Mesa eatery, where regulars suggest you "point to other tables to make your choices" and "go with a group

FOOD DECOR SERVICE COST

and share"; there's "not much" ambiance and service isn't noteworthy, but the "awesome" eats alone suffice.

Piatti *Italian*
26 | 23 | 25 | $36

La Jolla | 2182 Avenida de la Playa (Avenida De La Ribera) | 858-454-1589 | www.piatti.com

"Heavenly" bread and olive oil kicks off the "delicious" Italian feasts at this "reasonably priced" link in a regional chain deemed a "treasure" in La Jolla; with "first-class" service and a "crowded but delightful" setting plus an "atmospheric" patio, it's no wonder it's "hugely popular."

Pink Noodle ● *Thai*
▽ 22 | 18 | 20 | $26

Hillcrest | 406 University Ave. (4th Ave.) | 619-298-2929

This "fun little Thai restaurant" in Hillcrest offers "fresh, prepared-to-order" fare at "good prices", with a menu of both classic curries and offbeat offerings like the signature 'pink lady' noodle dish; a "kind, patient" owner oversees the "friendly" crew as they tend to the "austere" bi-level space.

Pizza Nova *Italian*
24 | 20 | 23 | $25

Solana Beach | Lomas Santa Fe Plaza | 945 Lomas Santa Fe Dr. (Santa Helena) | 858-259-0666
Point Loma | 5050 N. Harbor Dr. (Scott St.) | 619-226-0268
San Marcos | 141 N. Twin Oaks Valley Rd. (San Marcos Blvd.) | 760-736-8300
www.pizzanova.net

"Unusual" pizzas, "amazing little" garlic rolls and "classic" Italian entrees keep this midpriced trio "busy" with "smiling patrons"; with a "casual" vibe and "attentive" service, locals feel "lucky to have it" nearby, and though the contemporary settings aren't fancy, the Point Loma location boasts floor-to-ceiling windows overlooking the marina.

Pizza Port *Pizza*
25 | 18 | 19 | $18

Solana Beach | 135 N. Hwy. 101 (Lomas Santa Fe Dr.) | 858-481-7332
Carlsbad | 571 Carlsbad Village Dr. (Roosevelt St.) | 760-720-7007
Ocean Beach | 1956 Bacon St. (Santa Monica Ave.) | 619-224-4700
www.pizzaport.com

"Killer", "hand-tossed" pies with "chewy" crusts are washed down with an "amazing selection of beers" (many brewed on-site) at this "packed, popular" group of "cheap" "beach hangouts"; "noisy" patrons place orders at the counter with "patient" staffers and then circle "like pirates" to find a spot on the picnic tables while kids play "arcade-style" games in back and all "enjoy the cacophony."

Pizzeria Luigi *Pizza*
24 | 16 | 22 | $14

Golden Hill | 1137 25th St. (B St.) | 619-233-3309 ✉
North Park | 2121 El Cajon Blvd. (Alabama St.) | 619-294-9417
www.pizzerialuigi.com

Whether you "eat there or take it to go", fans "promise you'll love" the "NY-style" pizzas and calzones at Luigi Agostini's affordable Golden Hill–North Park pie parlors; the "to-die-for" goods are ordered at the counter and best washed down with one of many craft beers in the "laid-back" dining area or "nice" sidewalk seats.

| | FOOD | DECOR | SERVICE | COST |

Point Loma Seafoods *Seafood*
26 | 16 | 19 | $21

Point Loma | 2805 Emerson St. (Scott St.) | 619-223-1109 |
www.pointlomaseafoods.com

You "can't beat" the "amazingly delicious" seafood at Point Loma's
"ultracasual" fish house, where guests "push to the front" to place
"reasonably priced" orders of "to-die-for" calamari, crab sammies on
"chewy, tangy sourdough" and "very fresh" sushi via "somewhat chaotic" counter service; though recently renovated, it's still a "crowded
madhouse" inside but "breezy bay views" are available on the patio.

Ponce's ⌦ *Mexican*
24 | 20 | 23 | $23

Kensington | 4050 Adams Ave. (Terrace Dr.) | 619-282-4413 |
www.poncesrestaurant.com

"Killer" margaritas soaked up with "tasty" burritos, enchiladas and
chilaquiles have kept this affordable Kensington Mexican "popular"
for more than four decades; tended by "quick, friendly" staffers and
decorated with retro portraits, the "loud, riotous" room is especially
packed during the "decent" happy hour.

Po Pazzo *Italian/Steak*
∇ 20 | 20 | 19 | $42

Little Italy | 1917 India St. (bet. Fir & Grape Sts.) | 619-238-1917 |
www.popazzo.com

Diners are "never disappointed" with the "hearty" fare at this "expensive" Italian steakhouse in Little Italy and tabs are tempered by
half-price wine nights and happy-hour specials; staffers may be
"harried" in tending to the bricklined space and outdoor patio but
live music on weekends "really makes it a must-stop."

Poseidon *Californian*
21 | 24 | 21 | $35

Del Mar | 1670 Coast Blvd. (18th St.) | 858-755-9345 |
www.theposeidonrestaurant.com

"Only a few yards from the surfers and beachcombers" of Del Mar,
the "on-the-sand" patio at this midpriced Californian destination
"can't be surpassed" as a place to take in "unadulterated" eyefuls of
the Pacific while downing "cold beers" and "serviceable" seafood-
centric fare; sure, the food "isn't nearly as good" as the view, ditto
the service, but never mind – the "fabulous setting" ensures it remains "king of the sea."

Prado at Balboa Park *Californian*
24 | 27 | 24 | $36

Balboa Park | House of Hospitality | 1549 El Prado (Pan American Rd.) |
619-557-9441 | www.pradobalboa.com

Whether sitting in the "Spanish-style" dining room or out on the
"glorious" patio "overlooking the garden", guests say this "magical"
eatery in Balboa Park boasts "one of the most picturesque settings in
San Diego"; "silky-smooth" staffers proffer "consistent" Californian
fare at prices considered "reasonable for the area" in an atmosphere
that's "romantic or frenetic" depending on time of day.

Prepkitchen *American*
25 | 19 | 23 | $32

Del Mar | 1201 Camino del Mar (12th St.) | 858-792-7737
La Jolla | 7556 Fay Ave. (bet. Kline & Pearl Sts.) | 858-875-7737

(continued)
Prepkitchen
NEW Little Italy | 1660 India St. (Date St.) | 619-398-8383 ♪
www.prepkitchen.com

"Delicious, fresh, local" American fare – think "finger-lickin'-good" house-cured charcuterie, "healthy, gourmet" salads and "inventive" cocktails – is "prepared with care" at this "value"-oriented trio by the Whisknladle folks; all are "unpretentious" and boast "cool" spaces, with a smaller La Jolla branch, a newly renovated Del Mar location and a "big bar" prime for "low-key evening drinking" in Little Italy.

Primavera Ristorante *Italian*   ▽ 28 | 25 | 28 | $64
Coronado | 932 Orange Ave. (bet. 9th & 10th Sts.) | 619-435-0454 | www.primavera1st.com

"What a treat!" enthuse admirers of this "old-fashioned" Coronado "classic" whose "unmatched", appropriately "solicitous" staff – ranking No. 1 for Service in San Diego – delivers "mouthwatering" Northern Italian food with a "Tuscan flair", paired with a "lovely" wine list; softly lit and "lavishly decorated", the "intimate" setting makes the "special-occasion" prices nearly as palatable as the food.

Puerto La Boca *Argentinean*   ▽ 27 | 22 | 22 | $48
Little Italy | 2060 India St. (Hawthorn St.) | 619-234-4900 | www.puertolaboca.com

At this "uncompromisingly true" tribute to Buenos Aires in Little Italy, "you really can't beat" the "heavenly" empanadas, "melt-in-your-mouth" meats slathered with "too-good-to-describe" chimichurri and "reasonably priced" Malbecs, all served "with Argentinean flair"; "wonderfully friendly and fast" staffers and an "elegant, warm" space that hosts live musicians on weekends complete the "authentic" picture.

Rama *Thai*   25 | 24 | 22 | $27
Gaslamp Quarter | 327 Fourth Ave. (K St.) | 619-501-8424 | www.ramarestaurant.com

"Sexy" decor "sets the mood" at this "ethereal" Gaslamp Thai, where a "spiritual-meets-modernist" milieu of "diaphanous" curtains cushioned booths and a "striking" stone waterfall will "arouse your desires" for both a "romantic" night and a "delicious" meal; the midpriced menu offers some "traditional" dishes as well as more "innovative" ones, while the "just-right" service is "attentive but unobtrusive."

RA Sushi Bar *Japanese*   23 | 22 | 21 | $33
Downtown | 474 Broadway (bet. 4th & 5th Aves.) | 619-321-0021 | www.rasushi.com

"Inventive" sushi and "imaginative" Japanese entrees are matched with an "extensive" sake selection at this "hip" Downtown link of the Benihana-owned chain, where "twentysomethings" head "before club-hopping" to fill up "without spending a fortune"; "friendly" "young" staffers and "contemporary" decor add to the "lively" vibe.

	FOOD	DECOR	SERVICE	COST

Red Door Restaurant & Wine Bar *American* 23 | 23 | 24 | $37

Mission Hills | 741 W. Washington St. (Falcon St.) | 619-295-6000 |
www.thereddoorsd.com

"Quality ingredients" – they "grown their own" produce in an off-site
garden – combine with "skilled preparation" for "excellent results" at
this Mission Hills American "boîte", where the "always-changing",
midpriced menu of "delicious comfort food" is complemented by a
"nicely chosen" wine list; "charming" servers and an "upscale yet
homey" room make it "quite a find."

Red Fox Steakhouse ⦿ *Seafood/Steak* ▽ 23 | 20 | 22 | $38

North Park | Lafayette Hotel | 2223 El Cajon Blvd. (bet. Louisiana &
Mississippi Sts.) | 619-297-1313 | www.redfoxsd.com

"Something of a time warp", this "old-fashioned" steakhouse in
North Park's recently renovated Lafayette Hotel is fashioned from
a circa-1560 English inn that was shipped to the states in 1926; it
draws mature types and hipsters alike for midpriced surf 'n' turf
classics amid "dim" lighting and vinyl booths, and "continues to
shine" after decades thanks to its "interesting" piano bar, "comfortable" feel and solid service.

Red Pearl Kitchen *Asian* 21 | 23 | 21 | $34

Gaslamp Quarter | 440 J St. (4th Ave.) | 619-231-1100 |
www.redpearlkitchen.com

A "cool" "1930s Shanghai" look bolstered by "seductive" lighting
and "blaring" music lures "gorgeous people" to this Gaslamp
"hipster heaven" where "creative" cocktails go down well with
the kitchen's "deliciously zippy" Pan-Asian "concoctions"; a few
gripe about "less-than-spectacular" service, but at least the
staff's "cute", and dining at the "entertaining" chef's table in the
kitchen is perfect "for a hungry group."

Red Tracton's *Seafood/Steak* 22 | 19 | 23 | $49

Solana Beach | 550 Via de la Valle (Valley Ave.) | 858-755-6600 |
www.redtractonssteakhouse.com

"Even big eaters often take home leftovers" from this "pricey" Solana
Beach chophouse across from the Del Mar track, where "racing
fans" spend their winnings on "county fair–size" portions of "classic" American favorites, including solid steaks; its dining room suf-
fused in "old-time supper club atmosphere" is overseen by an able
staff, but it and the front piano bar are "major hangouts" in season,
so make reservations.

Rei do Gado *Brazilian* 26 | 24 | 24 | $46

Gaslamp Quarter | 939 Fourth Ave. (B'way) | 619-702-8464 |
www.reidogado.net

"Come hungry" to this "all-you-can-eat" Brazilian churrascaria in
Gaslamp, a "carnivore's dream" where "handsome" servers keep the
"huge spits" of barbecued beef, lamb, pork and chicken coming "until
you say stop" and the "insane" salad bar packs "hidden treasures"
like chilled crab and smoked salmon that make it "worth every penny";
no wonder the "small, intimate" space is usually "crowded."

FOOD | DECOR | SERVICE | COST

Rhinoceros Cafe & Grill *American*   ▽ 25 | 21 | 26 | $31

Coronado | 1166 Orange Ave. (Loma Ave.) | 619-435-2121 |
www.rhinocafe.com

"Well-cooked, tasty and interesting" New American "comfort" fare
at "reasonable" rates keeps 'em coming to this "small but lively"
Coronado cafe; "dependable" staffers "have it down", making patrons feel "welcome" while dining in the "airy" interior or "watching
the world go by" from the sidewalk tables.

Richard Walker's
Pancake House *American*   23 | 16 | 19 | $17

Downtown | Pinnacle Museum Tower | 520 Front St. (bet. Island Ave. &
Market St.) | 619-231-7777 | www.richardwalkers.com

"Come early or expect to wait" at this breakfast-and-lunch-only
Downtown link of the Illinois-based American chain, where "soufflé-
like" pancakes, "housemade" syrup and "thick-cut" bacon will "ruin
any diet" but keep wallets intact; "brisk" staffers "help offset" waits by
"rushing" patrons in and out of the "appealing", high-ceilinged space.

Ricky's Restaurant *American*   ▽ 23 | 14 | 21 | $19

Mission Valley | 2181 Hotel Circle S. (Hotel Circle Dr.) | 619-291-4498

"Known for its apple pancakes", "off-the-charts" French toast and
other Traditional American morning fare that comes out "piping
hot" in "huge" portions, this Mission Valley diner is "all about the
breakfast"; the "old-fashioned" decor is a "blast from the past", while
"decent" prices and solid service help make it "a family favorite."

Rimel's Rotisserie *Californian*   22 | 17 | 21 | $32

Cardiff-by-the-Sea | 2005 San Elijo Ave. (Birmingham Dr.) | 760-633-2202
La Jolla | 1030 Torrey Pines Rd. (Herschel Ave.) | 858-454-6045
www.rimelsrestaurants.com

Locals "never tire" of the "fresh-off-the-boat" grilled seafood and
"smoky" rotisserie birds at this "unpretentious" La Jolla Californian
and its Cardiff-by-the-Sea sib, which are also appreciated for their
"reasonable" prices; the LJ branch's "tiny strip-mall" locale is on the
"dingy" side and the service gets mixed reviews, leading many to reserve it for "take-out family dinners."

Ritual Tavern ●Ⓜ *American*   24 | 24 | 23 | $28

North Park | 4095 30th St. (Polk Ave.) | 619-283-1720 |
www.ritualtavern.com

"Inventive" American dishes built on "local seafood, organic vegeta-
bles and artisanal cheeses" are paired with pours from an "excellent
rotating beer selection" at this "cozy" neighborhood tavern "standout" on North Park's Restaurant Row; the "generous" portions and
"helpful" service shore up the overall "value."

Riviera Supper Club *Steak*   ▽ 23 | 23 | 23 | $26

La Mesa | 7777 University Ave. (Lee Ave.) | 619-713-6777 |
www.rivierasupperclub.com

From the former proprietors of Turf Supper Club, this midpriced "cook-
your-own-steak" place in La Mesa features a "big BBQ grill" where

"convivial" crowds gather to sear "tender, nicely aged" strips and sirloins while downing "tasty, massive, strong" cocktails; it boasts solid service and "killer atmosphere" ideal for "hanging with friends", and the attached Turquoise Room bar hosts live music nightly.

Rockin' Baja ● *Mexican*

| 22 | 20 | 20 | $31 |

Gaslamp Quarter | 310 Fifth Ave. (K St.) | 619-234-6333
Old Town | 3890 Twiggs St. (Congress St.) | 619-260-0305
www.rockinbaja.com

"Tourists" and locals alike vouch for the seafood-focused Mexican fare – especially the $2 Taco Tuesday deals, or cervezas and 'Baja buckets' of shrimp and crab – at these Old Town and Gaslamp links of the Cali mini-chain; factor in beachy settings and outdoor seating, and to many they're "worth the trip."

Rocky's Crown Pub ⊘ *Burgers*

| 26 | 12 | 18 | $14 |

Pacific Beach | 3786 Ingraham St. (La Playa Ave.) | 858-273-9140 | www.rockyburgers.com

You'd better like "juicy, tasty, dripping cheeseburgers" because "they don't serve anything else" but fries and beer at this cheap, cash-only Pacific Beach "dive bar"; "don't expect to be charmed by the ambiance" caution "loyal fans" – it's "very casual", "crowded" and offers "counter seating, for the most part", but "good food is worth a little sacrifice, no?"

Romano's Macaroni Grill *Italian*

| 22 | 22 | 22 | $29 |

Escondido | 202 E. Via Rancho Pkwy. (I-15) | 760-741-6309
Oceanside | 2655 Vista Way (El Camino Real) | 760-722-9905
Chula Vista | Otay Ranch Town Ctr. | 2015 Birch Rd. (Eastlake Pkwy.) | 619-656-0966
www.macaronigrill.com

"Better-than-average" Italian basics in "plentiful" portions at "reasonable" rates dished up by "friendly" staffers is the winning formula behind this national chain; sure, it can all feel a little "cookie cutter", and you've gotta like "intense garlic flavor", but it's just the thing for groups and families – hand your kids the complimentary crayons and "order some wine."

Roppongi *Asian*

| 24 | 22 | 22 | $47 |

La Jolla | 875 Prospect St. (Bishops Ln.) | 858-551-5252 | www.roppongiusa.com

With an "innovative" knack for "beautifully composed flavors", chef Stephen Window creates "delicious" sushi and Asian fusion small plates at this "pricey" La Jolla hangout manned by a capable crew; its "cool", sleek quarters host a "lively" crowd that gathers in "chic, playful" dining areas or around the "stylish" patio fire pit.

Royal India *Indian*

| ▽ 22 | 21 | 21 | $27 |

Gaslamp Quarter | 329 Market St. (4th Ave.) | 619-269-9999 | www.royalindia.com

"Wonderful smells of spices" greet "lovers of Indian food" at this Gaslamp eatery, where some call the offerings "Americanized" but others report "very good" vegetarian items, Halal meats and tandoori

FOOD DECOR SERVICE COST

dishes; an "elegant" dining room leads some to wonder if "you're paying more for the decor", but "warm, friendly" servers and a "terrific" lunch buffet add value; P.S. there are two "fantastic" fast-food siblings.

Royal Thai Cuisine *Thai*   ▽ 24 | 20 | 21 | $20

Gaslamp Quarter | 467 Fifth Ave. (Island Ave.) | 619-230-8424 |
www.royalthaicuisine.com
Serving "fresh", "reasonably priced" Thai, this "oft-overlooked" Gaslamp eatery "festooned with Asian artifacts" is a "solid choice"; the "convenient" location near the Convention Center and Petco Park is an added appeal.

Roy's *Hawaiian*   25 | 24 | 24 | $56

Downtown | San Diego Marriott Hotel & Marina | 333 W. Harbor Dr. (1st Ave.) | 619-239-7697
Golden Triangle | Costa Verde Ctr. | 8670 Genesee Ave. (bet. La Jolla Vill. & Nobel Drs.) | 858-455-1616
www.roysrestaurant.com
At the Downtown–Golden Triangle links of chef Roy Yamaguchi's national Hawaiian fusion chain, "wonderful" seafood and other "terrific" dishes will "satisfy everyone", while "personalized" service makes 'em feel "like royalty"; a "fun" feel completes the "special occasion"–worthy picture, and though "pricey" tabs make it best when "someone else is buying", the seasonal prix fixe packs "value."

Rubio's *Mexican*   25 | 17 | 22 | $12

College East | 5500 Campanile Dr. (Hardy Ave.) | 619-594-6656
Golden Triangle | University Town Ctr. | 4545 La Jolla Village Dr. (Nobel Dr.) | 858-587-1231
Golden Triangle | 8935 Towne Centre Dr. (Nobel Dr.) | 858-453-1666
Kearny Mesa | 3675 Murphy Canyon Rd. (Aero Dr.) | 619-715-1580
Kearny Mesa | 7420 Clairemont Mesa Blvd. (Convoy St.) | 858-268-5770
Mission Bay | 4504 E. Mission Bay Dr. (Tecolote Rd.) | 858-272-2801
Mission Valley | 10460 Friars Rd. (Zion Ave.) | 619-285-9985
Mission Valley | 2075 Camino de la Reina (Texas St.) | 619-299-6502
Mission Valley | 7007 Friars Rd. (Fashion Valley Rd.) | 619-718-9975
Pacific Beach | 910 Grand Ave. (Cass St.) | 858-270-4800
www.rubios.com
Additional locations throughout the San Diego area
"Hot, fresh" fish and shrimp tacos fly over the counter at the nothing-fancy local links of this "reliable" San Diego–based Mexican chain providing "fast food at its best" with "quality" ingredients (including sustainable seafood) and made-daily salsas; a wallet-minded few consider it "expensive" for the genre, but most just sigh *"me gusta."*

Ruby's Diner *Diner*   21 | 22 | 21 | $18

Mission Valley | Mission Valley Mall | 1640 Camino Del Rio N. (bet. Camino Del Este & Mission Center Rd.) | 619-294-7829
Carlsbad | Carlsbad Premium Outlets | 5630 Paseo Del Norte (Car Country Dr.) | 760-931-7829
Oceanside | 1 Oceanside Pier (Pacific St.) | 760-433-7829
www.rubys.com
For a "blast from the past", "take the family" to these links of the "'50s-type diner" chain offering a "bite of Americana" with its "drive-

in" classics – notably "mouthwatering" burgers and "over-the-top" shakes, floats and sundaes – delivered by "kind" staffers dressed like carhops; "reasonable" prices and "bright", "cute" interiors help "bring back memories of past decades."

Ruth's Chris Steak House *Steak* | 27 | 24 | 26 | $71 |

Del Mar | 11582 El Camino Real (Carmel Valley Rd.) | 858-755-1454
Downtown | 1355 N. Harbor Dr. (Ash St.) | 619-233-1422
www.ruthschris.com

Release your inner "caveman" on the "buttery" steaks "cooked to perfection" and paired with "gargantuan" sides, "sinful" desserts and "potent" drinks at these Downtown and Del Mar links in the "high-end" national chain; "superior" service and "fantastic" views from the "contemporary" dining room further support the "splurge" prices.

Saffron Noodles & Saté *Thai* | 24 | 10 | 18 | $18 |

Mission Hills | 3731 India St. (Washington St.) | 619-574-7737

Saffron Thai Grilled Chicken *Thai*

Mission Hills | 3731 India St. (Washington St.) | 619-574-0177
www.saffronsandiego.com

"Mouthwatering" rotisserie chicken and "amazing" sauces "rock" at chef Su-Mei Yu's Saffron Chicken in Mission Hills, while her adjacent "no-nonsense" Thai noodle house dishes up "healthy, tasty, affordable" dishes with "sophisticated" seasonings; there's little ambiance in the "sparse, overly bright" setups, so many rely on "prompt" counter service to supply "phenomenal takeout."

Saigon on Fifth ● *Vietnamese* | 25 | 23 | 24 | $28 |

Hillcrest | 3900 Fifth Ave. (University Ave.) | 619-220-8828

Treat your tongue to an "adventure" at this "classy" Hillcrest Vietnamese, where the "flavorful" pho and other "exquisite" dishes manage to be "subtle, intense, rich and light, all at the same time"; "warm" waitresses dressed in "traditional" garb oversee the "beautiful" room, which may "look expensive" but "don't be fooled" – tabs are "reasonable"; P.S. open till 3 AM, it's ideal for "late-night dinners."

Sally's Seafood on the Water *Asian/Seafood* | 24 | 23 | 21 | $47 |

Downtown | Manchester Grand Hyatt Hotel | 1 Market Pl. (Kettner Blvd.) | 619-358-6740 | www.sallyssandiego.com

"As fresh as it gets", the "outstanding", "Asian-influenced" fish dishes and solid sushi at this "high-end" seafooder in Downtown's Manchester Grand Hyatt have guests returning "again and again"; manned by an "able" team, its "open, modern" space "right on the waterfront" has most saying it's "worth every penny" of the "not-cheap" tab – and there's always the "excellent-deal" dinner prix fixe.

Saltbox *American* | ▽ 21 | 22 | 20 | $45 |

Downtown | Hotel Palomar | 1047 Fifth Ave. (B'way) | 619-515-3003 | www.saltboxrestaurant.com

Chic locals and hotel guests settle into "sleek banquettes" beneath "stylish" lighting fixtures at this "cool" self-described 'gastro-lounge' in Downtown's "trendy" Hotel Palomar; mixologists blend "fresh ingredients" into "craft" cocktails to accompany the "creative" New American small plates, and, by day, bargain-seekers tout the $12 'power-lunch' special.

Salvatore's 🔲 *Italian* ▽ 25 | 24 | 22 | $61

Downtown | 750 Front St. (G St.) | 619-544-1865 | www.salvatoresdowntown.com

A "grande dame" of "classic" Italian fare, this Downtowner "delights" with a "wonderful variety" of "housemade" pastas and "outstanding" sauces proffered by "cheerful" pro staffers; tabs are "high", but most declare it "worth the price" for "special occasions" and "romantic nights out" in "elegant", "white-tableclothed" environs.

Sammy's Woodfired Pizza *Pizza* 23 | 20 | 21 | $23

Del Mar | Del Mar Highlands Town Ctr. | 12925 El Camino Real (Del Mar Heights Rd.) | 858-259-6600
Downtown | 770 Fourth Ave. (F St.) | 619-230-8888
La Mesa | 8555 Fletcher Pkwy. (Trolley Ct.) | 619-460-8555
Golden Triangle | Costa Verde Ctr. | 8650 Genesee Ave. (La Jolla Village Dr.) | 858-404-9898
La Jolla | 702 Pearl St. (Draper Ave.) | 858-456-5222
Mission Valley | Mission Valley Mall | 1620 Camino de la Reina (Mission Center Rd.) | 619-298-8222
Carlsbad | 5970 Avenida Encinas (Palomar Airport Rd.) | 760-438-1212
Point Loma | Liberty Station | 2401 Truxtun Rd. (Womble Rd.) | 619-222-3111
San Marcos | 121 S. Las Posas Rd. (Grand Ave.) | 760-591-4222
Scripps Ranch | 10785 Scripps Poway Pkwy. (Spring Canyon Rd.) | 858-695-0900
www.sammyspizza.com

"Swing by" a branch of this ever-expanding chain of pizza-focused "price performers" for "light, crispy" artisan pies, "reliable" salads, "decadent" desserts and more, including "extensive" gluten-free choices; they "tend to be a little crowed and noisy", but that's the price of "popularity."

San Diego Chicken 23 | 13 | 22 | $13
Pie Shop *American*

North Park | 2633 El Cajon Blvd. (Oregon St.) | 619-295-0156

"Good old-fashioned" American "stick-to-your-ribs chow" ("the best" fried chicken, "excellent" coleslaw, "fresh" baked goods) is the lure at this North Park "institution"; it's definitely nothing fancy, but you "can't beat the price" – and you can always just pick up some pot pies "for the freezer."

Sapori *Italian* ▽ 24 | 23 | 22 | $39

Coronado | 120 Orange Ave. (bet. 1st & 2nd Sts.) | 619-319-5696 | www.saporicoronado.com

"Everything tastes homemade because it is" at this "perfect little" Coronado Italian, where "excellent, fresh, healthy" entrees and an "impressive" wine list offered at "reasonable prices" make it "a real step up" from nearby options; "wonderful, welcoming" owners and "delightful", stylish decor add to a "terrific experience."

Saska's ❶ *Seafood/Steak* ▽ 25 | 20 | 23 | $36

Mission Beach | 3768 Mission Blvd. (Redondo Ct.) | 858-488-7311 |
www.saskas.com

A Mission Beach "institution", this "dependable" "standby" has been
dispensing surf 'n' turf favorites and "good specials" at "reasonable"
rates since 1951; sure, its "red-vinyl-booth" decor is "a little dated",
but to fans that's just part of the "cozy" charm – plus nowadays there
are modern touches like a rooftop deck and sushi annex.

Sbicca *American* 23 | 19 | 22 | $40

Del Mar | 215 15th St. (Stratford Ct.) | 858-481-1001 |
www.sbiccabistro.com

"Creative" New American fare "with a fusion flair" and a "wonderful" wine list draw "foodies" to this Del Mar bistro, where "friendly"
staffers deliver "genuine California charm" and you "can smell the
ocean" while you dine; the rooftop terrace has a "killer" Pacific view
and inside there's a "lively" bar scene, especially on "hard-to-beat"
half-price vino nights or "after the horse races" at the nearby track.

Sea Rocket Bistro *Seafood* ▽ 27 | 22 | 23 | $30

North Park | 3382 30th St. (Upas St.) | 619-255-7049 |
www.searocketbistro.com

"Local/sustainable"-seekers "become regulars" at this "wholesome"
North Park seafooder where the catch netted nearby is so "very fresh",
it's practically "still moving"; diners "learn where their food comes
from" thanks to the "knowledgeable" staff, while "moderate" prices
and no-pretenses digs keep things casual.

Searsucker *American* 24 | 24 | 21 | $47

Gaslamp Quarter | 611 Fifth Ave. (Market St.) | 619-233-7327 |
www.searsucker.com

The "adventurous" New American fare is "well prepared" and "delicious" at celeb chef Brian Malarkey's "spendy", "trendy" Gaslamp
eatery; "sexy", luxe-industrial environs and a "lively" scene make it
a "perfect" place to "unwind and people-watch" – or "sit at the counter by the kitchen" and observe the chefs doing their thing.

Sessions Public *Eclectic* ▽ 24 | 22 | 21 | $31

Point Loma | 4204 Voltaire St. (Catalina Blvd.) | 619-756-7715 |
www.sessionspublic.com

"Delicious" Eclectic small plates meet a "pretty awesome beer selection" at this gastropub on an "unlikely corner" in Ocean Beach;
the "casual" feel and decor with a "creative edge" make it a "nice
place to hang out" – especially over a plate of duck-fat fries.

Shades Oceanfront Bistro *American* ▽ 25 | 23 | 24 | $24

Ocean Beach | 5083 Santa Monica Ave. (Abbott St.) | 619-222-0501 |
www.shadesob.com

This "reasonably priced" Ocean Beach American is known for its
breakfasts, but it's also lauded as a "laid-back" place to "sit on the
deck" for cocktails and "wonderful sunset views"; "caring" staffers
who "try to please, and succeed" complete the picture.

	FOOD	DECOR	SERVICE	COST

DINING

Sheerwater *Californian*
23 | 25 | 24 | $44

Coronado | Hotel del Coronado | 1500 Orange Ave. (Glorietta Blvd.) |
619-522-8490 | www.hoteldel.com

"The decor is the ocean" at the Hotel Del Coronado's "casual" eatery,
where "splendid" views of "sand and sea" (especially "awesome"
from the patio) make you feel like you're right "on the beach" as
you savor "delightfully modern" Californian fare, the "picturesque"
scene enhanced by "relaxed, unhurried" service helps justify "higher-
than-average" prices.

The Shores *Californian*
24 | 22 | 25 | $40

La Jolla | La Jolla Shores Hotel | 8110 Camino del Oro (Avienda de la Playa) |
858-456-0600 | www.theshoresrestaurant.com

Fans say the La Jolla Shores Hotel's "casual" Californian is "improv-
ing every day", offering "consistent" cuisine and a "well-priced, inventive" wine list; surpassing the moderately priced menu, though,
is the "unobstructed" view of the Pacific, so guests can enjoy "spectacular" sunsets even though the decor inside is getting "tired."

NEW Slater's 50/50 ● *Burgers*
25 | 20 | 22 | $18

Point Loma | Liberty Station | 2750 Dewey Rd. (bet. Cushing &
Historic Decatur Rds.) | 619-398-2600 | www.slaters5050.com

Endless options "wow" guests at the Point Loma branch of this SoCal
sports bar chain, where the beer list is lengthy and the build-your-
own burger choices include the namesake 50/50 beef-and-bacon
patty and fixin's like anchovies, grilled pineapple, country gravy and
peanut butter; tabs are affordable, staffers will "jump through hoops"
and everyone leaves satisfied – "can you say 'food coma'?"

Smoking Goat Ⓜ *American/French*
▽ 27 | 20 | 25 | $38

North Park | 3408 30th St. (Upas St.) | 619-955-5295 |
www.thesmokinggoatrestaurant.com

"Deliciousness awaits" for "adventurous eaters" at this midpriced
North Park bistro boasting "knowledgeable" staff and a "limited" menu
of "fresh, innovative" French-American fare offered with "great"
wine pairings; the "little gem" gives off an "upscale" farmhouse vibe
and a recent expansion will mitigate "hole-in-the-wall" proportions.

NEW Snooze *American*
27 | 26 | 25 | $19

Hillcrest | 3940 Fifth Ave. (University Ave.) | 619-500-3344 |
www.snoozeeatery.com

Those who "can stand the wait" at this "always-busy" Hillcrest
American are rewarded with "unique variations" on Bloodies, burritos, eggs Benny and other affordable "breakfast standards"; it's all
"executed extremely well" and served "fast" by the "amazing" staffers who tend its bright, airy space; P.S. closes at 2:30 PM.

Solare Ⓜ *Italian*
▽ 27 | 24 | 21 | $30

Point Loma | Liberty Station | 2820 Roosevelt Rd. (Historic Decatur Rd.) |
619-270-9670 | www.solarelounge.com

"Authentic" classic Italian dishes are "prepared with love" and presented by "warm, friendly" servers at this "chic" eatery in a historic

Spanish Revival building at Point Loma's Liberty Station, the former Naval Training Center; happy-hour deals and half-off wine nights slash prices, but "try the chef's table" for a "special treat."

South Beach   ▽ 26 | 18 | 17 | $14
Bar & Grill ●▱ *Mexican/Seafood*

Ocean Beach | 5059 Newport Ave. (Abbott St.) | 619-226-4577 | www.southbeachob.com

"Top-notch" fish tacos fly over the counter at this "laid-back beach bar" in Ocean Beach, where the "value"-oriented, cash-only seafood-meets-Mexican menu is possibly "the best this side of the border", matched with a "huge selection of microbrews"; service may be "so-so" but the staff is "easy on the eyes", and though the decor's strictly basic, "clear" ocean views and a "lively" vibe keep it "way crowded."

Spice & Rice   ▽ 23 | 20 | 22 | $24
Thai Kitchen   *Thai*

La Jolla | 7734 Girard Ave. (bet. Kline & Silverado Sts.) | 858-456-0466 | www.spiceandricethaikitchen.com

"Locals swear by" this "unpretentious" La Jolla Thai, where "exotic" dishes "spiced just right" certainly "set the bar" for local competitors and the "bargain" lunch combo keeps 'em coming back; "wonderful" staffers "wow" guests as they dine in the "cozy, intimate" interior or on the "tropical" patio "amid lots of plants."

Spicy City   *Chinese*   26 | 15 | 20 | $19

Kearny Mesa | 4690 Convoy St. (Engineer Rd.) | 858-278-1818 | www.spicycity.menutoeat.com

"Bursts of intense heat" await at this aptly named Kearny Mesa Chinese, where diners "sweat and drool" as they devour fiery specialties featuring frog, kidney and gizzards – or tamer standards like chicken, eggplant and tofu; there's "no ambiance" to speak of, but it's "reasonably priced" and that spicy kick takes diners "higher than a dragon kite."

The Spot ● *American*   ▽ 20 | 15 | 20 | $20

La Jolla | 1005 Prospect St. (Girard Ave.) | 858-459-0800 | www.thespotonline.com

"You can get anything you want" (or close to it) at this "reasonably priced" La Jolla American where the "broad" menu includes "big, juicy" build-your-own burgers, "delicious" Chicago-style pizza and more; "nothing-fancy" tavern surrounds keep things "casual", but the "dark wood" and "great" fireplace make it just "the spot" on "cold days", and it gets bonus points for being open "long after" other nearby choices are closed for the night.

Steakhouse at Azul La Jolla   *Steak*   ▽ 24 | 25 | 24 | $49

La Jolla | 1250 Prospect St. (bet. Cave St. & Ivanhoe Ave.) | 858-454-9616 | www.azul-lajolla.com

Take in "to-die-for" scenery at this "spectacular" surf 'n' turfer, where "huge windows overlooking La Jolla Cove" afford views of "dolphins jumping in the ocean" while diners savor "outstanding" steakhouse fare, "super-fresh" seafood and selections from a "robust" wine list; "exemplary" service and an overall "romantic" vibe are further endearments.

Stone World Bistro & Gardens *Eclectic* | 23 | 27 | 21 | $29 |

Escondido | 1999 W. Citracado Pkwy. (Auto Park Way) | 760-294-7866 | www.stoneworldbistro.com

"The place to be if you're a beer geek", this "unique" Escondido brewery/eatery pours a "huge" selection of "world-class" suds that are a "perfect match" for the midpriced, "hearty", "inventively prepared" Eclectic fare; the "grand" environs are "imaginative and bold", with "rich textures" inside and "verdant landscapes" in the "gorgeous" outdoor garden; P.S. pick up a "refill on your growler" or stick around and take "a tour of the brewery."

Studio Diner ❷ *Diner* | 22 | 22 | 22 | $23 |

Kearny Mesa | 4701 Ruffin Rd. (Spectrum Center Blvd.) | 858-715-6400 | www.studiodiner.com

Enjoy an enormous selection of "surprisingly tasty" American standards with some "modern touches" at this Kearny Mesa 24/7 diner located on a working TV studio lot, where breakfast is offered all day and "plenty-for-two" fish 'n' chips, burgers and blue-plate specials are served amid film gear and movie stills in a chrome-wrapped space; "who knows – you might just be discovered."

Sushi on the Rock *Japanese* | 25 | 23 | 24 | $26 |

La Jolla | 1025 Prospect St. (Girard Ave.) | 858-459-3208 | www.sushiontherock.com

"Everyone can be satisfied" at this "pricey" La Jolla Japanese, where a "gigantic" menu of "creative" rolls, "the freshest" entrees and "extensive" sake options also make it easy to "rack up a bill"; the "fun" staff and "cranked music" keep energy levels up in the stark space, while a patio offers "beautiful" ocean views.

Sushi Ota *Japanese* | 29 | 16 | 21 | $49 |

Pacific Beach | 4529 Mission Bay Dr. (Bunker Hill St.) | 858-270-5670 | www.sushiota.com

"Sushi purists" will "cry" tears of "pleasure" when "lucky enough" to snag a seat at this "incomparable" Pacific Beach Japanese, where "gracious" chef-owner Yukito Ota and his talented "army" earn the No. 1 Food score in San Diego with "simply magnificent" seafood "delicacies" and an "innovative" omakase tasting; frequently "hurried" service, a "random" strip-mall location and "shabby" interior certainly don't match the "phenomenal" fare and "pricey" tabs, but guests still need to make a reservation "well in advance."

NEW Table 926 Ⓜ *Californian* ▽ | 23 | 21 | 24 | $35 |

Pacific Beach | 926 Turquoise St. (Cass St.) | 858-539-0926 | www.table926.com

"Well-prepared", seasonally driven Californian fare will "awaken your palate and surprise you" at this Pacific Beach bistro, where "professional, knowledgeable" servers ensure guests are "greeted and well taken care of" upon arrival; lined with wine bottles and brick walls, the "simple" space is a bit "crammed" but still "romantic."

	FOOD	DECOR	SERVICE	COST

Tajima *Japanese*
25 | 19 | 22 | $16

Kearny Mesa | 4411 Mercury St. (Balboa Ave.) | 858-278-5367
Kearny Mesa | 4681 Convoy St. (Engineer Rd.) | 858-576-7244
www.tajimasandiego.com

"Stand out" ramen from the Convoy Street noodle house and "inventive, fresh, exciting" Japanese plates from the Mercury Street izakaya make this "reasonable" Kearny Mesa duo a "delightful respite" from the "made-for-Americans" sushi joints around town; the basic spaces are "crowded" with "returning customers" and tended by "friendly" staffers.

Taka *Japanese*
▽ 25 | 20 | 21 | $58

Gaslamp Quarter | 555 Fifth Ave. (Market St.) | 619-338-0555 |
www.takasushi.com

"Leave your fate in the hands" of the "personable" sushi "masters" at this Gaslamp Japanese and they'll "surprise you" with "treat after treat" of "serious, challenging" fare ("live shrimp" anyone?) prepared with "understated artistry" and priced "fairly" considering the quality; the "small, simple" space "isn't that glamorous" but linen tablecloths "raise the environs a touch", making it equally appealing to the "power-suited and sweat-suited."

Tao Ⓜ *Asian/Vegetarian*
28 | 21 | 24 | $19

Normal Heights | 3332 Adams Ave. (Felton St.) | 619-281-6888

Even though you're allowed to "write on the walls" with markers, don't be deceived by the "quirky" atmosphere at this Normal Heights Asian eatery – an affordable "favorite" for its "generous", "spicy" and "always-fresh" dishes that appeal to carnivores and vegetarians alike; what's more, the staff "always greets you warmly" and is "very willing to accommodate" any special requests.

Tapenade *French*
28 | 21 | 26 | $61

La Jolla | 7612 Fay Ave. (bet. Kline & Pearl Sts.) | 858-551-7500 |
www.tapenaderestaurant.com

Francophiles say *"merci"* to this "pricey" La Jolla French destination's "brilliant" chef Jean-Michel Diot, whose "creative" dishes feature "fantastically layered" flavors and "delightful presentations" and are complemented by a "well-balanced" wine list; the atmosphere is "bright" and "serene", and though a few detect a "mildly pretentious" air, most report "first-rate" service attuned to the "classy" clientele.

Tartine *European*
▽ 26 | 20 | 23 | $26

Coronado | 1106 First St. (Orange Ave.) | 619-435-4323 |
www.tartinecoronado.com

By day this "friendly little" European cafe in Coronado offers an affordable, "tasteful" selection of "fresh salads, lovely sandwiches" and "always-delicious" pastries, and by night it serves "simple" "bistro fare"; "attentive" servers tend to the "mostly well-heeled local crowd", and if you're lucky you can "snag a table" on the "relaxing" patio.

	FOOD	DECOR	SERVICE	COST

Tender Greens *American* | 26 | 18 | 21 | $16 |

Point Loma | Liberty Station | 2400 Historic Decatur Rd. (Womble Rd.) |
619-226-6254
University City | University Town Ctr. | 4545 La Jolla Village Dr.
(Nobel Dr.) | 858-455-9395
www.tendergreensfood.com

Fans say "even the picklest eaters" will enjoy this "healthy" American
chain link duo in Point Loma and University Town Center, where
"freshness abounds" in the "wonderfully prepared" "farm-to-table"
salads, soups and sandwiches ordered at the counter and then delivered by "quick" servers; the "casual" space can get "crowded",
but "value" prices keep most happy.

Terra American Bistro *American* | ▽ 24 | 18 | 23 | $26 |

East San Diego | Uptown Ctr. | 7091 El Cajon Blvd. (71st St.) |
619-293-7088 | www.terrasd.com

Chef/co-owner Jeff Rossman uses "all-natural, organic" ingredients
from local purveyors in his "fresh, tasty" small and large plates at
this "intimate, noisy" East San Diego New American; service scores
"great" marks, and the early dining prix fixe (Tuesday–Thursday and
Sunday) makes it even more affordable.

The 3rd Corner ● *Californian* | 23 | 21 | 23 | $35 |

Encinitas | 896 S. Coast Hwy. 101 (H St.) | 760-942-2104
Ocean Beach | 2265 Bacon St. (Point Loma Blvd.) |
619-223-2700 Ⓜ
www.the3rdcorner.com

Guests at this "swanky" but "reasonably priced" Ocean Beach bistro
and wine shop (with an Encinitas sib) can indulge in "delectable"
Californian small plates while sipping "wonderful wines", including
"under-the-radar" bottles pulled from cases that surround the dining room (for a "token corkage fee"); the "multiple" seating areas
are "always bustling" with "convivial" company, and "warm" staffers
add to the "thoroughly enjoyable experience."

333 Pacific *Seafood/Steak* | 25 | 25 | 24 | $46 |

Oceanside | Wyndham Suites | 333 N. Pacific St. (Pier View Way) |
760-433-3333 | www.333pacific.com

"Upscale" surf 'n' turf, "well-chosen" wine and vodka lists and a
"stunning" location beside the Wyndham Suites and across the
street from the Oceanside Pier make this one of "the best options"
in the area for "impressing a boss or mother-in-law"; prices are
"high", but "courteous" staffers, a "jumping" bar scene and "wonderful" views make for a "captivating" dining experience.

Tin Fish *Seafood* | 22 | 18 | 20 | $22 |

Imperial Beach | 910 Seacoast Dr. (bet. Imperial Beach Blvd. & Palm Ave.) |
619-628-8414
🆕 **Oceanside** | 302 The Strand (bet. 1st St. & Surf Rider Way) |
760-966-0007
Tin Fish Gaslamp *Seafood*
Gaslamp Quarter | 170 Sixth Ave. (L St.) | 619-238-8100
www.thetinfish.net

		FOOD	DECOR	SERVICE	COST

(continued)

Joao's Tin Fish Bar & Eatery   *Seafood*

Point Loma | Liberty Station | 2750 Dewey Rd. (bet. Cushing & Historic Decatur Rds.) | 619-794-2192 | www.joaostinfish.com

Serving what some say are the "best fish tacos" around, not to mention "great cioppino and scallops", this quick-fix chain might be "noisy", but service is fast and the affordable menu is full of "tasty seafood"; there are "good deals at lunch" and many insist there's "nothing better" than enjoying the Gaslamp outpost's outdoor patio "on a nice day."

Todai   *Chinese/Japanese*   19 | 17 | 16 | $35

Mission Valley | 2828 Camino Del Rio S. (I-8) | 619-299-8996 | www.todaisandiego.com

"Come with an appetite" because you can "stuff yourself" with a "wide" range of sushi, sashimi and hot Japanese and Chinese standards, plus a "whole room of dessert" at this all-you-can-eat Mission Valley buffet chain link; critics find the offerings "just average" and say prices are "high" for the genre, but enthusiasts excuse it all on account of the "huge selection."

Tom Ham's Lighthouse   *Californian/Seafood*   22 | 23 | 22 | $40

Harbor Island | 2150 Harbor Island Dr. (Harbor Dr.) | 619-291-9110 | www.tomhamslighthouse.com

"Beautiful" bay and skyline views star at this "touristy" Californian seafooder, a Harbor Island stalwart where the "solid" midpriced fare is perhaps best experienced at the "classic" Sunday champagne brunch; though critics deem the offerings "nothing special" they admit service is generally "friendly" and the location sure is "priceless."

Tony Roma's   *BBQ*   24 | 20 | 21 | $33

Pacific Beach | 4110 Mission Blvd. (Pacific Beach Dr.) | 858-272-7427 | www.tonyromas.com

"Ribs are king" at this midpriced BBQ chain link in Pacific Beach, where "succulent" meats, "delicious" sides and an array of sauces are "finger licking good"; service is "friendly", and even if a few say the "dark" space "could use updating", it still works for a "casual dinner out."

Top of the Market   *Seafood*   24 | 24 | 23 | $49

Downtown | 750 N. Harbor Dr. (G St.) | 619-234-4867 | www.thefishmarket.com

A Downtown harborside setting with "magnificent" views of San Diego Bay provides the backdrop for "high-quality" seafood that admirers say "matches" the "gorgeous" surrounds at this "classy" eatery located atop its more casual Fish Market sib; service gets solid marks too, and though it's not cheap, it's still a "great spot for a date."

Tractor Room   ◐ *American*   25 | 25 | 24 | $28

Hillcrest | 3687 Fifth Ave. (Pennsylvania Ave.) | 619-543-1007 | www.thetractorroom.com

"It takes a tractor to lift the portions" at this midpriced Hillcrest New American, where an "adventurous" meat-heavy menu (with lots of wild game items) makes it "the place for carnivores", though there are plenty of options for others too; "clever" cocktails, "knowledgeable" service and "funky" hunting lodge decor also work in its favor.

Trattoria Fantastica *Italian*

▽ 26 | 19 | 23 | $31

Little Italy | 1735 India St. (bet. Date & Fir Sts.) | 619-234-1735 | www.trattoriafantastica.com

Around since 1983, this Little Italy trattoria is still a "consistent" "favorite", turning out "authentic" "perfectly dressed pastas", *insalate* "worth writing home about" and "famous" cannoli, all at "affordable" prices; fans praise staffers who go "the extra mile" and if the space doesn't earn quite the same marks, the patio is "great for people-watching."

Trattoria I Trulli *Italian*

26 | 19 | 20 | $37

Encinitas | 830 S. Coast Hwy. 101 (bet. G & H Sts.) | 760-943-6800 | www.itrulli.signonsandiego.com

There's an *"abbondanza"* of Italian delights at this "little slice of Little Italy right in Encinitas", a sister to Buon Appetito that "gastronomes" praise for its "delicious, authentic" fare, "reasonable-for-the-quality" prices and "amicable" staffers; the "warm, cozy" room can be "cramped" and "noisy", especially when "mobbed on weekends", so "show up early" – and "bring earplugs."

Trattoria Ponte Vecchio *Italian*

▽ 28 | 21 | 26 | $33

Del Mar | 2334 Carmel Valley Rd. (bet. Via Cortina & Via Donada) | 858-259-9063 | www.pontevecchiodelmar.com

"Involved" Milanese chef-owner Daniel Nobili creates "masterpieces" at his "down-home" Del Mar *"cucina"*, focusing on "fresh, inventive" pastas and other dishes that "taste like Italy", all offered at moderate prices; "mature" servers manage the "cute, quaint" dining room, which is hidden behind an "unprepossessing" exterior that helps locals "keep it a secret."

Truluck's *Seafood/Steak*

27 | 26 | 27 | $61

Golden Triangle | Aventine | 8990 University Center Ln. (Lebon Dr.) | 858-453-2583 | www.trulucks.com

Some of the "sweetest crab legs in town" are featured on the "top-drawer" menu at this "upscale" surf 'n' turf chain link in the Golden Triangle, where fans say the "well-prepared" offerings are "pricey" but "worth every dollar", especially desserts "enormous" enough to "feed four"; "precise-but-not-pushy" staffers and a "swanky" setting further make it the "total package", and the "excellent" happy hour extends the appeal.

Turf Supper Club ◐ *Steak*

▽ 25 | 20 | 20 | $21

Golden Hill | 1116 25th St. (C St.) | 619-234-6363 | www.turfsupperclub.com

Among the first to employ the "cook-your-own concept", this circa-1956 Golden Hill "staple" "takes away the middleman" by letting the "cool, casual, young" 21-plus crowd sizzle its steaks over a center grill while sipping "no-nonsense" cocktails; the "kitschy cowboy decor" adds to the "unpretentious supper club" feel, and prices are "low."

	FOOD	DECOR	SERVICE	COST

25 Forty Bistro Ⓜ *Italian*

| | 23 | 22 | 23 | $38 |

Old Town | 2540 Congress St. (Twiggs St.) | 619-294-2540 |
www.25fortybistro.com

"Exceptional" pastas and "to-die-for" desserts make this "super-cute, atmospheric" Italian bistro "a real lifesaver" for those "tired of carnitas" in Mexican-heavy Old Town; dedicated chef-owner Mark Pelliccia, who spent many years cooking in Northern Italy, charges fair prices and carefully supervises "quick, easy service."

NEW Underbelly ⦿ *Japanese*

| | 23 | 23 | 22 | $19 |

Little Italy | 750 W. Fir St. (bet. India St. & Kettner Blvd.) |
619-269-4626 | www.godblessunderbelly.com

Partially owned by bar/resto impresario Arsalun Tafazoli, this Little Italy tribute to the Japanese noodle house is a "great concept" that "does not disappoint" say those "in the mood for ramen", high-quality sakes and craft beers; the small space has communal tables where diners sit after ordering at the counter, and prices are affordable.

Union Kitchen & Tap *American*

| | 21 | 22 | 21 | $32 |

Encinitas | 1108 S. Coast Hwy. 101 (J St.) | 760-230-2337 |
www.localunion101.com

"Good vibes" and a "trendy" reclaimed-chic motif keep this "hot spot" (from the owners of Pacific Beach Ale House) along Encinitas' burgeoning stretch of Highway 101 "packed" on weekends; the "fun" crowd is fueled by a "variety" of midpriced American gastro-pub plates and 20 rotating craft beers served by "friendly" waiters.

Urban Solace *American*

| | 26 | 22 | 24 | $32 |

North Park | 3823 30th St. (bet. Park Way & University Ave.) |
619-295-6464 | www.urbansolace.net

"Down-home cooking" takes on a "creative" bent at this "reasonably priced" American in "funky" North Park, where the "creamy comfort food" is made with "gourmet" ingredients and features "interesting, eclectic" twists; a "straightforward" staff tends to "relaxed yet hip" clientele in a "dim, romantic" space that gets especially "crowded" during the "bomb" Sunday bluegrass brunch; P.S. Encinitas offshoot Solace & The Moonlight Lounge has a similar style.

URBN Coal Fired Pizza ⦿ *Pizza*

| | 26 | 22 | 21 | $23 |

North Park | 3085 University Ave. (31st St.) | 619-255-7300 |
www.urbnnorthpark.com

"Smoky, crisp" "New Haven–style" pizza, "excellent" cocktails and "lots of specialty beers" from hefty glass growlers draw diners to this affordable North Park hangout; the "big, open" space with a "ware-house aesthetic" (and "mesmerizing giant ceiling fan") is tended by "welcoming" staffers, and prices are appropriately affordable.

Vagabond *Eclectic*

| | 21 | 22 | 21 | $34 |

South Park | 2310 30th St. (Juniper St.) | 619-255-1035 |
www.vagabondkitchen.com

Take a "culinary journey" at this midpriced South Park Eclectic, where the "broad, interesting" menu "represents recipes from around the world", and "boho-funky" artifacts help create a "globe-trotter ambiance" to match; service may get mixed marks ("efficient" vs. "uneven"), but a "hip" clientele keeps it "densely crowded" nonetheless.

NEW Veladora *Californian* | − | − | − | E |

Rancho Santa Fe | Rancho Valencia Resort & Spa | 5921 Valencia Circle (Rancho Valencia Dr.) | 858-759-6216 | www.ranchovalencia.com

After a $30 million renovation, the Rancho Valencia Resort & Spa boasts a new on-site eatery helmed by chef Eric Bauer, offering an ultralocal Californian menu including market veggies, housemade charcuterie and honey from beehives located on the property, and an extensive wine menu with over 600 bottles; valley views and outdoor fireplaces add an alfresco feel to the more formal dining room.

Venetian *Italian* | 25 | 21 | 24 | $33 |

Point Loma | 3663 Voltaire St. (bet. Chatsworth Blvd. & Poinsettia Dr.) | 619-223-8197 | www.venetian1965.com

"Consistently great" "hearty" Italian fare, including "excellent" pizzas, and strong service have kept this midpriced Point Loma eatery a "favorite among locals" since 1965; a few sniff it's "unspectacular", but it's still "always crowded", and if inside gets "a little noisy", fans say the covered patio has "the best atmosphere."

Via Italia Trattoria *Italian* | ▽ 24 | 21 | 23 | $35 |

Encinitas | 569 S. Coast Hwy. 101 (E St.) | 760-479-9757 | www.viaitaliatrattoria.com

This "authentic" Encinitas trattoria is "a little slice of Italy" say talliers touting the "moderately priced" Italian "standards" like "feather-light, crispy" thin-crust pizzas and "toothsome, flavorful" handmade pastas proffered by waiters with an "outstanding knowledge" of the menu; those who find the "quaint" dining room "cramped" can try for a seat outside.

Vigilucci's Cucina Italiana *Italian* | 24 | 22 | 23 | $44 |

Carlsbad | 2943 State St. (Grand Ave.) | 760-434-2500

Vigilucci's Ristorante *Seafood/Steak*

Coronado | 1330 Orange Ave. (Churchill Pl.) | 619-522-0946

Vigilucci's Seafood & Steakhouse *Seafood/Steak*

Carlsbad | 3878 Carlsbad Blvd. (Tamarack Ave.) | 760-434-2580

Vigilucci's Trattoria Italiana *Italian*

Encinitas | 505 S. Coast Hwy. 101 (D St.) | 760-942-7332 www.vigiluccis.com

Roberto Vigilucci's empire of Italian and surf 'n' turf spots peppers San Diego's coast from Coronado to Encinitas, offering "authentic" pastas, "fresh" seafood and "wonderful" chops, "professionally served" by staffers who "make you feel at home"; "noisy" crowds lend a "convivial" vibe, and "beautiful" decor and "lovely" views take the sting out of "not-cheap" tabs.

Villa Capri Cucina Italiana *Italian* | 23 | 22 | 23 | $31 |

Carmel Heights | Piazza Carmel | 3870 Valley Centre Dr. (Carmel View Rd.) | 858-720-8777 | www.villacapriristorante.com

(continued)

(continued)

Villa Capri 2 Family Style Trattoria *Italian*

Chula Vista | San Miguel Ranch | 2330 Proctor Valley Rd.
(Mt. Miguel Rd.) | 619-216-5900 | www.villacaprichulavista.com

**Villa Capri 2 Italian
Restaurant & Bar** *Italian*

Carmel Valley | 7875 Highland Village Pl. (Camino Del Sur) |
858-538-5884 | www.villacapri2.com

NEW **Villa Capri Trattoria & Wine Bar** *Italian*

Poway | 14771 Pomerado Rd. (Twin Peaks Rd.) | 858-391-9400 |
www.vc3.villacaprиristorante.com

Capri Blu Italian Bistro & Wine Bar *Italian*

Rancho Bernardo | 4S Commons Town Ctr. | 10436 Craftsman Way
(Reserve Dr.) | 858-673-5100 | www.capri-blu.com

Capri Cafe *Italian*

Carmel Valley | 12265 El Camino Real (Valley Centre Dr.) | 858-523-0221

The whole "comfort-food-loving" clan "always enjoys eating" at these "casual" Italian chain links offering "tasty" entrees and "family-size" plates that are a "good deal for large parties"; "uniformly pleasant" staffers "recognize regulars and treat them like family", creating a "loyal following" of "once-a-week" visitors.

Vincent's 🈲Ⓜ️ *French* | 27 | 23 | 24 | $49 |

Escondido | 113 W. Grand Ave. (B'way) | 760-745-3835 |
www.vincentsongrand.com

"World-class" chef Vincent Grumel serves up "delicious" New French plates at this Escondido bistro; "great" service and casually elegant decor score solid marks, and while it's not inexpensive, dinner prix fixes offered Tuesdays–Thursdays are a more affordable alternative.

Vivace *Italian* | ▽ 27 | 28 | 28 | $65 |

Carlsbad | Park Hyatt Aviara Resort | 7100 Aviara Resort Dr.
(Aviara Pkwy.) | 760-448-1234 | www.parkaviara.hyatt.com

"For special-occasion dining", this "excellent, creative" Italian in Carlsbad's luxe Park Hyatt Aviara is among "the best" around according to fans; able staffers tend a "lovely" room that matches "expensive" tabs and is enhanced by working fireplaces and "sunset dining" on the terrace.

Wahoo's Fish Taco *Mexican/Seafood* | 23 | 19 | 21 | $16 |

Carmel Mountain Ranch | 4S Commons Town Center |
10436 Craftsman Way (4S Ranch Pkwy.) | 858-487-0288
Encinitas | 1006 N. El Camino Real (Town Center Dr.) | 760-753-5060
La Jolla | 637 Pearl St. (bet. Cuvier St. & Draper Ave.) | 858-459-0027
Mission Valley | 2195 Station Village Way (Rio San Deigo Dr.) |
619-299-4550
Ocean Beach | 3944 W. Point Loma Blvd. (Ollie St.) | 619-222-0020
www.wahoos.com

Solid fish tacos and other Mexican-accented seafood, including some "healthy" options, make for "good eats" at these Cali-based chain links; the "laid-back" counter-service digs have a "cool" "skate and surfer vibe", and tabs are fittingly budget-friendly.

	FOOD	DECOR	SERVICE	COST

DINING

NEW Wang's North Park *Chinese*
24 | 25 | 23 | $29

North Park | 3029 University Ave. (Ohio St.) | 619-291-7500 |
www.wangsnorthpark.com

"Minimal, modern decor" lends an "elegant touch" to this "cavernous" North Park Chinese, which offers "interesting takes" on classics, including many vegetarian and gluten-free choices, all offered at "good prices overall", fans also vouch for "friendly" service and convenient parking in back – a "big plus" in this bustling 'hood.

West Coast Tavern ● *American*
▽ 21 | 20 | 20 | $16

North Park | North Park Theatre | 2895 University Ave. (29th St.) |
619-295-1688 | www.westcoasttavern.com

"Reasonably priced" American comfort fare like "hit-the-spot" sliders and daily mac 'n' cheese are on offer at this North Park standout, a "favorite" for happy hour thanks to its "fine beverage selection"; "helpful" staffers facilitate "quick seating" in the spacious, dimly lit space, and the "casual vibe" is another plus.

West Steak & Seafood *Seafood/Steak*
27 | 25 | 26 | $64

Carlsbad | 4980 Avenida Encinas (Cannon Rd.) | 760-930-9100 |
www.weststeakandseafood.com

"Terrific fine dining" thrives at this Carlsbad surf 'n' turfer, where "perfectly prepared" steaks and "outstanding" seafood – sided with seasonal produce from the restaurant's private farm – earn raves; upscale decor and "attentive" servers reinforce its "special-occasion" status, though the happy-hour bar menu is an "excellent" deal.

Whisknladle *Californian/French*
23 | 21 | 22 | $43

La Jolla | 1044 Wall St. (Herschel Ave.) | 858-551-7575 |
www.whisknladle.com

"Inventive, homey" Cali-French fare is made with "the freshest of the fresh" local ingredients and is augmented by "sublime" cocktails at this "whimsical" La Jolla "haven"; it has a "delightful", "bistro-in-Manhattan" vibe that's enhanced by "hip" "foodie" staffers, and though prices aren't cheap, many feel they are "fair."

Wild Note Cafe *Californian*
▽ 24 | 21 | 23 | $22

Solana Beach | Belly Up Tavern | 143 S. Cedros Ave. (Lomas Santa Fe Dr.) |
858-720-9000 | www.wildnote.com

"De rigueur" for a "pre-show" meal, this Solana Beach Californian attached to the legendary Belly Up Tavern offers "tasty" fare via "friendly" staffers; in keeping with the musical milieu, the "classy" interior features instrument displays, and affordable prices complete the picture.

WineSellar & Brasserie ☒Ⓜ *French*
26 | 21 | 25 | $62

Sorrento Mesa | 9550 Waples St. (Mira Mesa Blvd.) | 858-450-9557 |
www.winesellar.com

Set in a "far afield" Sorrento Mesa locale, this "sophisticated" brasserie is ideal for a "quiet evening away from the crowds" say fans applauding the "gourmet" French fare, "smooth" service and "intimate" setting; "excellent" vinos from the connected wine shop's "enormous" collection can be opened for a "minimal" corkage fee, which helps offset "pricey" tabs.

Wine Vault & Bistro 🅂🅜 *Eclectic*   27 | 22 | 25 | $45

Mission Hills | 3731 India St. (Washington St.) | 619-295-3939 | www.winevaultbistro.com

With "scrumptious, thoughtfully prepared" Eclectic fare, "well-chosen" wine pairings and "bargain" prix fixe meals, "you can't go wrong" at this "hidden treasure" in Mission Hills; the "simple" space holds "large communal tables" that create "great camaraderie with fellow guests", overseen by "dedicated" owners who "truly care about their patrons"; P.S. open Thursday–Saturday only (with winemaker dinners on other nights).

Woodstock's Pizza ◑ *Pizza*   25 | 19 | 22 | $17

East San Diego | 6145 El Cajon Blvd. (College Ave.) | 619-265-0999 | www.woodstockssd.com
Pacific Beach | 1221 Garnet Ave. (Everts St.) | 858-642-6900 | www.woodstockspb.com

SDSU students and alums call this College Area pizzeria's flagship an "institution" for its "cheesy" but "not greasy" pies, "unique crust style" and plethora of "tasty" toppings, all offered for "reasonable" prices; counter service staffers are "great", and the "fun atmosphere" carries over to a second, more "kid-friendly" spot in Pacific Beach.

World Famous *Seafood*   23 | 20 | 19 | $26

Pacific Beach | 711 Pacific Beach Dr. (Mission Blvd.) | 858-272-3100 | www.worldfamouspb.com

Fresh coastal cuisine, like "straight-from-the-ocean" lobster tacos and clam chowder, pairs with "impressive" ocean views enjoyed from the dining room or sand-abutting patio at this "well-located" Pacific Beach seafooder; service can get "backed up" but remains "pleasant", and prices are "affordable."

Yanni's Bistro *Greek/Italian*   24 | 21 | 23 | $32

Poway | Trident Plaza | 12205 Scripps Poway Pkwy. (Pomerado Rd.) | 858-527-0011 | www.yannisbistro.net

Proprietor Yanni Pihas makes for a "terrific host" at this Poway Greek-Italian, where guests receive a "warm" greeting before dining on "fabulously different" dishes served in "comfortable" surrounds that go beyond the "strip-mall" status quo; add in "reasonable" prices and "well-picked" wines and fans dub it a "perennial favorite."

Yard House ◑ *American*   22 | 20 | 21 | $27

Downtown | 1023 Fourth Ave. (B'way) | 619-233-9273 | www.yardhouse.com

"Friendly" servers proffer an "astounding selection of draft beer" and "diverse" menu of "solid" New American fare in a "bustling" setting, making this Downtown link of the "high-end sports bar" chain a "fun place to watch the game" or "kick it with buddies", especially during the weekday happy hour; but, even with "over 100" brews, a few say there are "better" options "now that San Diego has so many excellent beer bars."

	FOOD	DECOR	SERVICE	COST

Zenbu Sushi Bar & Restaurant *Japanese* | 22 | 21 | 21 | $37 |

Cardiff-by-the-Sea | 2003 San Elijo Ave. (Birmingham Dr.) | 760-633-2223
La Jolla | 7660 Fay Ave. (Kline St.) | 858-454-4540 Ⓜ
www.rimelsrestaurants.com

The sushi is "as fresh as you can get" (some even comes from the owner's own daily catch) says fans of the "nontraditional" rolls at this midpriced Japanese duo in La Jolla and Cardiff; the "dark" space is "trendy, sexy and hip – and so is the clientele", so even if the otherwise "efficient" service can get "slow" when it's "crowded", at least there's "interesting" people-watching.

Zinc Cafe *Vegetarian* | 23 | 20 | 21 | $22 |

Solana Beach | 132 S. Cedros Ave. (Lomas Santa Fe Dr.) |
858-793-5436 | www.zinccafe.com

Nestled in Solana Beach's Cedros Design District, this breakfast-and-lunch-only vegetarian "hits the mark" cheer fans applauding the "simple", "consistently good" fare, able counter service and affordable prices; it's "not fancy", but "cozy" coffee-shop decor and an outdoor patio help ensure a "pleasant" meal.

The Zodiac at Neiman Marcus Ⓩ *Californian/Eclectic* | 23 | 20 | 23 | $29 |

Mission Valley | Fashion Valley Mall | 7027 Friars Rd. (Fashion Valley Rd.) |
619-542-4450 | www.neimanmarcus.com

For a "relaxing, therapeutic" respite from "the rigors of shopping", "ladies who lunch" head to this "tasteful" midday cafe on the top floor of the Mission Valley Neiman Marcus that's praised for "always dependable" Cal-Eclectic fare; staffers take "good care" of you, and it all comes at prices considered "reasonable for a high-priced department store."

NIGHTLIFE

Most Popular

This list is plotted on the map at the back of this book.

- **1** Belly Up Tavern
- **2** 4th & B
- **3** House of Blues
- **4** Aero Club
- **5** Altitude Sky Bar
- **6** Pacific Beach B&G
- **7** Humphrey's Backstage Live
- **8** In Cahoots
- **9** Fluxx
- **10** Blind Lady Ale House

Top Atmosphere

28 Noble Experiment
Float
Top/Hyatt

27 Shout! House
R. O'Sullivan's

Sogno Di Vino*
Vin De Syrah

26 Prohibition
Humphrey's Backstage Live
Latitude Lounge

BY SPECIAL APPEAL

AFTER WORK

27 R. O'Sullivan's
Sogno Di Vino*

26 Whaling B&G
Altitude Sky Bar

25 Waterfront B&G

BEER SPECIALISTS

25 Blind Lady Ale House
Tiger!Tiger! Tavern
Pacific Beach AleHouse

24 Toronado

23 Hamiltons Tavern

COCKTAIL EXPERTS

28 Noble Experiment

27 Vin De Syrah

26 Prohibition

24 Bootlegger

22 El Dorado

DANCE CLUBS

25 Voyeur
Sevilla Nightclub
Side Bar
Fluxx

24 Stingaree

DIVES

25 Waterfront B&G

24 In Cahoots
Pacific Shores Cafe

Rosie O'Grady's

23 Live Wire

FIRST DATE

28 Noble Experiment
Float
Top/Hyatt

27 Shout! House

26 Altitude Sky Lounge

FRAT HOUSE

25 McGregor's
Sandbar

24 Bub's
Encinitas Ale House

23 McFadden's

GAY/LESBIAN

26 Lips

25 Urban Mo's B&G

24 Bourbon Street

23 Redwing B&G
Rich's

HOTEL BARS

28 Float (Hard Rock)
Top/Hyatt
(Manchester Grand Hyatt)

26 Latitude Lounge
(Marriott Gaslamp)
Whaling B&G (La Valencia)
Ivy Rooftop (Andaz)

Excludes places with low votes; *indicates a tie with place above

Share your reviews on plus.google.com/local

MUSIC/PERFORMANCE VENUES

26 Humphrey's Backstage Live
25 Loft at UCSD
   House of Blues
   Belly Up Tavern
23 Casbah

SINGLES SCENES

24 El Camino
   Firehouse

23 Whistle Stop
22 El Dorado
21 Nunu's

TRENDY

28 Noble Experiment
   Top/Hyatt
27 Shout! House
   Vin De Syrah
25 Fluxx

Top Decor

28 Noble Experiment
27 Vin De Syrah
26 Sogno Di Vino
   Float
   Top/Hyatt

25 Voyeur
   Fluxx
   Ivy Winebar
24 Ivy Nightclub
   Latitude Lounge

Top Service

27 Noble Experiment
26 ENO Wine Bar
25 Whaling B&G
   Redwing B&G
   Loft at UCSD

Grand on Grand
Tiger!Tiger! Tavern*
Sandbar
R. O'Sullivan's
Oasis Lounge

Nightlife Special Appeals

Listings cover the best in each category and include names, locations and Atmosphere ratings. Multi-location nightspots' features may vary by branch. These lists include low-vote places that do not qualify for tops lists.

AFTER WORK

R. O'Sullivan's | **Escondido**	27
Sogno Di Vino | **Little Italy**	27
Grape | **Gaslamp Qtr**	26
Whaling B&G | **La Jolla**	26
Altitude Sky | **Gaslamp Qtr**	26
Patricks | **Gaslamp Qtr**	26
Shakespeare Pub | **Mission Hills**	25
Urban Mo's | **Hillcrest**	25
Royal Dive | **Oceanside**	25
Tiger! Tiger! | **North Pk**	25
Splash | **North Pk**	25
Sandbar | **Mission Bch**	25
Waterfront B&G | **Little Italy**	25
OffShore Tav. | **Bay Pk**	25
Ivy Winebar | **Gaslamp Qtr**	25
Pacific Beach Ale | **Pacific Bch**	25
Tipsy Crow | **Gaslamp Qtr**	25
Mosaic Wine | **North Pk**	24
Toronado | **North Pk**	24
Wine Steals | **Hillcrest**	24
Go Lounge | **La Mesa**	24
Pacific Shores | **Ocean Bch**	24
Bub's | **multi.**	24
Main Tap Tav. | **El Cajon**	24
Encinitas Ale | **Encinitas**	24
Small Bar | **University Hts**	24
Rosie O'Grad. | **Normal Heights**	24
Toast Enoteca | **E Vill**	24
Ould Sod | **Normal Heights**	23
Monkey Paw | **E Vill**	23
Whistle Stop | **South Pk**	23
Triple Crown | **Normal Heights**	23
Hamiltons Tav. | **South Pk**	23
En Fuego | **Del Mar**	23
LOUNGEsix | **Gaslamp Qtr**	23
La Jolla Brew | **La Jolla**	23
Pacific Beach B&G | **Pacific Bch**	22
Beachcomber | **Mission Bay**	22
Beaumont's | **La Jolla**	22
Nunu's Cocktail | **Hillcrest**	21
Kraken | **Cardiff-by-the-Sea**	21
Bar Leucadian | **Encinitas**	21
Carriage Hse. | **Kearny Mesa**	21
Griffin | **Morena District**	20
Fifty Seven Deg. | **Middletown**	19

BACHELOR PARTIES

Float | **Gaslamp Qtr**	28
Patricks | **Gaslamp Qtr**	26
NEW Block No. 16 | **E Vill**	25
McGregor's | **Grantville**	25
Side Bar | **Gaslamp Qtr**	25
Sandbar | **Mission Bch**	25
Gaslamp Tav. | **Gaslamp Qtr**	25
OffShore Tav. | **Bay Pk**	25
Fluxx | **Gaslamp Qtr**	25
In Cahoots | **Mission Valley**	24
Bub's | **multi.**	24
Kristy's MVP | **Midway District**	24
Firehse. | **Pacific Bch**	24
Stingaree | **Gaslamp Qtr**	24
710 Beach | **Pacific Bch**	23
McFadden's | **Gaslamp Qtr**	23
Whiskey Girl | **Gaslamp Qtr**	22
Double Deuce | **Gaslamp Qtr**	22
Bar West | **Pacific Bch**	22
Pacific Beach B&G | **Pacific Bch**	22
Tavern/Beach | **Pacific Bch**	22
True North Tav. | **North Pk**	22
BeachWood | **Pacific Bch**	21
F6ix | **Gaslamp Qtr**	21
Jolt 'n Joe's | **Gaslamp Qtr**	21
Typhoon Saloon | **Pacific Bch**	21
Dirty Birds | **Pacific Bch**	21
U-31 | **North Pk**	20
Boar Cross'n | **Carlsbad**	18

BACHELORETTE PARTIES

Float | **Gaslamp Qtr**	28
Shout! Hse. | **Gaslamp Qtr**	27
Lips | **North Pk**	26
Ivy Rooftop | **Gaslamp Qtr**	26
Urban Mo's | **Hillcrest**	25
House of Blues | **Gaslamp Qtr**	25
Sevilla Nightclub | **Gaslamp Qtr**	25
Ivy Nightclub | **Gaslamp Qtr**	24
Firehse. | **Pacific Bch**	24
McFadden's | **Gaslamp Qtr**	23
Whiskey Girl | **Gaslamp Qtr**	22
Double Deuce | **Gaslamp Qtr**	22
Bar West | **Pacific Bch**	22
Tavern/Beach | **Pacific Bch**	22

Lamplighter | **Mission Hills**	21	High Dive | **Linda Vista**	25
BeachWood | **Pacific Bch**	21	In Cahoots | **Mission Valley**	24
Air Conditioned | **North Pk**	21	Go Lounge | **La Mesa**	24
Typhoon Saloon | **Pacific Bch**	21	Pacific Shores | **Ocean Bch**	24
NEW Johnny V | **Pacific Bch**	21	Rosie O'Grad. | **Normal Heights**	24
U-31 | **North Pk**	20	Champ's Lounge | **Clairemont**	23

CABARET

Lips | **North Pk**	26

COMEDY CLUBS

(Call ahead to check nights, times, performers and covers)

NEW Amer. Comedy | **Gaslamp Qtr**	25
Comedy Store | **La Jolla**	23

COOL LOOS

Prohibition | **Gaslamp Qtr**	26
Humphrey's/Live | **Shelter Is**	26
Whaling B&G | **La Jolla**	26
Ivy Rooftop | **Gaslamp Qtr**	26
Marble Rm. | **Gaslamp Qtr**	25
Blind Lady | **Normal Heights**	25
Sevilla Nightclub | **Gaslamp Qtr**	25
Fluxx | **Gaslamp Qtr**	25
Bootlegger | **E Vill**	24
El Camino | **Little Italy**	24
Bleu Bar | **Del Mar**	23
Aero Club | **Mission Hills**	23
207 | **Gaslamp Qtr**	23

DANCE CLUBS

Voyeur | **Gaslamp Qtr**	25
NEW Block No. 16 | **E Vill**	25
Sevilla Nightclub | **Gaslamp Qtr**	25
Side Bar | **Gaslamp Qtr**	25
Fluxx | **Gaslamp Qtr**	25
Ivy Nightclub | **Gaslamp Qtr**	24
Stingaree | **Gaslamp Qtr**	24
Spin | **Middletown**	23
Rich's | **Hillcrest**	23
El Dorado Cocktail | **E Vill**	22
Bar West | **Pacific Bch**	22
Air Conditioned | **North Pk**	21
Onyx Rm. | **Gaslamp Qtr**	21
F6ix | **Gaslamp Qtr**	21
Typhoon Saloon | **Pacific Bch**	21
Bar Dynamite | **Mission Hills**	21
U-31 | **North Pk**	20
Belo | **Gaslamp Qtr**	20

DIVES

Royal Dive | **Oceanside**	25
Waterfront B&G | **Little Italy**	25

High Dive | **Linda Vista**	25
In Cahoots | **Mission Valley**	24
Go Lounge | **La Mesa**	24
Pacific Shores | **Ocean Bch**	24
Rosie O'Grad. | **Normal Heights**	24
Champ's Lounge | **Clairemont**	23
Casbah | **Middletown**	23
Whistle Stop | **South Pk**	23
Live Wire | **University Hts**	23
Triple Crown | **Normal Heights**	23
Redwing B&G | **North Pk**	23
Hamiltons Tav. | **South Pk**	23
Club Marina | **Pt Loma**	23
Aero Club | **Mission Hills**	23
SRO Lounge | **Bankers Hill**	23
Flying Elephant | **Carlsbad**	23
Gallagher's | **Ocean Bch**	23
Loft | **Hillcrest**	22
Soda Bar | **Normal Heights**	22
Gilly's | **University Hts**	22
Beachcomber | **Mission Bay**	22
Ruby Rm. | **Hillcrest**	22
Hole | **Pt Loma**	22
Lamplighter | **Mission Hills**	21
Alibi | **Hillcrest**	21
Dirk's Niteclub | **Lemon Grove**	21
Duke's | **Cardiff-by-the-Sea**	21
CJ's Club | **Hillcrest**	21
Tower Bar | **City Heights**	21
Coaster Saloon | **Mission Bch**	21
Nunu's Cocktail | **Hillcrest**	21
Kraken | **Cardiff-by-the-Sea**	21
Shanty | **Cardiff-by-the-Sea**	21
Black Cat | **City Heights**	21
Bar Dynamite | **Mission Hills**	21
Catalina Lounge | **Pt Loma**	21
Number One Fifth | **Hillcrest**	21
Carriage Hse. | **Kearny Mesa**	21
Bar Pink | **North Pk**	20
Eleven | **Normal Heights**	20
Morena Club | **Linda Vista**	20
Tivoli B&G | **E Vill**	20
Brick/Brick | **Morena District**	19
Lancers | **University Hts**	19
Caliph | **Bankers Hill**	19
Kensington Club | **Kensington**	18
Daley Double | **Encinitas**	18
Til-Two | **City Heights**	18
Boar Cross'n | **Carlsbad**	18
Silver Spigot | **Bay Pk**	17
Tin Can | **Bankers Hill**	17
Chee-Chee | **E Vill**	13

NIGHTLIFE

SPECIAL APPEALS

DJs

Float | **Gaslamp Qtr**	28
Vin De Syrah | **Gaslamp Qtr**	27
Ivy Rooftop | **Gaslamp Qtr**	26
Altitude Sky | **Gaslamp Qtr**	26
Voyeur | **Gaslamp Qtr**	25
Urban Mo's | **Hillcrest**	25
Oasis Lounge | **Valley Center**	25
NEW Block No. 16 | **E Vill**	25
Sevilla Nightclub | **Gaslamp Qtr**	25
Side Bar | **Gaslamp Qtr**	25
Fluxx | **Gaslamp Qtr**	25
Tipsy Crow | **Gaslamp Qtr**	25
Ivy Nightclub | **Gaslamp Qtr**	24
Firehse. | **Pacific Bch**	24
Stingaree | **Gaslamp Qtr**	24
Kava Lounge | **Middletown**	23
Dreamcatcher/Viejas | **Alpine**	23
McFadden's | **Gaslamp Qtr**	23
Whistle Stop | **South Pk**	23
Live Wire | **University Hts**	23
Spin | **Middletown**	23
207 | **Gaslamp Qtr**	23
En Fuego | **Del Mar**	23
Rich's | **Hillcrest**	23
Soda Bar | **Normal Heights**	22
Whiskey Girl | **Gaslamp Qtr**	22
El Dorado Cocktail | **E Vill**	22
Double Deuce | **Gaslamp Qtr**	22
Bar West | **Pacific Bch**	22
Pacific Beach B&G | **Pacific Bch**	22
PB Shore Club | **Pacific Bch**	22
Tavern/Beach | **Pacific Bch**	22
Flicks | **Hillcrest**	22
True North Tav. | **North Pk**	22
Air Conditioned | **North Pk**	21
Onyx Rm. | **Gaslamp Qtr**	21
F6ix | **Gaslamp Qtr**	21
Jolt 'n Joe's | **La Mesa**	21
Typhoon Saloon | **Pacific Bch**	21
Bar Dynamite | **Mission Hills**	21
Numbers | **Hillcrest**	20
U-31 | **North Pk**	20
Belo | **Gaslamp Qtr**	20
Office Bar | **North Pk**	20

DRINK SPECIALISTS

BEER

Shakespeare Pub | **Mission Hills**	25
Blind Lady | **Normal Heights**	25
Tiger! Tiger! | **North Pk**	25
Pacific Beach Ale | **Pacific Bch**	25

Toronado | **North Pk**	24
Encinitas Ale | **Encinitas**	24
Small Bar | **University Hts**	24
Monkey Paw | **E Vill**	23
Live Wire | **University Hts**	23
Hamiltons Tav. | **South Pk**	23
Aero Club | **Mission Hills**	23
La Jolla Brew | **La Jolla**	23
El Cajon Brew | **El Cajon**	22
San Diego Brew | **Grantville**	22
Tin Can | **Bankers Hill**	17

CHAMPAGNE

Vin De Syrah | **Gaslamp Qtr**	27
Grape | **Gaslamp Qtr**	26
ENO | **Coronado**	25
Splash | **North Pk**	25
Ivy Winebar | **Gaslamp Qtr**	25
Wine Steals | **Hillcrest**	24
Toast Enoteca | **E Vill**	24

COCKTAILS

Noble Experimt. | **E Vill**	28
Vin De Syrah | **Gaslamp Qtr**	27
Prohibition | **Gaslamp Qtr**	26
Ivy Rooftop | **Gaslamp Qtr**	26
Marble Rm. | **Gaslamp Qtr**	25
NEW Block No. 16 | **E Vill**	25
Bootlegger | **E Vill**	24
Firehse. | **Pacific Bch**	24
Bleu Bar | **Del Mar**	23
El Dorado Cocktail | **E Vill**	22
Beaumont's | **La Jolla**	22
Nunu's Cocktail | **Hillcrest**	21
Office Bar | **North Pk**	20
NEW Propagandist | **Gaslamp Qtr**	-

MARTINIS

Top/Hyatt | **Downtown**	28
Latitude Lounge | **Gaslamp Qtr**	26
Whaling B&G | **La Jolla**	26
Altitude Sky | **Gaslamp Qtr**	26
Grand/Grand | **Escondido**	24
Bleu Bar | **Del Mar**	23

RUM

Blue Parrot | **Ocean Bch**	23

SCOTCH/SINGLE MALTS

Shakespeare Pub | **Mission Hills**	25
Gaslamp Tav. | **Gaslamp Qtr**	25
Dublin Sq. | **Gaslamp Qtr**	24
Hennessey's | **La Jolla**	24
Ould Sod | **Normal Heights**	23
Aero Club | **Mission Hills**	23

Maloney's Tav. | **Gaslamp Qtr** 21
NEW Seven Grand | **North Pk** –

TEQUILA

Ivy Rooftop | **Gaslamp Qtr** 26
Ivy Nightclub | **Gaslamp Qtr** 24
El Camino | **Little Italy** 24
En Fuego | **Del Mar** 23

FRAT HOUSE

McGregor's | **Grantville** 25
Sandbar | **Mission Bch** 25
OffShore Tav. | **Bay Pk** 25
Bub's | **multi.** 24
Main Tap Tav. | **El Cajon** 24
Kristy's MVP | **Midway District** 24
Encinitas Ale | **Encinitas** 24
710 Beach | **Pacific Bch** 23
McFadden's | **Gaslamp Qtr** 23
Flying Elephant | **Carlsbad** 23
Whiskey Girl | **Gaslamp Qtr** 22
Bar West | **Pacific Bch** 22
Pacific Beach B&G | **Pacific Bch** 22
PB Shore Club | **Pacific Bch** 22
Tavern/Beach | **Pacific Bch** 22
Beachcomber | **Mission Bay** 22
True North Tav. | **North Pk** 22
BeachWood | **Pacific Bch** 21
Miller's Field | **Pacific Bch** 21
Winstons | **Ocean Bch** 21
Duke's | **Cardiff-by-the-Sea** 21
Jolt 'n Joe's | **Gaslamp Qtr** 21
Typhoon Saloon | **Pacific Bch** 21
Kraken | **Cardiff-by-the-Sea** 21
Dirty Birds | **Pacific Bch** 21
NEW Johnny V | **Pacific Bch** 21
Tivoli B&G | **E Vill** 20
Plum Crazy | **Pacific Bch** 20
Brick/Brick | **Morena District** 19
Silver Fox | **Pacific Bch** 19
Boar Cross'n | **Carlsbad** 18

GAY

(See also Lesbian)
Lips | **North Pk** 26
Urban Mo's | **Hillcrest** 25
Bourbon St. | **University Hts** 24
Redwing B&G | **North Pk** 23
SRO Lounge | **Bankers Hill** 23
Rich's | **Hillcrest** 23
Loft | **Hillcrest** 22
Cheers | **University Hts** 22
Flicks | **Hillcrest** 22
Hole | **Pt Loma** 22

Brass Rail | **Hillcrest** 21
Number One Fifth* | **Hillcrest** 21
Numbers | **Hillcrest** 20
Caliph | **Bankers Hill** 19

HAPPY HOUR

R. O'Sullivan's | **Escondido** 27
NEW Amer. Comedy | **Gaslamp Qtr** 25
House of Blues | **Gaslamp Qtr** 25
Belly Up Tav. | **Solana Bch** 25
Side Bar | **Gaslamp Qtr** 25
Waterfront B&G | **Little Italy** 25
Pacific Beach Ale | **Pacific Bch** 25
Dublin Sq. | **Gaslamp Qtr** 24
Bourbon St. | **University Hts** 24
Go Lounge | **La Mesa** 24
Grand/Grand | **Escondido** 24
Stingaree | **Gaslamp Qtr** 24
Ould Sod | **Normal Heights** 23
Whistle Stop | **South Pk** 23
Redwing B&G | **North Pk** 23
Aero Club | **Mission Hills** 23
En Fuego | **Del Mar** 23
LOUNGEsix | **Gaslamp Qtr** 23
Bluefoot | **North Pk** 22
Pacific Beach B&G | **Pacific Bch** 22
El Cajon Brew | **El Cajon** 22
Maloney's Tav. | **Gaslamp Qtr** 21
Air Conditioned | **North Pk** 21
Duke's | **Cardiff-by-the-Sea** 21
Porter's Pub | **La Jolla** 21
Bar Dynamite | **Mission Hills** 21
Number One Fifth | **Hillcrest** 21
Jimmy O's | **Del Mar** 20
Bar Pink | **North Pk** 20
Eleven | **Normal Heights** 20
Tivoli B&G | **E Vill** 20
Plum Crazy | **Pacific Bch** 20

HOTEL BARS

Andaz San Diego
  Ivy Rooftop | **Gaslamp Qtr** 26
  Ivy Winebar | **Gaslamp Qtr** 25
  Ivy Nightclub | **Gaslamp Qtr** 24
del Coronado
  ENO | **Coronado** 25
Hard Rock Hotel
  Float | **Gaslamp Qtr** 28
  207 | **Gaslamp Qtr** 23
L'Auberge Del Mar Hotel
  Bleu Bar | **Del Mar** 23

La Valencia Hotel
Whaling B&G | **La Jolla** 26

Manchester Grand Hyatt Hotel
Top/Hyatt | **Downtown** 28

Pala Casino Spa Resort
Center Bar | **Pala** 21

San Diego Marriott Gaslamp
Latitude Lounge | **Gaslamp Qtr** 26

Solamar
LOUNGEsix | **Gaslamp Qtr** 23

W San Diego
Living Room | **Downtown** 24

KARAOKE BARS

(Call to check nights, times
and prices)

Lamplighter | **Mission Hills** 21
Carriage Hse. | **Kearny Mesa** 21

LESBIAN

Urban Mo's | **Hillcrest** 25
Bourbon St. | **University Hts** 24
Redwing B&G | **North Pk** 23
SRO Lounge | **Bankers Hill** 23
Loft | **Hillcrest** 22
Cheers | **University Hts** 22
Flicks | **Hillcrest** 22
Hole | **Pt Loma** 22
Brass Rail | **Hillcrest** 21
Number One Fifth* | **Hillcrest** 21
Numbers | **Hillcrest** 20
Caliph | **Bankers Hill** 19

LOUNGES

Float | **Gaslamp Qtr** 28
Top/Hyatt | **Downtown** 28
Latitude Lounge | **Gaslamp Qtr** 26
Ivy Rooftop | **Gaslamp Qtr** 26
Altitude Sky | **Gaslamp Qtr** 26
Oasis Lounge | **Valley Center** 25
Pasha Lounge | **Gaslamp Qtr** 25
Living Room | **Downtown** 24
LOUNGEsix | **Gaslamp Qtr** 23
Bluefoot | **North Pk** 22
El Dorado Cocktail | **E Vill** 22
Air Conditioned | **North Pk** 21
Nunu's Cocktail | **Hillcrest** 21
Catalina Lounge | **Pt Loma** 21
NEW Propagandist | -
Gaslamp Qtr

MATURE CROWDS

Noble Experimt. | **E Vill** 28
Shout! Hse. | **Gaslamp Qtr** 27

R. O'Sullivan's | **Escondido** 27
Sogno Di Vino | **Little Italy** 27
Vin De Syrah | **Gaslamp Qtr** 27
Humphrey's/Live | **Shelter Is** 26
Latitude Lounge | **Gaslamp Qtr** 26
Whaling B&G | **La Jolla** 26
ENO | **Coronado** 25
Oasis Lounge | **Valley Center** 25
Tiger! Tiger! | **North Pk** 25
Waterfront B&G | **Little Italy** 25
Wine Steals | **Hillcrest** 24
Grand/Grand | **Escondido** 24
Toast Enoteca | **E Vill** 24
Hennessey's | **La Jolla** 24
Bleu Bar | **Del Mar** 23
Arizona Café | **Ocean Bch** 23
Dreamcatcher/Viejas | **Alpine** 23
Comedy Store | **La Jolla** 23
En Fuego | **Del Mar** 23
LOUNGEsix | **Gaslamp Qtr** 23
La Jolla Brew | **La Jolla** 23
98 Bottles | **Little Italy** 22
Beaumont's | **La Jolla** 22
Bar Leucadian | **Encinitas** 21
Jimmy O's | **Del Mar** 20

MUSIC CLUBS

The Loft at UCSD | **La Jolla** 25
House of Blues | **Gaslamp Qtr** 25
Belly Up Tav. | **Solana Bch** 25
SOMA | **Midway District** 24
Kava Lounge | **Middletown** 23
Casbah | **Middletown** 23
Dreamcatcher/Viejas | **Alpine** 23
98 Bottles | **Little Italy** 22
4th & B | **Downtown** 22
Ruby Rm. | **Hillcrest** 22
Winstons | **Ocean Bch** 21
Porter's Pub | **La Jolla** 21
Stage | **Gaslamp Qtr** 21
Griffin | **Morena District** 20
Che Café | **La Jolla** 20
Eleven | **Normal Heights** 20
Brick/Brick | **Morena District** 19
Epicentre | **Mira Mesa** 19
Tin Can | **Bankers Hill** 17

NEWCOMERS

Amer. Comedy | **Gaslamp Qtr** 25
Block No. 16 | **E Vill** 25
Barleymash | **Gaslamp Qtr** -
Commons | **Gaslamp Qtr** -
Seven Grand | **North Pk** -

Propagandist | **Gaslamp Qtr** —|
Uptown Tavern | **Hillcrest** —|

OLD SAN DIEGO

(50+ yrs.; Year opened; * building)

1885 | Tivoli B&G | **E Vill** 20
1899 | Waterfront B&G | **Little Italy** 25
1920 | Jimmy O's* | **Del Mar** 20
1930 | En Fuego* | **Del Mar** 23
1932 | Tower Bar | **City Heights** 21
1933 | Patricks | **Gaslamp Qtr** 26
1933 | Stingaree* | **Gaslamp Qtr** 24
1933 | Chee-Chee | **E Vill** 13
1934 | Hole | **Pt Loma** 22
1935 | Kensington Club | **Kensington** 18
1938 | Air Conditioned* | **North Pk** 21
1940 | Bar Leucadian | **Encinitas** 21
1941 | Pacific Shores | **Ocean Bch** 24
1948 | Aero Club | **Mission Hills** 23
1950 | Whaling B&G | **La Jolla** 26
1950 | Club Marina | **Pt Loma** 23
1950 | Beachcomber | **Mission Bay** 22
1954 | Belly Up Tav.* | **Solana Bch** 25
1958 | Boar Cross'n | **Carlsbad** 18
1960 | Redwing B&G | **North Pk** 23
1960 | Gallagher's | **Ocean Bch** 23
1960 | Morena Club | **Linda Vista** 20
1961 | Nunu's Cocktail | **Hillcrest** 21
1961 | Lancers | **University Hts** 19
1961 | Daley Double | **Encinitas** 18

OUTDOOR SPACES

Float | **Gaslamp Qtr** 28
R. O'Sullivan's | **Escondido** 27
Sogno Di Vino | **Little Italy** 27
Humphrey's/Live | **Shelter Is** 26
Latitude Lounge | **Gaslamp Qtr** 26
Ivy Rooftop | **Gaslamp Qtr** 26
Altitude Sky | **Gaslamp Qtr** 26
Patricks | **Gaslamp Qtr** 26
Marble Rm. | **Gaslamp Qtr** 25
Shakespeare Pub | **Mission Hills** 25
ENO | **Coronado** 25
Oasis Lounge | **Valley Center** 25
House of Blues | **Gaslamp Qtr** 25
Tiger! Tiger! | **North Pk** 25
McGregor's | **Grantville** 25
Sandbar | **Mission Bch** 25
Waterfront B&G | **Little Italy** 25
OffShore Tav. | **Bay Pk** 25
High Dive | **Linda Vista** 25
Pasha Lounge | **Gaslamp Qtr** 25

Pacific Beach Ale | **Pacific Bch** 25
Dublin Sq. | **Gaslamp Qtr** 24
In Cahoots | **Mission Valley** 24
Bourbon St. | **University Hts** 24
Bootlegger | **E Vill** 24
Wine Steals | **multi.** 24
Go Lounge | **La Mesa** 24
Bub's | **E Vill** 24
Main Tap Tav. | **El Cajon** 24
Kristy's MVP | **Midway District** 24
Small Bar | **University Hts** 24
Firehse. | **Pacific Bch** 24
Grand/Grand | **Escondido** 24
Toast Enoteca | **E Vill** 24
Hennessey's | **multi.** 24
Stingaree | **Gaslamp Qtr** 24
Bleu Bar | **Del Mar** 23
Ould Sod | **Normal Heights** 23
Whistle Stop | **South Pk** 23
Blue Parrot | **Ocean Bch** 23
Spin | **Middletown** 23
Triple Crown | **Normal Heights** 23
Redwing B&G | **North Pk** 23
207 | **Gaslamp Qtr** 23
Gallagher's | **Ocean Bch** 23
En Fuego | **Del Mar** 23
LOUNGEsix | **Gaslamp Qtr** 23
La Jolla Brew | **La Jolla** 23
Bluefoot | **North Pk** 22
Pacific Beach B&G | **Pacific Bch** 22
Gilly's | **University Hts** 22
Tavern/Beach | **Pacific Bch** 22
Callahan's | **Mira Mesa** 22
True North Tav. | **North Pk** 22
Beaumont's | **La Jolla** 22
BeachWood | **Pacific Bch** 21
Maloney's Tav. | **Gaslamp Qtr** 21
Alibi | **Hillcrest** 21
Miller's Field | **Pacific Bch** 21
Jolt 'n Joe's | **multi.** 21
Nunu's Cocktail | **Hillcrest** 21
Typhoon Saloon | **Pacific Bch** 21
Shanty | **Cardiff-by-the-Sea** 21
Carriage Hse. | **Kearny Mesa** 21
Plum Crazy | **Pacific Bch** 20
Til-Two | **City Heights** 18
NEW Commons | **Gaslamp Qtr** —|

PEOPLE-WATCHING

Float | **Gaslamp Qtr** 28
Vin De Syrah | **Gaslamp Qtr** 27
Prohibition | **Gaslamp Qtr** 26
Lips | **North Pk** 26

Ivy Rooftop	**Gaslamp Qtr**	26
Voyeur	**Gaslamp Qtr**	25
Urban Mo's	**Hillcrest**	25
Fluxx	**Gaslamp Qtr**	25
Bourbon St.	**University Hts**	24
El Camino	**Little Italy**	24
Firehse.	**Pacific Bch**	24
Casbah	**Middletown**	23
SRO Lounge	**Bankers Hill**	23
Bluefoot	**North Pk**	22
Whiskey Girl	**Gaslamp Qtr**	22
El Dorado Cocktail	**E Vill**	22
Double Deuce	**Gaslamp Qtr**	22
True North Tav.	**North Pk**	22
Lamplighter	**Mission Hills**	21
Typhoon Saloon	**Pacific Bch**	21
Center Bar	**Pala**	21
Brass Rail	**Hillcrest**	21
U-31	**North Pk**	20
ꓠꓰꓪ Seven Grand	**North Pk**	–

PIANO BARS

Shout! Hse.	**Gaslamp Qtr**	27
Caliph	**Bankers Hill**	19

POOL HALLS

Jolt 'n Joe's	**multi.**	21
Boar Cross'n	**Carlsbad**	18

ROMANTIC

Noble Experimt.	**E Vill**	28
Top/Hyatt	**Downtown**	28
Sogno Di Vino	**Little Italy**	27
Vin De Syrah	**Gaslamp Qtr**	27
Prohibition	**Gaslamp Qtr**	26
Whaling B&G	**La Jolla**	26
ENO	**Coronado**	25
Sevilla Nightclub	**Gaslamp Qtr**	25
Splash	**North Pk**	25
Pasha Lounge	**Gaslamp Qtr**	25
Mosaic Wine	**North Pk**	24
Toast Enoteca	**E Vill**	24
Stingaree	**Gaslamp Qtr**	24
Bleu Bar	**Del Mar**	23
LOUNGEsix	**Gaslamp Qtr**	23
98 Bottles	**Little Italy**	22
Fifty Seven Deg.	**Middletown**	19

SPORTS BARS

Sandbar	**Mission Bch**	25
Gaslamp Tav.	**Gaslamp Qtr**	25
OffShore Tav.	**Bay Pk**	25
High Dive	**Linda Vista**	25
Bub's	**E Vill**	24

Kristy's MVP	**Midway District**	24
Tavern/Beach	**Pacific Bch**	22
Miller's Field	**Pacific Bch**	21
Jolt 'n Joe's	**multi.**	21
Bar Leucadian	**Encinitas**	21
Dirty Birds	**Pacific Bch**	21
Jimmy O's	**Del Mar**	20
Plum Crazy	**Pacific Bch**	20
ꓠꓰꓪ Commons	**Gaslamp Qtr**	–

SUITS

Noble Experimt.	**E Vill**	28
Vin De Syrah	**Gaslamp Qtr**	27
Prohibition	**Gaslamp Qtr**	26
Whaling B&G	**La Jolla**	26
Ivy Rooftop	**Gaslamp Qtr**	26
ꓠꓰꓪ Seven Grand	**North Pk**	–

SWANKY

Noble Experimt.	**E Vill**	28
Float	**Gaslamp Qtr**	28
Top/Hyatt	**Downtown**	28
Vin De Syrah	**Gaslamp Qtr**	27
Prohibition	**Gaslamp Qtr**	26
Latitude Lounge	**Gaslamp Qtr**	26
Whaling B&G	**La Jolla**	26
Ivy Rooftop	**Gaslamp Qtr**	26
Voyeur	**Gaslamp Qtr**	25
Side Bar	**Gaslamp Qtr**	25
Fluxx	**Gaslamp Qtr**	25
Stingaree	**Gaslamp Qtr**	24
Bleu Bar	**Del Mar**	23
207	**Gaslamp Qtr**	23
LOUNGEsix	**Gaslamp Qtr**	23
Beaumont's	**La Jolla**	22
Onyx Rm.	**Gaslamp Qtr**	21

THEME BARS

Noble Experimt.	**E Vill**	28
Prohibition	**Gaslamp Qtr**	26
Lips	**North Pk**	26
Marble Rm.	**Gaslamp Qtr**	25

TRENDY

Noble Experimt.	**E Vill**	28
Shout! Hse.	**Gaslamp Qtr**	27
Vin De Syrah	**Gaslamp Qtr**	27
Prohibition	**Gaslamp Qtr**	26
Altitude Sky	**Gaslamp Qtr**	26
Voyeur	**Gaslamp Qtr**	25
Sevilla Nightclub	**Gaslamp Qtr**	25
Side Bar	**Gaslamp Qtr**	25
Waterfront B&G	**Little Italy**	25
Fluxx	**Gaslamp Qtr**	25

El Camino | **Little Italy** _24_
Stingaree | **Gaslamp Qtr** _24_
LOUNGEsix | **Gaslamp Qtr** _23_
El Dorado Cocktail | **E Vill** _22_
Onyx Rm. | **Gaslamp Qtr** _21_
NEW Barleymash | **Gaslamp Qtr** _–_
NEW Seven Grand | **North Pk** _–_

VELVET ROPE

Noble Experimt | **E Vill** _28_
Float | **Gaslamp Qtr** _28_
Vin De Syrah | **Gaslamp Qtr** _27_
Prohibition | **Gaslamp Qtr** _26_
Altitude Sky | **Gaslamp Qtr** _26_
Voyeur | **Gaslamp Qtr** _25_
Sevilla Nightclub | **Gaslamp Qtr** _25_
Side Bar | **Gaslamp Qtr** _25_
Fluxx | **Gaslamp Qtr** _25_
Firehse. | **Pacific Bch** _24_
Stingaree | **Gaslamp Qtr** _24_
207 | **Gaslamp Qtr** _23_

Rich's | **Hillcrest** _23_
Whiskey Girl | **Gaslamp Qtr** _22_
El Dorado Cocktail | **E Vill** _22_
True North Tav. | **North Pk** _22_
BeachWood | **Pacific Bch** _21_
Onyx Rm. | **Gaslamp Qtr** _21_
F6ix | **Gaslamp Qtr** _21_
Typhoon Saloon | **Pacific Bch** _21_
Belo | **Gaslamp Qtr** _20_

VIEWS

Float | **Gaslamp Qtr** _28_
Top/Hyatt | **Downtown** _28_
Humphrey's/Live | **Shelter Is** _26_
Ivy Rooftop | **Gaslamp Qtr** _26_
Altitude Sky | **Gaslamp Qtr** _26_
Firehse. | **Pacific Bch** _24_
Stingaree | **Gaslamp Qtr** _24_
LOUNGEsix | **Gaslamp Qtr** _23_
PB Shore Club | **Pacific Bch** _22_
BeachWood | **Pacific Bch** _21_

NIGHTLFE

SPECIAL APPEALS

Nightlife Locations

Includes names and Atmosphere ratings. These lists include low-vote places that do not qualify for tops lists.

ALPINE

Dreamcatcher/Viejas	23

BANKERS HILL

SRO Lounge	23
Caliph	19
Tin Can	17

BAY PARK

OffShore Tav.	25
Silver Spigot	17

CARDIFF-BY-THE-SEA

Wine Steals	24
Duke's	21
Kraken	21
Shanty	21

CITY HEIGHTS

Tower Bar	21
Black Cat	21
Til-Two	18

CLAIREMONT

Champ's Lounge	23

COASTAL TOWNS

Belly Up Tav.	25
Encinitas Ale	24
Bleu Bar	23
En Fuego	23
Bar Leucadian	21
Jimmy O's	20
Daley Double	18

CORONADO

ENO	25

DOWNTOWN

Top/Hyatt	28
Living Room	24
4th & B	22

EAST COUNTY

Go Lounge	24
Jolt 'n Joe's	21

EAST VILLAGE

Noble Experimt.	28
NEW Block No. 16	25
Bootlegger	24
Bub's	24

Toast Enoteca	24
Monkey Paw	23
El Dorado Cocktail	22
Tivoli B&G	20
Chee-Chee	13

EL CAJON

Main Tap Tav.	24
El Cajon Brew	22

GASLAMP QUARTER

Float	28
Shout! Hse.	27
Vin De Syrah	27
Grape	26
Prohibition	26
Latitude Lounge	26
Ivy Rooftop	26
Altitude Sky	26
Patricks	26
Voyeur	25
Marble Rm.	25
NEW Amer. Comedy	25
House of Blues	25
Sevilla Nightclub	25
Side Bar	25
Gaslamp Tav.	25
Fluxx	25
Pasha Lounge	25
Ivy Winebar	25
Tipsy Crow	25
Dublin Sq.	24
Ivy Nightclub	24
Hennessey's	24
Stingaree	24
Lime Tequila	24
McFadden's	23
207	23
LOUNGEsix	23
Whiskey Girl	22
Double Deuce	22
Maloney's Tav.	21
Xhale Hookah	21
Onyx Rm.	21
F6ix	21
Jolt 'n Joe's	21
Stage	21
Belo	20

NIGHTLFE

LOCATIONS

Bar Pink 20
Office Bar 20
NEW Seven Grand –

OCEAN BEACH

Pacific Shores 24
Arizona Café 23
Blue Parrot 23
Gallagher's 23
Winstons 21

OCEANSIDE

Royal Dive 25

PACIFIC BEACH

Pacific Beach Ale 25
Bub's 24
Firehse. 24
710 Beach 23
Bar West 22
Pacific Beach B&G 22
PB Shore Club 22
Tavern/Beach 22
BeachWood 21
Miller's Field 21
Typhoon Saloon 21
Australian Pub 21
Dirty Birds 21
NEW Johnny V 21

Plum Crazy 20
Silver Fox 19

PALA

Center Bar 21

POINT LOMA

Wine Steals 24
Club Marina 23
Hole 22
Catalina Lounge 21

SHELTER ISLAND

Humphrey's/Live 26

SOUTH PARK

Whistle Stop 23
Hamiltons Tav. 23

UNIVERSITY HEIGHTS

Bourbon St. 24
Small Bar 24
Live Wire 23
Gilly's 22
Cheers 22
Lancers 19

VALLEY CENTER

Oasis Lounge 25

Nightlife

Ratings & Symbols

Atmosphere, **Decor** & **Service** are rated on a 30-point scale.

Cost reflects the price of a typical single drink.

<u>I</u> below $7   <u>E</u> $11 to $14
<u>M</u> $7 to $10   <u>VE</u> $15 or above

Aero Club
$$23 \quad 21 \quad 22 \quad M$$
Mission Hills | 3365 India St. (bet. Sassafras & Upas Sts.) | 619-297-7211 | www.aeroclubbar.com

The "off-the-beaten-path" locale doesn't stop patrons from descending upon this "old-school" Mission Hills dive bar where "lots of drink options", including an "impressive" collection of 100 plus whiskeys (with some "hard-to-find" options), are all offered at "reasonable" prices; "cool bartenders" and a "laid-back" feel help give it "more character than typical SD spots", and a pool table is an added draw.

Air Conditioned Lounge
$$21 \quad 20 \quad 19 \quad M$$
North Park | 4673 30th St. (bet. Adams & Madison Aves.) | 619-501-9831 | www.airconditionedbar.com

You can "relax" over "strong drinks" or "bust a move on the dance floor" at this somewhat "clubby" North Park lounge, where "serious DJs" spin all kinds of music, including hip-hop, house and dubstep; "competent, efficient" servers keep most guests happy.

Alibi ⇗
$$21 \quad 17 \quad 21 \quad I$$
Hillcrest | 1403 University Ave. (Richmond St.) | 619-295-0881

A "quintessential dive bar", this Hillcrest hang delivers "cheap" yet "potent" drinks in a "cool little" space with pool tables and a jukebox; even if you should "not expect anything fancy", it's still a "good place when you've had a bad day", especially since the staff is "friendly."

Altitude Sky Bar
$$26 \quad 24 \quad 21 \quad E$$
Gaslamp Quarter | San Diego Marriott Gaslamp Quarter | 660 K St. (bet. 6th & 7th Aves.) | 619-450-2437 | www.altitudeskybar.com

"Check out the view – both of San Diego and the ladies" at this "swanky" lounge atop the Gaslamp Marriott, where the all-outdoor setting offers "divine" eyefuls of Petco Park during the day and its "hip" clientele "shaking booty" after dark; it has an "upscale" vibe and "friendly" staff, so the "expensive" tabs are "what you would expect."

NEW American Comedy Co.
$$25 \quad 22 \quad 23 \quad E$$
Gaslamp Quarter | 818B Sixth Ave. (bet. E & F Sts.) | 619-795-3858 | www.americancomedyco.com

An "unparalleled" lineup of "top" comedians (like Kevin Nealon, Tom Arnold and Tim Meadows) can mean "great laughs" at this club in "the heart of the Gaslamp"; its "spacious" yet "cozy" underground setting is enhanced by a "knowledgeable" staff, and though it's not cheap, prices are "typical" for the genre.

Arizona Café
23 | 21 | 23 | M

Ocean Beach | 1925 Bacon St. (bet. Newport & Santa Monica Aves.) | 619-223-7381 | www.theazcafe.com

"Great happy hour" is a draw at this spacious Ocean Beach "local fave" where the "friendly" staff also earns praise; prices are affordable, and pool tables and big-screen plasmas add to the appeal.

Australian Pub
21 | 21 | 21 | I

Pacific Beach | 1014 Grand Ave. (Cass St.) | 858-273-2363

It's a "true dive bar" say mates of this Pacific Beach hang known for "cheap beer", including Aussie imports of course; Packers fans crowd in on game days when it can be hard to find a seat, but "friendly" service helps.

Bar Dynamite
21 | 18 | 20 | M

Mission Hills | 1808 W. Washington St. (San Diego Ave.) | 619-295-8743 | www.bardynamite.com

It has "no decor or windows" and is located "between a liquor store and a taco shop" but this Mission Hills haunt still "carries its name" say fans touting the DJs who spin "consistently good house music", "awesome hip-hop beats" and more, plus drinks that "pack a punch" and a "friendly" staff; "yes, it's small" and can "get packed quick", but "if you don't mind catching the body sweat from the person dancing next to you", it's an all-around "cool" pick.

Bar Leucadian ⊅
21 | 16 | 21 | I

Encinitas | 1542 N. Coast Hwy. 101 (bet. Avocado & Jupiter Sts.) | 760-753-2094

One of the "friendliest bars around" say fans of this Encinitas "dive" that's a "great place to stop after a day at the beaches" and mix with "lots of cool locals" over "cheap" drinks; pool tables and multiple TVs further the appeal.

NEW Barleymash
- | - | - | M

Gaslamp Quarter | 600 Fifth Ave. (bet. G & Market Sts.) | 619-255-7373 | www.barleymash.com

This Gaslamp resto-bar from the crew behind Tavern at the Beach and True North attracts a mixed crowd with a large variety of craft beers, bourbon and cocktails, as well as local DJs spinning standard crowd-pleasers; the modern space is heavy on reclaimed wood and has many large-screen TVs for watching the game.

Bar Pink ⊅
20 | 19 | 18 | I

North Park | 3829 30th St. (bet. Park Way & University Ave.) | 619-564-7194 | www.barpink.com

A "cross between a divey neighborhood bar and indie nightclub", this "sassy" North Parker hosts live music from "local talent" in a "dark, retro" space boasting arcade games and "cool old films" playing behind the bar; drinks are "cheap (and stiff)", and service is pretty "fast."

Bar West

22 | 21 | 20 | E

Pacific Beach | 959 Hornblend St. (bet. Bayard & Cass Sts.) | 858-273-9378 | www.barwestsd.com

A "taste of Downtown in Pacific Beach", this "hip" dance club features a "swanky" setting and "more upscale" vibe that make it "a nice change" from other places nearby; "popular" music from DJs helps fuel "lots of dancing", and even if it's "more expensive" than its neighbors, at least the "people-watching is better than some reality shows."

Beachcomber

22 | 18 | 20 | I

Mission Bay | 2901 Mission Blvd. (San Gabriel Pl.) | 858-488-2644

It's a "dive bar with a heart of gold" say fans of this "old-school" Mission Bay "institution", where "typical Southern California beach bums" and "college" kids mix over "cheap drinks" poured by "always friendly" servers; it also has a pool table and an overall "relaxed" vibe that make it tops for just "hanging out."

BeachWood

21 | 21 | 19 | M

Pacific Beach | 4190 Mission Blvd. (bet. Pacific Beach Dr. & Reed Ave.) | 858-750-2512 | www.thebeachwood.com

"Chill during the day, crazy at night", this bar and club with an "optimum" Pacific Beach location offers something for everyone; the ground level has copious flat-screens, a mechanical bull and pub grub served with a "country" soundtrack, while the "beautiful people" beeline for the rooftop, where "dance music" and a beach view make up for "crowded" conditions that can "overwhelm the staff."

Beaumont's

22 | 19 | 20 | E

La Jolla | 5662 La Jolla Blvd. (bet. Bird Rock Ave. & Forward St.) | 858-459-0474 | www.beaumontseatery.com

"You'll be happy" you found this La Jolla resto-bar say fans citing the weekend live music and "all-around good times"; "attentive" staffers work the deco-inspired space, and if prices are on the high side, a "reasonable" happy hour helps – just don't plan to settle in for the whole night, as last call comes at 10 PM.

Belly Up Tavern

25 | 21 | 22 | M

Solana Beach | 143 S. Cedros Ave. (bet. Lomas Santa Fe Dr. & Rosa St.) | 858-481-9022 | www.bellyup.com

"Always a favorite" say fans of this "laid-back, yet lively" and "well-managed" rock club in Solana Beach, where "quality bands" play in an "intimate, homey" setting that allows you to "feel close to the music" and earns it No. 1 Most Popular honors in the SD Nightlife Survey; prices are "reasonable" and service is "dependable", so though "you have to be in the mood for loud noise and crowds" as it can get "crammed to the gills."

Belo

20 | 20 | 18 | E

Gaslamp Quarter | 919 Fourth Ave. (bet. B'way & E St.) | 619-231-9200 | www.belosandiego.com

"Dance and drink the night away" at this Gaslamp club, where a "young" crowd grooves to Top 40 tunes from a "booming" sound

ATMOS. | DECOR | SERVICE | COST

system in a big, 20,000-sq.-ft. space; though there's "good energy", some say it "isn't worth the cover" for an "overcrowded" room, "overwhelmed" bartenders and "tasteless" bar food – but, then again, "who wants to eat" in a "dark basement" anyway?

Black Cat Bar
21 | 19 | 21 | I

City Heights | 4246 University Ave. (Van Dyke Ave.) | 619-280-5834

Even if it's in the "middle of nowhere", this "fun" City Heights dive draws hipsters with pool, pinball, cheap beers and a rather stately chandelier; "top-notch" cocktails paired with "authentic Mexican street food" from the taco truck parked outside add up to a "purrfectly great night."

Bleu Bar
23 | 21 | 20 | VE

Del Mar | L'Auberge Del Mar Hotel | 1540 Camino Del Mar
(bet. 15th St. & L'Auberge Del Mar) | 858-259-1515 |
www.laubergedelmar.com

Guests "feel like they're on holiday" when visiting this "beautiful" poolside lounge at the bourgeois L'Auberge Del Mar resort, where tourists and locals recline on fireside chaises while sampling from a "clever" menu of craft cocktails and charcuterie platters; the "awesome" seaside location offers ocean views, making it a natural for a "special night."

Blind LadyAle House
25 | 24 | 23 | I

Normal Heights | 3416 Adams Ave. (34th St.) | 619-255-2491 |
www.blindladyalehouse.com

Already a "beacon" for craft beer fans thanks to a "second-to-none" selection of housemade ales, this midpriced Normal Heights bar is also touted for its "warm" staff and "wood-fired" pizzas; the "open", "urban" space features "communal" tables that "encourage merriment", so it can be "hard to find a seat" – or a parking spot, even though many "hipsters ride their bikes" over.

NEW Block No. 16
∇ 25 | 27 | 23 | M
Union & Spirits

East Village | 344 Seventh Ave. (bet. J & K Sts.) | 619-255-7625 |
www.blockno16.com

This former warehouse across from the East Village's Petco Park is now a gigantic, Vegas-esque mega-club and "awesome" entertainment space complete with LED lighting and a posh upstairs mezzanine; guests can expect a variety of club nights ranging from Top 40 dance parties to Americana-style music concerts, and fans say "we need more of these" in San Diego.

Bluefoot Bar & Lounge
22 | 18 | 23 | I

North Park | 3404 30th St. (Upas St.) | 619-756-7891 |
www.bluefootsd.com

"Relaxed hipsters" and cool locals unwind at this "wonderful" North Park neighborhood bar with a game of pool, a "quality" craft beer (there are "tons" to choose from) or a spin on the dance floor; there's "not much in the way of decor", but "friendly" staffers and fair prices compensate.

	ATMOS.	DECOR	SERVICE	COST

Blue Parrot
23 | 20 | 20 | M

Ocean Beach | 4993 Niagara Ave. (Bacon St.) | 619-222-1722

Ocean Beach locals assemble at this "chill", dog-friendly bar "a block off the main strip" for its "attractive" waitresses, "decent" grub and fairly priced hooch; a "partying" crowd swigs margaritas on the "crowded" patio, so expect "loud" decibels.

Boar Cross'n
18 | 14 | 15 | I

Carlsbad | 390 Grand Ave. (bet. Christiansen & Grand Aves.) | 760-729-2989 | www.boarcrossn.net

The decor's "shabby" and it "takes forever to get a drink", but this Carlsbad dive still draws "military" types from nearby Camp Pendleton to "play pool and hang out"; its "trashy" clientele digs its "cheap" drinks, "heavy metal" soundtrack and occasional live music.

Bootlegger
24 | 23 | 23 | E

East Village | 804 Market St. (8th Ave.) | 619-794-2668 | www.bootleggersd.com

With "plenty" of TVs and a big bartop to "cozy up to", this "lively" East Village tavern is a "great spot to watch sports", but locals also give props to its specialty cocktails, "not-too-shabby" gastropub grub and "knowledgeable" servers; "open windows" lend airy appeal, while a "secret" back bar supplies a speakeasy vibe.

Bourbon Street
24 | 22 | 22 | M

University Heights | 4612 Park Blvd. (bet. Adams & Madison Aves.) | 619-291-4043 | www.bourbonstreetsd.com

Nestled inside a "New Orleans–style" University Heights building, this "straight-friendly gay bar" boasts "awesome" drink deals and "speedy" servers with "no attitude"; "strong" cocktails and "fun" events – like the "wet underwear party" and "ladies' Jell-O wrestling" – supply a "French Quarter feel", but there's also a "lovely" courtyard for just enjoying the "fresh air."

Brass Rail
21 | 18 | 20 | I

Hillcrest | 3796 Fifth Ave. (Robinson Ave.) | 619-298-2233 | www.thebrassrailsd.com

"Drinks are cheap and so are the boys" at this "rowdy" Hillcrest gay bar where "cut, sexy" men let loose to "'80s music" in "dark, inviting" digs perfect for "when you want to stay a stranger"; "crazy fun" times and on-the-ball service – "talk about being treated like a queen!" – have kept this "icon" around for over two decades.

Brick By Brick
19 | 16 | 19 | M

Morena District | 1130 Buenos Ave. (Naples Pl.) | 619-275-5483 | www.brickbybrick.com

Offering "ample" seating and "tons of space", this "rocking" music venue in the Morena District draws a "mixed crowd" with "decent" acts, though it's probably best known for its "cheesy cover bands and dated metal"; despite "poor sound", a "cold vibe" and "dive" looks, it's "crowded" nonetheless with patrons supporting their "favorite underground" groups.

ATMOS. DECOR SERVICE COST

Bub's
24 | 21 | 23 | M

East Village | 715 J St. (7th Ave.) | 619-546-0815 | www.bubssandiego.com
Pacific Beach | 1030 Garnet Ave. (bet. Cass & Dawes Sts.) |
858-270-7269 | www.bubsdive.com

"College" types convene for "great drink specials" and "delicious wings" at these "kick-back" sports bars in Pacific Beach and East Village, but ladies avoid "wearing heels" lest they trip over the "peanut shells on the ground"; staffers are "friendly" in spite of the "crowded" conditions during football season.

Caliph
19 | 16 | 21 | M

Bankers Hill | 3100 Fifth Ave. (Redwood St.) | 619-298-9495

"Cross-dressing singers" and karaoke nights make for "entertaining" times at this "old-school" Bankers Hill cabaret/piano lounge; it's "been around for many years" (as the "totally dive" decor demonstrates), drawing an "eclectic" LGBT crowd with "great drinks" and "great prices."

Callahan's Pub & Brewery
22 | 19 | 22 | M

Mira Mesa | 8111 Mira Mesa Blvd. (Reagan Rd.) | 858-578-7892 |
www.callahanspub.com

"Traditional" Irish grub washed down with a "great" suds selection has been drawing locals to this Mira Mesa pub for over 20 years; it's a "great little neighborhood bar" where fans watch the game on a multitude of TVs from the comfort of vintage leather booths.

Carriage House
21 | 18 | 21 | I

Kearny Mesa | 7945 Balboa Ave. (bet. Convoy & Mercury Sts.) |
858-278-2597 | www.carriagehousesandiego.com

"No frills, no food, just drinks, pool and karaoke" sums up the scene at this "dark" Kearny Mesa "dive" where "friendly regulars" swig "cheap" cocktails and sing songs from a "thicker-than-the-bible" roster while a "funny" host moderates; "hole-in-the-wall" decor earns middling marks, but pool tables and flat-screens add to the "fun."

The Casbah
23 | 19 | 22 | I

Middletown | 2501 Kettner Blvd. (Laurel St.) | 619-232-4355 |
www.casbahmusic.com

Around since 1989, this "dark" Middletown "icon" has "showcased many of the greatest bands ever" (e.g. Nirvana, The White Stripes) and remains an "excellent place to see up-and-coming acts", including "indie and alternative" musicians, thanks in part to "fast service", "good pours" and an "intimate", "nothing fancy, but cozy" space; it's often "jam-packed", but an outdoor patio and separate room with pool tables and arcade games can provide a "quick break from loud rocking in the main room."

Catalina Lounge ⊄
21 | 17 | 20 | I

Point Loma | 4202 Voltaire St. (Catilana Blvd.) | 619-224-4979

This cash-only "ultimate dive bar" in Point Loma features "old-school" decor that's a match for the "inexpensive, non-froufrou drinks" served by "attentive" staffers who seem to have been on duty "since the place opened"; TVs, pool tables, shuffleboard and a jukebox make it the "bar of choice" for a "nice" neighborhood crowd that's "always ready for a chat."

Center Bar
21 | 20 | 21 | E

Pala | Pala Casino Spa Resort | 11154 Hwy. 76 (bet. Lilac Rd. & Rancho Luna Ranch) | 760-510-5100 | www.palacasino.com
High rollers watch cover bands perform while sipping pricey cocktails and playing video poker at this bar surrounding a stage inside the Pala Casino; the acts are only "sometimes" worthwhile and staffers "act like they've never seen you before" even if you're a regular, but it can be a "nice" enough spot "for a drink after winning."

Champ's Lounge ⊘
23 | 18 | 23 | I

Clairemont | 3050 Clairemont Dr. (Iroquois Ave.) | 619-276-3760
Like an "encyclopedia" example of a dive bar, this "old-school" Clairemont neighborhood joint lures an "eclectic" group of "locals" with "cheap", "stiff" drinks, "timely" service and a "no-drama" setting; lookswise, it's "nothing special", but pool tables, karaoke, dartboards and "lots of laughter" make it a "great hangout."

Che Café
20 | 17 | 22 | -

La Jolla | University of California, San Diego | 9500 Gilman Dr. (Scholars Dr.) | 858-534-2311 | www.thechecafe.blogspot.com
"Still a UCSD hot spot", this "convenient" La Jolla venue "hidden" in a graffitied shack on campus provides music lovers of all ages with an "intimate" setting for watching "not-on-the-radar" acts and eating "good" vegan food; despite being alcohol-free and only open for shows, it's still a "favorite."

Chee-Chee Club ⊘
∇ 13 | 14 | 16 | I

East Village | 929 Broadway (10th Ave.) | 619-234-4404
There's "no line, no waiting, no dress code and no b.s." at this East Village "dive of all dives", where a "friendly" mix of hipsters, LGBTers and "ordinary, everyday" regulars gather for "cheap" drinks and games of pool; some of the "nicest bartenders around" brighten up the otherwise "dark", "hole-in-the-wall" setting.

Cheers
22 | 20 | 24 | I

University Heights | 1839 Adams Ave. (bet. Georgia St. & Park Blvd.) | 619-298-3269 | www.cheerssandiego.com
Naturally, "everybody knows your name" at this "friendly" University Heights gay bar where "fun-loving" servers are "quick" in proffering "fairly priced" drinks to a "welcoming" crowd; sure, it's a "dive", but regulars say it works as a "starter for a night out" or as the main event.

CJ's Club ⊘
21 | 19 | 21 | I

Hillcrest | 222 W. Washington St. (bet. Albatross & Front Sts.) | 619-296-2721
"Watch a football game", "play some darts" or "just bump and dance" to the jukebox at this "great little dive bar" on the outskirts of Hillcrest; look for kitschy decor, plenty of TVs and "lovely" bartenders preparing "simple" cocktails for "neighborhood" folks.

⌐ Marina 🚭   23 | 20 | 23 | I

Point Loma | 1310 Scott St. (bet. Dickens & Emerson Sts.) | 619-222-5932

"Smell the ocean" and "mix with fishermen" at this "tiny" Point Loma dive bar where people from "all walks of life" gather as early as 9 AM to throw back "strong, cheap" drinks; the bartenders are "friendly", the decor as seafaring as the crowd and the jukebox and pool tables provide added entertainment.

Coaster Saloon   ▽ 21 | 18 | 18 | I

Mission Beach | 744 Ventura Pl. (bet. Mission Blvd. & Strand Way) | 858-488-4438 | www.coastersaloon.com

Seats "right near the boardwalk" provide "perfect sunset views" at this Mission Beach "staple" next to Belmont Park's roller coaster, where folks quaff a "great" selection of California-brewed beers and down "excellent" breakfasts at reasonable tabs; alright, this "quintessential open-air beach bar" is definitely a "dive", yet locals have "loved it" for decades.

The Comedy Store   23 | 18 | 21 | M

La Jolla | 916 Pearl St. (bet. Drury Ln. & Fay Ave.) | 858-454-9176 | www.comedystore.com

When "your funny bone is in dire need of tickling", this "reasonably priced" La Jolla comedy club fits the bill say fans applauding its "up-and-coming" acts, "casual atmosphere" and "competently done drinks"; service gets solid marks too, and even if "some nights are better than others", fans agree it's "not a bad way to spend some hard-earned dollars."

NEW The Commons   - | - | - | I

Gaslamp Quarter | 901 Fourth Ave. (B'way.) | 619-696-8888 | www.tcbsandiego.com

While sports bars are certainly not uncommon in the Gaslamp, this new bi-level space across from Horton Plaza stands out with industrial-modern decor, chicken wings that are already locally beloved (the same recipe as Dirty Birds in Pacific Beach) and an upstairs game room that has shuffleboard, foosball and board games; tons of TVs and a classic-rock soundtrack fit the genre.

Daley Double Saloon   18 | 16 | 18 | I

Encinitas | 546 S. Coast Hwy. 101 (bet. D & E Sts.) | 760-753-1366

"Lots of regulars" and "local workers" hit this Encinitas "bar by the beach" during the daytime but it draws a "young crowd at night" for "good drinks" and a "totally fun" atmosphere; some guests relish the "funky, unpretentious" setting of wood-paneled walls and vintage Naugahyde booths but others say it "could be better."

Dirk's Niteclub 🚭   21 | 20 | 20 | I

Lemon Grove | 7662 Broadway (bet. Buena Vista Ave. & Olive St.) | 619-469-6344 | www.dirksniteclub.com

Lemon Grove isn't known for nightlife, so this "low-key" bar draws "hard-working", blue-collar types with its "reasonably priced" hooch and competitive pool games; it's certainly a "dive", but a "good-size dance floor" and live "rock music every weekend" provide distraction.

Dirty Birds

21 | 19 | 22 | M

Pacific Beach | 4656 Mission Blvd. (bet. Diamond & Emerald Sts.) | 858-274-2473 | www.dirtybirdspb.com

A "great mix of people" gathers at this Pacific Beach bar for "cheap" happy-hour specials matched with "amaaazing wings" and "juicy" burgers from a largely "greasy" menu; "lots of flat-screens" keep it "packed" during sporting events but it manages to maintain a "comfortable", "friendly" air.

Double Deuce

22 | 21 | 19 | M

Gaslamp Quarter | 528 F St. (bet. 5th & 6th Aves.) | 619-450-6522 | www.doubledeucesd.com

With its honky-tonk theme, "frat-party" feel and "freakin' mechanical bull" ("yeehaw!"), this Gaslamp Deuce is certainly "wild", and a favorite of an "off-the-wall" crowd heavy with birthday girls and bachelorettes; the "happy-go-lucky" service can be "slow" when the place is "packed", but at least the tabs are "affordable."

Dreamcatcher at Viejas

23 | 23 | 23 | E

Alpine | Viejas Casino | 5000 Willows Rd. (Brown Rd.) | 619-445-5400 | www.viejasentertainment.com

Get "up close and personal" with the performers at this "intimate" concert venue at Alpine's Viejas Casino, where both "tribute bands" and bigger talents "perform with gusto" for a "merry" crowd on weekends; the prices fit the venue, service is "friendly" and the seating "comfortable", with a bonus "dance floor just below the stage."

Dublin Square

24 | 23 | 23 | M

Gaslamp Quarter | 554 Fourth Ave. (bet. Island Ave. & Market St.) | 619-239-5818 | www.dublinsquareirishpub.com

"As close to Dublin as you can get" while staying in Gaslamp, this "welcoming" pub draws "friendly faces" with "above-par pub food" and "tall pours" of Irish beers and whiskey; "authentic" decor (fabricated in Ireland) and live renditions of "traditional folk songs" are reasons why it's usually so "busy."

Duke's Cardiff Office

21 | 14 | 20 | I

Cardiff-by-the-Sea | 110A Aberdeen Dr. (bet. New Castle & San Elijo Aves.) | 760-753-7766

"If you like dive bars, you'll be in heaven" at this local watering hole where a "priceless cast of characters" gathers for "cheap drinks" after a day of surfing or camping in "laid-back" Cardiff; there's no decor, but its pet friendliness is a plus – it sometimes seems like there's "one dog for every two imbibers."

El Cajon Brewing Co.

22 | 20 | 21 | I

El Cajon | 110 N. Magnolia Ave. (bet. Cypress Ave. & Main Sts.) | 619-873-0222 | www.elcajonbrewingco.com

They "take their craft seriously" at this El Cajon brewpub where "wonderful" housemade stouts, IPAs and ales come at "reasonable" prices and complement the "just ok" American fare (even so, "anything tastes good" after a few drinks); the decor is plain and the service "hit-or-miss", but live music, theme nights and special events have been added in an attempt to "step it up."

El Camino
24 | 23 | 21 | E

Little Italy | 2400 India St. (W. Kalmia St.) | 619-685-3881 | www.elcaminosd.com

"Day of the Dead" decor and planes flying over the patio make for a "festive" feel at this "funky" Mexican cantina in Little Italy where a "fun" crowd "shakes their buns" to "old-school jams" and watches "'70s flicks" playing behind the bar; sometimes "snobby" service is offset by "dee-lish" margaritas and "sangria to define all sangria."

El Dorado Cocktail Lounge
22 | 20 | 23 | M

East Village | 1030 Broadway (bet. 10th & 11th Aves.) | 619-237-0550 | www.eldoradobar.com

Escape the "upscale wannabe attitude" of other area watering holes and hit this Western-themed East Village cocktail den for "special" seasonal libations (the "friendly" staff is "always reinventing" the list); regulars turn up to dance to some of the "best house music" around spun by local DJs.

Eleven
20 | 19 | 20 | I

Normal Heights | 3519 El Cajon Blvd. (bet. 35th St. & Wilson Ave.) | 619-450-4292 | www.elevensandiego.com

"Not as sceney" as other clubs, this Normal Heights dive books "decent" hard rock acts that attract rockabilly and punk fans; patrons pick from an "awesome" craft beer list and sip at one of the back tables or watch the show next to a wall of vintage performance posters.

Encinitas Ale House
24 | 20 | 22 | M

Encinitas | 1044 S. Coast Hwy. 101 (bet. I & J Sts.) | 760-943-7180 | www.encinitasalehouse.com

"New kegs" from "all over the world" are "tapped daily" by "in-tune" barkeeps at this "laid-back" Encinitas beer bar, where the patrons are "friendly" and the suds are paired with "locally sourced" eats; the "tiny" space gets "crowded", so be prepared to "wait for a seat."

En Fuego
23 | 21 | 19 | E

Del Mar | 1342 Camino Del Mar (bet. 13th & 14th Sts.) | 858-792-6551 | www.enfuegocantina.com

"Young, single" folks plus random "cougars on the prowl" populate the "comfy" interior and "romantic" patio at this Mexican bar/restaurant in the heart of Downtown Del Mar; it's especially "packed" during racing season but remains "on fire" year-round thanks to "spirited bartenders" concocting some of the "strongest drinks" around.

ENO Wine Bar
25 | 22 | 26 | E

Coronado | Hotel del Coronado | 1500 Orange Ave. (bet. Avenida Del Sol & Rh Dana Pl.) | 619-522-8546 | www.enowinerooms.com

If you want to "impress a date" or need a "great place to bring out-of-town guests", look no further than this "elegant" wine bar nestled in the historic Hotel Del Coronado; "fantastic" small plates and chocolate pairings are the perfect match to its "extensive" wine list.

The Epicentre
| 19 | 14 | 19 | - |

Mira Mesa | 8450 Mira Mesa Blvd. (bet. Camino Ruiz & Reagan Rd.) | 858-271-9737 | www.epicentreconcerts.org

While the "warehouse" setting of this "all-ages" Mira Mesa venue suits the "local bands" (including "high school garage bands") and their "teenager" fans, the 21-plus crowd laments the lack of food or alcohol; still, it can be a "great place to hang out" if you're underage.

Excalibur Hookah Lounge
| 22 | 20 | 22 | M |

Hillcrest | 3858 Fifth Ave. (bet. Robinson & University Aves.) | 619-260-8099 | www.excaliburhookahlounge.com

There's a "wide variety" of flavored tobaccos on offer at this "secluded" Hillcrest hookah bar, where a "polite" staff "keeps the coals – as well as the tradition – alive and well"; ornate knickknacks, Turkish textiles and "mood lighting" enhance the "Middle Eastern ambiance", ditto the live music and belly dancers.

Fifty Seven Degrees
| 19 | 19 | 18 | M |

Middletown | 1735 Hancock St. (Washington St.) | 619-234-5757 | www.fiftysevendegrees.com

A wine bar, bottle shop and event space all in one, this "cavernous" Middletown spot "can handle a large crowd" thanks to a "snazzy", 16,500-sq.-ft. setting complete with an outdoor patio that gives customers "room to breathe" while browsing, imbibing or nibbling on small plates; despite a "weird" location and staffers that sometimes can't "be bothered", it's still "a neat idea."

Firehouse American Eatery & Lounge
| 24 | 22 | 21 | E |

Pacific Beach | 722 Grand Ave. (bet. Mission & Ocean Blvds.) | 858-274-3100 | www.firehousepb.com

Whether it's the "swanky" weekday crowd or the "rowdy twentysomethings" on weekends, everyone enjoys the "fruity" drinks and "killer" rooftop lounge (with "live DJs nightly") at this "trendy" bi-level bar/restaurant that's "a stone's throw" from the water in Pacific Beach; critics contend they "overcharge", but no one cares since the staff "looks good enough to put on the platter and eat."

Flicks
| 22 | 21 | 19 | M |

Hillcrest | 1017 University Ave. (bet. 10th Ave. & Vermont St.) | 619-297-2056 | www.sdflicks.com

On the scene for nearly 30 years, this "treasure" of a Hillcrest gay bar draws dudes with "friendly" staffers, affordable drinks and "great theme nights" (think karaoke, wet underwear contests and movie nights); it's a "great place to hook up" for "those who are looking."

Float
| 28 | 26 | 21 | E |

Gaslamp | Hard Rock Hotel | 207 Fifth Ave. (L St.) | 619-764-6924 | www.hardrockhotelsd.com

Weekends turn this "gorgeous, open-air club" on the rooftop of Gaslamp's Hard Rock Hotel into a "super-charged party machine", but stop by on a weekday to "dip your feet" in the pool, huddle around "chill" fire pits or lounge in the "VIP cabanas"; service can be "hit-or-miss" and the drinks and covers "overpriced", but "you can't argue with that view."

Fluxx
25 | 25 | 19 | E

Gaslamp Quarter | 500 Fourth Ave. (bet. Island Ave & Market St.) | 619-232-8100 | www.fluxxsd.com

"Be prepared to drop some cash" at this "ever-exclusive" Gaslamp "version of Vegas", where "beautiful women and trendy guys" turn up for "eye-catching" decor and "big-name" DJs blasting music from a "next-level" sound system; "rude" service and "traffic-jam" lines come with the territory, so insiders advise you better "know somebody" if you want to get into the "most epic nightclub" around.

Flying Elephant
23 | 22 | 22 | M

Carlsbad | 850 Tamarack Ave. (Jefferson St.) | 760-434-2660 | www.flyingelephantpub.com

"Comfortable even when it's busy", this Carlsbad pub exudes a "good neighborhood vibe" and attracts a mixed crowd with bil-liards, live music, "friendly" service and "fairly priced" food and drink; the crowd can get raucous depending on what band is playing and how many Marines show up from the neighboring base, so plan accordingly.

4th & B
22 | 18 | 19 | E

Downtown | 345 B St. (4th Ave.) | 619-231-4343 | www.4thandbevents.com

You can "let loose" while taking in some "big-name" musical acts, comedians and more at this "no-frills" Downtown venue; it's not cheap, and a few say the space "could use some upgrading", but the "decent sound", spacious dance floor and stage set "so high up that even shorties can see" all help make up for it.

F6ix
21 | 20 | 18 | E

Gaslamp Quarter | 526 F St. (bet. 5th & 6th Aves.) | 619-238-0138 | www.f6ixsd.com

One of the few places in the Gaslamp to "get your crunk on" to hip-hop, this cavernous underground dance club supplies a "party-hard" mood via a colorful metallic interior complete with a disco ball and subwoofer-heavy sound system; covers are gentler and the crowds sparser if you arrive early, but after 11 PM it gets, to paraphrase Nelly, "hot in there."

Gallagher's Irish Pub
23 | 20 | 22 | I

Ocean Beach | 5046 Newport Ave. (bet. Abbot & Bacon Sts.) | 619-222-5300 | www.gallagherspubob.com

"Be prepared to yell to have a conversation" at this "genuine" Ocean Beach Irish pub that draws "young, casual" folks with "in-expensive pints"; "playful" servers, reggae nights and frequent drink deals are reasons why this "lively, vibrant" spot is not just "good for St. Patty's Day."

	ATMOS.	DECOR	SERVICE	COST

Gaslamp Tavern
25 | 22 | 24 | M

Gaslamp Quarter | 868 Fifth Ave. (E St.) | 619-239-3339 |
www.gaslamptavern.com

With a "super" Gaslamp location "in the middle of the action", this
"laid-back" bar offers a "plentiful" selection of beers, spirits and
"great" food, all served "with a smile" by a "friendly" team; an "inviting", open-air layout and plenty of "huge" TVs make it a natural
for "taking in a game" or "people-watching" on the patio.

Gilly's
22 | 17 | 22 | I

University Heights | 2306 El Cajon Blvd. (Louisiana St.) | 619-298-6008 |
www.gillysbarnorthpark.com

"Everyone seems to know each other" at this University Heights bar
where the "eclectic" crowd gets "silly" with "insane" karaoke nights,
"champion" pool games and strong, "inexpensive" drinks poured by
"welcoming" bartenders; it has the "grit" that comes with a "classic
dive", but its "friendly" mien makes it a "favorite pit stop."

Go Lounge
▽ 24 | 21 | 24 | I

La Mesa | 7123 El Cajon Blvd. (bet. 71st & 72nd Sts.) | 619-644-2317 |
www.thegoloungesd.com

"Cheap" drinks and "great live music" lure young locals to this "hidden gem" in La Mesa; the interior shows "character" with rock 'n' roll
decor and red leather booths, while outside there's a "super-cool"
backyard that's "perfect for warm summer nights."

The Grand on Grand
24 | 22 | 25 | M

Escondido | 150 W. Grand Ave. (bet. B'way & Maple St.) |
760-871-4178 | www.thegrandongrand.com

This Escondido stop is a "nice place to chill", whether at the long bar,
in the dining area or on the fire pit–enhanced patio; it gets "loud"
with DJs, live bands or karaoke but the "local crowd" still approves.

The Grape
▽ 26 | 22 | 23 | M

Gaslamp Quarter | 823 Fifth Ave. (bet. E & F Sts.) | 619-238-8010 |
www.thegrapebar.com

Offering a "huge selection of wines", a "romantic, cozy" vibe and a
"friendly" staff that "really knows" its vino, this moderate Gaslamp
spot is "recommended to anyone" by fans; with a "great" menu of
salads and pizzas to boot, it's a "quiet place for an upscale evening."

The Griffin
20 | 19 | 21 | M

Morena District | 1310 Morena Blvd. (bet. Savannah St. & Tecolote Rd.) |
619-684-1816 | www.thegriffinsd.com

Once a notoriously seedy dive bar, this Morena Districter is now a "casual" music venue with hardwood floors and leather booths; moderate
tabs and a "friendly" staff help make it a "good place to hang out."

Hamiltons Tavern
23 | 20 | 22 | I

South Park | 1521 30th St. (bet. Beech & Cedar Sts.) | 619-238-5460 |
www.hamiltonstavern.com

South Park's "cool characters" think they've "died and gone to beer
heaven" at this "superb" dive bar/gastropub where an "expansive"

selection of "hard-to-find" brews and "awesome" grub (including housemade sausages) make it a "shrine" for both guzzlers and gourmands; a "standing-room-only" setting and "slow" service irk some, but most feel like kids in a "candy store."

Hennessey's Carlsbad
24 | 22 | 23 | M

Carlsbad | 2777 Roosevelt St. (bet. Beech & Grand Aves.) | 760-729-6951

Hennessey's Gaslamp

Gaslamp Quarter | 708 Fourth Ave. (G St.) | 619-239-9994

Hennessey's La Jolla

La Jolla | 7811 Herschel Ave. (bet. Silverado & Wall Sts.) | 858-551-8772
www.hennesseystavern.com

This "party"-hearty Irish chain is "always a good choice" for sports fans thanks to game-day specials and TVs tuned to football, but guests also come for "great" pub grub and "awesome" drinks like the signature vodka-laced lemonade; "dependable" servers help cultivate the "relaxed" vibe.

High Dive Bar & Grill
▽ 25 | 25 | 27 | I

Linda Vista | 1801 Morena Blvd. (Asher St.) | 619-275-0460 | www.highdiveinc.com

An "out-of-the-way" location ensures that this "delightful dive" in Linda Vista's Bay Park "doesn't get too crowded" on weekdays, yet given its selection of "exotic" local suds and an "awesome" staff that "makes you feel like part of the family", it can get "uncomfortably full" with "USD kids" on weekends.

The Hole
22 | 15 | 21 | M

Point Loma | 2820 Lytton St. (St. Charles St.) | 619-226-9019 | www.thehole.com

"Loud and funner than heck" say regulars of this "no-attitude" Point Loma gay bar that's especially "packed" at its "Sunday funday" beer bust, when guys form "long lines down the sidewalk" for a chance to mingle and hang on the spacious patio; the staff is "laid-back", but just be aware the "large", affordable drinks can "knock you out if you aren't careful", so sip slowly.

House of Blues
25 | 24 | 22 | E

Gaslamp Quarter | 1055 Fifth Ave. (bet. B'way & B St.) | 619-299-2583 | www.houseofblues.com

There's "always something happening" at this big, multilevel Gaslamp branch of the "touristy" music venue chain, where fans can get "up close and personal" with "fantastic" regional and national performers; "expensive" cocktails, "above-average" food and "Louisiana juke joint" decor come with the territory.

Humphrey's Backstage Live
26 | 23 | 23 | E

Shelter Island | 2241 Shelter Island Dr. (Anchorage Ln.) | 619-224-3577 | www.humphreysbackstagelive.com

Not to be confused with neighboring Humphrey's by the Bay, this "relaxed but upscale" Shelter Island lounge offers a roster of "won-

derfully entertaining" bands while also serving as a "favorite" hangout for pre-show drinks and bites; its outside deck is cooled by "gentle
breezes blowing off the bay."

In Cahoots
24 | 22 | 22 | M

Mission Valley | 5373 Mission Center Rd. (bet. Frairs Rd. &
Hazard Centre Dr.) | 619-291-1184 | www.incahoots.com
"Dress in Western gear" for a night out at this Mission Valley "cowboy" club where "lively" patrons gather for country music and "line
dancing at its finest" on a "crowded" dance floor decked out with
disco balls and American flags; those who don't know the steps can
learn at free evening classes or just nurse midpriced drinks and shoot
pool on the second floor.

Ivy Nightclub
24 | 24 | 19 | E

Gaslamp Quarter | Andaz San Diego | 600 F St. (bet. 6th & 7th Aves.) |
619-814-2055 | www.ivyentertainmentsandiego.com
A "Las Vegas" sensibility meets Miami chic at this "sleek" multilevel club in Gaslamp's "plush" Andaz Hotel, where "beautiful
people" "dress to impress" to get "beyond the red ropes"; "way
expensive" tabs and "pounding" music come with the territory, and
though it can be "hard to get a drink", VIP tables offer the "luxury
of personalized service."

Ivy Rooftop
26 | 24 | 20 | E

Gaslamp Quarter | Andaz San Diego | 600 F St. (bet. 6th & 7th Aves.) |
619-814-2055 | www.ivyentertainmentsandiego.com
"Stellar" views of the Gaslamp, "plenty of space for socializing" and
"chill" poolside cabanas make this "sexy" roof atop the Andaz Hotel
the ultimate in "high-end partying"; despite "expensive" drinks, "long
waits" and staffers with "attitude", its "cool" cat following remains
"lively but relaxed."

Ivy Winebar
25 | 25 | 23 | E

Gaslamp Quarter | Andaz San Diego | 600 F St. (bet. 6th & 7th Aves.) |
619-814-2055 | www.ivyentertainmentsandiego.com
"Wine adventures" await at this "beautifully decorated" bar in
Gaslamp's Andaz Hotel, where "self-service" machines allow patrons to pour their own Pinots while sampling small plates and
reclining in "comfy" booths; some wonder why it isn't busier, but
others are happy to "skip club nights" elsewhere in favor of its
more "slow" pace.

Jimmy O's
20 | 18 | 21 | M

Del Mar | 225 15th St. (Stratford Ct.) | 858-350-3735 |
www.jimmyosbardelmar.com
"Get hammered, dance with everybody and make out with
strangers" at this affordable Del Mar "standout", an "average"
sports bar by day turned "crazy-busy" scene after dark when DJs
spin Top 40 hits and "super-friendly" bartenders always "keep
your drink full"; ok, the decor "could be updated" and the "extremely
loud" decibels make "conversation difficult", but ultimately "everyone has a good time."

	ATMOS.	DECOR	SERVICE	COST

Johnny V
21 | 20 | 20 | M

Pacific Beach | 945 Garnet Ave. (bet. Bayard & Cass Sts.) |
858-274-4833 | www.johnnyvsd.com

Serving solid food in a "charming" brick-and-wood setting, this multi-room bar/restaurant is about as "upclass" as it gets in Pacific Beach, yet it also draws "just-turned-21" types with "awesome drink specials", pool tables and tons of TVs; while some find it "overcrowded" and "impossible" to get a beverage, it's still a "great place for dancing."

Jolt 'n Joe's
21 | 19 | 21 | M

La Mesa | 8076 La Mesa Blvd. (bet. Acacia & Normal Aves.) |
619-466-2591
Gaslamp Quarter | 379 Fourth Ave. (bet. J & K Sts.) | 619-230-1968
www.joltnjoes.com

This double-decker warehouse space in Gaslamp (with a La Mesa sib) is an "all-in-one establishment", offering a "mellow sports bar" vibe where patrons sample "reasonably priced" pub food and local brews while playing pool, Ping-Pong or Jenga; those seeking a less "chill atmosphere" hit the "wild" dance floor.

Kava Lounge
23 | 20 | 22 | M

Middletown | 2812 Kettner Blvd. (bet. Olive & Palm Sts.) |
619-543-0933 | www.kavalounge.com

An "addiction" for fervent fans, this "strange" Middletown music club showcases "niche, experimental and all-around crazy" acts along with "amazing" DJs and random "underground" performers; "amazing" mixologists concoct "eccentric" craft cocktails, though it may be too dark to see the "whimsical" decor and "interesting trinkets" lining the walls; P.S. cover and hours vary.

Kensington Club ⊅
18 | 14 | 22 | I

Kensington | 4079 Adams Ave. (bet. Kensington & Terrace Drs.) |
619-284-2848

Unusual in rather "traditional" Kensington, this circa-1935 "San Diego icon" serves "affordable", cash-only drinks to an "alternative" crowd that shows up to check out a "friend's band"; "sticky" seats and "musty" decor suggest it's "seen better days", though it's just the ticket when you want to "avoid huge crowds and big scenes."

The Kraken ⊅
21 | 14 | 21 | I

Cardiff-by-the-Sea | 2531 S. Coast Hwy. 101 (near Cardiff State Beach) |
760-436-6483

It's the "funkiest spot on Highway 101" according to the "good mix" of Cardiff locals who love this "old-school beach bar" located on the strip between the ocean and San Elijo Lagoon; "nothing-special" decor and "great local bands" make it a "dive in the best possible sense", and "bartenders are generous with the pours"; P.S. cash only.

Kristy's MVP Sports Bar & Grill
∇ 24 | 21 | 22 | M

Midway District | 3225 Midway Dr. (bet. Riley & Wing Sts.) |
619-222-0388 | www.kristysmvp.com

"Represent your team" at this Midway District sports bar where the "no-drama" crowd is ever "friendly", regardless of your affiliation –

though Saints and Raiders fans are particularly prevalent; 30 big-screen TVs and every major package guarantee your game will be on, but Kristy herself "walks around with a paddle, ready to spank your butt into place" if you get too rowdy.

La Jolla Brew House

`23` `21` `22` `M`

La Jolla | 7536 Fay Ave. (bet. Kline & Pearl Sts.) | 858-456-6279 | www.lajollabrewhouse.com

Microbrews and housemade beers star at this La Jolla brewpub where the "great" bevvie selection can be paired with "decent" chow in "casual, sporty" digs; it may be "priced higher" than the competition and bartenders are occasionally "overstretched", but happy hours, trivia nights and pet-friendly events make for "fond memories" here.

Lamplighter ⊅

`21` `15` `20` `I`

Mission Hills | 817 W. Washington St. (Goldfinch St.) | 619-298-3624

"Rock out to some Journey" at this Mission Hills "hole-in-the-wall" where a "fun-loving" crowd enjoys nightly karaoke fueled by "strong" drinks; moderate tabs and "dim lighting" compensate for the "divey" surrounds, while "cool" staffers man the bar from 6 AM until 2 AM.

Lancers ⊅

∇ `19` `16` `18` `I`

University Heights | 4671 Park Blvd. (Adams Ave.) | 619-298-5382

"What's not to like?" ask fans of this "divey" University Heights "neighborhood bar" where "cheap, stiff" drinks, a jukebox and pool tables keep it "humming all night" with a funky mix of "hipsters" and "old men"; there's "not much" going on in the decor department, but "there are worse places to hang out."

Latitude Lounge

`26` `24` `23` `E`

Gaslamp Quarter | San Diego Marriott Gaslamp Quarter | 660 K St. (bet. 6th & 7th Aves.) | 619-450-2437 | www.latitudeloungesd.com

While rooftop club Altitude is the Gaslamp Marriott's primary hot spot, this lobby-adjacent lounge is the hotel's "hidden gem", offering craft cocktails and a limited array of appetizers, sandwiches and flatbreads; like any place that neighbors Petco Park, the atmosphere can feel "a little sports bar–ish", but stylish decor and pricier tabs help weed out the cap-wearing crew.

Lime Tequila Bar

`24` `23` `23` `M`

Gaslamp Quarter | 653 Fifth Ave. (bet G & Market Sts.) | 619-238-5463 | www.mylimebar.com

Lime is only one of many flavors at this "small" but "comfortable" Gaslamp tequila bar, known for its signature margaritas that come in peach, passionfruit and even gingerbread almond varieties; although service can be variable, a "great selection" of spirits and "decent" drink specials make up for it.

Lips

`26` `24` `24` `E`

North Park | 3036 El Cajon Blvd. (bet. Ohio & 30th Sts.) | 619-295-7900 | www.lipssd.com

"Over the top in every way", this "campy" North Park drag club has patrons "falling out of their seats" with laughter at the "hilarious" revues, gospel brunches and bitchy bingo hosted by a bevy of "sassy, feisty" beauties; the food and drinks are "a bit pricey", but it's usually "packed" with a crowd that feels the "entertainment is worth the cost."

Live Wire   23 | 18 | 23 | I

University Heights | 2103 El Cajon Blvd. (bet. Alabama & Mississippi Sts.) | 619-291-7450 | www.livewirebar.com

"Even before San Diego became a beer town", this University Heights "rock 'n' roll dive" was serving "cheap" pints from an "extraordinary" menu of "flavorful" brews; "dark, homey and reeking of 10-year-old spills", it offers plenty of chances to "hang in the shadows" or jam to "upbeat" tunes from the "excellent" jukebox or occasional DJs.

Living Room Lounge   24 | 21 | 21 | E

Downtown | W San Diego | 421 W. B St. (bet. Columbia) | 619-398-3100 | www.thewsandiegohotel.com

Redefining the lobby bar, this Downtown W Hotel lounge has an "allure of awesomeness" that draws "international hobnobbers" with bespoke cocktails, plush couches and occasional performances by DJs or live bands; high prices make it "nothing to write home about" as far as bargains go, but that's par for the course in this genre.

The Loft   22 | 16 | 25 | I

Hillcrest | 3610 Fifth Ave. (bet. Brookes & Pennsylvania Aves.) | 619-296-6407

"Friendly", "playful" bartenders "welcome all" to this Hillcrest "hang" to drink "strong" cocktails and "make friends"; a "comfy" vibe and "cheap" tabs help keep it packed with a "mostly gay" crowd of "good people" on weekends, even if a few say the space "needs updating."

The Loft at UCSD   25 | 23 | 20 | M

La Jolla | University of California, San Diego | 9500 Gilman Dr. (Lyman Ave.) | 858-534-4090 | www.theloft.ucsd.edu

It's hard to find this performance venue on La Jolla's UCSD campus but, once discovered, it's a "charming" place to take in "offmainstream" music, film and literature in a "no-pretension" atmosphere; guests can also grab bites and beverages at the Zanzibar cafe inside; P.S. hours vary depending on time of year and show schedule.

LOUNGEsix   ∇ 23 | 23 | 22 | E

Gaslamp Quarter | Hotel Solamar | 616 J St. (6th Ave.) | 619-531-8744 | www.jsixsandiego.com

For a "cool, loungey" spot "without the chaos" typical in the Gaslamp, this rooftop above the JSix restaurant in the Hotel Solamar hits the mark, offering "excellent" bar bites and signature cocktails via "attentive" servers; with fire pits and poolside cabanas, it's "perfect for couples", especially on "nice summer weekends."

Main Tap Tavern   ∇ 24 | 21 | 22 | M

El Cajon | 518 E. Main St. (bet. Ballantyne St. & Roanoke Rd.) | 619-749-6333 | www.maintaptavern.com

You'll "always feel welcome" at this "fantastic" beer bar on El Cajon's main drag, where "knowledgeable" servers proffer a "wonderful" selection of drafts and bottles from breweries both local and foreign, plus some house suds; the beverages wash down a modest pub grub menu, while live music, HDTVs and an outdoor patio add to its allure.

Maloney's Tavern 　　21 | 21 | 21 | M

Gaslamp Quarter | 777 Fifth Ave. (bet F & G Sts.) | 619-232-6000 | www.maloneystavern.com

A wee bit of Gaslamp gloss adds appeal to this high pub, where "clever" decor and "hot girls" upstairs distract from the "dark, dank" downstairs; "well-prepared" bar food and staffers that "treat you like regulars" make it a "nice change" from the usual, though it can feel like a "bad frat party" on an off night.

Marble Room 　　▽ 25 | 25 | 24 | E

Gaslamp Quarter | 535 Fifth Ave. (bet. Island Ave. Market St.) | 619-702-5595 | www.themarbleroom.com

"Sparkling" chandeliers, "risqué" nude paintings and "friendly" waitresses dressed up like "old-school prostitutes" provide the eye candy at this Gaslamp saloon/supper club that harkens back to a time when the area was mostly made up of brothels and speakeasies; live soul singers add to the "sexy" scene, and "wicked good" Californian fare and "perfectly mixed" cocktails come at fair prices that won't ruin the mood.

McFadden's Restaurant & Saloon 　　23 | 20 | 22 | M

Gaslamp Quarter | 731 Fifth Ave. (bet. F & G Sts.) | 619-795-2500 | www.mcfaddenssandiego.com

The "staff knows how to keep the party rolling" at this "loud, rowdy" Gaslamp pub chain link, where a "frat boy"–style set goes to "get its drink on"; tabs are affordable, and the digs include a dance floor, sit-down section and more "quiet" outdoor area, so enthusiasts say it offers "whatever atmosphere you desire."

McGregor's Grill & Ale House 　　25 | 22 | 24 | I

Grantville | Rancho Mission Plaza | 10475 San Diego Mission Rd. (bet. Friars & Rancho Mission Rds.) | 619-282-9797

You can "watch a game" or just "meet people" at this "all-around reliable" Grantville sports bar near Qualcomm Stadium where a somewhat "bro-tastic", "easygoing" crowd bonds over pool, darts and shuffleboard; "attentive, quick" bartenders, "reasonably priced" drinks and "surprisingly spacious" surrounds are other reasons fans find it "an easy choice", especially when "meeting up with friends."

Miller's Field 　　21 | 19 | 20 | I

Pacific Beach | 4465 Mission Blvd. (Hornblend St.) | 858-483-4143 | www.millersfield.com

"Tons" of "quality TVs" in "every possible location" make this Pacific Beach sports bar one of "the best" places to cheer on your team, while "great drink specials" and all-around affordable prices further draw a "young, fun" crowd; outdoor seating adds appeal, and though service can be "hit-or-miss" when it gets "crowded" (which is often), staffers are generally "friendly."

Monkey Paw
23 | 21 | 24 | I

East Village | 805 16th St. (F St.) | 619-358-9901 |
www.monkeypawbrewing.com

An "awesome selection of beer", including "stellar" craft brews,
stars at this "funky" East Village pub; "knowledgeable" staffers, a
"friendly" vibe and "great prices" have many "swinging from the
trees" – though that may have to do with the "high alcohol content"
of some of the beverages.

Morena Club
20 | 17 | 21 | I

Linda Vista | 1319 Morena Blvd. (Tecolote Rd.) | 619-276-1620

Drawing "clubsters, rockers and seniors of the nearby trailer park",
this "strange little bar" in Linda Vista "caters to everyone" looking to
"have a good time with friends" and "save some money" with budget
beers; keep in mind, the "weirdos" inside sometimes make this "hole-
in-the-wall" feel like a night on the set of the *Jerry Springer Show*",
so don't expect anything glamorous.

Mosaic Wine Bar
24 | 24 | 22 | M

North Park | 3422 30th St. (bet. Myrtle Ave. & Upas St.) | 619-906-4747 |
www.mosaicwinebar.com

Oenophiles "hang with friends" and "unwind" while sipping solid
vinos at this "trendy" North Park wine bar; the "large" space is
"group"-friendly, with high ceilings and plush couches, and while
tabs can get "pricey", happy-hour deals help; P.S. guests can also
purchase wines to take home.

98 Bottles
22 | 20 | 21 | M

Little Italy | 2400 Kettner Blvd. (bet. Juniper & Laurel Sts.) |
619-255-7885 | www.98bottlessd.com

A "cool spot", this Little Italy bar draws a stylish crowd with its "great
selection" of wine, sake and craft beer dispensed by a "friendly" crew;
regulars say one of its "best features" is the speakeasy-inspired Back
Room, which hosts art shows and live jazz.

Noble Experiment
28 | 28 | 27 | E

East Village | 777 G St. (8th Ave.) | 619-888-4713 |
www.nobleexperimentsd.com

"Hidden" behind a "secret" entrance in The Neighborhood restaurant, this "trendy" East Village speakeasy "gets it right from A to Z",
with "excellent" cocktails "well crafted" by "friendly" mixologists
and "swanky" stylings like golden skulls, sparkling chandeliers and
"sideways TVs", all of which earn it top Atmosphere, Service and
Decor honors in San Diego's Nightlife Survey; the "intimate" space
is "teeny tiny" and tabs are predictably "pricey", but hey, that just
helps it maintain its "exclusive" vibe.

Number One Fifth Avenue
21 | 17 | 23 | I

Hillcrest | 3845 Fifth Ave. (bet. Robinson & University Aves.) |
619-299-1911

Expect "lots of local color" at this "laid-back, easygoing" Hillcrest
gay bar that draws "devoted regulars" with solid service and "cheap,

strong cocktails"; the "small" digs have a "hole-in-the-wall" vibe, and there's also a back patio with pool tables.

Numbers   20 | 18 | 20 | M

Hillcrest | 3811 Park Blvd. (Essex St.) | 619-294-7583 | www.numberssd.com

"What's not to like" about this Hillcrest gay club say fans citing the inviting vibe, "friendly" barkeeps and DJs spinning hits, hip-hop and electro over various dance floors; and even if others find it "just ok", different theme nights can still make for a "fun night with the boys."

Nunu's Cocktail Lounge & Grill   21 | 15 | 23 | I

Hillcrest | 3537 Fifth Ave. (Ivy Ln.) | 619-295-2878 | www.nunuscocktails.com

"Cool, laid-back vibes", "heavy pours" and "throwback" environs with red Naugahyde booths and dim lighting make this Hillcrest "legend" "the definition of a dive bar"; prices are "affordable", and a "friendly" cast of "regulars" makes for "interesting people-watching."

Oasis Lounge at Harrah's Rincon   25 | 23 | 25 | E

Valley Center | Harrah's Rincon Casino | 777 Harrah's Rincon Way (bet. Arviso & Boucher Heights Rds.) | 760-751-3100 | www.harrahsrincon.com

"It's never boring" at this glossy bar and performance venue in Valley Center's Harrah's Rincon Casino, where local bands, stand-up comedians, DJs and karaoke participants provide entertainment that leaves guests "flush with excitement"; tabs aren't cheap, but drinks are "stiff" and service is "aces."

Office Bar   20 | 18 | 20 | M

North Park | 3936 30th St. (bet. Lincoln & University Aves.) | 619-450-6632 | www.officebarinc.com

Formerly a punk-rock dive, this North Park bar is now a place where you can chat over "decently priced" drinks in the early evening until it "turns into a dance club" at night, when occasional live bands and "loud but pretty good" DJs spinning a "different mix of music" keep the crowd moving; the "minimal" space is "dark", but patrons can still glimpse stylized illustrations of working girls in office-inappropriate attire.

OffShore Tavern & Grill   ▽ 25 | 20 | 26 | I

Bay Park | 2253 Morena Blvd. (Lister St.) | 619-276-2253 | www.offshoretavern.com

"Kind, helpful" staffers and a "solid draft beer selection" win "kudos" at this midpriced Bay Park sports bar where the many TVs "throughout" lend "game-day" appeal; there's also a covered patio and "plenty of good" pub grub – more reasons fans vow to "definitely go back."

Onyx Room   21 | 20 | 19 | M

Gaslamp Quarter | 852 Fifth Ave. (bet. E & F Sts.) | 619-235-6699 | www.onyxroom.com

A "variety of music" (there are Latin, hip-hop and soul-themed nights) played over a "nice" sound system fuels the dancing scene at this "trendy" bi-level club in the Gaslamp; some say service is "friendly" while others call it "not the best" and the vibe merely "ok" – either way, it's "always crowded."

Ould Sod
`23` `21` `22` `I`

Normal Heights | 3373 Adams Ave. (bet. Felton & 34th Sts.) | 619-284-6594 | www.theouldsod.com

"Friendly" is the operative word at this "real-deal" Irish pub in Normal Heights where "welcoming" brogue-bearing barkeeps "call you lad" while "pulling a terrific pint of Guinness"; the "small", "comfortable" digs have a "cozy" vibe, prices are affordable and locals say the whole experience is "even better" when there's live music (karaoke also provides entertainment).

Pacific Beach AleHouse
`25` `21` `23` `M`

Pacific Beach | 721 Grand Ave. (Mission Blvd.) | 858-581-2337 | www.pbalehouse.com

A "happening" place to "lounge with friends", this midpriced Pacific Beach "hang" offers "quality" housebrewed suds and a wide variety of pub grub in spacious surrounds complete with a deck and "beautiful" fire pit–enhanced patio; "plenty of TVs" bring in sports fans, and a "relaxed vibe" broadens the appeal, so many are forgiving if the otherwise "accommodating" service is sometimes just "ok."

Pacific BeachBar & Grill
`22` `18` `21` `I`
(aka PB Bar & Grill)

Pacific Beach | 860 Garnet Ave. (bet. Bayard St. & Mission Blvd.) | 858-272-4745 | www.pbbarandgrill.com

It's a "cool place to hang" and "relax without the snobbery of a club", say fans of this "cheap" Pacific Beach bar that draws a "young", sometimes "fratty" crowd with "strong drinks", "good music" and "friendly" service; it's "nothing upscale" and can "get packed and crazy on weekends", but that just ensures it's a "sociable" place to "meet ladies."

Pacific Shores Cafe ⊉
`24` `21` `25` `I`

Ocean Beach | 4927 Newport Ave. (bet. Bacon & Cable Sts.) | 619-223-7549

"Blast-from-the-past" environs and "affordable" tabs are equally "retro" at this Ocean Beach "gem", where "friendly natives" and dive-loving hipsters down "stiff" cocktails from "not chatty" but certainly solid bartenders; "old-timey", "underwater-themed" decor and "mood lighting" make it feel like "the Rat Pack could walk in at any time."

Pasha Lounge
`▽ 25` `25` `23` `E`

Gaslamp Quarter | 425 Market St. (bet. 4th & 5th Aves.) | 619-338-0100 | www.pashasd.com

Decidedly more "upscale" than the average hookah bar, this Gaslamp getaway features plush sofas, dangling lanterns, colorful wall hangings and Moroccan tiles, all of which help foster an "interesting atmosphere"; solid servers tend to guests as they "chill" and try out smoke flavored with fruits like kiwi, white peach or mint.

Patricks Gaslamp Pub
26 | 22 | 22 | M

Gaslamp Quarter | 428 F St. (bet. 4th & 5th Aves.) | 619-233-3077 | www.patricksgaslamppub.com

Known for its "thriving local music scene", this circa-1933 Gaslamp pub is a "sure bet" thanks to its "always great" blues performers and "warm, comfy atmosphere"; "affordable" drinks are poured by a "friendly" crew, just be prepared to go "early" as it gets "crowded."

PB Shore Club
22 | 19 | 22 | I

Pacific Beach | 4343 Ocean Blvd. (bet. Grand & Thomas Aves.) | 858-272-7873 | www.pbshoreclub.com

Regulars say it does "not get more So-Cal" than this "affordable" Pacific Beach bar, where a "right-on-the-beach" locale affords "unbelievable" ocean views that are complemented by a "good beer selection"; the "big, open" space, adorned with "vintage skateboards and framed surf mag covers", can get "loud and busy", especially on weekends when it's often "packed" with "singles on the prowl."

Plum Crazy Saloon
20 | 17 | 21 | I

Pacific Beach | 1060 Garnet Ave. (bet. Cass & Dawes Sts.) | 858-270-1212 | www.plumcrazypb.com

Considered "cheap for its great location" on Pacific Beach's main strip, this "good old dive" used to lack in the decor department (unless "cute" bartenders and "peanuts on the floor" count), but scores don't reflect a recent reno; with a pool table and TVs tuned to the game, it works if you're just looking to "relax with a drink."

Porter's Pub
21 | 16 | 19 | I

La Jolla | University of California, San Diego | 9500 Gilman Dr. (bet. Myres & Scholars Drs.) | 858-213-3890 | www.porterspub.com

Students say "yes please" to this bar and music venue on the UCSD La Jolla campus, where an all-ages crowd can enjoy "indie bands", dance parties and such; sure, some say the space could stand a "remodel", but the substantial craft beer list and "cheap" prices work in its favor; P.S. open Monday–Friday and some weekends.

Prohibition
26 | 24 | 22 | E

Gaslamp Quarter | 548 Fifth Ave. (bet. Island Ave. & Market St.) | No phone | www.prohibitionsd.com

You'll feel like you've been "transported to the 1930s" at this below-ground Gaslamp bar where the "swanky", "speakeasy"-like surrounds provide the backdrop for "well-made" cocktails crafted by a "skilled" crew; the "cozy" space is "pretty small" and tabs can be "pricey", but that doesn't keep the "sophisticated crowd" (mind the dress code) from deeming it a "don't-miss", especially when there's live music; P.S. open Wednesday–Saturday only.

NEW The Propagandist
- | - | - | E

Gaslamp Quarter | 835 Fifth Ave. (E St.) | 619-238-7117

A change from the typical Gaslamp scene, this stylish, edgy basement bar has a more sophisticated sensibility with decor that includes church pews and walls lined with World War II–style propaganda posters; atypical entertainment like movie nights, indie bands and DJs spinning just about anything but Top 40 keep it cool.

Redwing Bar & Grill

23 | 19 | 25 | I

North Park | 4012 30th St. (bet. Lincoln & Polk Aves.) | 619-281-8700 | www.redwingbar.com

"Everyone is welcome" at this "gay-friendly" North Park "hang", a "great place to be" say fans cheering its "casual", "comfy" setting, "popular" karaoke and a highly rated staff; a solid bar food menu and affordable prices further explain why fans call it an "easy" pick when you want to "enjoy a round or two."

Rich's

23 | 18 | 19 | M

Hillcrest | 1051 University Ave. (bet. 10th Ave. & Vermont St.) | 619-295-2195 | www.richssandiego.com

"Get your dance on" at this "poppin'" Hillcrest gay club, where bartenders keep the "drinks flowing" while the "lively" crowd gets down to "uplifting house and pop"; the "warehousey" space features strobe lights and lots of "eye candy", and "if you have it going on the go-go boys will sometimes let you join them on their perch."

Rosie O'Grady's

24 | 19 | 23 | I

Normal Heights | 3402 Adams Ave. (35th St.) | 619-284-7666 | www.rosieogradyspub.com

"Reasonably priced drinks", including "stiff" cocktails and a wide beer selection, have fans cheering you "can't go wrong" at this "Irish-themed" Normal Heights "hole-in-the-wall", a "classic old neighborhood bar" with "homey" environs, solid service and an active "pickup" scene; there's live music on weekends, and multiple TVs also make it a "great place to catch a game."

R. O'Sullivan's Irish Pub

27 | 24 | 25 | M

Escondido | 118 E. Grand Ave. (bet. B'way & Kalmia St.) | 760-737-0954 | www.rosullivans.com

"Chatty" patrons sing along to live music at this "sweet little" Irish pub in otherwise sleepy Escondido, where it's "cozy, warm and inviting" and you can "browse the passersby" on the outdoor patio; "attentive" staffers offer a "great selection of beers", and tabs are "not bad."

Royal Dive

∇ 25 | 23 | 24 | I

Oceanside | 2949 San Luis Rey Rd. (bet. Airport & Benet Rds.) | 760-722-1911

As its name suggests, this "out-of-the-way" Oceanside stop is a dark, divey bar, and one that offers a vast beer selection and solid specials; it has frequent live bands, ranging from metal to reggae, and the scene can vary from packed to "relaxing."

Ruby Room

22 | 18 | 20 | I

Hillcrest | 1271 University Ave. (bet. Richmond & Vermont Sts.) | 619-299-7372 | www.rubyroomsd.com

It "feels like everyone knows each other" at this Hillcrest destination, a "rock 'n' roll version of *Cheers*", where the staff is "friendly" and music from "obscure" metal, punk and electro bands is pumped from a "top-notch" sound system; while the "dingy" decor is "a bit on the dive side", it still gets props for its "good selection of beer" and "cheap" prices.

Sandbar Sports Bar & Grill `25` `23` `25` `I`

Mission Beach | 718 Ventura Pl. (bet. Mission Blvd. & Strand Way) | 858-488-1274 | www.sandbarsportsgrill.com

"Before hitting the beach", sun worshipers visit this bi-level Mission Beach sports bar "just steps" from the ocean, where the "windowed" space has "sand on the ground" and a rooftop patio offers "board-walk views"; local DJs spin hits well into the night, and staffers treat patrons like "friends" while slinging affordable food and drinks.

San Diego Brewing Company `22` `21` `22` `I`

Grantville | 10450 Friars Rd. (bet. Riverdale St. & Zion Ave.) | 619-284-2739 | www.sandiegobrewing.com

The "strip-mall" setting is basic but the beers are anything but at this Grantville brewpub, where an "astronomical" menu of "local and big-name" drafts plus "tasty" house ales bring hopsheads in hordes; "witty" waitresses and reasonable tabs reinforce the "down-to-earth" vibe, and a "bunch of sports-blasting TVs" provide entertainment.

NEW Seven Grand `-` `-` `-` `M`

North Park | 3054 University Ave. (bet. Illinois & Ohio Sts.) | 619-269-8820 | www.sevengrandbars.com

Sibling to the LA original, this speakeasy-style whiskey lounge draws North Park's cool crowd with seasonal cocktails, an extensive bour-bon menu and local craft beers on tap; the dim, dark wood–lined space is also home to occasional blues and live jazz performances.

710 Beach Club `23` `19` `22` `I`

Pacific Beach | 710 Garnet Ave. (Mission Blvd.) | 858-483-7844 | www.710bc.com

An "easygoing", "friendly" vibe greets patrons at this "divey" Pacific Beach seaside bar where you can often catch some "good local bands" or just "chill" and "hang out with friends"; service is "quick", drinks are "inexpensive" and multiple TVs add game-day appeal.

Sevilla Nightclub `25` `23` `23` `E`

Gaslamp Quarter | Café Sevilla | 353 Fifth Ave. (bet. J & K Sts.) | 619-233-5979 | www.sevillanightclub.com

"Lots of Latin music" will "get anyone moving" at this subterranean "Spanish-themed" Gaslamp nightclub, where "fierce" flamenco per-formances, "free" salsa lessons and "dark" surrounds all help fuel a "sultry" scene; "friendly" servers pour "must-try" sangria, and while it may be a "little pricey", the "can't-beat" happy hour has "good prices."

Shakespeare Pub & Grille `25` `22` `23` `M`

Mission Hills | 3701 India St. (Winder St.) | 619-299-0230 | www.shakespearepub.com

You can "pretend you're in England" at this "traditional" Mission Hills pub, where "warm welcomes" from "witty yet courteous" staffers and "heavy pours" of British ales provide expats a "taste of home"; decor is "authentic", and a "laid-back" vibe encourages "conversations with mates" over plates of "classic" fish 'n' chips.

Shanty Cocktail Lounge ⇸

▽ 21 | 18 | 22 | I

Cardiff-by-the-Sea | 126 Chesterfield Dr. (bet. Newcastle & San Elijo Aves.) | 760-753-1548

Beloved by locals, this "fun" Cardiff shack off Highway 101 certainly lives up to its name, with spare, no-frills decor, except for the requisite pool tables, video games and foosball; with "cheap, strong" drinks, admirers call it the "perfect neighborhood dive."

Shout! House

27 | 22 | 21 | E

Gaslamp Quarter | 655 Fourth Ave. (bet. G & Market Sts.) | 619-231-6700 | www.theshouthouse.com

"Dueling pianos and audience sing-alongs" make for "rollicking good times" at this Gaslamp resto-bar, where an "exuberant" crowd gathers to watch "hilarious", "amazingly talented" entertainers and sip on "pricey" cocktails; it's "so darn crowded" that service gets "slow", but "everyone leaves with great memories" despite the wait; P.S. make reservations "way in advance" or else there's "nowhere to sit."

Side Bar

25 | 23 | 23 | E

Gaslamp Quarter | 536 Market St. (6th Ave.) | 619-696-0946 | www.sidebarsd.com

"Upscale but not over the top", this "New York–style" Gaslamp club provides one of the "most memorable" experiences in town, with "tasty" (if "expensive") cocktails fueling a "smoking hot" crowd that moves to Top 40 and house music on a "cramped" dance floor; the "plush" scarlet setting is as "well-dressed" as the clientele, though some complain of "snooty" service despite solid scores.

Silver Fox Lounge ⇸

19 | 15 | 22 | I

Pacific Beach | 1833 Garnet Ave. (bet. Kendall & Lamont Sts.) | 858-270-1343 | www.silverfoxlounge.com

Whether you need a place to "start the night" or get a beer when "everywhere else is closed" at 6 AM, this cash-only Pacific Beach bar does the trick; a "dive in every sense of the term", it has "cheap" beers, billiards and ancient "cheetah-print" carpet.

Silver Spigot

▽ 17 | 11 | 18 | I

Bay Park | 2221 Morena Blvd. (bet. Lister & Milton Sts.) | 619-276-1030 | www.silverspigot.com

"Juan Cabrillo could have had a drink" here when he discovered San Diego joke patrons of this Bay Park "hole-in-the-wall" that's "been around forever", plying "locals" with "cheap" drinks; "divey" surrounds include dartboards and pool tables, and service is "pleasant."

Small Bar

24 | 21 | 24 | I

University Heights | 4628 Park Blvd. (bet. Adams & Madison Aves.) | 619-795-7998 | www.smallbarsd.com

It may be "small" but the "super-chill, local" clientele is big on this "unpretentious" University Heights tavern, where an "insane" craft beer selection and "delicious" gastropub grub can be had "without killing the budget"; it's "always packed" ("get ready to get cozy with your neighbor"), but "rad" staffers tend to crowds with aplomb and "make sure your glass is never empty."

Soda Bar
22 | 21 | 23 | I

Normal Heights | 3615 El Cajon Blvd. (36th St.) | 619-255-7224 | www.sodabarmusic.com

Though some say it "doesn't look like much", this Normal Heights "hole-in-the-wall" has "become an elite place to see live music" say fans cheering the "cheap covers" and "real talent" from a variety of genres (electro, folk, hip-hop, indie rock); "easygoing" bartenders and "can't-be-beat" pricing mean the "hipsters" stay after the show is over.

Sogno Di Vino
27 | 26 | 24 | M

Little Italy | 1607 India St. (bet. Cedar & Date Sts.) | 619-531-8887 | www.sognodivino.signonsandiego.com

It "really feels like you're in Italy" say *amici* at this Little Italy wine bar, where "fabulous" vintages and "helpful" service do the motherland proud; the small, "quaint" setting, with rustic walls, ornate chandeliers and a "sunny" patio, helps make it perfect for "a date or girls' night out."

SOMA
24 | 16 | 17 | -

Midway District | 3350 Sports Arena Blvd. (bet. Camino Del Rio & Hancock St.) | 619-226-7662 | www.somasandiego.com

"Underage San Diegans" crowd this 18-plus "alternative and indie" music venue in the Midway District of Point Loma, which hosts mostly "new and local artists" but occasionally scores a national act; housed in a "converted cinema", it's "a little run-down" and gets pretty "crowded and sweaty" when the "younger generation" starts to "mosh", which is rough since there's "no alcohol" to cool you down.

Spin
∇ 23 | 21 | 25 | E

Middletown | 2028 Hancock St. (Noell St.) | 619-294-9590 | www.spinnightclub.com

Though it's one of the city's "premier spots for electronic dance music", this "killer" three-level club in Middletown maintains its "underground" appeal with "bumpin'" DJs, the "hottest" events and an overall "great combination" of "quality sound, lighting and talent"; there's "ample" space on the dance floor, but those looking to "get away" from the masses hit the rooftop bar for late-night food and "expensive" drinks from "stellar" servers.

Splash Wine Lounge
25 | 22 | 23 | M

North Park | 3043 University Ave. (Grim Ave. & Ray St.) | 619-296-0714 | www.asplashofwine.com

North Park natives "love the concept" of this "affordable" wine lounge, where they can "explore" a "vast" selection of bottles "from around the world" via self-serve dispensing machines; "friendly, helpful, quick" servers "always have good suggestions", and the "kick-back" setting makes you want to "curl up on one of the sofas and chill."

SRO Lounge

▽ 23 | 18 | 26 | I

Bankers Hill | 1807 Fifth Ave. (bet. Elm & Fir Sts.) | 619-232-1886
"If you blink, you'll miss" this unassuming Bankers Hill "landmark"
where LGBTers and crossdressers mix with hipsters and "stumblers-
by", but "everyone is accepting of one another" (maybe the "cheap"
drinks help); "friendly" bartenders really "get to know you", and
the "creatively decorated" space – think red walls and sparkling
chandeliers – begs the question "can a dive bar be glam?"

Stage

▽ 21 | 18 | 22 | M

Gaslamp Quarter | 762 Fifth Ave. (F St.) | 619-651-0707 |
www.stagebarsd.com
Bands of all genres take the stage upstairs and DJs play hip-hop and
Top 40 downstairs at this Gaslamp "dive bar that rocks", making it a
"fun place to get your drink on" while taking in the tunes; with "fair"
prices and mostly solid staffers, it's a place "music lovers need to
support" say fans.

Stingaree

24 | 24 | 18 | VE

Gaslamp Quarter | 454 Sixth Ave. (Island Ave.) | 619-544-9500 |
www.stingsandiego.com
Even after six years, this "posh" Vegas-inspired nightclub in
Gaslamp is still *the* "ultrahot" spot for San Diego's "plastic people",
whether in the "tasteful" lobby restaurant, "packed" VIP dance club,
"sweet" open-air rooftop or just waiting behind the "velvet rope";
staffers can be "inconsiderate" and the cocktails may "bust your
wallet", but at least they're "potent" and come with "plenty of eye
candy" on the side.

Tavern at the Beach

22 | 20 | 19 | I

Pacific Beach | 1200 Garnet Ave. (Everst St.) | 858-272-6066 |
www.tavernatthebeach.com
A "typical Pacific Beach bar", this "spacious" hang is a "great place to
grab a cocktail and party", attracting a "young crowd" with "cheap,
strong" drinks and DJs spinning nightly; it also has pool tables, outdoor patios and tons of TVs tuned to the game, and while it can get
"loud", it's still a "fun place to people-watch."

Tiger! Tiger! Tavern

25 | 24 | 25 | I

North Park | 3025 El Cajon Blvd. (bet. Ohio & 30th Sts.) |
619-487-0401 | www.tigertigertavern.com
It's all about the "amazing beer selection" at this midpriced North
Park pub where "unique" craft brews are poured by "friendly",
"knowledgeable" staffers; a "cool" vibe and "clever" "foodie" eats
extend the appeal, and "long" picnic tables are just right for "getting
to know your neighbor."

Til-Two

▽ 18 | 18 | 17 | I

City Heights | 4746 El Cajon Blvd. (bet. Euclid Ave. & 47th St.) |
619-516-4746 | www.tiltwoclub.com
From "comedy and karaoke to punk bands and hip-hop nights", a "wide
variety of entertainment" results in a "good time" "almost every

night of the week" at this "cute, hipster" City Heights "dive"; afford-able local beers, "inspired" drinks (try the whipped cream-topped Cupcake cocktail) and "cool" servers enhance the experience.

Tin Can Ale House
∇ 17 | 16 | 18 | I

Bankers Hill | 1863 Fifth Ave. (Fir St.) | 619-955-8525 | www.thetincan1.wordpress.com

Canned beers are the "gimmick" at this moderate Bankers Hill bar, where a "hipsterville" crowd sips from a "surprising" selection of suds while watching "one of the most eclectic mixes" of live music in town; it can get "crowded and steamy" during concerts, but it maintains its "pretty chill" vibe nonetheless.

Tipsy Crow
25 | 24 | 24 | M

Gaslamp Quarter | 770 Fifth Ave. (F St.) | 619-338-9300 | www.thetipsycrow.com

"Three different levels with three different themes" attract a "lively, varied" crowd to this Gaslamp "favorite", featuring a "classic" ground-floor bar, a fireplace-enhanced second-floor lounge complete with a pool table and an "energetic" basement nightclub that has DJs and dancing; staffers "treat you special" no matter which you choose, and regulars suggest you check out the "drink exchange" happy hour, where beverage prices fluctuate like a cocktail "stock market" for an "interactive drinking" experience.

Tivoli Bar & Grill
20 | 15 | 21 | I

East Village | 505 Sixth Ave. (Island Ave.) | 619-232-6754 | www.tivolibargrill.com

"Close enough to the action" Downtown but "far enough away to avoid unbearable crowds", this Gaslamp "hole-in-the-wall" claims to be the area's oldest bar, as the "decor, or lack thereof", might sug-gest; it's still "roomy and comfortable", and bartenders will gladly "bend a listening ear" while proffering "affordable" drinks.

Toast Enoteca & Cucina
∇ 24 | 22 | 24 | E

East Village | 927 J St. (bet. 7th & 10th Sts.) | 619-269-4207 | www.toastenoteca.com

You can "try really expensive wine without having to commit to a full bottle" at this East Village enoteca, where guests can taste many different varieties by loading cash onto a card and using self-serve machines, but can also order by the glass or bottle; "caring, atten-tive" staffers tend the industrial-chic dining room and patio, while happy-hour specials further the appeal.

Top of the Hyatt
28 | 26 | 24 | E

Downtown | Manchester Grand Hyatt | 1 Market Pl. (Harbor Dr.) | 619-232-1234 | www.manchestergrand.hyatt.com

"Astounding" views make this "classic penthouse bar" atop Downtown's Manchester Grand Hyatt an "elegant, romantic" place to "wow out-of-town guests" or "woo the woman of your dreams"; it's predictably "pricey", but tabs are matched by "top-notch" servers that make sure you feel "like a high roller."

ATMOS. DECOR SERVICE COST

Toronado
| 24 | 19 | 24 | I |

North Park | 4026 30th St. (bet. Lincoln & Polk Aves.) | 619-282-0456 |
www.toronadosd.com

There are "so many good beers to chose from" cheer hopsheads at
this "reasonably priced" North Park bar where an "outstanding array
of local and regional brews on tap" and hundreds of craft bottles (including some "elusive" picks) make up the "mind-boggling selection";
luckily, "helpful" bartenders are "knowledgeable" about what to
pick, and "loud" conditions don't prevent it from getting "packed."

Tower Bar
| 21 | 17 | 21 | I |

City Heights | 4757 University Ave. (Reno Dr.) | 619-284-0158 |
www.thetowerbar.com

Often "packed to the gills" with "PBR-toting hipsters", this dive located
in an "iconic" City Heights building has been plying locals with "cheap"
drinks since 1932; "personable" bartenders tend to crowds as they
take in "intimate" live shows or play the jukebox – just know that an
upstairs tattoo parlor means you might "end up with some fresh ink."

Triple Crown Pub
| 23 | 18 | 23 | I |

Normal Heights | 3221 Adams Ave. (bet. Bancroft & 32nd Sts.) |
619-281-0263 | www.triplecrownpubsd.com

You can play "practically all bar games known to man" at this inexpensive Normal Heights sports bar where Ping-Pong, pool, darts,
foosball, shuffleboard and even casual drinking competitions are
encouraged with a wink from the "friendly" staff; it also has "plenty
of TVs" for watching the game, and large surrounds complete with
"a lot" of patio space mean it's "never too crowded."

True North Tavern
| 22 | 20 | 20 | M |

North Park | 3815 30th St. (bet. Park Way & University Ave.) |
619-291-3815 | www.truenorthtavern.com

"Cool and mellow during the day", this "popular" North Park tavern is
more "energetic" at night when a "loud" group "lines up around the
block" to "eat, then drink, then dance all night"; "plenty of seating",
loads of TVs and a "friendly staff" also attract "sports fanatics."

207
| 23 | 22 | 21 | E |

Gaslamp Quarter | Hard Rock Hotel | 207 Fifth Ave. (L St.) |
619-764-6924 | www.207sd.com

Set in the ground floor of Gaslamp's Hard Rock Hotel, this "large"
club has "plenty of space to hang", whether on plush leather booths
or red satin couches, or at the "giant bar" tended by "solid" staffers;
local DJs spin Thursday–Sunday nights, multiple TVs add appeal
and tabs are predictably "expensive" given the venue.

Typhoon Saloon
| 21 | 18 | 20 | I |

Pacific Beach | 1165 Garnet Ave. (bet. Everts & Dawes Sts.) |
858-373-3474 | www.typhoonsaloon.com

If you like "cheap" drinks, including "good margs", plus "poppin'" Top
40 music and fellow "fresh 21 year olds" then fans say this Pacific
Beach bar is "what you're looking for"; the "beachy-industrial" space

(complete with stripper pole) gets "packed", but "bartenders know what they're doing", so even if it's not for everyone, many find it a "fun" place to "dance and go wild."

U-31 Cocktail Lounge

| 20 | 19 | 21 | M |

North Park | 3112 University Ave. (31st St.) | 619-584-4188 | www.u31bar.com

With "awesome" music from SoCal DJs, Sunday football on "every TV" and "fair prices", "great" specials and "strong" pours every day of the week, this "cool" North Park club always draws a "noisy", "youthful" crowd; some say the clientele is "a bit much" and service can be "hit-or-miss" but most agree it's "fun on some nights."

NEW Uptown Tavern

| - | - | - | M |

Hillcrest | 1236 University Ave. (Richmond St.) | 619-241-2710 | www.uptowntavernsd.com

Taking a super-local approach to food and drink, this Hillcrest tavern offers over 20 microbrews on tap, many from San Diego breweries, plus an American menu of shareable plates sourced from nearby purveyors; the rustic setting includes a fireplace-equipped back patio.

Urban Mo's Bar & Grill

| 25 | 21 | 23 | M |

Hillcrest | 308 University Ave. (3rd Ave.) | 619-491-0400 | www.urbanmos.com

"Always happening", "always a blast" say fans of this midpriced Hillcrest gay bar and restaurant that's often "packed" from dance floor to patio with a "great mix of people" ("everyone is welcome") and helmed by "friendly" bartenders pouring "strong", affordable drinks; though "different nights have different themes and activities" (line dancing, drag shows, showtune revues), it's generally "lively" and "busy" "no matter what time of day or night."

Vin De Syrah Spirit & Wine Parlor

| 27 | 27 | 21 | E |

Gaslamp Quarter | 901 Fifth Ave. (E. St.) | 619-234-4166 | www.syrahwineparlor.com

"Whimsical", "straight-out-of-*Alice-in-Wonderland*" stylings, like "grassy walls", "oversized chairs" and "outrageous centerpieces", make guests "feel lost in a different world" at this subterranean "wine parlor" turned "fantasy land" in the Gaslamp; it's "quite pricey", but with "superb" vino tastings, "experienced" sommeliers and entertainment from DJs, magicians and burlesque performers, many happily "fall down the rabbit hole" – if they can find the "hidden" entrance, that is.

Voyeur

| 25 | 25 | 21 | E |

Gaslamp Quarter | 755 Fifth Ave. (bet. F & G Sts.) | 619-756-7678 | www.voyeursd.com

"If nightclubs are your thing" you'll "enjoy" this "cool", "sexy" Gaslamp venue say fans touting the "thumping, state-of-the-art sound system", "ridiculously awesome" LED wall and "lots of great DJs", including some of "the best electronic acts"; it's not cheap, often gets a "bit too crowded" and can be a "major scene to get in", but devotees proclaim it one of "San Diego's dopest clubs."

	ATMOS.	DECOR	SERVICE	COST

Waterfront Bar & Grill

| 25 | 19 | 23 | I |

Little Italy | 2044 Kettner Blvd. (bet. Grape & Hawthorn Sts.) | 619-232-9656 | www.waterfrontbarandgrill.com

Sure, it's "no longer on the waterfront" since the bay was filled in decades ago, but this "old" Little Italy "institution" remains "busy", drawing an "eclectic" crowd of "bikers, surfers", "professionals" and more to enjoy "inexpensive" drinks and "fine burgers" in "relaxed" "dive"-like surrounds; it's constantly "crowded", but "warm" servers remain "attentive" despite the masses.

Whaling Bar & Grill

| 26 | 23 | 25 | E |

La Jolla | La Valencia Hotel | 1132 Prospect St. (Girard Ave.) | 858-551-3765 | www.lavalencia.com

"Bring your date" to this "classy" bar inside La Jolla's oceanside La Valencia Hotel, where an "upscale" crowd relishes the "traditional" Golden Age setting of tufted leather booths, rich red walls, sea-centric accents and a gleaming bar that once hosted '50s-era movie stars; since it's "expensive", some save it for that "special occasion" or go for just "one drink."

Whiskey Girl

| 22 | 20 | 20 | M |

Gaslamp Quarter | 702 Fifth Ave. (bet. F & G Sts.) | 619-236-1616 | www.whiskeygirl.com

You can "shake that boring work day out" on the dance floor at this "popular" Gaslamp sports bar and club, where "frat boy" types and "girls in heels" engage in "late-night mischief" over midpriced drinks and Top 40 tunes; it can be "crowded", and service can range from "friendly" to merely "decent", but those who go to "mingle and flirt" barely notice.

Whistle Stop ⊅

| 23 | 19 | 22 | I |

South Park | 2236 Fern St. (bet. Ivy & Juniper Sts.) | 619-284-6784 | www.whistlestopbar.com

This South Park "watering hole" is a "local" "favorite" for its "house party vibe", "fantastic beer", "well-made" cocktails and "friendly" staff; it also has a "great lineup" of entertainment, including live bands, art shows, game nights and spoken word performances, and since prices are affordable, most aren't bothered if it's "not pretty" to look at.

Wine Steals

| 24 | 22 | 23 | M |

Cardiff-by-the-Sea | 1953 San Elijo Ave. (bet. Birmingham Dr. & Mozart Ave.) | 760-230-2657
Hillcrest | 1243 University Ave. (bet. Richmond & Vermont Sts.) | 619-295-1188
Point Loma | 2970 Truxtun Rd. (Lytton St.) | 619-221-1959
www.winestealssd.com

A "vast" selection of bottles and "great happy hour" are draws at these "chill" wine bars, where "pleasant" staffers "impress" with their "knowledge and enthusiasm" as they guide guests through well-priced tastings; the "homey" digs and "sunshine"-drenched patios are "busy, busy, busy", so "arrive early."

	ATMOS.	DECOR	SERVICE	COST

Winstons Beach Club
21 | 18 | 20 | I

Ocean Beach | 1921 Bacon St. (bet. Newport & Santa Monica Aves.) |
619-222-6822 | www.winstonsob.com
You can "unwind and socialize with locals" at this "laid-back" Ocean
Beach hangout, known for its live music scene, "cool", "laid-back"
vibe and "reasonable drink prices"; the "dance floor is the place to
be" on some nights when it can get "noisy and crowded", but luckily
the "chill" staff "handles it really well."

Xhale Hookah Lounge
21 | 20 | 21 | -

Gaslamp Quarter | 635 C St. (bet. 6th & 7th Aves.) | 619-255-2458
If you "don't want to go out drinking", fans say this "casual" Gaslamp
hookah lounge is a "good alternative"; guests sit on couches in the
"smoky, dark" space and can bring their own beer or wine to accompany the many flavors of tobacco on offer.

SHOPPING

Local Favorites

The top five on this list are plotted on the map at the back of this book.

1 Jerome's Furniture
2 San Diego Zoo Gift Shop
3 Geppetto's
4 Great News!
5 Adelaid's Flowers

6 Bazaar Del Mundo
7 Warwick's
8 Babette Schwartz
9 Play It Again Sports
10 Leaping Lotus

Top Quality

29 Apple Store

28 Great News!
Burberry
Warwick's

27 Gucci

Neiman Marcus
Kiehl's
Geppetto's

26 Williams-Sonoma
Sony Style

BY CATEGORY

ACCESSORIES/JEWELRY

26 Swarovski
25 Sunglass Hut
Village Hat
Jessop Jeweler
22 Harold Stevens

APPAREL

28 Burberry
27 Gucci
26 Lululemon Athletica
Brooks Brothers
25 Levi's

GARDEN/HOME

25 Mission Hills Nursery
Adelaide's Flowers
24 Ethan Allen
22 Jerome's Furniture
CoHabitat

GIFTS/NOVELTIES

28 Warwick's
25 Contemporary Art Museum
SD Zoo Gift Shop
24 Babette Schwartz
23 Vintage Religion

SPORTING GOODS

26 REI
Golfsmith
23 Route 44
Overload Skateboard
Ray's Tennis*

SURF SHOPS

24 Surf Hut
Rusty Del Mar
23 Mitch's Surf Shop
22 PB Surf Shop
18 Bessell Surfboards

Top Display

27 Apple Store
Gucci

26 SD Zoo Gift Shop
Warwick's
Burberry

Neiman Marcus
Swarovski

25 Williams-Sonoma
Contemporary Art Museum
Geppetto's

Excludes places with low votes; * indicates a tie with place above

Top Service

<u>26</u> Nordstrom
Great News!
Apple Store

<u>25</u> Warwick's
Movin Shoes

Gypsy Treasure

<u>24</u> Burberry
Neiman Marcus
REI
Gucci

Good Values

Blumenthal Jewelers
Casa Artelexia
Great News!
Hunt & Gather
Mint

Noon Designs
Play It Again Sports
Progress
Rusty Surf Shop
Warwick's

Shopping: Merchandise

Includes store names, locations and Quality ratings. These lists include low-vote places that do not qualify for tops lists.

ACCESSORIES

Store	Location	Rating
Sunglass Hut	**multi.**	25
Village Hat	**multi.**	25
Enchantress	**Mission Valley**	25
Fairen Del	**Del Mar**	22
Motu Hawaii	**Pacific Bch**	21
Ooh La La	**Carlsbad**	20
Temptress	**Ocean Bch**	20
Aphrodite's Closet	**Pt Loma**	19
Pretty Please	**multi.**	19
Noon Designs	**multi.**	19

ANTIQUES/ FLEA MARKETS

Store	Location	Rating
Architect. Salvage	**Little Italy**	21
Ark Antiques	**La Jolla**	19

APPAREL

Store	Location	Rating
Burberry	**Mission Valley**	28
Gucci	**Mission Valley**	27
Lululemon	**multi.**	26
Brooks Brothers	**La Jolla**	26
Movin Shoes	**multi.**	25
Levi's	**Gaslamp Qtr**	25
Gone Bananas	**Mission Bch**	25
Gypsy Treasure	**La Mesa**	25
Rusty Surf/Boardhse.	**multi.**	24
Mitch's Surf Shop	**multi.**	23
Fresh Produce	**La Jolla**	23
Hanger 94	**La Mesa**	22
PB Surf Shop	**Pacific Bch**	22
Five/Dime	**E Vill**	22
Pomegranate	**La Jolla**	22
House Boi	**Hillcrest**	21
Hillside Artisans	**multi.**	21
Frock You	**North Pk**	21
TRE Boutique	**multi.**	21
Blue Jeans/Bikinis	**multi.**	20
Ooh La La	**Del Mar**	20
Hunt/Gather	**North Pk**	20
Ascot Shop	**La Jolla**	20
Lola Luna	**Ocean Bch**	19
Pretty Please	**multi.**	19
Magical Child	**Encinitas**	19
Baby Mabel's	**Solana Bch**	18
Gerhard	**multi.**	18

Store	Location	Rating
Haven Boutique	**Gaslamp Qtr**	17
Le Bel Age	**Mission Hills**	17
NEW Adrenalina	**La Jolla**	17
Mimi & Red	**multi.**	16
Le Chauvinist	**La Jolla**	16

ART SUPPLIES

Store	Location	Rating
Blick Art	**multi.**	26

BABY GEAR

Store	Location	Rating
Baby Frenzy	**El Cajon**	18
Baby Mabel's	**Solana Bch**	18
Agana Baby	**Kearny Mesa**	18

BEAUTY/GROOMING

(See also Department Stores)

Store	Location	Rating
Kiehl's	**multi.**	27
Origins	**Mission Valley**	26
M.A.C.	**multi.**	26
Sephora	**multi.**	25
Fresa	**Chula Vista**	18

BICYCLES

Store	Location	Rating
PB Surf Shop	**Pacific Bch**	22

BRIDAL

Store	Location	Rating
White Flower	**Bankers Hill**	23
D'Angelo	**Mission Valley**	22
Sparrow Bridal	**La Mesa**	20

CAMERAS/VIDEO

Store	Location	Rating
Nelson Photo	**Little Italy**	26

COOKWARE

Store	Location	Rating
Great News!	**Pacific Bch**	28
Williams-Sonoma	**multi.**	26

DEPARTMENT STORES

Store	Location	Rating
Neiman Marcus	**Mission Valley**	27
Nordstrom	**multi.**	26

ELECTRONICS

Store	Location	Rating
Apple Store	**multi.**	29
Sony Style	**Mission Valley**	26
Nelson Photo	**Little Italy**	26

FABRICS

Store	Location	Rating
Home Fabrics/Rugs	**Clairemont**	21
Aja Rugs	**La Jolla**	18

FURNITURE/ HOME FURNISHINGS

(See also Antiques)

GARDEN

GIFTS/NOVELTIES

JEANS

JEWELRY

MATERNITY

MUSIC/MUSICAL INSTRUMENTS

PETS/PET SUPPLIES

SHOES

SNEAKERS

SPORTING GOODS

STATIONERY

TOYS

SHOPPING

MERCHANDISE

Shopping: Locations

Includes store names, merchandise type (if necessary) and Quality ratings.
These lists include low-vote places that do not qualify for tops lists.

BANKERS HILL

White Flower | *Bridal* — 23

CARMEL MOUNTAIN RANCH

Geppetto's | *Toys* — 27

CARMEL VALLEY

Pretty Please | *Apparel* — 19

CLAIREMONT

Home Fabrics/Rugs | *Fabrics* — 21

COASTAL TOWNS

Geppetto's | *Toys* — 27
REI | *Sporting Gds.* — 26
Movin Shoes | *Shoes* — 25
Rusty Surf/Boardhse. | *Apparel* — 24
Muttropolis | *Pets/Supplies* — 24
Mitch's Surf Shop | *Apparel* — 23
Leaping Lotus | *Gifts/Novelties* — 22
Fairen Del | *Apparel* — 22
Hillside Artisans | *Apparel* — 21
TRE Boutique | *Apparel* — 21
Ooh La La | *Apparel* — 20
Pretty Please | *Apparel* — 19
Magical Child | *Children's* — 19
Noon Designs | *Jewelry* — 19
Baby Mabel's | *Children's* — 18
Gerhard | *Apparel* — 18
Aja Rugs | *Carpets/Rugs* — 18

COLLEGE EAST

Blick Art | *Art* — 26

CORONADO

Sunglass Hut | *Eyewear* — 25
Blue Jeans/Bikinis | *Apparel* — 20
Pretty Please | *Apparel* — 19

DOWNTOWN

SD Zoo Gift | *Gifts/Novelties* — 25

EAST COUNTY

Movin Shoes | *Shoes* — 25
Gypsy Treasure | *Theme* — 25
Hanger 94 | *Activewear* — 22

Blumenthal Jewelers | *Jewelry* — 22
Sparrow Bridal | *Bridal* — 20

EAST VILLAGE

Five/Dime | *Apparel* — 22

EL CAJON

Jerome's | *Furniture/Home* — 22
Blue Jeans/Bikinis | *Apparel* — 20
Baby Frenzy | *Baby Gear* — 18

GASLAMP QUARTER

Lululemon | *Activewear* — 26
Nordstrom | *Dept Stores* — 26
M.A.C. | *Beauty/Groom* — 26
Sunglass Hut | *Eyewear* — 25
Levi's | *Jeans* — 25
Harold Stevens | *Jewelry* — 22
Haven Boutique | *Apparel* — 17

GOLDEN HILL

Progress | *Furniture/Home* — 23
So Childish | *Toys* — 21

HILLCREST

Village Hat | *Accessories* — 25
Babette Schwartz | *Gifts/Novelties* — 24
Ray's Tennis | *Sporting Gds.* — 23
Cathedral | *Gifts/Novelties* — 22
Column One | *Gifts/Novelties* — 22
CoHabitat | *Furniture/Home* — 22
House Boi | *Apparel* — 21
Mint | *Shoes* — 20
Pretty Please | *Apparel* — 19

IMPERIAL BEACH

Surf Hut | *Sporting Gds.* — 24

KEARNY MESA

REI | *Sporting Gds.* — 26
Ethan Allen | *Furniture/Home* — 24
Agana Baby | *Baby Gear* — 18

LA JOLLA

Warwick's | *Gifts/Novelties* — 28
Geppetto's | *Toys* — 27
Lululemon | *Activewear* — 26

SHOPPING

LOCATIONS

Shopping

Ratings & Symbols

Quality, Display & **Service** are rated on a 30-point scale.

Cost reflects our surveyors' estimate of the price range:

| Inexpensive   E| Expensive
M| Moderate   VE| Very Expensive

● usually open after 7 PM   Ⓜ closed on Monday
Ⓢ closed on Sunday

Adelaide's Flowers   25 | 24 | 23 | E |

La Jolla | 7766 Girard Ave. (bet. Kline & Silverado Sts.) | 858-454-0146 |
www.adelaides.com

The "fresh", "exotic" flowers at this "fantastic" La Jolla Village florist
are a "definite splurge", but the displays are so "inviting" and the
"exquisite" "long-lasting" arrangements are "sure to impress", plus
the "experienced" staffers ensure bouquets arrive in "perfect condition"; the finishing touch: "gorgeous" garden accessories and "hostess gifts" for your "have-everything friends."

NEW Adrenalina   17 | 15 | 16 | M |

La Jolla | 5726 La Jolla Blvd. (Bird Rock Ave.) | 858-456-2061 |
www.adrenalinaonlinestore.com

Set in the Bird Rock shops south of La Jolla, this action sports retailer
boasts "good" skateboard equipment for men, women and kids, much
of which is displayed strikingly on the walls of the spare space; local
boarders find a selection of decks, wheels, and "up-to-date" apparel,
and diehards can also don their duds in the lifestyle brand's 26.2-mile
Adrenalina Skateboard Marathon.

Agana Baby   18 | 16 | 16 | M |

Kearny Mesa | 7420 Clairemont Mesa Blvd. (bet. Convoy &
Ruffner Sts.) | 858-277-3262 | www.aganababy.com

Surveyors swear staffers are "helpful" in "understanding what you
really need" and aiding guests in navigating the selection of high-end
strollers, cribs, carriers and car seats at this Kearny Mesa baby boutique, though middling service scores may suggest otherwise; some
customers would "love to see more inventory", but rewards points
and in-store events like kids' sign language classes lead customers
to "drive out here" in lieu of other options.

Aja Rugs   18 | 16 | 16 | E |

Solana Beach | 143 S. Cedros Ave. (bet. Lomas Sante Fe Dr. & Rosa St.) |
858-523-9570

La Jolla | 955 Prospect St. (Girard Ave.) | 858-459-0333
www.ajadesign.com

Loyal customers say this store in La Jolla and the Solana Beach design
district is "the only place to go for carpets", praising the "beautiful"

collection of antique and new Persian rugs, though others wish the offerings were more "diverse"; educated clerks "know their stuff", and the care staff offers cleaning, repair and restoration services.

Ananas ●

16 | 15 | 15 | M

Pacific Beach | 714 Garnet Ave. (Mission Blvd.) | 858-274-4006
Hard to miss with its iconic lime-green exterior, this standout at Pacific Beach's Crystal Pier stocks a "good variety" of items, from touristy trinkets like shot glasses and picture frames to SoCal-style tees, hoodies, board shorts and summer dresses; the shelves are filled to the brim, making it a "fun place to go" for "girlfriends" looking to score souvenirs.

Aphrodite's Closet ⌧

19 | 17 | 16 | M

Point Loma | 3304 Midway Dr. (bet. East Dr. & Fordham St.) | 619-225-1491
A "godsend" for dancers, clubgoers and party animals, this Point Loma shop offers a "huge variety" of apparel and footwear that "only a unique person" could pull off, like faux-fur boots, neon tops, colorful wigs and sparkly bikinis with stage appeal; it's also "nice to browse" for "cute masks" and Halloween costumes, and you can even treat yourself to a "custom-made" ensemble.

Apple Store ●

29 | 27 | 26 | E

Mission Valley | Fashion Valley Mall | 7007 Friars Rd. (Cabrillo Frwy.) | 619-682-3477
Carlsbad | The Forum Carlsbad | 1923 Calle Barcelona (El Camino Real) | 760-697-9800
Escondido | Westfield North County Mall | 272 E. Via Rancho Pkwy. (Avocado Hwy.) | 760-317-2484
Chula Vista | Otay Ranch Town Ctr. | 2015 Birch Rd. (Hwy. 125) | 619-205-6400
University City | University Town Ctr. | 4505 La Jolla Village Dr. (bet. Genesee Ave. & La Jolla Village Dr.) | 858-795-6870
www.apple.com
You'll "wish you were a nerd all along" at these "jaw-dropping" showrooms for Apple's "tantalizing" devices, combining "flashy" "hands-on displays" with "one-stop shopping and support" from a staff of "egghead maestros" who are "unfailingly" helpful to "techies and nontechies alike"; the "cutting-edge" wares "command a hefty price", and the crowds of "e-nuts" "can be maddening", but "once bitten", it's "futile to resist."

Architectural Salvage

21 | 18 | 19 | E

Little Italy | 2401 Kettner Blvd. (bet. Juniper & Laurel Sts.) | 619-696-1313 | www.architecturalsalvagesd.com
"Who knows what you'll find" – the "goods are always changing" at this "unique" architectural salvage specialist in Little Italy staffed with "friendly" folk; you may have to "dig" to uncover that "particular object" with "character" you "covet", be it "fantastic old hardware", "amazing" chandeliers, Victorian and Craftsman doors, stained-glass windows or "vintage" garden accessories, but this "treasure hunt" always "stimulates your creative juices."

SHOPPING

	QUALITY	DISPLAY	SERVICE	COST

Ark Antiques ⊠

	19	17	17	M

La Jolla | 7620 Girard Ave. (bet. Kline & Pearl Sts.) | 858 459 7755 |
www.arkantiques.org

There's "no junk" at this nonprofit organization's 5,000-sq.-ft. vintage
shop in La Jolla, where the donated and consigned pieces (antique
jewelry, art, furniture, rugs, china, sterling silver) are "prescreened
for quality" and a portion of proceeds benefit animal-related charities; more reasons to climb onboard: it's "fun to rummage" for "unusual" finds and there are even "occasional bargains to be had."

Ascot Shop ⊠

	20	18	19	E

La Jolla | 7750 Girard Ave. (bet. Kline & Silverado Sts.) | 858-454-4222 |
www.ascotshop.com

Established over 60 years ago in La Jolla, this family-owned, formerly
"old-school" haberdashery with double-Dutch doors, mahogany
cabinetry and state-of-the-art lighting continues to "move to more
fashionable" menswear lines like Robert Graham and Hickey Freeman
and also stocks jeans, tees and casual attire; while price tags "trend
upward", the "quality is equally high", plus seasoned staffers "know
exactly how to create that up-to-date, elegant look."

Babette Schwartz ●

	24	24	21	M

Hillcrest | 421 University Ave. (bet. 4th & 5th Aves.) | 619-220-7048 |
www.babette.com

As "eclectic" as the community it's in, this "consistently quirky"
Hillcrest novelty shop is a "mainstay" for "gays and straights with
good taste"; the hodgepodge of "silly" gag gifts, "raunchy" bachelorette party favors and "dirty" birthday cards makes you "laugh out
loud" and you won't find these "kitschy", "irreverent" tchotchkes
"anyplace else"; customers are "always entertained" – fitting considering this "fabulous" store is "owned by a drag queen."

Baby Frenzy ⊠Ⓜ

	18	17	16	E

El Cajon | 1529 N. Cuyamaca St. (bet. Bradley Ave. & Vernon Way) |
619-456-9094

"Environmentally conscious parents" go gaga for the "natural" products for mother and child at this El Cajon baby gear shop that also
stocks its own line of "top-quality" Happy Heiny's reusable nappies
for "cloth diaper lovers"; the "excellent selection" also includes covers, liners, "cute" toys and infant carriers from brands such as Ergo
and Moby, making shopping an "enjoyable experience."

Baby Mabel's

	18	16	15	E

Solana Beach | 136 S. Cedros Ave. (bet. Lomas Santa Fe Dr. & Rosa St.) |
858-794-0066 | www.babymabels.com

Owned by three like-minded sisters and named after their grandmother Mabel, this "adorable" Solana Beach cottage houses all
the "special treats" that fashion-conscious moms and moms-to-be
could want for themselves and their "little princes and princesses";
the selection of "adorable" diaper bags, maternity clothes and baby
gear changes "practically daily", while the "helpful" staffers round
out the experience.

QUALITY | DISPLAY | SERVICE | COST

Bazaar Del Mundo ❷
23 | 24 | 22 | M

Old Town | 4133 Taylor St. (Juan St.) | 619-296-3161 |
www.bazaardelmundo.com

"Take a quick trip" to Mexico and the Southwest "without crossing the border" at this "charming" giftware bazaar in Old Town offering a "tantalizing adventure for avid shoppers"; the "exciting" series of "colorful" shops boasts "artistic displays" full of "unique", "hand-crafted" clothing, jewelry, folk art, ceramics and home goods, plus the clerks won't "hound you" but are "there when you need" assistance.

Beads of La Jolla
20 | 19 | 19 | M

La Jolla | 5645 La Jolla Blvd. (bet. Bird Rock Ave. & Forward St.) |
858-459-6134 | www.beadsoflajolla.com

"Sit, socialize and make beautiful jewelry" at this La Jolla enclave that "carries every kind of bead you can think of", made from glass, stones, shells and more, along with "a vast supply of materials" to work with, all for a "modest cost"; staffers put "extra effort" into "helping you design" your masterpiece, and they're also on hand to make repairs and modifications.

Bessell Surfboards ⊠
18 | 16 | 15 | E

La Jolla | 515 Westbourne St. (La Jolla Blvd.) | 858-456-2591 |
www.bessellsurf.com

Professionals and weekend warriors ride over to "super"-talent Tim Bessell's La Jolla shop for his "beautifully manufactured", "custom"-shaped surfboards that resemble "works of functional art"; made from "innovative" materials that "push the boundaries", his "hand-crafted" long, short and paddleboards help surfers "catch the biggest waves" around; adorned with "abstract" sculptures, the digs also "feel more like a gallery than surf shop", which seems appropriate for such creations.

Blick Art Materials
26 | 22 | 21 | M

College East | San Diego State University | 5500 Campanile Dr.
(Hardy Dr.) | 619-594-7560
Little Italy | 1844 India St. (Fir St.) | 619-687-0050 ❷
www.dickblick.com

"Wow!" – "they have everything" in the way of "quality art supplies" at this "well-stocked" national chain where you'll find an "incredible selection" of paints, pencils, canvas, paper, frames and craft materials; "reasonable prices" make it an "excellent resource" that "hobbyists and professionals" alike "love to get lost in."

Blue Jeans & Bikinis
20 | 20 | 19 | E

Coronado | 917 Orange Ave. (bet. 9th & 10th Sts.) | 619-319-5858
El Cajon | 14860 Olde Hwy. 80 (Labrador Ln.) | 619-328-6745 ⊠Ⓜ
www.bluejeansandbikinis.com

"Everything you need" for "beach and nightlife" is on offer at these "cute" boutiques in Coronado and El Cajon (attached to the W Salon and Spa); true-blue fans "love" shopping the "unique" selection of, you guessed it, jeans and bikinis, choosing from "quality" brands like Rock Revival and True Religion, plus "trendy" apparel and accessories.

	QUALITY	DISPLAY	SERVICE	COST

Blumenthal Jewelers ⊠Ⓜ | 22 | 21 | 21 | E |

La Mesa | 8353 La Mesa Blvd. (3rd St.) | 619-463-8663 |
www.blumenthaljewelers.com

La Mesans' jeweler of choice, this "longtime fixture" offers "reasonable pricing" on both brand-name and "custom-designed" necklaces, earrings and engagement rings that leave gift-givers and betrothed couples "very pleased"; what's more, the "trustworthy" staff offers "personal service" whether you're "getting a battery replaced or making a major purchase."

Bowers Jewelers ⊠Ⓜ | 19 | 17 | 19 | E |

La Jolla | 7860 Girard Ave. (bet. Prospect & Silverado Sts.) | 858-459-3678

Since Ron and Margaret Bowers first opened the doors in 1945, this La Jolla "gem" has set "the standard" in the Village for fine jewelry and gifts; "satisfied" patrons "love" that the same crew has worked there "forever" offering "determined-to-please" service in intimate surrounds complete with comfy chairs.

Brooks Brothers | 26 | 24 | 24 | E |

La Jolla | 1055 Wall St. (Herschel Ave.) | 858-456-2104 |
www.brooksbrothers.com

"A bastion of old-school style without living in the past", this "classic" chain hasn't lost its touch, with devotees calling it "the gold standard for all-American tailored clothing" thanks to "quality" suits, "wrinkle-free" dress button-downs and preppy rep ties; edgier sorts call the women's fashions "staid", but "excellent service" and "interesting bargains" come sale time keep customers loyal.

Buddha For You Two Ⓜ | 21 | 20 | 20 | M |

Rolando | 6145 El Cajon Blvd. (bet. College Ave. & 62nd St.) |
619-582-1100 | www.buddha-for-you.com

Fill "all your deity needs" at this Rolando gallery, which stocks an "astonishing array" of "Asian artifacts", "spiritual items" and "beautiful Buddhas" in "all price ranges"; "just being in the store is a calming, uplifting experience" confirm New Agers, who also applaud the on-site free concerts, Buddhism classes and group meditations, some led by staffers themselves.

Burberry ◕ | 28 | 26 | 24 | VE |

Mission Valley | Fashion Valley Mall | 7007 Friars Rd. (Cabrillo Frwy.) |
619-291-9500 | www.us.burberry.com

"The ubiquitous plaid" "has become just as recognizable as the flag of England itself", but this "classy" chain also boasts "well-tailored", "avant-posh" "riffs on the classics" for him and her alike; all this finery is priced for the "swanky" "one percent" – but this "British luxury collection" is proof positive that you've "succeeded in life."

Burns Drugs | 23 | 20 | 22 | M |

La Jolla | 7824 Girard Ave. (bet. Prospect & Silverado Sts.) |
858-459-4285 | www.burnsdrugs.com

Entering this "old-fashioned" drug store "in the heart of La Jolla" is like "stepping back in time" to the "1960s", with a "Mayberry"-style setting and "well-thought-out" selection of "hard-to-find" presents, cards, candy, medical equipment and bath products that "the big chains don't" carry; the "knowledgeable" staffers "care so much about taking care of you", whether you're looking for a "quick treat" or "unusual gift", plus they have "marvelous sales."

California Candle Gallery ❶   19 | 19 | 19 | M

Marina District | 823 W. Harbor Dr. (Kettner Blvd.) | 619-338-9902 | www.globalcandlegallery.com

An offshoot of the Madeira Beach, Florida, chainlet, this candle purveyor set in tourist hot spot Seaport Village's maze of stores spotlights "handmade" paraffin wax creations carved with landscapes, sea creatures and intricate patterns and dipped, using a patented process, so they glow when lit; crafted on-site by "incredible" artists, the "unique" items make the store "smell wonderful" and are such "perfect gifts."

NEW Casa Artelexia Ⓜ   ∇ 19 | 18 | 18 | M

Little Italy | 2400 Kettner Blvd. (bet. Juniper & Laurel Sts.) | 619-544-1011 | www.artelexia.com

"Mexican treasures" abound at this "wonderful" Little Italy shop, offering "handmade" jewelry, artwork, leather goods, textiles and rustic furniture from south of the border in a "colorful" setting that's "totally unique"; the finishing touch: "attentive, friendly" owners who "make the effort to be part of the community" by hosting parties, classes, toy drives and other events for "locals and tourists alike."

Cathedral   22 | 20 | 19 | M

Hillcrest | 435 University Ave. (bet. 4th & 5th Aves.) | 619-296-4046 | www.shopcathedral.com

Find "gifts for anyone on your list" and "something special for yourself" at this Hillcrest boutique stocked to the rafters with "beautiful" soy, vegetable and food grain paraffin candles in "great scents" from makers like Diptyque, Red Flower and Votivo; rounding out the mix: home fragrances, lotions and "amazing" decor items like vases and wall hangings; the "knowledgeable" staffers apply "no pressure", which further enhances the "relaxing environment."

CoHabitat ❶   22 | 22 | 20 | M

Hillcrest | 1433 University Ave. (bet. Herbert & Richmond Sts.) | 619-688-1390 | www.cohabitathome.com

"Get your Zen on" at this Hillcrest home furnishings fixture with a "calm, welcoming" aura and a selection of "fun and funky international items" made for "browsing"; the "unique collection" of Buddhas, "beautiful silk" textiles, hand-painted furniture and other "inspirational" Indian artifacts appeal to "all budgets" and speak to your "inner hippie", plus it's all sold by a "friendly, knowledgeable" staff.

Column One ❶   22 | 18 | 22 | E

Hillcrest | 401 University Ave. (bet. 4th & 5th Aves.) | 619-299-9074 | www.columnonesd.com

Patrons are "always impressed" with the "astounding" selection of fountains, statues, waterfalls, gargoyles and other "beautiful, unique"

| | QUALITY | DISPLAY | SERVICE | COST |

home and garden items at this Hillcrest showroom; these "dream purchases" tend to be "expensive" but the goods last for years and the "patient, competent" salespeople are "a pleasure to do business with."

Contemporary Art Museum
25 | 25 | 23 | E

La Jolla | 700 Prospect St. (bet. Eads Ave. & Cuvier St.) | 858-454-3541 | www.mcasd.org

It's "always worth a visit" to this "treasure" in the Contemporary Art Museum, where "excellent" salespeople proffer "unique" housewares, books, stationery and toys arranged in displays so "excellent" they compete with the "divine" La Jolla setting; with provocative, "leading-edge" artwork on exhibit next door, it's no wonder that the gifts here "make you think."

D'Angelo Couture
22 | 16 | 19 | M

Mission Valley | Plaza Del Rio | 1400 Camino De La Reina (bet. Camino Del Este & Mission Center Rd.) | 619-497-1949 | www.dangelocouture.com

They "rock the wedding world" and try to "stick with your budget" at this "small, intimate" Mission Valley salon say even "somewhat hard-to-please" brides who put themselves in the "caring" hands of designer Diane D'Angelo and her "willing" staff; the location may be "hard to find" but never mind – prices are "spot-on" and the selection of "amazing" gowns, bridesmaid dresses and the owner's "one-of-a-kind jewelry" and headpieces fill every nuptial need.

The Enchantress
25 | 21 | 23 | E

Mission Valley | 1400 Camino De La Reina (bet. Camilo Del Este. & Mission Center Rd.) | 619-294-4544 | www.lingerie4brides.com

"Well-endowed" ladies "love, love, love" this "sexy" Mission Valley lingerie shop thanks to "super" shopkeepers that scour the racks of "pretty, feminine" bras to help those "abundantly blessed in the bust" find "the perfect fit" – and gals with "small" chests are also in luck; it's "pricey" but considered "worth every penny", and the selection is also ready-made for a "bachelorette gift" or "illicit affair."

Ethan Allen
24 | 25 | 22 | E

Kearny Mesa | 7341 Clairemont Mesa Blvd. (Ruffner St.) | 858-560-4404
San Marcos | 1040 Los Vallecitos Blvd. (Bingham Dr.) | 760-744-3919
www.ethanallen.com

"Traditional" styles, "well-made" mean this circa-1932 chain is a "favorite" for "high-end, conservative" pieces, though its more "youthful" offerings have surveyors swearing it's "not your mother's Ethan Allen"; the "furniture lasts and lasts", making it "worth the investment", and their "talented" interior decorators "will design your home for free if you purchase products."

Eye of Buddha
23 | 22 | 22 | E

North Park | 4247 Park Blvd. (El Cajon Blvd.) | 619-296-1150 | www.eyeofbuddha.com

There's a "treasure trove of goodies waiting to be explored" at this North Park home furnishings find, where customers discover an "eclectic", "interesting" global mix of "beautiful" bedding, "rich" textiles, rugs, "fine" art and "treasures" (think prayer flags, Buddhas and bongos) from far-flung places like Bali, India, Egypt and Turkey; staffers are "helpful", and though items "aren't cheap", nether are most "family possessions" you want to "last a lifetime."

Fairen Del
22	21	19	M

Del Mar | 2690 Via De La Valle (San Andres Dr.) | 858-259-1120 | www.fairendel.com

What a "wonderful" experience exclaim enthusiasts who find shopping this Del Mar boutique a bona fide "pleasure"; the "excellent selection" runs the gamut, from Pandora jewelry, Isabella Fiore handbags and Tumi luggage to travel-ready women's clothing, jeans and accessories; though some items challenge budgets, others offer "*Vogue*" looks at "Cost Plus" prices.

Five & A Dime ❶
22	21	21	E

East Village | 701 Eighth Ave. (G St.) | 619-236-0364 | www.fiveandadime.com

For "the biggest selection of popular streetwear south of LA", this East Village menswear shop hits the spot, offering "unique, urban clothing" in a "cool, NYC-style" setting; prices are "moderate to expensive", as to be expected at a "top-shelf" place with "baller" product and "inviting" service.

Fresa ❶
18	17	17	I

Chula Vista | Plaza Bonita | 3030 Plaza Bonita Rd. (Sweetwater Rd.) | 619-470-8300

Members of the "teen set" "love" this beauty shop in Chula Vista's Plaza Bonita, snapping up "cheap" cosmetics from the likes of E.L.F., NYX and Profusion; the "nicely organized" goods range from shimmery eyeshadows and foundation to false lashes, and prices are "great", allowing makeup mavens to change up their look whenever the urge strikes.

Fresh Produce Clothing ❶
23	21	21	M

La Jolla | 1147 Prospect St. (Ivanhoe Ave.) | 858-456-8134 | www.freshproduceclothes.com

Loyalists laud the "comfortable, casual beach-style" womenswear and kids' clothing at this national chain's "lovely" La Jolla link, stocking up on tops, tunics, shorts and dresses that "wash well and hold their shape" and are "perfect for traveling"; while some of "summery styles" may be "more cozy than stylish", that's just what the "wife and mother" clientele craves.

Frock You Ⓜ
21	21	20	E

North Park | 4121 Park Ave. (bet. Howard & Polk Aves.) | 619-220-0630 | www.frockyouvintage.com

Patrons "feel welcome" at this "stylish, well-organized vintage shop" in North Park, where "cute" clothing, "intricate" accessories and other "well-chosen gems" from the 1920s–1980s make shopping "very worthwhile"; if a few feel that the retro goods "should not be that expensive", supporters retort that the flea-market-esque 'Huge Frocking Sale' event every other month tempers pricey tags.

	QUALITY	DISPLAY	SERVICE	COST

Geppetto's

| | 27 | 25 | 24 | E |

Carmel Mountain Ranch | 10436 Craftsman Way (45 Ranch Pkwy.) | 858-674-9990 ◑

Del Mar | 2670 Via de la Valle (San Andres Dr.) | 858-755-2100

Del Mar | 3435 Del Mar Heights Rd. (El Camino Real) | 858-350-9038 ◑

La Jolla | 7850 Girard Ave. (bet. Prospect & Silverado Sts.) | 858-456-4441

Mission Valley | 7007 Friars Rd. (Fashion Valley Rd.) | 619-294-8878 ◑

Carlsbad | 1935 Calle Barcelona (Woodfern Ln.) | 760-632-1107 ◑

Old Town | 2754 Calhoun St. (Juan St.) | 619-293-7520 ◑

Chula Vista | 2015 Birch Rd. (Eastlake Pkwy.) | 619-216-3471 ◑

www.geppettostoys.com

Stocked with "toys galore", this "old-fashioned", well-"organized" chain is every child's "dream" and a "treat for parents" too, offering a "wide variety" of "imaginative" items, from "clever" games, "classic" wooden playthings and "handcrafted" doodads to "educational and interactive" science kits and "favorite" books; "be prepared to shell out some cash", though "happy" staffers "love kids and not just their parents' dollars."

Gerhard

| | 18 | 17 | 16 | E |

NEW **Solana Beach** | 143 S. Cedros Ave. (bet. Lomas Santa Fe Dr. & Via De La Valle) | 858-345-1153

Del Mar | Del Mar Plaza | 1555 Camino Del Mar (bet. 15th St. & Seaview Ave.) | 858-481-9709

www.gerharddelmar.com

"Like shopping in New York without the hassle" say fans of this well-edited boutique from owner David Fifield, offering high-end designer clothing that's not readily "available anywhere else in San Diego"; the "minimally designed" Del Mar and Solana Beach spaces artfully showcase covetables from Lanvin, L'Wren Scott and Narciso Rodriguez that, as to be expected, are a "definite splurge."

Golfsmith ◑

| | 26 | 24 | 23 | M |

Mission Valley | 824 Camino Del Rio N. (Auto Circle) | 619-497-0568 | www.golfsmith.com

"Golf nuts" report that this national chain has all you need "to play your best game" with its "top-notch", "fairly priced" clubs, balls, gear and apparel; with staffers who are as "knowledgeable" as "teaching pros" and an in-store practice range for swing tests, it's a duffer's "dream" – "don't tee off without them."

Gone Bananas ◑

| | 25 | 24 | 21 | E |

Mission Beach | 3785 Mission Blvd. (bet. Santa Clara & San Jose Pls.) | 858-488-4900 | www.gonebananasbeachwear.com

A staple in Mission Beach since 1975, this swimwear boutique offers "something for everyone", accommodating "all shapes and sizes" with its "awesome" selection of "pricey but worth it" suits, including "mix-and-match", "one-of-a-kind bikinis"; the "cute" wares are "color-coded", so it's "easy to shop", and staffers help you find the "perfect" piece that's sure to make a splash.

QUALITY | DISPLAY | SERVICE | COST

Great News! Cookware & Cooking ❶   28 | 24 | 26 | E

Pacific Beach | 1788 Garnet Ave. (bet. Jewell & Lamont Sts.) |
858-270-1582 | www.great-news.com

"Every cooking gadget, bowl or pan you can think of" is on offer at
this "foodie's delight" in Pacific Beach, a "gourmet" cookware haven
stocking an "extensive supply" of "everything culinary" you "never
knew you needed but now can't live without" and hosting "premier"
classes by "guest chefs"; if few find the shelves a "bit "overcrowded",
even they concede that the "expert" salespeople are "trained to answer your questions before you even ask."

Gucci ❶   27 | 27 | 24 | VE

Mission Valley | Fashion Valley Mall | 7007 Friars Rd. (Cabrillo Frwy.) |
619-298-0748 | www.gucci.com

Customers prosperous enough to be "greeted by name" and aspirants
alike are gluttons for this "iconic brand" that's "always reinventing"
itself to make sure there's "always something to want"; the selection
of "ultimate status items" includes "excellent" shoes ("best men's
loafers" around), "timeless" bags, "great sunglasses" and a host of
accessories; staffers "dote" "hand and foot" while you contemplate
the perilously posh array.

Gypsy Treasure Costumes ⌧   25 | 24 | 25 | M

La Mesa | 8119 La Mesa Blvd. (bet. Acacia & Date Aves.) |
619-466-2251 | www.gypsytreasure.com

Dress yourself "from head to toe" at this "year-round" La Mesa costume shop, which eschews "crummy, pre-packaged stuff" in favor of
"beautiful" masks, "great" theater makeup, "arghh-thentic-looking
pirate boots" and "fantastic" period wear, all at "reasonable" prices;
it "can be hard to find something on your own" in the "tightly woven"
space, but "knowledgeable" salespeople "know their stock" and are
"more than willing to help."

Hanger 94 ❶   22 | 22 | 20 | E

La Mesa | 5270 Jackson Dr. (bet. Center Dr. & Glen St.) |
619-469-9494 | www.hanger94.com

"If you love skating, surfing and snowboarding" then make tracks to
this La Mesa extreme sports leviathan, stocking an "unbelievable
selection" of "pricey" bikes, boards, wetsuits, shoes and sunglasses
alongside apparel from Roxy, Quiksilver, Billabong and Toms; shoppers are divided about staffers, with most lauding the "stoked" crew of
"total bros", and others deeming service "hit-or-miss."

Harold Stevens Jewelers ⌧   22 | 20 | 19 | E

Gaslamp Quarter | 525 B St. (bet. 5th & 6th Aves.) | 619-231-0520 |
www.haroldstevens.com

Create the bespoke "piece of your dreams" at this Gaslamp jeweler
where guests choose "lovely settings" and "gorgeous" gems for
"custom" designs – or peruse the "nice selection" of brand-name
baubles and "beautiful diamond" rings and things; the "knowledgeable" salespeople dole out "great advice at every step along the way"
and "work within any budget", making this a shop "you can trust."

	QUALITY	DISPLAY	SERVICE	COST

Haven Boutique 🅂🅼 | 17 | 16 | 16 | M |

Gaslamp Quarter | 751 Fifth Ave. (F St.) | 619-450-5872
"You never know what you'll find" at this "trendy" Gaslamp boutique, where "unique" and "affordable" items from designers like Beulah and English Rose are "up to date" and the jewelry is, according to one impressed shopper, "way cooler than I am"; the "small" space is connected to nightclub Voyeur, so clubgoers can strut their "funky finds" on the dance floor.

Hillside Artisans & Children's Boutique | 21 | 19 | 20 | E |

Del Mar | 1412 Camino Del Mar (bet. 14th & 15th Sts.) | 858-794-0134
Mission Hills | 827 W. Washington St. (Goldfinch St.) | 619-293-0134
www.hillsideartisans.com
There are "so many toys to choose from" at these Mission Hills and Del Mar children's boutiques, where owner Karen Dole makes it her mission to stock clothing, baby items and playthings "made with quality materials" for a range of ages; some find the inventory is "so cute but so expensive", making it mostly for "Christmas gifts" and generous "grandmas."

Home Fabrics & Rugs ◐ | 21 | 20 | 19 | M |

Clairemont | 4711 Clairemont Dr. (bet. Clairemont Mesa Blvd. & Lakehurst Ave.) | 858-581-3975 | www.homefabricsonline.com
What a "great source of upholstery fabric and rugs" agree home decorators and interior designers who make this Clairemont chain branch their "first stop" whenever they have "a new project"; the "unbelievable" selection of textiles, tassels and hardware "can't be beat for the quality and price", and the "arranged-by-color" setup makes for "easy" shopping; if a few feel service is lacking, others find staffers "helpful" and full of "suggestions."

House Boi ◐ | 21 | 22 | 18 | E |

Hillcrest | 1435 University Ave. (bet. Herbert & Richmond Sts.) | 619-298-5200 | www.houseboisandiego.com
Men who "don't want to look like they only shop at the mall" appreciate the "unique designer brands" available at this concept store, where "delightful, knowledgeable" owner Ari Clare carefully curates a "trendy, cool" mix for his Hillcrest clientele; but there's more: he also proffers "amazing home furnishings", and patrons who appreciate the aesthetic can even enlist him for interior design projects.

Hunt & Gather | 20 | 20 | 18 | M |

North Park | 2871 University Ave. (bet. Granada Ave. & 29th St.) | 619-297-3040 | www.huntandgathershop.com
"It's almost impossible to walk out" of this North Park "place of discovery" without finding a "unique" item from the "original" array of "super-chic" vintage and reworked vintage wear, "stylish" new pieces from local artisans, "handmade" accessories, "rare" vinyl and "amazing" artwork; the "awesome, artsy" owners, husband-wife team Lee Reynolds and Zoe Crenshaw, make it "so much more

than a clothing store", creating a "hub" for "San Diego designers, artists, musicians and friends."

Jerome's Furniture ❶   22 | 23 | 22 | M

El Cajon | 333 N. Johnson Ave. (bet. Madison Ave. & Main St.) | 866-633-4094
Linda Vista | 1190 W. Morena Blvd. (Buenos Ave.) | 866-633-4094
San Marcos | 780 Los Vallecitos Blvd. (bet. Knoll Rd. & Vallecitos De Oro) | 866-633-4094
Scripps Ranch | 10724 Treena St. (bet. Carroll Canyon Rd. & Mira Mesa Blvd.) | 866-633-4094
Chula Vista | 775 Plaza Ct. (Paseo Del Rey) | 866-633-4094
www.jeromes.com

Shoppers can furnish the "whole house" at this "moderately priced" home store chain, where "well-made" sofas, bedroom sets and kitchen tables are arranged in "nice displays" all "under one roof" earning it No. 1 Most Popular honors in the San Diego Shopping Survey; "informative" staffers are "helpful" in guiding the crowd of "first-time" and "budget-conscious" buyers around a store-room so "huge" you could "get lost."

Jessop Jeweler ⊠   25 | 24 | 23 | E

Little Italy | 401 W. C St. (bet. 4th & 5th Aves.) | 619-234-4137 | www.jessopjewelers.com

Faithful shoppers "wouldn't go anywhere else" for their baubles, pledging their allegiance to this "exceptionally nice", family-owned Little Italy stalwart with a "long history" (it first opened in 1892) of creating custom pieces and stocking "gorgeous, top-quality" fine jewelry at "reasonable" prices; "helpful" employees offer "old-fashioned" service, and staff gemologists make sure "you know ex-actly what you're getting."

Kiehl's ❶   27 | 24 | 24 | E

Mission Valley | Fashion Valley Mall | 7007 Friars Rd. (Cabrillo Frwy.) | 619-294-4732
NEW **University City** | University Town Ctr. | 4545 La Jolla Village Dr. (bet. Genesee Ave. & La Jolla Village Dr.) | 858-455-9720
www.kiehls.com

Bringing dull complexions "back to life" since 1851, this "time-warp chemist" peddles "hard-to-live-without" cosmetics, "natural" sham-poos, "herbal" toners and body butter ("Crème de Corps: nothing moisturizes better") in "old-school" settings; "as luxuries go, it's comparatively cheap", and the "ego-boosting" staff is "generous" with both kind words and free samples.

Leaping Lotus   22 | 22 | 18 | M

Solana Beach | 240 S. Cedros Ave. (bet. Lomas Santa Fe Dr. & Via De La Valle) | 858-720-8283 | www.leapinglotus.com

It's a "treasure trove" inside this Solana Beach "warehouse of artistic booths", where over 100 vendors peddle "unusual" gifts, "vintage" housewares and other "unique, special" finds that "cater to every taste and budget"; the setup can be "cluttered and overwhelming" and salespeople are "scarce", but guests "easily spend hours browsing", saying "if you can't find it here, they don't make it."

Le Bel Age ⊠Ⓜ `17` `16` `16` `M`

Mission Hills | 1607 W. Lewis St. (bet. Palmetto Way & Stephens St.) | 619-297-7080

When it comes to "date night or party clothes", fans of this Mission Hills boutique trust owner Valerie Ferrari, whose "eclectic, supergirlie, lots of glam" style informs the store's stock of apparel and accessories; prices range from "totally affordable to splurge", and "magnificent" Halloween displays may be reason enough to visit.

Le Chauvinist Consignment Store `16` `14` `12` `E`

La Jolla | 7709 Fay Ave. (bet. Kline & Silverado Sts.) | 858-456-0117 | www.lechauvinist.com

"Handsome, fashionable" men "wish there were more stores like this", say fans of the La Jolla consignment shop, which stocks an ever-evolving collection of clothing and accessories from the likes of Burberry, John Lobb and Zegna; the guy goods run the gamut, from ascots, silk ties and cowboy hats to trench coats and smoking jackets, keeping customers despite mixed service reviews.

The Levi's Store ◑ `25` `21` `20` `M`

Gaslamp Quarter | Westfield Horton Plaza Mall | 67 Horton Plaza (F St.) | 619-702-6254 | www.levi.com

"The daddy" of denim offers a "nice selection" of "all-American casualwear" at "reasonable prices" in its worldwide storefronts, where the "classic" brand is "still rocking" after 160 years; devotees believe "everyone should have a pair", and the "kind and willing" salespeople will help you choose just the right one.

Lola Luna ◑ `19` `18` `20` `M`

Ocean Beach | 4985 Newport Ave. (bet. Bacon & Cable Sts.) | 619-222-6811

Fashionistas find "fresh styles all year" long at this "small" Ocean Beach boutique, where "funky" designs and "hard-to-find" womenswear brands at "moderate" prices are likely to draw "compliments everywhere" you go; with "personable" shopkeepers that "keep you looking good" and "always make customers feel welcome", the service may even "exceed the products."

Lululemon Athletica `26` `23` `24` `E`

Gaslamp Quarter | 675 G St. (7th Ave.) | 619-234-0292
La Jolla | 7835 Girard Ave. (Silverado St.) | 858-459-4407 ◑
Carlsbad | The Forum Carlsbad | 1923 Calle Barcelona (El Camino Real) | 760-479-0183 ◑
www.lululemon.com

"Get your sweat on in style" at this "yoga heaven", where the "amazing activewear makes you want to" bend and stretch, and the "high-end" prices are "worth it" thanks to "fabulous" quality and those "flattering" "pants that make every butt look great"; the "staff of perky yogis" is "skilled and sweet", and you might even find them downward dogging in storefront windows.

QUALITY DISPLAY SERVICE COST

M.A.C. Cosmetics
26 | 24 | 22 | M

Gaslamp Quarter | 204 Fifth Ave. (K St.) | 619 237 0488
Mission Valley | Fashion Valley Mall | 7007 Friars Rd. (Cabrillo Frwy.) |
619-296-9955
Carlsbad | The Forum Carlsbad | 1923 Calle Barcelona (El Camino Real) |
760-753-1425
www.maccosmetics.com
Makeup junkies go wild at this cosmetics chain that's a "grown-up's
playland" with its house brand of "all the new lipstick colors", "richly
pigmented" blushes and "a rainbow assortment of look-at-me shadows and liners"; stylists "know their stuff" and stand ready "to give
you a new look" – they'll even do makeovers on the spot.

Magical Child
19 | 19 | 18 | E

Encinitas | 967 S. Coast Hwy. 101 (bet. E & I Sts.) | 760-633-1326 |
www.magicalchild.com
The "mystically presented" displays of "beautiful things" for infants
and kids are so appealing that even browsers without offspring wish
they "had an excuse to come" to this Encinitas children's store more
often; from the eco-friendly PlanToy playthings to clothing from the
likes of Tea Collection, everything is "delicate and natural looking" –
perfect for the "vegan, meditating child" joke surveyors.

Mimi & Red
16 | 15 | 15 | M

La Jolla | 5630 La Jolla Blvd. (bet. Bird Rock Ave. & Forward St.) |
858-456-7933
North Park | 3032 University Ave. (bet. Ohio & 30th Sts.) | 619-298-7933
www.mimiandred.com
Catering to the "hippest" Bird Rock residents, this La Jolla and
North Park twosome is "always stocked with the latest trends"
for women from brands such as BB Dakota, Dolce Vita and Yumi
Kim according to supporters; "fun, cheap things" are merchan-
dised alongside "nicer, more expensive options", making this
stylish apparel and accessories stop one of the more "unique
boutiques" in town.

Mint ◗
20 | 22 | 18 | E

Hillcrest | 525 University Ave. (bet. 5th & 6th Aves.) | 619-291-6468 |
www.mintshoes.com
Shoe lovers "make it a point to check out" this "trendy" Hillcrest
footwear find, where "helpful" staffers tend an "amazing selection"
of "hip, hot, cool, retro" styles, all arranged to "great" visual effect;
some prices "may be a bit expensive" but it "depends on the brand",
and "twentysomething" guys and girls are apt to leave with "no less
than three new pairs" of kicks.

Mission Hills Nursery
25 | 24 | 24 | E

Mission Hills | 1525 Fort Stockton Dr. (Randolph St.) | 619-295-2808 |
www.missionhillsnursery.com
Entering this Mission Hills nursery is "like visiting an English garden"
muse green thumbs who "could wander for hours" watching "cute
flocks of chicks roam the yard" and perusing a "wide array" of

"healthy" shrubs, annuals, perennials and supplies; the botanicals are "on the pricey side", but well "worth it", plus the "well-informed" staff is "willing to help and offer advice."

Mitch's Surf Shop
23 | 20 | 22 | E

Solana Beach | 363 N. Hwy. 101 (Cliff St.) | 858-481-1354
La Jolla | 631 Pearl St. (bet. Cuvier St. & Draper Ave.) | 858-459-5933
www.mitchssurfshop.com

An "institution" since 1967, this La Jolla "classic" surf shop (with a Solana Beach offshoot) is a "mandatory stop for tools of the trade", offering a stock of longboards, fins, wetsuits, T-shirts, sunnies and more that's "surprisingly good" given the "small" space; beach bums also give the "low-pressure" staffers a thumbs-up, adding they help "figure out the best equipment for your needs."

Motu Hawaii
21 | 18 | 21 | E

Pacific Beach | 4150 Mission Blvd. (bet. Pacific Beach Dr. & Reed Ave.) | 858-272-6688 | www.motuhawaii.com

Bringing the South Pacific to Pacific Beach, this "awesome" Hawaiian specialty store attracts "islander transplants", who "naturally migrate here" to find fresh flower leis, ukuleles, tropical-print fabrics, Tahitian black pearls, hula supplies and other "special touches they miss from home"; it's "worth a trip to see if there's something that you cannot find anywhere else" or to get a welcome dose of aloha.

Movin Shoes Running Centers
25 | 20 | 25 | E

Encinitas | 897 S. Coast Hwy. 101 (H St.) | 760-634-2353
La Mesa | 6105 Lake Murray Blvd. (bet. Dallas & El Paso Sts.) | 619-466-1656
Pacific Beach | 1892 Garnet Ave. (Lamont St.) | 858-373-2310
www.movinshoes.com

"Active" types "swear by" this local trio, where "knowledgeable" salespeople who are "actual runners" fit you with footwear that's right "for your sport and gait" and athletes can join group runs and races; the selection of sneakers, workout-wear and accessories from names like Adidas, Asics, Nike and Saucony is also among the "best" – little wonder "loyal customers" vow that they'll "never go anywhere else again."

M-Theory Music ●
22 | 20 | 21 | E

Mission Hills | 915 W. Washington St. (bet. Goldfinch & Hawk Sts.) | 619-220-0485 | www.mtheorymusic.com

This Mission Hills record shop is "one of the best in town" say fans who pore over the collection of rock, indie, jazz and soul and score "fresh" new LPs and vintage vinyl you "can't find anywhere else"; "cool, honest" staffers "pay well for trade-ins" and the bargain bin holds "gems", but the real plus may be occasional in-store performances from artists like Chuck D, The Hold Steady and Nada Surf.

Muttropolis
24 | 23 | 22 | E

Solana Beach | 227 S. Cedros Ave. (bet. Lomas Santa Fe Dr. & Via De La Valle) | 858-755-3647

(continued)

QUALITY DISPLAY SERVICE COST

(continued)

Muttropolis

La Jolla | 7755 Girard Ave. (bet. Kline & Silverado Sts.) |
858-459-9663
www.muttropolis.com

"Everything you need for your pet" is sold at these "cute" La Jolla and
Solana Beach boutiques, where animal lovers "spoil" their pups with
"beautiful" collars, "favorite" toys and "healthy" foods; "friendly"
salespeople are "on your heels helping you", and "fun" events and
"awesome" on-site training classes draw "woofs" of approval; if a
few bark that it's "pricey", even they concede that Fido is "worth it."

Neiman Marcus   27 | 26 | 24 | VE

Mission Valley | 7027 Friars Rd. (Cabrillo Hwy.) | 619-692-9100 |
www.neimanmarcus.com

This circa-1907 department store chain oozes "class" and "luxury",
from the "upscale" fashions by an "eclectic" mix of "top-of-the-line"
designers to the prices that are best suited to "the one percent"; even
those who "can't afford" the goods find it "inspiring" to "wander"
among the "posh splendor", and staffers, who are mostly "polished"
and "welcoming" (only occasionally coming across as "snooty"),
add icing to an already "stunning" cake.

Nelson Photo Supplies ☒   26 | 20 | 24 | E

Little Italy | 1909 India St. (Fir St.) | 619-234-6621 |
www.nelsonphotosupplies.com

A "port in the storm" for shutterbugs, this "well-stocked" Little Italy
photography vet boasts a "wide selection of cameras and accessories" that go "from darkroom to digital"; "readily available" salesfolk
assure "there are no stupid questions", and while the wares may "cost
more" than online sources, the staff's "wisdom" is "well worth it."

Noon Designs   19 | 19 | 19 | M

Solana Beach | 349 N. Hwy. 101 (bet. Cliff & Estrella Sts.) |
858-436-7417 ☒ Ⓜ
Ocean Beach | 4993 Niagara Ave. (bet. Bacon & Cable Sts.) |
619-523-1744
www.noondesignshop.com

Loyalists are "blown away" by this Ocean Beach–Solana Beach duo,
a "favorite" "go-to for gifts" owned by RISD-grad designers who
stock their own "unique", "made-by hand" jewelry, plus "simple"
home goods and "beautiful" stationery (including custom wedding
invitations); the talented twosome are not only as "crafty as you can
get", they're also "accommodating to requests" and "make sure you
love the products you receive."

Nordstrom ◑   26 | 24 | 26 | E

Gaslamp Quarter | Westfield Horton Plaza Mall | 103 Horton Plaza
(1st Ave.) | 619-239-1700
Mission Valley | Fashion Valley Mall | 6997 Friars Rd. (Cabrillo Frwy.) |
619-295-4441
Escondido | 270 E. Via Rancho Pkwy. (Avocado Hwy.) |
760-740-0170

(continued)

Nordstrom

University City | University Town Ctr. | 4321 La Jolla Village Dr.
(bet. Genesee Ave. & La Jolla Village Dr.) | 858-457-4575
www.nordstrom.com

Starting off as a Seattle shoe store back in 1901, this "lovely", "civi-
lized" national department store chain now offers "tasteful" fashions for the whole family, a "fabulous" footwear department and
service that is "second to none" – it's no wonder fans call it "god's
gift to retail"; still, the wares can be "pricey", which is why many
"live for their sales."

Ooh La La
20 | 20 | 19 | E

Del Mar | 1555 Camino Del Mar (bet. 15th St. & Seaview Ave.) |
858-523-1896 ◐
Carlsbad | 2972 State St. (bet. Carlsbad Village Dr. & Grand Ave.) |
760-434-1897
www.shopoohlala.com

Reviews are mixed on this "upscale" women's boutique in Carlsbad
and Del Mar, where some praise the "unique" selection for an "older"
crowd and others deem the apparel "ritzy rags" for "middle-aged
teens"; whatever their style, shoppers "most often" find something
to buy, though said patrons may be "tourists, not locals."

Origins
26 | 23 | 23 | E

Mission Valley | Fashion Valley Mall | 7007 Friars Rd. (Cabrillo Frwy.) |
619-295-9681 | www.origins.com

No matter your complexion type, the paraban-free products offered at this chain of "natural" skincare stop-offs will leave you
feeling beautiful and virtuous; the "smell good, feel good" cosmetics, "amazing staff" and corporate commitment to sustain-
ability and "animal"-friendly practices are a hit, particularly with
the "under-25 set."

OTM Fight Shop ◐
18 | 17 | 16 | E

Pacific Beach | 975 Garnet Ave. (bet. Cass & Dawes Sts.) |
858-270-5425 | www.otmfightshops.com

Black belts buy their supplies from this specialty sports and
mixed martial arts emporium in Pacific Beach stocking a "good
selection" of gear for Jiu Jitsu, Muay Thai, Judo, wrestling and
boxing; enthusiasts also get a kick out of the "knowledgeable"
staffers who guide them toward the right product and prove "helpful
in fitting" them properly.

Overload Skateboarding
23 | 19 | 21 | M

North Park | 3064 University Ave. (bet. Illinois & Ohio Sts.) |
619-296-9018 | www.shopoverload.com

North Park boarders buy "most of their gear" at this "rad" skateboarding shop, offering "sweet" decks, wheels, trucks and helmets
at "good" prices, with discounts for first-time customers; sporty
types also load up on shoes, shades and apparel from heavy-hitter
brands including Converse, Oakley, Vans and RVCA.

QUALITY | DISPLAY | SERVICE | COST

Paper Tales
20 | 18 | 17 | E

Midway District | 3960 W. Point Loma Blvd. (Sports Arena Blvd.) |
619-222-2510 | www.papertales.typepad.com

Crafters call this "super-cute" Midway District scrapbook store
a "must" for its "wide selection" of stamps, stickers, paper goods
and more; creative types looking to gain some expertise can at-
tend classes on making holiday cards, canvas collages and travel
albums, and turn to the "knowledgeable" shopkeepers for "personalized" service and advice.

PB Surf Shop
22 | 22 | 20 | E

Pacific Beach | Promenade at Pacific Beach | 4150 Mission Blvd.
(bet. Pacific Beach Dr. & Reed Ave.) | 858-373-1138
Pacific Beach | 4208 Oliver Ct. (bet. Oliver & Reed Aves.) |
858-270-1695
Pacific Beach | 707 Grand Ave. (Oliver Pl.) | 858-270-2466
www.pbsurfshop.com

"All the stuff you need for the ocean" can be found at this surf
trio in Pacific Beach, where wave-riders score "gnarly" boards,
wetsuits and accessories at a cost "comparable" to competitors;
both beginners and advanced boarders can benefit from the out-
fit's private lessons and camps, where they get to "hang loose"
with "amazing" instructors.

Play It Again Sports ❂
19 | 17 | 20 | M

Mira Mesa | 9841 Mira Mesa Blvd. (Treena St.) | 858-695-3030
Pacific Beach | 1401 Garnet Ave. (Gresham St.) | 858-490-0222
www.playitagainsportssd.com

When "frantic parents" are "awash in kids' sports", these Mira
Mesa–Pacific Beach equipment stores are a "life preserver" for "gen-
tly used" goods from bicycles to bodyboards, which are "second hand"
but still in "good condition" – and there's plenty for grown-ups too;
sure, there's some "junk" to sift through, but "helpful" staffers assist
in the search and help you "save big bucks."

Pomegranate
22 | 20 | 18 | E

La Jolla | 1152 Prospect St. (bet. Coast Blvd. & Girard Ave.) |
858-459-0629 | www.pomegranatelajolla.com

Serving La Jolla's style set since 1983, this women's boutique stocks
"to-die-for" jewelry, "charming, quaint" home accents "like you've
never seen" and "fabulous, unusual, trendy" clothing from international designers; devotees say they'll happily "buy all their clothes
and accessories here" – that is, "when they win the lottery."

Pretty Please ❂
19 | 18 | 20 | E

Carmel Valley | 11835 Carmel Mountain Rd. (bet. Highland Ranch Rd. &
Stoney Peak Dr.) | 858-676-1188
Carmel Valley | Del Mar Highlands | 12925 El Camino Real
(bet. Del Mar Heights Rd. & Townsgate Dr.) | 858-720-1188
Solana Beach | 427 S. Cedros Ave. (bet. Loma Santa Fe Dr. &
Via De La Valle) | 760-518-4553
NEW **Coronado** | 961 Orange Ave. (bet. 9th & 10th Sts.) |
619-437-1188

(continued)

Pretty Please

Hillcrest | 1220 Cleveland Ave. (Vermont St.) | 619-296-1188
www.prettypleasefashion.com

What began as a women's shop in Del Mar has expanded to include five stores across the city, all welcome additions to their respective 'hoods thanks to a "great selection" of "beautiful" clothing, shoes and accessories from the likes of Michael Stars and Joe's Jeans; generally the merchandise is "expensive" – as "smaller boutiques tend to be" – but that doesn't deter loyal shoppers.

Progress

▽ 23 | 22 | 21 | E

Golden Hill | 2225 30th St. (bet. Ivy & Juniper Sts.) | 619-280-5501 | www.progresssouthpark.com

"Design-lovers" adore this Golden Hill boutique furniture shop that caters to a "hip, young, trendy" clientele looking to reinvent abodes with midcentury-modern and sleek contemporary sofas, chairs, entertainment centers and bedroom sets; there are also "unique" gift items that make it the "perfect" place to buy for "difficult-to-shop-for" friends, and "great" staffers will tell you where to find items they don't stock.

Ray's Tennis Shop

23 | 16 | 20 | M

Hillcrest | 1434 University Ave. (bet. Normal & Richmond Sts.) | 619-295-5362

Everyone from "tournament players" to those just looking to "hit an occasional ball" find what they need at this "reasonable" Hillcrest tennis shop, "highly recommended" for more than four decades thanks to its "excellent" (if slightly "disorganized") selection of apparel, accessories and rackets that patrons can try out on a small indoor court "before they commit"; it's often too "swamped" for them to "get to you right away" but, once available, the "honest" staffers "know what they're talking about."

REI ◑

26 | 23 | 24 | M

Encinitas | 1590 Leucadia Blvd. (El Camino Real) | 760-944-9020
Kearny Mesa | 5556 Copley Dr. (Copley Park Pl.) | 858-279-4400
Chula Vista | Otay Ranch Town Ctr. | 2015 Birch Rd. (Hwy. 125) | 619-591-4924
www.rei.com

"Activities" addicts turn to the branches of Seattle's reigning sporting goods champion for "excellent" outdoor clothes and gear "galore" that provide "inspiration for doing exercise" and propel you "into the wild"; add "top-notch service" and "fair" pricing (with "a healthy rebate" for members), and the "adventure" "fix" "is complete."

Route 44 Skateboards ◑

23 | 22 | 22 | M

University Heights | 2002 El Cajon Blvd. (Florida St.) | 619-291-9051 | www.routefortyfour.com

Those who "skate and grind" should "love" this University Heights skateboarding shop, where the solid selection includes decks, shoes, apparel and more ("they even sell records!") and they "cut you some slack" on pricing; "knowledgeable" staffers will "hook you up" with all you need and won't "treat you like a poser if you're not a pro."

Rusty Boardhouse

| 24 | 21 | 21 | E |

La Jolla | 2170 Avenida De la Playa (Calle de la Plata) | 858-551-0262 | www.rustyboardhouse.com

Rusty Del Mar Surf Shop

Del Mar | 201 15th St. (Stratford Ct.) | 858-259-3200 | www.rustydelmar.com

"Everything a real surfer needs" is arranged in "attractive" displays at this "Del Mar institution" (with an affiliated La Jolla boardhouse), a "busy, quaint seaside shop" selling "good brands" of boards, accessories and "comfortable" clothing for the wave rider; best of all, the "knowledgeable" staffers always give off "the best vibes."

San Diego Zoo Gift Shop ●

| 25 | 26 | 22 | E |

Downtown | 2000 Zoo Dr. (Park Blvd.) | 619-231-1515 | www.sandiegozoo.org

"After a long day of adventure", visitors to the world-renowned San Diego Zoo in Balboa Park make this "outstanding" souvenir shop their "last stop before leaving"; with the aid of "helpful" staffers, shoppers of "all ages" unearth a "treasure trove" of "cute, clever" (and predictably "pricey") animal-themed clothing, stuffed toys, books and crafts that are "beautifully arranged" and sure to preserve "so many memories" of the trip.

Sephora ●

| 25 | 24 | 22 | M |

Mission Valley | Fashion Valley Mall | 7007 Friars Rd. (Cabrillo Frwy.) | 619-220-0771

Chula Vista | Otay Ranch Town Ctr. | 2015 Birch Rd. (Hwy. 125) | 619-482-4400

University City | University Town Ctr. | 4545 La Jolla Village Dr. (bet. Genesee Ave. & La Jolla Village Dr.) | 858-457-1983 www.sephora.com

All hail the "candy store of cosmetics" carrying "your favorite brands" in makeup, skin treatments, haircare, fragrance and beauty tools for every age and ethnicity; reviewers adore the "well-trained" staff, loyalty card "perks" and return policy, not to mention the on-site makeup artists – just "be careful, it's seductive" and the "impulse to buy" reigns supreme.

So Childish Ⓜ

| 21 | 21 | 19 | E |

Golden Hill | 1947 30th St. (bet. Fir & Grape Sts.) | 619-238-0800 | www.sochildish.com

"The cutest stuff" for children is in stock at this "moderate-to-expensive" Golden Hills boutique, where "they're always updating their inventory" of "unique, creative, high-quality" toys, clothes, books and games, from both local purveyors and bigger brands; the "personable" proprietor "always has time for questions", and a "super-cool" back play room keeps the kids occupied.

QUALITY | DISPLAY | SERVICE | COST

Sony Style ◑   26 | 24 | 22 | E

Mission Valley | Fashion Valley Mall | 7007 Friars Rd. (Cabrillo Frwy.) |
619-220-7482 | www.store.sony.com

These nationwide stores from "a brand that has stood the test of
time" show off "all the newest Sony equipment", including a vast array of cameras, computers, gaming consoles, televisions and home
theater goods, it skews "expensive", but the "knowledgeable" salespeople "won't rush you" and most techies "couldn't be more pleased."

Sparrow Bridal Boutique Ⓜ   20 | 19 | 19 | M

La Mesa | 8332 La Mesa Blvd. (bet. Palm Ave. & Third St.) |
619-985-6525 | www.sparrowbridal.com

Whether seeking "new, used, retro or vintage", the betrothed find
"the perfect dress for the perfect price" at this La Mesa bridal boutique, where the "varied" selection of consigned styles "changes" often; "helpful" staffers "think outside the box" when outfitting brides,
helping to create an "honest, easy, special" shopping experience.

St. James Gift Shop   22 | 20 | 20 | M

La Jolla | 743 Prospect St. (Eads Ave.) | 858-456-1105 |
www.stjamesgiftshop.com

It's "almost like a museum" inside this "quaint little store" under the
bell tower of La Jolla's St. James by-the-Sea Episcopal Church, where
"friendly" staffers tend "organized" displays of "unusual" jewelry,
nativities and books, as well as folk and religious art "from everywhere" around the globe; the wares make "interesting items for gifts",
and better still, proceeds help support the church's ministries.

Sunglass Hut ◑   25 | 23 | 22 | E

Coronado | 950 Orange Ave. (10th St.) | 619-522-0551
Gaslamp Quarter | Westfield Horton Plaza Mall | 324 Horton Plaza
(F St.) | 619-557-8405
Mission Valley | Mission Valley Ctr. | 1640 Camino del Rio N.
(Mission Center Rd.) | 619-858-0478
Mission Valley | Fashion Valley Mall | 7007 Friars Rd. (Cabrillo Frwy.) |
619-299-8846
www.sunglasshut.com

"Your reliable source for those Wayfarers", these ubiquitous
branches offer a comprehensive roll call of the big names in
shades along with "attentive service" to "make suggestions" till
you meet your match among the myriad designs; while views vary
on whether the prices are "fair" or "expensive", sunny supporters
say they "intend to return."

Surf Hut   24 | 22 | 23 | E

Imperial Beach | 710 Seacoast Dr. (bet. Dahlia & Daisy Aves.) |
619-575-7873 | www.surfhutinc.com

Fittingly located "right on the beach", this "beloved" surf shop is an
Imperial Beach "institution", stocking "all top brands" in surfboards,
wetsuits, shoes and apparel, and also offering "build-your-own"
skateboards; the "friendly" staffers are "always willing to help" their
wave-riding clientele, while yearly sales mitigate high prices.

	QUALITY	DISPLAY	SERVICE	COST

Swarovski ◗
26 | 26 | 23 | E

Mission Valley | Fashion Valley Mall | 7007 Friars Rd. (Cabrillo Frwy.) |
619-298-7451
Escondido | Westfield North County Mall | 272 E. Via Rancho Pkwy.
(Avocado Hwy.) | 760-489-9818
Chula Vista | Otay Ranch Town Ctr. | 2015 Birch Rd. (Hwy. 125) |
619-482-1929
www.swarovski.com

It's hard to "resist all the bling" at this glittery chain where acolytes
consider the "gorgeous" crystal-spangled jewelry "the next best
thing to diamonds"; the sparklers are "always on trend", while other
options, such as figurines, sunglasses and home accessories, also
dazzle; if some items are "not that expensive", others require a "huge
wad of cash."

Temptress
20 | 20 | 21 | E

Ocean Beach | 1918 Bacon St. (bet. Newport & Santa Monica Aves.) |
619-224-2284 | www.temptressfashion.com

Modern-day pinups shop the "'50s-style garments" and "sexy,
cute" lingerie that fill the racks at this retro Ocean Beach boutique, where patrons are "prepared to pay a little more" for the
"stylish, gorgeous" threads and true fashionistas participate in an
annual beauty pageant; for shyer folk, "helpful" staffers "always
have great fashion tips."

Traveler's Depot
23 | 17 | 21 | M

Pacific Beach | 1655 Garnet Ave. (bet. Ingraham & Jewell Sts.) |
858-483-1421 | www.travelersdepot.com

"All the gadgets, guides, goodies, luggage" and "stuff you don't know
you need" for your next trip is on offer at "reasonable" prices at this
Pacific Beach travel shop; the "knowledgeable" staffers have "lots of
experience" and offer "good advice" when pointing patrons toward
"invaluable" items for vacations and venturing overseas.

TRE Boutique
21 | 17 | 17 | E

Del Mar | 2710 Via De La Valle (San Andres Dr.) | 858-755-7227
Carlsbad | 1923 Calle Barcelona (Leucadia Blvd.) |
760-942-0227 ◗

These très "trendy" boutiques stock "nice-quality, cute" apparel and
accessories by BB Dakota, BCBG and Steve Madden, all selected by
an owner with "style"; a few complain of "crammed" displays that
"you have to dig through", but many still "love the stuff here."

Underground Furniture
21 | 18 | 20 | M

Pacific Beach | 1345 Garnet Ave. (bet. Fanuel & Gresham Sts.) |
858-581-0229 | www.undergroundfurniture.com

Patrons are "pleasantly surprised" at this Pacific Beach home
store, where those seeking "unique" furniture and "custom" sofas at "reasonable prices" have "found the right place"; its showroom can feel a bit "cluttered", but "polite" staffers offer "service
with a smile" whether answering questions or letting shoppers
"walk the floor."

	QUALITY	DISPLAY	SERVICE	COST

Village Hat Shop
25 | 23 | 21 | M

Hillcrest | 3821 Fourth Ave. (bet. Robinson & University Aves.) | 619-683-5533

Marina District | Seaport Village | 853 W. Harbor Dr. (bet. Kettner Blvd. & Pacific Hwy.) | 619-233-7236 ◑

www.villagehatshop.com

There's "something for every head" at these specialty hat shops in Hillcrest and Seaport Village, with a "vast inventory" of "fine" Panamas, "old-fashioned" caps, "novelty" toppers and other "unexpected" lids; costs range from "cheap to pricey", and "knowledgeable" salesfolk help scour the "top-notch" displays.

Vintage Religion
23 | 23 | 24 | M

North Park | 3821 32nd St. (bet. Park Way & University Ave.) | 619-280-8408 | www.vintagereligion.com

"Different cultures and religions" are the inspiration for this "funky" North Park shop that stocks a "clever" mix of Buddhist, Christian and Jewish art, antiques, jewelry and home decor items; it "can be pricey", but the "unusual" wares and an owner who "remembers his customers" make it "exactly what a local shop should be."

Warwick's
28 | 26 | 25 | E

La Jolla | 7812 Girard Ave. (bet. Prospect & Silverado Sts.) | 858-454-0347 | www.warwicks.com

Readers relish the "fantastically deep selection" at this "fabulous indie bookseller" in La Jolla, where there's also "amazing" stationery and "utterly unique" gifts; "knowledgeable, warm" staffers tend the "cozy" space and "terrific" appearances by "popular" authors help make it a favorite "place to just hang out", so "serious" bookworms urge "please patronize" this local "institution."

White Flower Bridal Boutique ⊠Ⓜ
▽ 23 | 21 | 21 | E

Bankers Hill | 2525 Fifth Ave. (bet. Laurel & Maple Sts.) | 619-501-1700 | www.thewhiteflower.com

Brides-to-be have the store "all to themselves" at this appointment-only Bankers Hill bridal boutique, where a "lovely" selection of "classic, elegant" gowns, veils and jewelry are presented in a "personal" setting with "plenty of space and privacy"; a "warm, welcoming" owner gives patrons her "undivided attention" in finding the right dress and even doles out "celebratory champagne."

Williams-Sonoma ◑
26 | 25 | 23 | E

Mission Valley | Fashion Valley Mall | 7007 Friars Rd. (Cabrillo Frwy.) | 619-295-0510

University City | University Town Ctr. | 4417 La Jolla Village Dr. (bet. Genesee Ave. & La Jolla Village Dr.) | 858-597-0611 | www.williams-sonoma.com

An "indispensable" source of "kitchen fantasy fulfillment", this popular chain is guaranteed to "lend culinary cachet" with a "comprehensive selection" of "first-rate" cookware "classics" and "obscure" gadgets; between the "customer service" and "enticing displays", "discerning" home chefs "don't mind paying top dollar" – "case closed."

SHOPPING: FOOD & WINE

Local Favorites

The top five on this list are plotted on the map at the back of this book.

1 99 Ranch | *Major Mkt.*

2 Jimbo's | *Health/Natural*

3 Bristol Farms | *Produce*

4 Iowa Meat | *Meat/Poultry*

5 Mitsuwa Mktpl. | *Spec. Shops*

6 V.G. Donut | *Baked Gds.*

7 Zion Market | *Spec. Shops*

8 Nothing Bundt Cakes | *Baked Gds.*

9 Keil's Food Store | *Maj. Mkt.*

10 Windmill Farms | *Maj. Mkt.*

Top Quality

29| Suzie's Farm

28| Chuao Chocolatier
Port Brewing/Lost Abbey
Venissimo Cheese
Iowa Meat

Siesel's Meats
Hans & Harry Bakery
Bristol Farms
Temecula Olive Oil Co.

27| Nothing Bundt Cakes

BY CATEGORY

BAKED GOODS

28| Hans & Harry Bakery
27| Nothing Bundt Cakes
26| Uncle Biff's Killer Cookies
V.G. Donut*
European Cake Gallery

BREWERIES

28| Port Brewing/Lost Abbey
26| Green Flash Brewing Co.
Ballast Point Brewery
25| Stone Company Store
24| Alpine Beer Co.

MAJOR MARKETS

28| Bristol Farms
27| Seaside Market
Windmill Farms
Harvest Ranch Market
25| Olive Tree Marketplace

MEAT/POULTRY/SEAFOOD

28| Iowa Meat
Siesel's Meats

25| Catalina Offshore Products
22| Butcher Block Meat Market
20| Lucky Seafood

PRODUCE

29| Suzie's Farm
27| Chino Farms
24| Specialty Produce
23| Farmers Outlet
21| North Park

SPECIALTY SHOPS

28| Temecula Olive Oil Co.
27| World Foods
Mona Lisa Italian Foods
26| Mitsuwa Mktpl.
25| Nijiya Market

WINE/LIQUOR STORES

26| Pizza Port Bottle Shop
San Diego Wine Co.
Holiday Wine Cellar
25| Chris' Liquor & Deli
KnB Wine Cellars

Top Display

27| Bristol Farms
Chuao Chocolatier

26| Nothing Bundt Cakes
Venissimo Cheese

25| Hans & Harry Bakery

Harvest Ranch Market
Temecula Olive Oil Co.
World Foods
Hot Licks
Windmill Farms

Excludes places with low votes; *indicates a tie with place above

Top Service

Best Buys

In order of Bang for the Buck rating.

Shopping: Food & Wine Types

Listings cover the best in each category and include names, locations and Quality ratings. These lists include low-vote places that do not qualify for tops lists.

BAKED GOODS

Hans/Harry Bakery | **Bonita**	28
Nothing Bundt | **multi.**	27
Uncle Biff's | **Hillcrest**	26
V.G. Donut/Bakery | **Cardiff-by-the-Sea**	26
European Cake | **Pt Loma**	26
Edelweiss Bakery | **multi.**	26
SD Desserts | **City Heights**	26
Charlie's Best Bread | **Pacific Bch**	25
Twiggs Bakery | **University Hts**	25
Cupcakes/Beyond | **Poway**	25
Cupcakes Squared | **Pt Loma**	25
NEW Cupcake Store | **Santee**	24
Azucar | **Ocean Bch**	24
Cups | **La Jolla**	24
Cupcake Love | **Solana Bch**	23
Panchitas Bakery | **multi.**	23
Heaven. Cupcake | **Gaslamp Qtr**	22
Cake | **Mission Hills**	21
2Good2B | **Encinitas**	21
CB's Cupcakes | **Carlsbad**	21
Batter Up! | **Rancho Bernardo**	21
Stephanie's Bakery | **Ocean Bch**	21
Frosted Robin | **Marina District**	19
Arely French | **Clairemont**	19

CANDY & NUTS

Chuao Chocolatier | **multi.**	28
Eclipse Chocolat | **South Pk**	26
Chi Chocolate | **Pt Loma**	23
Elegant Truffle | **Shelter Is**	22
Dallman Fine Choc. | **Del Mar**	22

CHEESE & DAIRY

Venissimo Cheese | **multi.**	28
Cheese Shop | **La Jolla**	25

COFFEE & TEA

My Cup/Tea | **Chula Vista**	25
Café Moto | **Barrio Logan**	24
Café Virtuoso | **Barrio Logan**	20

HEALTH & NATURAL FOODS

Bristol Farms | **University City**	28
Seaside Mkt. | **Cardiff-by-the-Sea**	27
Windmill Farms | **Del Cerro**	27
Harvest Ranch | **multi.**	27

Jimbo's | **multi.**	26
Ocean Beach People's Mkt. | **Ocean Bch**	26
Boney's Bayside | **Coronado**	25
Baron's Mkt. | **multi.**	24
Jonathan's Mkt. | **La Jolla**	24
Lisko Artisan | **City Heights**	20
Krisp | **Downtown**	17

MAJOR MARKETS

Bristol Farms | **University City**	28
Seaside Mkt. | **Cardiff-by-the-Sea**	27
Windmill Farms | **Del Cerro**	27
Harvest Ranch | **Encinitas**	27
Jimbo's | **Carmel Mountain Ranch**	26
Olive Tree Mkpl. | **Ocean Bch**	25
Valley Farm Mkt. | **Spring Valley**	25
Baron's Mkt. | **multi.**	24
Jonathan's Mkt. | **La Jolla**	24
Keil's Food | **multi.**	24
Stump's Family Mktpl. | **Ocean Bch**	23
99 Ranch | **Clairemont**	22
Pancho Villa Farmer's Mkt. | **Normal Heights**	21
Krisp | **Downtown**	17
Northgate Mkt. | **multi.**	-

MEAT, POULTRY & GAME

Iowa Meat Farms | **Del Cerro**	28
Siesel's Meats | **Bay Pk**	28
Bristol Farms | **University City**	28
Seaside Mkt. | **Cardiff-by-the-Sea**	27
Windmill Farms | **Del Cerro**	27
Valley Farm Mkt. | **Spring Valley**	25
Jonathan's Mkt. | **La Jolla**	24
Keil's Food | **multi.**	24
Stump's Family Mktpl. | **Ocean Bch**	23
99 Ranch | **Clairemont**	22
Butcher Block Meat | **Barrio Logan**	22
Miller's Mkt. | **Golden Hill**	17

OLIVES & PICKLES

Bristol Farms | **University City**	28
Temecula Olive Oil | **Old Town**	28
Seaside Mkt. | **Cardiff-by-the-Sea**	27
Mona Lisa Ital. | **Little Italy**	27
Seaport Oil/Vinegars | **Marina District**	25

Baron's Mkt. | **Pt Loma** — 24
Specialty Produce | **Middletown** — 24
Grant's Mkpl. | **South Pk** — 24
Zanzibar | **E Vill** — 24
Baker/Olive | **Del Mar** — 23
Assenti's Pasta | **Little Italy** — 23
Stump's Family Mktpl. | **Ocean Bch** — 23
We Olive | **La Jolla** — 22
Market/Buon Appetito | **Little Italy** — 22
Shakespeare Corner | **Mission Hills** — 22
North Park Prod. | **Normal Heights** — 21
El Cajon Int'l | **El Cajon** — 21
La Bodega Mkt. | **Chula Vista** — 21
Balboa Int'l Mkt. | **Clairemont** — 20
Lucky Seafood | **Mira Mesa** — 20
Vine Ripe Mkt. | **La Mesa** — 20
Andres Latin Mkt. | **Linda Vista** — 19
Krisp | **Downtown** — 17
Hing Long Orient. | **City Heights** — 16

PASTAS

Mona Lisa Ital. | **Little Italy** — 27
Assenti's Pasta | **Little Italy** — 23
Market/Buon Appetito | **Little Italy** — 22

PRODUCE

Suzie's Farm | **Imperial Beach** — 29
Bristol Farms | **University City** — 28
Chino Farms | **Rancho Santa Fe** — 27
Seaside Mkt. | **Cardiff-by-the-Sea** — 27
Windmill Farms | **Del Cerro** — 27
Harvest Ranch | **multi.** — 27
Jimbo's | **multi.** — 26
Boney's Bayside | **Coronado** — 25
Baron's Mkt. | **multi.** — 24
Specialty Produce | **Middletown** — 24
Jonathan's Mkt. | **La Jolla** — 24
Keil's Food | **multi.** — 24
Farmers Outlet | **Grantville** — 23
Stump's Family Mktpl. | **Ocean Bch** — 23
99 Ranch | **Clairemont** — 22
North Park Prod. | **multi.** — 21

SEAFOOD

Bristol Farms | **University City** — 28
Seaside Mkt. | **Cardiff-by-the-Sea** — 27
Catalina Offshore | **Bay Pk** — 25
Valley Farm Mkt. | **Spring Valley** — 25
Jonathan's Mkt. | **La Jolla** — 24
Keil's Food | **multi.** — 24
99 Ranch | **Clairemont** — 22
Lisko Artisan | **City Heights** — 20
Lucky Seafood | **Mira Mesa** — 20
Bo's Seafood Mkt. | **Hillcrest** — 19

SPECIALTY SHOPS

Temecula Olive Oil | **multi.** — 28
World Foods | **City Heights** — 27
Mona Lisa Ital. | **Little Italy** — 27
Mitsuwa Mkpl. | **Kearny Mesa** — 26
Cheese Shop | **La Jolla** — 25
Nijiya Mkt. | **Kearny Mesa** — 25
Seaport Oil/Vinegars | **Marina District** — 25
Grant's Mkpl. | **South Pk** — 24
Zanzibar | **E Vill** — 24
Hot Licks | **multi.** — 24
Otay Farms Mkt. | **Chula Vista** — 24
Baker/Olive | **Del Mar** — 23
Valley Foods | **El Cajon** — 23
Zion Mkt. | **Kearny Mesa** — 23
Assenti's Pasta | **Little Italy** — 23
Marukai | **Kearny Mesa** — 23
We Olive | **La Jolla** — 22
Market/Buon Appetito | **Little Italy** — 22
Shakespeare Corner | **Mission Hills** — 22
El Cajon Int'l | **El Cajon** — 21
All Things Bright/Brit. | **La Mesa** — 21
La Bodega Mkt. | **Chula Vista** — 21
Lisko Artisan | **City Heights** — 20
Balboa Int'l Mkt. | **Clairemont** — 20
Vine Ripe Mkt. | **La Mesa** — 20
Ibis Mkt. | **Mission Hills** — 20
JNC Pinoy | **Chula Vista** — 20
Azteca Mex. | **Mira Mesa** — 19
Andres Latin Mkt. | **Linda Vista** — 19
La Tiendita Mex. | **multi.** — 19
Minh Hoa | **City Heights** — 18
Fiesta Mkt. | **University Hts** — 18
African Caribbean | **City Heights** — 17
Miller's Mkt. | **Golden Hill** — 17
Hing Long Orient. | **City Heights** — 16
Northgate Mkt. | **Rolando** — -

WINES, BEER & LIQUOR

Port Brewing/Lost Abbey | **San Marcos** — 28
Green Flash Brew. | **Mira Mesa** — 26
Ballast Point Brew | **Linda Vista** — 26
Pizza Port Bottle | **Carlsbad** — 26
San Diego Wine Co. | **Miramar** — 26
Holiday Wine | **Escondido** — 26
Stone Co. | **multi.** — 25
Chris' Liquor/Deli | **Ocean Bch** — 25
KnB Wine | **Del Cerro** — 25
Olive Tree Mkpl. | **Ocean Bch** — 25
Alpine Beer Co. | **Alpine** — 24

Share your reviews on plus.google.com/local

Shopping: Food & Wine Locations

Includes names, categories and Quality ratings. These lists include low-vote places that do not qualify for tops lists.

ALPINE
Alpine Beer Co. | *Wine/Beer/Liq.* 24

BARRIO LOGAN
Café Moto | *Coffee/Tea* 24
Panchitas Bakery | *Baked Gds.* 23
Butcher Block Meat | *Meat/Poultry* 22
Café Virtuoso | *Coffee/Tea* 20

BAY PARK
Siesel's Meats | *Meat/Poultry* 28
Catalina Offshore | *Seafood* 25

BONITA
Hans/Harry Bakery | *Baked Gds.* 28

CARDIFF-BY-THE-SEA
Seaside Mkt. | *Maj. Mkt.* 27
V.G. Donut/Bakery | *Baked Gds.* 26

CARMEL MOUNTAIN RANCH
Jimbo's | *Health/Natural* 26

CARMEL VALLEY
Jimbo's | *Health/Natural* 26

CITY HEIGHTS
World Foods | *Spec. Shops* 27
SD Desserts | *Baked Gds.* 26
Panchitas Bakery | *Baked Gds.* 23
Lisko Artisan | *Seafood* 20
Minh Hoa | *Spec. Shops* 18
African Caribbean | *Spec. Shops* 17
Hing Long Orient. | *Spec. Shops* 16

CLAIREMONT
Keil's Food | *Maj. Mkt.* 14
99 Ranch | *Maj. Mkt.* 22
Balboa Int'l Mkt. | *Spec. Shops* 20
Arely French | *Baked Gds.* 19
La Tiendita Mex. | *Spec. Shops* 19

COASTAL TOWNS
Chuao Chocolatier | *Candy/Nuts* 20
Venissimo Cheese | *Cheese/Dairy* 28
Temecula Olive Oil | *Spec. Shops* 28
Nothing Bundt | *Baked Gds.* 27
Harvest Ranch | *Produce* 27
Cupcake Love | *Baked Gds.* 23

Baker/Olive | *Spec. Shops* 23
Dallman Fine Choc. | *Candy/Nuts* 22
2Good2B | *Baked Gds.* 21

CORONADO
Boney's Bayside | *Produce* 25
WineStyles | *Wine/Beer/Liq.* 23

DEL CERRO
Iowa Meat Farms | *Meat/Poultry* 28
Windmill Farms | *Maj. Mkt.* 27
KnB Wine | *Wine/Beer/Liq.* 25

DOWNTOWN
Best Damn Beer | *Wine/Beer/Liq.* 20
Krisp | *Wine/Beer/Liq.* 17

EAST COUNTY
All Things Bright/Brit. | *Spec. Shops* 21
Vine Ripe Mkt. | *Spec. Shops* 20

EAST VILLAGE
Venissimo Cheese | *Cheese/Dairy* 28
Zanzibar | *Spec. Shops* 24
Bacchus Wine Mkt. | *Wine/Beer/Liq.* 19

EL CAJON
Harvest Ranch | *Produce* 27
Valley Foods | *Spec. Shops* 23
El Cajon Int'l | *Spec. Shops* 21

ESCONDIDO
Jimbo's | *Health/Natural* 26

GASLAMP QUARTER
Heaven. Cupcake | *Baked Gds.* 22
Wine Bank | *Wine/Beer/Liq.* 11

GOLDEN HILL
Panchitas Bakery | *Baked Gds.* 23
Miller's Mkt. | *Spec. Shops* 17

GOLDEN TRIANGLE
Chuao Chocolatier | *Candy/Nuts* 28

GRANTVILLE
Farmers Outlet | *Produce* 23

HILLCREST
Uncle Biff's | *Baked Gds.* 26
Bo's Seafood Mkt. | *Seafood* 19

IMPERIAL BEACH

Suzie's Farm | *Produce* 29

KEARNY MESA

Mitsuwa Mkpl. | *Spec. Shops* 26
Nijiya Mkt. | *Spec. Shops* 25
Zion Mkt. | *Spec. Shops* 23
Marukai | *Spec. Shops* 23
Societe Brew. | *Wine/Beer/Liq.* 21

KENSINGTON

Clem's Bottle Hse. | *Wine/Beer/Liq.* 23

LA JOLLA

Cheese Shop | *Cheese/Dairy* 25
Jonathan's Mkt. | *Maj. Mkt.* 24
Cups | *Baked Gds.* 24
Wine Time | *Wine/Beer/Liq.* 23
We Olive | *Spec. Shops* 22

LINDA VISTA

Ballast Point Brew | *Wine/Beer/Liq.* 26
Andres Latin Mkt. | *Spec. Shops* 19
La Tiendita Mex. | *Spec. Shops* 19

LITTLE ITALY

Mona Lisa Ital. | *Spec. Shops* 27
Bottlecraft Beer | *Wine/Beer/Liq.* 23
Assenti's Pasta | *Pastas* 23
Market/Buon Appetito | 22
   Spec. Shops

MARINA DISTRICT

Seaport Oil/Vinegars | *Spec. Shops* 25
Hot Licks | *Spec. Shops* 24
Frosted Robin | *Baked Gds.* 19

MIDDLETOWN

Specialty Produce | *Produce* 24
57 Degrees | *Wine/Beer/Liq.* 18

MIRAMAR

San Diego Wine Co. | 26
   Wine/Beer/Liq.
Vintage Wines | *Wine/Beer/Liq.* 24
AleSmith | *Wine/Beer/Liq.* 23
Hess Brewing | *Wine/Beer/Liq.* 22

MIRA MESA

Green Flash Brew. | *Wine/Beer/Liq.* 26
Edelweiss Bakery | *Baked Gds.* 26
Lucky Seafood | *Seafood* 20
Azteca Mex. | *Spec. Shops* 19

MISSION HILLS

Venissimo Cheese | *Cheese/Dairy* 28
Shakespeare Corner | *Spec. Shops* 22

Cake | *Baked Gds.* 21
Ibis Mkt. | *Spec. Shops* 20

MISSION VALLEY

Nothing Bundt | *Baked Gds.* 27

NORMAL HEIGHTS

Pancho Villa Farmer's Mkt. | 21
   Maj. Mkt.
Bine/Vine Bottle | *Wine/Beer/Liq.* 21
North Park Prod. | *Produce* 21

NORTH COUNTY

Chino Farms | *Produce* 27
Jimbo's | *Health/Natural* 26
Edelweiss Bakery | *Baked Gds.* 26
Pizza Port Bottle | *Wine/Beer/Liq.* 26
Holiday Wine | *Wine/Beer/Liq.* 26
Stone Co. | *Wine/Beer/Liq.* 25
Baron's Mkt. | *Maj. Mkt.* 24
Bernardo Wine. | *Wine/Beer/Liq.* 23
CB's Cupcakes | *Baked Gds.* 21
Batter Up! | *Baked Gds.* 21
Northgate Mkt. | *Maj. Mkt.* –

OCEAN BEACH

Ocean Beach People's Mkt. | 26
   Health/Natural
Chris' Liquor/Deli | *Wine/Beer/Liq.* 25
Olive Tree Mkpl. | *Maj. Mkt.* 25
Azucar | *Baked Gds.* 24
Stump's Family Mktpl. | *Maj. Mkt.* 23
Stephanie's Bakery | *Baked Gds.* 21

OLD TOWN

Temecula Olive Oil | *Spec. Shops* 28
Hot Licks | *Spec. Shops* 24
Old Town Liquor | *Wine/Beer/Liq.* 23

PACIFIC BEACH

Charlie's Best Bread | *Baked Gds.* 25

POINT LOMA

European Cake | *Baked Gds.* 26
Charlie's Best Bread | *Baked Gds.* 25
Cupcakes Squared | *Baked Gds.* 25
Baron's Mkt. | *Maj. Mkt.* 24
Chi Chocolate | *Candy/Nuts* 23

POWAY

Nothing Bundt | *Baked Gds.* 27
Cupcakes/Beyond | *Baked Gds.* 25
North Park Prod. | *Produce* 21

ROLANDO

Northgate Mkt. | *Maj. Mkt.* –

SAN CARLOS

Keil's Food | *Maj. Mkt.* 24

SAN MARCOS

Port Brewing/Lost Abbey | 28
  Wine/Beer/Liq.

CB's Cupcakes | *Baked Gds.* 21

SANTEE

NEW Cupcake Store | *Baked Gds.* 24

SAN YSIDRO

Northgate Mkt. | *Maj. Mkt.* -

SHELTER ISLAND

Elegant Truffle | *Candy/Nuts* 22

Grape Connections | 20
  Wine/Beer/Liq.

SOUTH BAY

My Cup/Tea | *Coffee/Tea* 25

Otay Farms Mkt. | *Spec. Shops* 24

La Bodega Mkt. | *Spec. Shops* 21

JNC Pinoy | *Spec. Shops* 20

Northgate Mkt. | *Maj. Mkt.* -

SOUTHCREST

Northgate Mkt. | *Maj. Mkt.* -

SOUTH PARK

Eclipse Chocolat | *Candy/Nuts* 26

Stone Co. | *Wine/Beer/Liq.* 25

Grant's Mkpl. | *Spec. Shops* 24

SPRING VALLEY

Valley Farm Mkt. | *Maj. Mkt.* 25

UNIVERSITY CITY

Bristol Farms | *Produce* 28

UNIVERSITY HEIGHTS

Twiggs Bakery | *Baked Gds.* 25

Fiesta Mkt. | *Spec. Shops* 18

VISTA

Iron Fist Brew. | *Wine/Beer/Liq.* 24

Northgate Mkt. | *Maj. Mkt.* -

SHOP: FOOD/WINE

LOCATIONS

Shopping: Food & Wine

Ratings & Symbols

Quality, Display & **Service** are rated on a 30-point scale.

Cost reflects our surveyors' estimate of the price range:

⌞I⌟ Inexpensive   ⌞E⌟ Expensive
⌞M⌟ Moderate   ⌞VE⌟ Very Expensive

◗ open until 8:30 PM or later

African Caribbean Foods   *Specialty Shops*   17 | 16 | 16 | M

City Heights | 4811 El Cajon Blvd. (bet. Estrella Ave. & 48th St.) | 619-229-0032

One of the "very few" local places catering to African and Caribbean communities, this small, no-frills ethnic market in City Heights stocks its shelves with hard-to-find spices and condiments, produce, seafood and meats that give shoppers a taste of home; "great prices" and "nice, patient" owners prompt loyalists to vow they'll be "visiting soon."

AleSmith   *Wines, Beer & Liquor*   23 | 19 | 21 | M

Miramar | 9368 Cabot Dr. (bet. Arjons Dr. & Miramar Rd.) | 858-549-9888 | www.alesmith.com

Known for its "to-die-for" handcrafted beers and "insightful" weekly tours by an owner who takes "obvious pride in his passion", this artisanal microbrewery in Miramar is the "perfect place to bring visiting" suds lovers or fill up your growler; the "unassuming" tasting room is always "bustling" and has no seating so "don't get too tipsy" – these "heavy" ales are "not for the novice."

All Things Bright & British ◗   *Specialty Shops*   21 | 18 | 21 | E

La Mesa | 8401 La Mesa Blvd. (4th St.) | 619-464-2298 | www.brightandbritish.com

Get your "Brit fix" at this "tiny, idiosyncratic" store in La Mesa, where Anglophiles scour "crowded" shelves to score "hard-to-find" specialty items "from bangers to Branston pickles" imported from the U.K.; sure it's "slightly pricey" but "much cheaper than airfare" for expats seeking "a taste of home."

Alpine Beer Company   *Wines, Beer & Liquor*   24 | 19 | 22 | M

Alpine | 2351 Alpine Blvd. (bet. Marshall & Ramsey Rds.) | 619-445-2337 | www.alpinebeerco.com

"All fans of hoppy beer" in particular and "top-notch" ales in general "must" visit this "high-quality" craft brewery in Alpine, where enthusiasts fill up growlers, buy branded tees and "sample different brews" amid the "convivial" atmosphere of a "well-worn, comfy" tasting room; "decent" prices and an on-site pub serving "fresh" food make it "worth the drive" from San Diego to "spend a Sunday afternoon."

	QUALITY	DISPLAY	SERVICE	COST

Andres Latin Market *Specialty Shops*   19 | 17 | 19 | M

Linda Vista | 1249 Morena Blvd. (Buenos Ave.) | 619-275-6523
Latin America meets Linda Vista at this "small" but "organized"
Hispanic specialty food shop, where you can get your "Cuban and
Puerto Rican fix", score rare-to–San Diego Peruvian goods and peruse
the large selection of yerba maté; the "exotic" items are "clustered by
country of origin", making it a cinch to find the "right stuff."

Arely French Bakery ❷ *Baked Goods*   19 | 18 | 18 | M

Clairemont | 4961 Clairemont Dr. (Clairemont Mesa Blvd.) |
858-270-1910 | www.arelyfrenchbakery.com
"Buttery" croissants, "sinfully wonderful" desserts and French sandwiches (*oui*, croque monsieur) make this "little" patisserie tucked in
a Clairemont shopping center a "great neighborhood breakfast" and
lunch spot and a "popular" place for picking up "tasty" baked goods
to go; prices are "competitive" and "best of all, no lines!"

Assenti's Pasta ✂ *Pastas*   23 | 20 | 21 | E

Little Italy | 2044 India St. (bet. Grape & Hawthorn Sts.) | 619-239-5117 |
www.assentispasta.com
Like grandma's "home cooking", the "uniquely flavored" fresh pastas,
"excellent" sauces, "great-quality" imported cheeses and other
"*delizioso*" ingredients are "gratifying to the tongue" attest admirers
of this Italian market, a family-owned fixture that "adds to the authentic charm of Little Italy"; the selection is "small but well thought-
out", and the proprietors are "proud of their heritage" and willing "to
share" it with shoppers by offering "spot-on fantastic" suggestions.

Azteca Mexican Market ❷ *Specialty Shops*   19 | 18 | 19 | M

Mira Mesa | Camino Ruiz Plaza | 11277 Camina Ruiz (bet. Capricorn Way &
Zapata Ave.) | 858-547-9930
For a solid selection of goods "representing the Latino culture", head
to this Mira Mesa "go-to", a Mexican market stocking "fresh" meat
and produce, "homemade" salsa, tamales and other south-of-the-
border ingredients that remind patrons "of home"; from pollo asado
to piñatas, affordable items pack the petite space.

Azucar *Baked Goods*   24 | 22 | 22 | M

Ocean Beach | 4820 Newport Ave. (bet. Cable St. & Sunset Cliffs Blvd.) |
619-523-2020 | www.iloveazucar.com
Living up to its sugary name, this Ocean Beach bakery "impresses"
with "gourmet confections" like "to-die-for" scones, "fantastic" cookies, "affordable" wedding cakes and other "treats", plus Cuban sandwiches that are "worth the trip alone"; "friendly" staffers create a
"special" experience so patrons pledge they'd "go back in a heartbeat."

Bacchus Wine Market & Tasting Room ❷ *Wines, Beer & Liquor*   19 | 17 | 17 | E

East Village | 647 G St. (bet. 6th & 7th Aves.) | 619-236-0005 |
www.bacchuswinemarket.com
"Tucked away" in the East Village, this "intimate" wine shop and
tasting room feels like a "private" cellar thanks to its below-ground

location and crates of vino lining the brick-and-burgundy-walled space; "simple" food "complements" a "wide selection" of varietals and "knowledgeable" servers oversee tastings; P.S: several local restaurants will waive corkage fees on Bacchus-bought bottles.

Baker & Olive *Specialty Shops* | 23 | 22 | 21 | E |

Encinitas | 165 S. El Camino Real (bet. Crest Dr. & Encinitas Blvd.) | 760-944-7840

NEW Baker & Olive *Specialty Shops*

Del Mar | Del Mar Highlands Town Ctr. | 12925 El Camino Real (bet. Del Mar Heights Rd. & Townsgate Dr.) | 858-350-1300 | www.bakerandolive.com

"Delicious" infused vinegars and oils that "rival the best Napa Valley has to offer" bring "happy" customers to these Del Mar and Encinitas specialty shops; you could spend "days in here" sampling the "pricey" selection (if you think EVOO isn't worth the dough, "boy are you wrong") and perusing cheeses, olives and fresh breads, plus "well-trained" staffers offer tastings and "give suggestions on pairings."

Balboa International Market ● *Specialty Shops* | 20 | 17 | 17 | M |

Clairemont | Balboa Mesa Shopping Ctr. | 5907 Balboa Ave. (Mt. Alifan Dr.) | 858-277-3600 | www.balboamarket.com

Recreate "any style of cooking" from almost "any country" in the Middle East and beyond at this "well-stocked" Clairemont market, where an "expansive" selection of Persian, Arabic, Mediterranean and Eastern European products is on offer at "reasonable prices"; many of the "international" items can't be found elsewhere, and expats attest that prepared specialties like "delicious kebabs" make them "feel at home."

Ballast Point Brewery *Wines, Beer & Liquor* | 26 | 22 | 24 | M |

Linda Vista | Presidio Pl. | 5401 Linda Vista Rd. (Riley St.) | 619-295-2337 | www.ballastpoint.com

In a town known for its craft beer, this Linda Vista microbrewery is lauded as one of the "best"; hops lovers gladly endure "outrageous" lines to "fill up growlers" and sample "unique", "reasonably" priced suds like the "spectacular" Sculpin IPA, dispensed by "friendly" servers; the tasting room "could use a few couches" and growing "popularity" means it's often "crowded", nevertheless it's a "must" for "novices" and connoisseurs alike.

Baron's Market *Major Market* | 24 | 22 | 22 | M |

Rancho Bernardo | 11828 Rancho Bernardo Rd. (Bernardo Center Dr.) | 858-485-8686

Point Loma | 4001 W. Point Loma Blvd. (Groton St.) | 619-223-4397 ● | www.baronsmarket.com

"Things you can't find other places" line the shelves at these "well-conceived" markets in Point Loma and Rancho Bernardo, where "fresh" local produce, "high-quality" specialty meats, "healthy" snacks, "nice" bulk goods and "the best IPA selection" around come at prices more "reasonable" than similar stores; salespeople are "quick" at the check-out and offer "personal" service when "helping you find what you're looking for."

Batter Up! Cupcakes *Baked Goods*   21 | 20 | 22 | E

Rancho Bernardo | Plaza at Rancho Bernardo | 16769 Bernardo Center Dr. (Lomica Dr.) | 858-676-2253 | www.batterupcupcakes.com

"Fresh, moist, not extremely sweet" cupcakes draw fans to this friendly Rancho Bernardo bakery, where "perfectly sized", "super-cute" bites in flavors like s'mores and caramel apple pie (plus vegan options) make the ideal dessert or party favor; a handful feels the treats are small "for what you spend" but most just keep "coming back for more"; P.S "go early to get the best selection."

Bernardo Winery *Wines, Beer & Liquor*   23 | 23 | 23 | M

Rancho Bernardo | 13330 Paseo Del Verano Norte (Cumana Terr.) | 858-487-1866 | www.bernardowinery.com

"Tucked away" in the Rancho Bernardo countryside, this "quaint" circa-1889 winery offers "delicious" samples and chocolate pairings for a "small fee" in a "relaxing" tasting room plus "delightful" shops stocked with "gourmet options" galore and "interesting" knickknacks; the "picturesque" grounds hold "blooming plants" and "rustic" buildings, and the Friday farmer's market is among "the best locally."

Best Damn Beer Shop ☻ *Wines, Beer & Liquor*   20 | 18 | 18 | M

Downtown | Super Jr. Market | 1036 Seventh Ave. (bet. B'way & C St.) | 619-232-6367

The name says it all at this Downtown beer emporium inside Krisp natural foods market that's "great to have in the area" thanks to its "unbelievable" selection of "fantastic" brews from San Diego County and around the globe; hard-core hops lovers also appreciate the staffers' "great knowledge" and can even shop for home brew supplies.

Bine & Vine
Bottle Shop ☻ *Wines, Beer & Liquor*   21 | 18 | 20 | E

Normal Heights | 3334 Adams Ave. (bet. Felton & 33rd Sts.) | 619-795-2463 | www.bineandvine.com

"Very focused" on craft beer, this "great addition" to Normal Heights stocks an "amazing" array of suds from local and international breweries, plus a "growing selection" of handpicked wines, ciders, sakes and "mead – yes, mead!"; also worthy of a toast: "knowledgeable, helpful" purveyors who are "honest" enough to steer customers away from "skunky" bottles.

Boney's Bayside
Market ☻ *Health & Natural Foods*   25 | 22 | 24 | M

Coronado | 155 Orange Ave. (bet. 1st & 2nd Sts.) | 619-435-0776 | www.baysidemarket.com

A "plethora" of "fresh-off-the-farm" produce, "much of it local", is a "true feast for the eyes" proclaim loyalists who also tout the "wide range" of "amazing healthy foods", deli items and "exceptional-quality" meat and fish at this "upscale market without upscale prices" in Coronado; the environs are "nice and comfortable" and the goods are rung up at the "efficient check-out" by "friendly" staffers.

QUALITY · DISPLAY · SERVICE · COST

Bo's Seafood Market *Seafood*
19 | 16 | 19 | E

Hillcrest | 1040 University Ave. (bet. 10th Ave. & Vermont St.) | 619-574-2800 | www.bosseafoodmarketandgrill.com

Head to this Hillcrest market for a "nice choice" of "super-fresh" seafood caught by local fishermen or go for a "delicious" bite of grilled fish tacos or albacore sandwiches with "tasty" San Diego beers to "pull the whole meal together"; it can be "a little pricey", but it's a "thoroughly satisfying experience" and heck, "you get what you pay for."

Bottlecraft
Beer Shop ❶ *Wines, Beer & Liquor*
23 | 22 | 22 | E

Little Italy | 2161 India St. (bet. Hawthorn & Ivy Sts.) | 619-487-9493 | www.bottlecraftbeer.com

"What an awesome concept" cheer fans of this "unique" Little Italy brew shop where "knowledgeable" staffers tend rows of beer from San Diego and the world over; suds fans can wrap up purchases or sit and drink in the wood-lined tasting room while "mixing and mingling" with others; adding to the "cool" experience: art shows and parties.

Bristol Farms ❶ *Major Market*
28 | 27 | 24 | E

University City | 8510 Genesee Ave. (bet. La Jolla Village & Nobel Drs.) | 858-558-4180 | www.bristolfarms.com

"Premium" products are the norm at this "pricey" UTC market, a SoCal-born chain link that earns Top Display honors among San Diego's food shops; customers are "dazzled" by "excellent" produce, "can't-be-beat" seafood, "the best" in-store butcher and "unique" specialty items you "can't find elsewhere", all overseen by "polite" staffers; but while most agree it's a "worthwhile splurge", it's "not a weekly grocery shopping" stop – unless you're part of the "upper-crust set."

Butcher Block
Meat Market *Meat & Poultry*
22 | 20 | 21 | E

Barrio Logan | 2670 National Ave. (26th St.) | 619-232-9960

Those seeking the "best cuts" of "amazing" beef, pork and poultry "return over and over" to this Barrio Logan butcher; though "a bit pricey" tabs may be "more expensive than supermarkets", consensus says it's "well worth it" for "great"-quality product and a "friendly" staff.

Café Moto *Coffee & Tea*
24 | 23 | 24 | E

Barrio Logan | 2619 National Ave. (bet. 26th & 27th Sts.) | 619-239-6686 | www.cafemoto.com

"True coffee lovers" are "hooked" on this caffeine "heaven" in Barrio Logan, where a "huge variety" of "world-class" beans, teas and sweets is sold by "cheerful" staffers who give "expert advice"; a "funky" setting of reclaimed wood and graphic art makes it feel like a "modern brewery", and the "people-watching" may be better than the brew.

Café Virtuoso *Coffee & Tea*
20 | 20 | 20 | M

Barrio Logan | 1616 National Ave. (bet. Sigsbee & 16th Sts.) | 619-550-1830 | www.cafevirtuoso.com

"Watch them roast the beans as you sip" at this "hole-in-the-wall" coffee shop in Barrio Logan, where "top-quality" java and "very

QUALITY　DISPLAY　SERVICE　COST

fresh" teas easily "convert" passersby into regulars and bagels and muffins provide carb sustenance; the "friendly" staffers "believe in their product", in fact, they're "thrilled to share samples" of their fair trade and organic beverages.

Cake *Baked Goods* `21` `21` `21` `M`

Mission Hills | 3085 Reynard Way (Eagle St.) | 619-295-2253 | www.fabcakes.com

The "cute, creative, unique" cakes from this Mission Hills bakery are ideal "for your special day", be it a wedding, birthday or baby shower – in fact, the "positively delicious" confections can be tailored to any theme; adding to the appeal are solid staffers, "fair" prices and a seasonal cafe (open October–May) that satisfies sugar cravings with brownies, cupcakes and tarts.

Catalina Offshore Products *Seafood* `25` `18` `22` `M`

Bay Park | 5205 Lovelock St. (Sherman St.) | 619-704-3639 | www.catalinaop.com

"Sustainable", "fresh" and "local" describes this well-respected Bay Park seafood market, where San Diego's top chefs come for "absolutely the freshest fish anywhere" at "prices that can't be beat"; started by a professional sea urchin diver, the store employs third-generation fishmongers that greet regulars with "a hug" and visiting chefs that offer "wonderful" bites.

CB's Cupcakes *Baked Goods* `21` `22` `22` `E`

Carlsbad | 5620 Paseo del Norte (bet. Car Country Dr. & Palomar Airport Rd.) | 760-431-1003 ◗
San Marcos | 137 Las Posas Rd. (Grand Ave.) | 760-736-8000
www.cbscupcakes.com

"Unique, delicious" cupcakes come in "all sizes, cake choices, icing flavors and toppings" at these Carlsbad–San Marcos bakeries, where sweet tooths can buy singles or "purchase a bunch" for an event or party; tabs may be "a little expensive" but most don't mind given the solid service and "quality" product.

Charlie's Best Bread *Baked Goods* `25` `20` `21` `M`

Pacific Beach | 1808 Garnet Ave. (bet. Jewell & Lamont Sts.) | 858-272-3521
Point Loma | 1110 Rosecrans St. (Cañon St.) | 619-487-0227
www.charliesbestbread.com

They "bake love right into their bread" at this "friendly" Pacific Beach bakery (with a cafe sibling in Point Loma), where the "wonderful" selection of "superb" organic loaves both sweet and savory is considered some of the "best in San Diego"; "generous samples" slathered in butter and reasonable prices are other endearments.

Cheese Shop *Cheese & Dairy* `25` `21` `23` `M`

La Jolla | 2165 Avenida de la Playa (bet. Calle De La Plata & El Paseo Grande) | 858-459-3921 | www.cheeseshoplajolla.com

"You could easily walk right by" this "small" La Jolla Shores specialty shop, but you'd be missing out on the "excellent" selection of goudas, stiltons, raclettes and other "wonderful" fromages, plus "freshly made" sandwiches, "disco-era" candies, "handcrafted" beverages and other "unique" treats offered at reasonable rates; the "helpful" counter staff is one more reason this "old-time" (since 1972) purveyor remains a local standby.

Chi Chocolate *Candy & Nuts* | 23 22 22 E

Point Loma | 2690 Historic Decatur Rd. (Dewey Rd.) | 619-546-0650 | www.chichocolat.net

Just a "small bite" of the "decadent" chocolate at this "quiet, quaint" shop in Point Loma's Liberty Station will "satisfy" your sweet tooth; the "pricey-but-delicious" offerings include "liquid-gold" hot cocoa and "amazing" flavors of truffles, bars, pastries and dipped fruits, all proffered by staffers who demonstrate "willingness to please."

Chino Farms *Produce* | 27 22 21 E

Rancho Santa Fe | 6123 Calzada del Bosque (bet. Hwy. S6 & Via De Santa Fe) | 858-756-3184

"When only the best, most perfect produce will do", this "ultimate roadside farm stand" in Rancho Santa Fe is a "true treasure", drawing "celebrity chefs" and "the public" alike for its seasonal fruits, veggies and herbs (both the "staples" and "new favorites"); while "prices are on the high end", devotees insist "you can't get fresher or higher quality anywhere."

Chris' Liquor & Deli ☻ *Wines, Beer & Liquor* | 25 21 24 M

Ocean Beach | 2275 Sunset Cliffs Blvd. (Point Loma Blvd.) | 619-222-0518 | www.chrisliquor.com

"In business a very long time", this circa-1956 Ocean Beach deli and liquor store owes its longevity to "great" sandwiches, "always cold" drinks and hundreds of craft beers from breweries local and international, making it the place to score items "not carried in a regular market"; adding to the appeal, prices are affordable and an "excellent" staff makes sure your stop is "quick."

Chuao Chocolatier *Candy & Nuts* | 28 27 26 VE

Del Mar | Del Mar Highlands Shopping Ctr. | 3485 Del Mar Heights Rd. (bet. Carmel Country Rd. & El Camino Real) | 858-755-0770
Encinitas | 937 S. Coast Hwy. 101 (bet. H & I Sts.) | 760-635-1444
Golden Triangle | Westfield University Towne Ctr. | 4465 La Jolla Village Dr. (bet. Genessee Ave. & Towne Centre Dr.) | 858-546-1463 ☻
www.chuaochocolatier.com

"A temple for those who worship chocolate", this "delightful, decadent" chocolatier trio "will impress anyone" with its "subtle but luxurious" bonbons, bars and cocoas in "exotic" flavors like rosemary salt caramel and spiced Napa Valley Cabernet; it's a "second-to-none" shopping experience, and though a visit may leave your wallet "a little lighter, your stomach will thank you."

Clem's Bottle House ☻ *Wines, Beer & Liquor* | 23 22 21 M

Kensington | 4100 Adams Ave. (Kensington Dr.) | 619-284-2485 | www.clemsbottlehouse.com

You'll find a "fantastic" variety of wine and liquor at this "Kensington classic", plus a "tremendous" craft brew selection (they "keep the new beers coming") and a "recently opened" taproom next door that offers IPA flights and flat-screen TVs; it's "never a problem to get recommendations" from the staff, and "great" sandwiches complement the beverages.

Cupcake Love *Baked Goods*
| 23 | 24 | 24 | E |

Solana Beach | Beachwalk Shopping Ctr. | 437 S. Hwy. 101 (bet. Border Ave. & Dahlia Dr.) | 858-755-5506 | www.cupcake-love.com

"Appealing" displays "tickle your interest through the window" at this "quaint, cute" Solana Beach cupcakery, and "very moist, not too sweet, just right" confections in "plentiful" flavors "delight the palate" inside the rose-colored quarters; some say the goods are "expensive for what you get" but "professional" staffers that are "great with last minute requests" help justify tabs.

Cupcakes & Beyond *Baked Goods*
| 25 | 22 | 24 | E |

Poway | 14791 Pomerado Rd. (Ted Williams Pkwy.) | 760-755-9998 | www.cupcakesnbeyond.com

"Just thinking about" the confections at this Poway cupcakery may be enough to "raise your blood sugar and make your mouth water" – the "delectable" desserts come in varieties like cookie dough and limoncello, and the frosting decorations are just as "commendable" as the flavors; some say "they charge a lot for a little cupcake" but others will happily pay the price for the "yummy", from-scratch sweets.

Cupcakes Squared *Baked Goods*
| 25 | 24 | 25 | E |

Point Loma | 3772 Voltaire St. (Worden St.) | 619-226-3485 | www.cupcakesquared.com

A "vast" array of "delicious", "unusual" flavors means "there's nothing square" about the cupcakes ("except the shape" of course) at this Point Loma bakery say fans cheering the "well-presented", "moist" treats and their "crispy edges"; it also sells gluten-free options and a variety of bars, and since "customer service is also a plus", it's easier to overlook tabs considered a "bit expensive."

NEW Cupcake Store *Baked Goods*
| 24 | 23 | 24 | E |

Santee | 9225 Carlton Hills Blvd. (Carlton Oaks Dr.) | 619-749-7777

"So many different varieties" of "moist, tasty" cupcakes, from German chocolate to bacon-topped "mancakes", "get those taste buds smacking" at this "well-priced" Santee bakery, and it's also "worth the drive" for the vegan, gluten-free and sugar-free options; "awesome" service and an "elegant" space add more reasons why it "rocks."

Cups ◑ *Baked Goods*
| 24 | 22 | 21 | E |

La Jolla | 7857 Girard Ave. (bet. Silverado & Wall Sts.) | 858-459-2877 | www.cupslj.com

"All organic" is the mantra at this La Jolla Village bakery, where the "well-done" cupcakes come in "surprising" flavors, the sugar-free options would pass a "blind taste test" and patrons can wash down their desserts with strawberry milk on tap; it may be "pricey", but with a "cute" lounge area and full-scale teaching kitchen – and "delicious" offerings, of course – it can be a "once-in-a-lifetime experience."

QUALITY | DISPLAY | SERVICE | COST

Dallman Fine Chocolates *Candy & Nuts*   22 | 21 | 22 | E

Del Mar | 2760 Via De La Valle (San Andres Dr.) | 858-720-1933 |
www.dallmannconfections.com

"Chocoholics are made" at this Del Mar shop in the Flower Hill Mall,
where the "incredible" selection includes "deliciously different"
truffles, bars and Austrian specialties that reflect its heritage (the
first was opened in Austria in 1954); the confections are handmade
by the original proprietor's granddaughter, and though pricey, fans
gush they're "worth their weight in gold."

Eclipse Chocolat ● *Candy & Nuts*   26 | 24 | 24 | E

South Park | 2145 Fern St. (Ivy St.) | 619-578-2984 |
www.eclipsechocolate.com

"Addicts of chocolate" may get a "well-earned tummy ache"
from overindulging in the "divine" truffles, bars and caramels in
"creative, delectable" flavors at this recently relocated South Park
shop, which now includes a full restaurant and craft beer bar; "spectacular" sweet-centric brunches and tasting dinner parties offer
more opportunities to "spoil yourself", while "personal" service further helps justify "pricey" tabs.

Edelweiss European   26 | 22 | 24 | E
Bakery *Baked Goods*

Mira Mesa | Mira Mesa Mall | 8270 Mira Mesa Blvd. (Camino Ruiz) |
858-578-6777
Rancho Bernardo | 11639 Duenda Rd. (Bernardo Dr.) | 858-487-4338
www.edelweissbakerysandiego.com

"They believe in butter" at this "European-style" Mira Mesa and
Rancho Bernardo bakery, where the "out-of-this-world" sweets are
"delicious", especially the "moist, delicate" cakes; staffers are
"helpful", and while tabs can be "expensive", "satisfied" fans say it's
"worth every penny."

El Cajon International   21 | 19 | 21 | M
Foods ● *Specialty Shops*

El Cajon | 502 E. Main St. (bet. Ballantyne St. & Roanoke Rd.) |
619-444-5800

"Unusual items, flavors and smells" bring patrons to this El Cajon market specializing in Middle Eastern foods, where "priced-right" items
appease adventurous eaters or expats seeking a taste of home; the atmosphere may not be up "to par" with the offerings but staffers who
go "out of their way to help" still make it "fun to explore."

Elegant Truffle *Candy & Nuts*   ∇ 22 | 20 | 20 | E

Shelter Island | 1111 Scott St. (bet. Avenida De Portugal & Canon St.) |
619-222-1889 | www.trufflemaker.com

"Hands-on" proprietor Jennifer Muratore "hails from a long line of
candy makers" and uses "handwritten recipes" to create "to-die-
for" "handmade" truffles, "decadent" brownies and "signature"
cakes at this Shelter Island chocolatier; smitten sweet tooths also
give service solid marks, and say while it's "a bit pricey", it's "worth
every sinful bite."

QUALITY DISPLAY SERVICE COST

European Cake Gallery ⇴ Baked Goods | 26 | 22 | 23 | E |

Point Loma | 3661 Voltaire St. (Chatsworth Blvd.) | 619-222-3377 |
www.europeancakegallery.com

"Calories be damned" cheer patrons at this Point Loma sweet shop,
where "moist, fluffy" "special-occasion" cakes are "beautiful and
taste excellent"; staffers are "accommodating" in the somewhat
"hole-in-the-wall" digs, and while prices are "high" (cash-only),
given the "quality" many "would go back in a heartbeat."

Farmers Outlet Produce | 23 | 19 | 19 | M |

Grantville | 10407 Friars Rd. (Riverdale St.) | 619-563-9165

You can "support your local farmers" at this Grantville market, where
"basic displays" of "locally grown" fruits, veggies and herbs will
"tantalize your senses" and a selection of candies, nuts, dried fruit
and regionally famous Julian pies ups its status as a "real gem"; make
sure to take advantage of the "friendly" service and "reasonable"
prices before the 6 PM closing time.

Fiesta Market Specialty Shops | 18 | 18 | 20 | M |

University Heights | 3015 Adams Ave. (bet. Ohio & 30th Sts.) |
619-284-5142

Though it specializes in Mexican staples like carne asada and
housemade salsa, this "convenient" University Heights grocery also
offers a "great market selection", including an aisle devoted to craft
beer; it's "not expensive" and locals say salespeople "seem to actually care", which can be "rare nowadays."

57 Degrees ◑ Wines, Beer & Liquor | 18 | 18 | 17 | E |

Middletown | 1735 Hancock St. (Washington St.) | 619-234-5757 |
www.fiftysevendegrees.com

"Not only a retail wine" and beer shop but also an "artsy" tasting bar
with a "small" menu, this "spacious" Middletown venue provides an
"excellent selection" of large-format bottles and small-producer selections in "attractive displays"; "knowledgeable, warm" staffers
tend to patrons, and if a few whine that the nibbles are "tasty" but
"overpriced", most agree it's a "a fun place to go with friends", especially for weekly events.

Frosted Robin Cupcakes ◑ Baked Goods V | 19 | 19 | 20 | E |

Marina District | 859 W. Harbor Dr. (Pacific Hwy.) | 619-702-7188 |
www.frostedrobincupcakes.com

"Once you see them you can't resist" say fans of the cupcakes at this
"pricey" Marina District dessert shop, where confections are complemented by organic coffee and artisan tea, and employees offer
"personal recommendations based on your specific occasion"; like
the sweets themselves, the space is "colorfully painted", reflecting
the owner's Cayman Island roots.

Grant's Marketplace ◑ Specialty Shops ▽ | 24 | 21 | 21 | E |

South Park | 2953 Beech St. (Dale St.) | 619-231-0524

"Everything the average superstore is not" attest admirers of this
"quaint" South Park market that's stocked with "personality" aplenty,

not to mention craft beverages, "lots of organic options" and "some of the best sandwiches", all at prices that fans find "expensive" but "worth paying"; "friendly" clerks "seem to like working there" as much as guests like "dining, meeting, browsing and mingling."

Grape Connections *Wines, Beer & Liquor* ▽ 20 | 17 | 20 | E

Shelter Island | 1130 Scott St. (bet. Avenida De Portugal & Canon St.) | 619-523-6441 | www.grapeconnections.com

Specializing in vino from "small, boutique vineyards", this Shelter Island bottle shop stocks some "outstanding wines not available at the larger retailers" and prices them "competitively"; the owner "knows customer service" and enthusiasts say he "never fails to produce a gem" when asked for recommendations.

Green Flash Brewing Company ◗ *Wines, Beer & Liquor* 26 | 21 | 24 | M

Mira Mesa | 6550 Mira Mesa Blvd. (bet. Flanders & Genetic Center Drs.) | 858-622-0085 | www.greenflashbrew.com

"Incredible" ales will "awaken any true beer lover's taste buds" tout talliers "highly recommending" this "reasonably priced" Mira Mesa brew "haven"; the "smell of hops permeates every inch" of the "open" "warehouse"-like setting, and with "prompt" service, it's one of the "perfect places to grab a pint" or fill a growler.

Hans & Harry Bakery *Baked Goods* 28 | 25 | 26 | M

Bonita | 5080 Bonita Rd. (Central Ave.) | 619-475-2253 | www.hans-harry.com

"You can't go wrong" with the "sublime pastries", "unbeatable" cakes, "famous fruit strudels" and other "world-class" sweets made with the "freshest ingredients" and doled out by "friendly" staffers at this Bonita bakery; Holland-born owners lend a "distinctive European quality", and high-ish prices are "fair" since it's all "delicious."

Harvest Ranch Market *Major Market* 27 | 25 | 24 | E

Del Mar | 1555 Camino Del Mar (15th St.) | 858-847-0555 ◗
Encinitas | 162 Rancho Sante Fe Rd. (Los Morros) | 760-944-6898
El Cajon | 759 Jamacha Rd. (bet. Granite Hills Dr. & Washington Ave.) | 619-442-0355
www.harvestranchmarkets.com

"High-quality" "gourmet" goods, like "prime meats", "top-notch" wines and "just-harvested" produce, define this "upscale" trio; true, tabs are priced for those "with money to burn", but devotees swear the "helpful" service and "organized" aisles create a "shopping experience that compensates for the extra expense."

Heavenly Cupcake ◗ *Baked Goods* 22 | 22 | 22 | E

Gaslamp Quarter | 518 Sixth Ave. (Island Ave.) | 619-235-9235 | www.heavenlycupcake.com

"Sweet tooths" get a "pick-me-up" at this "heavenly" Gaslamp cupcakery where "moist, decadent" treats come in "interesting flavors" and are handed out by a mostly "helpful" crew, though a few grumble about "snippy" service; while nitpickers find certain offerings just "so-so", more declare them "worth every penny and calorie."

QUALITY | DISPLAY | SERVICE | COST

Hess Brewing *Wines, Beer & Liquor* | 22 | 18 | 21 | M |

Miramar | 7995 Silverton Ave. (bet. Dowdy Dr. & Trade Pl.) |
619-786-4377 | www.hessbrewing.com

Hopsheads "love" this "tiny" Miramar "nano brewery" where the focus
is on small-batch brewing; given the size of the kegs, certain taps
"run out fast", but it's "not expensive" and the "delicious" beer is the
ultimate "prize", P.S. a North Park location is in the works.

Hing Long Oriental Food Market *Specialty Shops* | ∇ 16 | 17 | 16 | M |

City Heights | 4644 El Cajon Blvd. (Menlo Ave.) | 619-563-9986

A decent "alternative" to other Asian markets, this "small" City
Heights spot has all the staples and carries a "decent" selection of
vegetarian options and "always in stock" specialty beverages; prices
are fair and cashiers make check-outs "quick and easy", helping guests
overlook the "tight" parking situation and less-than-pristine setting.

Holiday Wine Cellar *Wines, Beer & Liquor* | 26 | 22 | 24 | E |

Escondido | 302 W. Mission Ave. (Escondido Blvd.) | 760-745-1200 |
www.holidaywinecellar.com

"Around for decades" this Escondido bottle shop is "the place to go
if you know wine" say fans who cite "knowledgeable" service and an
"excellent" selection that includes "rare" vintages and other booze
("anything alcoholic"); though it can be pricey, it does stock some
vinos to "fit all price ranges."

Hot Licks *Specialty Shops* | 24 | 25 | 23 | E |

Marina District | Seaport Village Shopping Ctr. | 865 W. Harbor Dr.
(Pacific Hwy.) | 619-235-4000 ◖
Old Town | 2754 Calhoun St. (Juan St.) | 619-293-3111
www.2hotlicks.com

Prepare to get "fired up" at these somewhat spendy Seaport Village
and Old Town specialty shops that "have it covered" when it comes
to "spicy foods", like sauces, salsas and seasonings in "every level of
hotness you can imagine"; staffers are on hand to dole out samples,
just be careful as "the only thing they don't have is a fire extinguisher
for your mouth."

Ibis Market *Specialty Shops* | 20 | 15 | 21 | M |

Mission Hills | 1112 Ft. Stockton Dr. (Ibis St.) | 619-298-5081

"Delicious", "filling" sandwiches are a standout at this Mission Hills
market, a "local favorite" where you can also find an "eclectic" selection of goods from beers and craft sodas to "quality meats", making it "perfect" when you need to "grab a hostess gift"; a "courteous"
staff and moderate prices also work in its favor.

Iowa Meat Farms *Meat & Poultry* | 28 | 24 | 26 | E |

Del Cerro | 6041 Mission Gorge Rd. (bet. Mission Gorge Pl. &
Twain Ave.) | 619-281-5766 | www.iowameatfarms.com

"Carnivorous gourmets" in search of "melt-in-your-mouth" steaks,
"top-notch" ribs and some "exotic" proteins (kangaroo, pheasant,
alligator) find "it all" at this "old-fashioned butcher" in Del Cerro,

where devotees say meat "so fresh it may bite you" is "worth the extra expense"; "honest" staffers will "help you select and give you tips for cooking", and since it also sells an "interesting variety of non-meat items", you may find yourself "leaving with an armload of goodies."

Iron Fist Brewing
Company *Wines, Beer & Liquor*

24 | 20 | 22 | M

Vista | 1305 Hot Spring Way (Sycamore Ave.) | 760-216-6500 | www.ironfistbrewing.com

Located "a bit off the beaten path", this midpriced Vista microbrewery is a "cozy place to hang out", with solid staffers pouring from an "excellent selection" of "tasty" craft brews in an "open warehouse" setting "surrounded by beer barrels"; the "strong" sips "aren't made for the occasional drinker", so consider supplementing the suds with bites from the food trucks often parked out front.

Jimbo's Naturally ● *Health & Natural Foods*

26 | 24 | 24 | M

Carmel Mountain Ranch | 10511 4S Commons Dr.
(bet. Camino del Norte & Rancho Bernardo Rd.) | 858-432-7755
Carmel Valley | 12853 El Camino Real (Townsgate Dr.) | 858-793-7755
Carlsbad | 1923 Calle Barcelona (Leucadia Blvd.) | 760-334-7755
Escondido | 1633 S. Centre City Pkwy. (Felicita Rd.) | 760-489-7755
www.jimbos.com

"Healthy, organic, sustainable" is the mantra at this "natural foods" market mini-chain, selling an "excellent selection" of "thoughtfully purchased" "top-quality" products; "friendly" staffers are "willing to help" and prices are moderate.

JNC Pinoy Food Mart *Specialty Shops*

20 | 17 | 19 | M

Chula Vista | 943 Otay Lakes Rd. (Gotham St.) | 619-421-1090

"Get your *pancit*, *lumpia* and *siopao* on" at this "affordable" Filipino market and eatery in Chula Vista, which stocks these regional foods along with other "delicious" Southeast Asian staples; "friendly" staffers serve the neighborhood well at this "great little establishment", and guests can order platters to eat in or take to go.

Jonathan's Market ● *Major Market*

24 | 22 | 22 | E

La Jolla | 7611 Fay Ave. (bet. Kline & Pearl Sts.) | 858-459-2677 | www.harvestranchmarkets.com

"If you're looking for something exotic" or "hard-to-find", this "La Jolla institution" "either has it or can get it" say loyalists also praising the "quality meats, cheese, wine" and other "specialty items"; the staff gets solid marks, especially butchers who "know their business", and while it's a "little more expensive than the chains", many consider it "worth it."

Keil's Food Store *Major Market*

24 | 22 | 23 | E

Clairemont | Clairemont Vill. | 3015 Clairemont Dr. (bet. Burgener Blvd. & Iroquois Ave.) | 619-275-7060 ●
San Carlos | 7403 Jackson Dr. (Hyde Park Dr.) | 619-667-2750
www.keils.com

"A hometown market with a hometown feeling", this independent Clairemont grocery (with a San Carlos twin) lures "locals" with a "large variety" of "well-displayed" goods and an "excellent deli" in a space that's "small enough to not be overwhelming"; staffers are "personable", and though it's "more expensive" than what some may be used to, fans say "it's worth a few extra bucks" given the "quality."

KnB Wine Cellars ◑ *Wines, Beer & Liquor* | 25 | 23 | 21 | M |

Del Cerro | 6380 Del Cerro Blvd. (bet. College & Madra Aves.) | 619-286-0321 | www.knbwinecellars.com

You can "discover new favorites" at this "reasonably priced" Del Cerro emporium where "shelves reaching up to the ceiling" are "stocked full" of "hard-to-find" wines, "high-end" spirits and a "great selection" of craft beers; "knowledgeable" staffers can help "if you're looking for a particular bottle", and you can "hang out with friends and neighbors" at the attached eatery.

Krisp Beverages & Natural Foods ◑ *Health & Natural Foods* | ▽ 17 | 15 | 17 | M |

Downtown | Super Jr. Market | 1036 Seventh Ave. (bet. B'way & C St.) | 619-232-6367 | www.krispsd.com

"Good deals" on grass-fed beef, organic produce, local seafood and more bring locals to this "small" Downtown market; "office workers" in search of deli sandwiches keep it "crowded" at lunch, while hopsheads appreciate the "fantastic selection of beers."

La Bodega Market ◑ *Specialty Shops* | 21 | 17 | 19 | E |

Chula Vista | 1193 Broadway (Oxford St.) | 619-476-0900 | www.labodegamarket.com

"All the authentic spices, fruits and veggies" you desire plus meats and some "hard-to-find" items too help make this "nothing-fancy" Chula Vista market a "one-stop shop" for any Mexican-cooking needs; fans also applaud the prepared items and "cheap" prices.

La Tiendita Mexican Market *Specialty Shops* | 19 | 16 | 19 | I |

Clairemont | 3851 Clairemont Mesa Blvd. (Onondaga Ave.) | 858-270-2221 ◑

Linda Vista | 2187 Ulrich St. (Clairemont Mesa Blvd.) | 858-999-3802

www.latienditamexicanmarketsd.com

Known for prepared foods like pollo asada and "to-die-for" tacos, this "authentic" Mexican market in Clairemont (with a Linda Vista sib) also stocks a "good selection" of produce, spices and other grocery items; the space is "small", but prices are "cheap" and the employees "friendly."

Lisko Artisan Deli & Fish Market *Seafood* | ▽ 20 | 18 | 20 | E |

City Heights | 6548 El Cajon Blvd. (Rolando Ct.) | 619-252-7687 | www.liskoartisandeliandfishmarket.com

"Fish delivered daily" is one of the draws at this City Heights deli and seafood market, where shoppers can also stock up on a number of gourmet items, including some of "the best pestos and hummus"; "knowledgeable" staffers are "willing to help", and prices are predictably higher than at big chains.

QUALITY | DISPLAY | SERVICE | COST

Lucky Seafood Super Market *Seafood*   20 | 17 | 16 | M

Mira Mesa | Mira Mesa Sq. | 9326 Mira Mesa Blvd.
(bet. Black Mountain Rd. & Westview Pkwy.) | 858-586-7979

An "incredible variety" of items fill this "big" Mira Mesa Asian market, where regulars say wandering through aisles stocked with "still-jumping" fish, meats, produce, spices and other groceries "you can't just get anywhere" feels like a "cultural experience"; it also offers prepared foods like banh mi and pho, and though it can be "difficult to find help", "reasonable" prices win the day.

Market by Buon Appetito ● *Specialty Shops*   ∇ 22 | 20 | 20 | E

Little Italy | 1605 India St. (bet. Cedar & Date Sts.) | 619-237-1335 | www.marketbyba.com

You can "pick up a few things for dinner" or stock up on a "nice selection" of "quality Italian goodies", like pastas, canned goods and more at this "tiny" Little Italy market, where the prepared foods come from the adjacent sister restaurant, Buon Appetito; "you may pay a little extra", but that's to be expected.

Marukai ● *Specialty Shops*   23 | 20 | 20 | M

Kearny Mesa | 8151 Balboa Ave. (Mercury St.) | 858-384-0248 | www.marukai.com

"All things Nippon" line the aisles at this Kearny Mesa Asian market, where an "extensive" selection of Japanese sundries, including "top-notch" fish, meat and produce and "ready-made" sushi platters, make for an "international-style" shopping experience; a lack of English signage can make it feel like you're "in another country", but relatively "frugal" prices make it worth the trip for items "you can't find anywhere else."

Miller's Market *Specialty Shops*   ∇ 17 | 13 | 15 | M

Golden Hill | 2985 C St. (30th St.) | 619-234-0684

It's a "great little neighborhood market" say fans at this "convenient" Golden Hill shop where the "fresh, affordable meat" is a highlight; it may be "small", but it still "has most things you may need in a hurry."

Minh Hoa SuperMarket ● *Specialty Shops*   18 | 16 | 16 | I

City Heights | 4690 El Cajon Blvd. (bet. 47th St. & Menlo Ave.) | 619-528-0333

For a "good variety" of foods, "locals" go to this no-frills City Heights Vietnamese market where some "unusual" and "interesting" imported items make for "fun shopping"; "low" prices seal the deal.

Mitsuwa Marketplace *Specialty Shops*   26 | 23 | 21 | M

Kearny Mesa | 4240 Kearny Mesa Rd. (bet. Armour St. & Othello Ave.) | 858-569-6699 | www.mitsuwa.com

"One-stop shopping for all your Japanese needs" say fans of this "well-set-up" Kearny Mesa emporium, where you can get "a little bit of everything", from the "specialty produce", "fresh fish" and more in the grocery section, to other "useful" goods, like books, dishes and toys, from the "little shops around the sides"; there's also a food court vending "pretty good grub", and though prices are generally considered "competitive", it "can be pricey depending on what you are looking for."

Mona Lisa Italian Foods ◑ *Specialty Shops*   27 | 22 | 23 | E

Little Italy | 2061 India St. (Hawthorn St.) | 619-239-5367 |
www.monalisalittleitaly.com

Shoppers say it's "just like being in Italy" at this "old-world deli" in Little Italy where you can "pick up authentic foods and wines", including "top-quality produce, meats, pastas" and other "imported delicacies"; it's "slightly crowded with people and products" and "fantastic" made-to-order sandwiches create a "meal-time rush", but the "staff remains friendly and helpful", and while prices aren't exactly low, fans deem them "better than expected."

My Cup of Tea   *Coffee & Tea*   ▽ 25 | 24 | 24 | E

Chula Vista | 242 Third Ave. (bet. Davidson & E Sts.) | 619-691-1347

It's always tea time at this "cute little" Chula Vista shop, where guests can sample from 100 varieties of tea, munch on "delicious" scones and peruse the gift selection; prices aren't cheap, but service is "congenial" and it also hosts monthly bingo.

Nijiya Market ◑ *Specialty Shops*   25 | 21 | 21 | M

Kearny Mesa | 3860 Convoy St. (Ostrow St.) | 858-268-3821 |
www.nijiya.com

"Excellent sashimi", "sushi-grade fish" and "interesting" specialty items are just some of the "quality" offerings at this "well-stocked" Japanese market in Kearny Mesa; what's "pricey" to some is "reasonable" to others, but most agree that service is "helpful", making for a "pleasant" shopping experience overall.

99 Ranch ◑ *Major Market*   22 | 18 | 17 | M

Clairemont | 7330 Clairemont Mesa Blvd. (bet. Ruffiner & Shawline Sts.) |
858-974-8899 | www.99ranch.com

Take an "instant trip to a Hong Kong market" via this "invaluable" Clairemont Mesa branch of an Asian grocery chain, which ranks as the No. 1 Local Favorite among San Diego food shops, featuring an "astounding variety" of "inexpensive" "foreign delicacies", "hard-to-find" produce, "unusual" meats and seafood that's so "fresh" some of it is still swimming in counterside tanks; English speakers are nearly "nonexistent" so "be sure to know what you're looking for."

Northgate Market   *Major Market*   23 | 22 | 21 | M

Escondido | 606 N. Escondido Blvd. (Washington Ave.) | 760-745-5701
Rolando | 5403 University Ave. (54th St.) | 619-265-9701 ◑
San Ysidro | 2909 Coronado Ave. (bet. Madden Ave. & 30th St.) |
619-429-8212
Chula Vista | 1058 Third Ave. (C St.) | 619-425-5700
Southcrest | 1410 S. 43rd St. (bet. Alpha & Gamma Sts.) |
619-266-6080 ◑
Vista | 1150 E. Vista Way (Bobier Dr.) | 760-724-4900
www.northgatemarkets.com

You can taste the flavors of Tijuana "without crossing the border" at these Mexican markets, where tortillas are "made right before your

QUALITY DISPLAY SERVICE COST

eyes" and the other "authentic" Hispanic sundries "galore" include "fresh-baked" breads and "mouthwatering" prepared foods; prices are "cost-sensitive", and "knowledgeable" clerks are "always ready with help, advice, samples or suggestions."

North Park Produce *Produce*   21 | 17 | 18 | M

Normal Heights | 3551 El Cajon Blvd. (bet. 36th St. & Wilson Ave.) | 619-516-3336 ●
Poway | 12342 Poway Rd. (bet. Oak Knoll & Pomerado Rds.) | 858-391-9100
www.northparkproduceonline.com

"Exotic" produce, "hard-to-find" meats and "interesting" international sundries make these "affordable" specialty markets "worth going to", especially for those seeking Middle Eastern staples and hookah supplies; check-out can "take a while" and surveyors say the building is "a bit run-down", but "affordable" prices make up for the less-than-"fancy" setting.

Nothing Bundt Cakes *Baked Goods*   27 | 26 | 25 | E

Del Mar | 2720 Via de la Valle (San Andres Dr.) | 858-764-7521
Mission Valley | 5624 Mission Center Rd. (Friars Rd.) | 619-294-2253
Poway | 12205 Scripps Poway Pkwy. (Pomerado Rd.) | 858-566-2863
www.nothingbundtcakes.com

Whether it's for a "special occasion", "hostess gift" or just a "once-in-a-while indulgence", this "niche" bakery chain "never disappoints" with its "creative" "moist and tasty" Bundt cakes in various sizes and "amazing" flavors, all arranged in "beautiful" displays; employees are "accommodating", and though some feel it's "too expensive", others consider prices "reasonable for the quality."

Ocean Beach People's Organic Food Market ● *Health & Natural Foods*   26 | 22 | 24 | E

Ocean Beach | 4765 Voltaire St. (Sunset Cliffs Blvd.) | 619-224-1387 | www.obpeoplesfood.coop

It's like a "trip back to the '60s" at this "local treasure", one of Ocean Beach's "original organic food shops", where they stock "hippie" must-haves like "locally sourced" produce, "natural remedies" and "specialty" items to fill every "conscious shopper's" gluten-free, vegan and health food needs, all selected by "picky" purchasers; "prices are high for some things" but those with a co-op membership enjoy discounted prices; P.S. don't miss the "delicious" upstairs cafe.

Old Town Liquor & Deli ● *Wines, Beer & Liquor*   23 | 21 | 23 | M

Old Town | 2304 San Diego Ave. (Old Town Ave.) | 619-291-4888 | www.zeetequila.com

"Boy have they got tequila" remark fans at this "nothing-fancy" Old Town liquor store and deli that stocks everything from "low-end" offerings to some of the "world's finest" spirits sure to "impress" even "connoisseurs"; the sandwiches are also "delicious", and "knowledgeable" service is another plus.

QUALITY | DISPLAY | SERVICE | COST

Olive Tree Marketplace ● *Major Market* | 25 | 22 | 22 | M

Ocean Beach | 4805 Narragansett Ave. (Sunset Cliffs Blvd.) |
619-224-0443 | www.olivetreemarket.com

"Indispensable in the neighborhood", this Ocean Beach market impresses with "top-shelf breads and meats", "delicious" deli sandwiches, "amazing" craft beers (sample some in the "great" tasting room) and other "high-quality products"; prices aren't inexpensive but service is "fast", and it comes "recommended" overall.

Otay Farms Market *Specialty Shops* | 24 | 19 | 21 | I

Chula Vista | 1716 Broadway (bet. Faivre & Main Sts.) | 619-423-1735

Budget-watchers head to this "mom and pop" market in Chula Vista for a "good selection" of "quality" groceries, including "fresh produce", "delicious" hot food and "tasty" housemade tortillas, all at "low prices"; solid service is another reason loyalists "love" it.

Panchitas Bakery ●⊅ *Baked Goods* | 23 | 19 | 20 | I

Barrio Logan | 1879 Logan Ave. (Cesar E. Chavez Pkwy.) | 619-338-9331
City Heights | 4414 University Ave. (bet. 44th St. & Highland Ave.) |
619-281-6662
Golden Hill | 2519 C St. (bet. 25th & 26th Sts.) | 619-232-6662
www.panchitasbakery.com

"Five dollars goes a long way" at this bakery trio that earns No. 1 Bang for your Buck in the SD Survey, where guests "feast on" an "impressive" array of the "freshest" Mexican baked goods for cheap; around for 30 years, it comes "highly recommended" by those who've been going here "since they were kids."

Pancho Villa Farmer's Market ● *Major Market* | 21 | 20 | 20 | I

Normal Heights | 3245 El Cajon Blvd. (bet. Iowa & 33rd Sts.) |
619-584-4595 | www.panchovillamarket.com

You'll find "a little bit of Mexico at every turn" at this "lively" Normal Heights grocer, where "fresh tortillas" are made on-site and sold alongside "quality baked goods", prepared foods "from carnitas to carne asada", "tons of produce" and much more; prices are "cheap", and "helpful" staffers make it "easy to find what you want."

Pizza Port Bottle Shop ● *Wines, Beer & Liquor* | 26 | 21 | 23 | M

Carlsbad | 571 Carlsbad Village Dr. (bet. Roosevelt & Tyler Sts.) |
760-720-7007 | www.pizzaport.com

"Every type of beer you could want" plus "lots no one has heard of" can be found at this Carlsbad bottle shop, a "staple of San Diego culture" where guests can peruse the "interesting" selection and drink their purchases on the outdoor patio; it's "always crowded", but if you score a seat you can also enjoy "gourmet" pies from the attached pizzeria.

Port Brewing/ The Lost Abbey *Wines, Beer & Liquor* | 28 | 22 | 25 | M

San Marcos | 155 Mata Way (Rancheros Dr.) | 800-918-6816 |
www.lostabbey.com

"Heaven for any beer drinker", this "top" San Marcos microbrewery offers "excellent tasting options" and affordable bottle fills of their "phenomenal" craft creations in a "rustic" setting that's "brimming with character"; a "laid-back" feel and "personable" staffers who are "willing to help" keep it "crowded" with "hops-happy" San Diegans.

San Diego Desserts ◐ *Baked Goods* | 26 | 23 | 23 | M |

City Heights | 5987 El Cajon Blvd. (60th St.) | 619-287-8186 | www.sandiegodesserts.net

The praise is "well deserved" say admirers of this City Heights bakery, where "high-quality, tasty" sweets are doled out by "knowledgeable" staffers; part cafe, it also offers "reasonably priced" wines and a savory menu that includes salads, pastas and more, so it works for a "relaxing dinner", though you can also just "pick up some desserts" to go.

San Diego Wine Co. *Wines, Beer & Liquor* | 26 | 22 | 24 | M |

Miramar | 7080 Miramar Rd. (bet. Distribution & Production Aves.) | 858-586-9463 | www.sandiegowine.net

Oenophiles find "plenty of pleasant surprises" at this "moderately priced" Miramar vino purveyor that stocks an "expertly curated selection" of everything from basic bottles to "highly rated cult wines"; and if some say it can "sometimes be hard to find what you're looking for", most agree the "courteous" staff is "more than happy to help" you select the right libation "based on your budget."

Seaport Oil & Vinegars ◐ *Specialty Shops* | 25 | 24 | 23 | E |

Marina District | 809 W. Harbor Dr. (Kettner Blvd.) | 619-232-6096 | www.seaportoilandvinegars.com

It's a "total treat for your mouth" attest admirers of the "high-quality oils and vinegars" available in some "amazing flavors" at this Marina District specialty shop in Seaport Village; staffers can help suggest "great combinations" and though not cheap, prices are "decent."

Seaside Market ◐ *Major Market* | 27 | 23 | 24 | E |

Cardiff-by-the-Sea | 2087 San Elijo Ave. (Liverpool Dr.) | 760-753-5443 | www.seasidemarket.com

"Exceptional cuts of meat or fish", "delicious deli foods" and baked goods worthy of "breaking your diet" have fans "hooked" on this "boutique grocer" in Cardiff; the "intimate" space is often "crowded" with "old and young surfers, hippies, yuppies and beautiful people", but "laid-back" staffers keep things moving, and while prices are "high", many remind "you get what you pay for."

Shakespeare Corner Shoppe *Specialty Shops* | 22 | 21 | 21 | E |

Mission Hills | 3719 India St. (Winder St.) | 619-683-2748 | www.ukcornershoppe.com

A "nice selection of authentic English foods" proves this Mission Hills market "knows what Brits are missing from the homeland" cheer expats of the crisps, drinks, cheese, sausage and other "traditional goods" often "not available in American shops"; true, the costs may "reflect the price of importing", but staffers are "ready to lend a hand", and the afternoon tea also makes for an "enjoyable" experience.

	QUALITY	DISPLAY	SERVICE	COST

Siesel's Meats *Meat & Poultry* | 28 | 24 | 25 | E |

Bay Park | 4131 Ashton St. (bet. Chicago St. & Morena Blvd.) |
619-275-1234 | www.iowameatfarms.com

"If you are into meat", this Bay Park "staple" is a "must-see" say fans
applauding the "fine" cuts, "wonderful" marinated items, "indispensable" rubs and other "gourmet foods"; "knowledgeable" butchers
will "cut anything to order" and "tell you exactly how to cook" what
you purchase, and though it's "not cheap, the quality is excellent."

Societe Brewing | 21 | 20 | 19 | E |
Company *Wines, Beer & Liquor*

Kearny Mesa | 8262 Clairemont Mesa Blvd. (Industrial Park Dr.) |
858-495-5409 | www.societebrewing.com

One of the more recent additions to the rapidly exploding San Diego
craft brewery scene, this "great" Kearney Mesa venue is considered
a "must-visit for any beer lover" say enthusiasts who appreciate its
focus on IPAs, Belgian-inspired suds and wine barrel–aged sours; it's
not cheap, but a large tasting space with unobstructed views of the
barrel room and brew center extend the appeal.

Specialty Produce *Produce* | 24 | 17 | 22 | M |

Middletown | 1929 Hancock St. (Noell St.) | 619-295-3172 |
www.specialtyproduce.com

A "hidden jewel", this "no-frills" Middletown spot is filled with "fabulous, fresh produce" offered in "large quantities", so it's no wonder
"it's where the local restaurateurs shop"; a "helpful staff and good
prices" further compensate for the "warehouse"-like surrounds.

Stephanie's Bakery *Baked Goods* | ∇ 21 | 19 | 19 | E |

Ocean Beach | 4879 Voltaire St. (bet. Cable St. & Sunset Cliffs Blvd.) |
619-221-0285 | www.stephaniesbakery.com

"Even non-vegans" become "lifetime customers" after sampling the
"delicious" cakes, "flaky" pastries and other dairy-, egg- and meat-free
offerings (including pizzas and salads) at this Ocean Beach bakery;
staffers who "greet you with a warm smile" are another reason it
comes "recommended" – just expect high prices on certain items.

Stone Company Store *Wines, Beer & Liquor* | 25 | 24 | 22 | E |

Escondido | 1999 Citracado Pkwy. (Auto Park Way) | 760-471-4999 ◐
South Park | 2215 30th St. (bet. Ivy & Juniper Sts.) | 619-501-3342
www.stonecompanystore.com

Hopsheads "celebrate their endless love" for these "amazing" brewery
stores in South Park and Escondido by stocking up on "awesome
gear" for an "envious brother back east" or visiting the filling station
to score growlers of "unique" stouts and IPAs; some wish it were "a
bit cheaper" but have no complaints about the "quick" staffers.

Stump's Family Marketplace ◐ *Major Market* | 23 | 20 | 21 | M |

Ocean Beach | 3770 Voltaire St. (Worden St.) | 619-226-9575 |
www.stumpssandiego.com

"Family-owned, full-service grocers" may be a "vanishing breed" but
this "great neighborhood market" in Ocean Beach fits the bill with

QUALITY DISPLAY SERVICE COST

"well-displayed" butchered meats, "from-scratch" prepared foods and "fresh" produce arranged in "well-marked" aisles; cashiers are mostly "friendly", and though some say it's "overpriced" others call costs "just right."

Suzie's Farm ⊘ *Produce* — 29 | 23 | 27 | E

Imperial Beach | 2570 Sunset Ave. (Hollister St.) | 619-662-1780 | www.suziesfarm.com

Both "top local restaurants" and the produce-loving public fill their fridges with the organic fruits and veggies displayed with "artistry" at this Imperial Beach farm that receives Top Quality and Service honors among San Diego's food shops; "amazing" staffers give tours of the urban grounds, and though goods may be "expensive", fans say it's "worth a little extra" since you can "taste the difference in quality."

Temecula Olive Oil — 28 | 25 | 25 | E
Company *Specialty Shops*

Solana Beach | 342 S. Cedros Ave. (Rosa St.) | 858-847-9007
Old Town | 2754 Calhoun St. (Taylor St.) | 619-269-5779
www.temeculaoliveoil.com

"Even the worst cook will seem like Martha Stewart" after using the "wonderful tasting", locally grown olive oils from these "real-deal" Old Town and Solana Beach boutiques say supporters touting the "distinct" dressings, vinegars and artisan foods; the "high-quality" products, "quaint" decor and "down-to-earth" staffers ensure it stays "busy" despite "pricey" tabs.

Twiggs Bakery *Baked Goods* — 25 | 22 | 24 | M

University Heights | 4590 Park Blvd. (Madison Ave.) | 619-296-0616
University Heights | 2804 Adams Ave. (Idaho St.) | 619-296-4077 ◗
www.twiggs.org

"Yum" is the word at this "cute" University Heights bakery and coffee-shop duo known for "delicious" baked goods and "awesome" sandwiches, though the real highlight may be the "unique, delicate, fresh" wedding cakes; with "reasonably priced" tabs and "efficient", "unpretentious service", patrons "can't wait" to "order from them again."

2Good2B Bakery *Baked Goods* — 21 | 19 | 20 | E

Encinitas | 204 N. El Camino Real (Via Molena) | 760-942-4663 | www.2good2b.com

Deemed a "gluten-free haven", this North County bakery/cafe also forgoes corn and soy, serving "divine" "fresh-daily" desserts, artisan breads, Neapolitan pizzas, pressed sandwiches, even "delicious" wedding cakes that are "so tasty" they truly seem "too good to be true"; fair prices and "friendly" staffers offering "personalized attention" help it "live up" to its name.

Uncle Biff's Killer Cookies *Baked Goods* — 26 | 22 | 23 | E

Hillcrest | 650 University Ave. (bet. 6th & 7th Aves.) | 619-291-2433 | www.unclebiffskillercookies.com

"The name says it all" cheer fans at this Hillcrest bakery, where the "indulgent" cookies are so "delicious" it's easy to "walk in to get one and walk out with a dozen"; the staff is "friendly", and though it's "slightly pricey", consensus says they're "worth every cent."

Valley Farm Market ❶ *Major Market* 25 | 19 | 24 | E

Spring Valley | 9040 Campo Rd. (Bancroft Dr.) | 619-463-9595 | www.valleyfarmmarkets.com

Though on the "smaller" side, this "old-fashioned" Spring Valley market is "well stocked" with a solid array of items, like "unusual marinades", "locally sourced" produce and a "terrific" craft beer selection, though the "real star" is one of the "best butcher" counters around; prices are on the high side, but service scores strongly and many find tabs "reasonable" for the "quality."

Valley Foods ❶ *Specialty Shops* 23 | 21 | 22 | M

El Cajon | 1275 E. Main St. (bet. Ballard & 2nd Sts.) | 619-749-8355 | www.valleyfoodsmed.com

"One of the better Middle Eastern markets" in East County say admirers of this "mom and pop"–style El Cajon spot that offers "good customer service" and "affordable" produce, meat, seafood and international groceries in a "clean, organized, not-too-cramped" space; those seeking a hot meal can also hit up the kitchen counter for eats like Halal lamb kebabs and rotisserie chicken.

Venissimo Cheese *Cheese & Dairy* 28 | 26 | 26 | E

Del Mar | 2650 Via de la Valle (San Andres Dr.) | 858-847-9616
East Village | 871 G St. (bet. 8th & 9th Aves.) | 619-358-9081
Mission Hills | 754 W. Washington St. (bet. Eagle & Falcon Sts.) | 619-491-0708
www.venissimo.com

You can "tour the entire world" by sampling the "exceptional selection" of international "artisanal" cheeses at these "expensive-but-worth-it" chain links where you can also find "eclectic" accompaniments, including some "devilishly addictive" options; those who need guidance turn to "patient" staffers, who are "comparable to sommeliers" in their knowledge and can offer "great suggestions" and pairing recommendations.

V.G. Donut & Bakery ❶ *Baked Goods* 26 | 22 | 24 | M

Cardiff-by-the-Sea | 106 Aberdeen Dr. (San Elijo Ave.) | 760-753-2400 | www.vgbakery.com

"A legend in its own time", this "long-standing" Cardiff "standby" draws a "loyal base" of "surfers, families and everyone else" with "unbeatable" baked goods, like "just-out-of-the-oven" donuts and "wonderful" cakes; "fast" service and affordable prices also work in its favor.

Vine Ripe Market ❶ *Specialty Shops* 20 | 18 | 17 | M

La Mesa | 8191 Fletcher Pkwy. (Jackson Dr.) | 619-462-7800

"Good, cheap and convenient" say enthusiasts of this La Mesa market that serves an international community with "exotic, hard-to-find" Middle Eastern sundries, "fine" produce, "fresh-cooked" hot foods and some "different types of meats not found in regular grocery stores"; service and display earn middling marks but no one's complaining about the "good prices."

QUALITY DISPLAY SERVICE COST

Vintage Wines   *Wines, Beer & Liquor*   24 | 21 | 23 | M

Miramar | 6904 Miramar Rd. (bet. Commerce & Production Aves.) | 858-549-2112 | www.vintagewinessd.com

"Wines to fit any budget" bring customers to this Miramar bottle shop that offers "variety and value" with its "nice selection" of more than 2,000 international vinos; "knowledgeable" staffers administer Saturday tastings and offer "reliable" recommendations, and patrons can sip from a by-the-glass menu at the bar.

We Olive   *Specialty Shops*   22 | 22 | 21 | E

La Jolla | 1158 Prospect St. (Herschel Ave.) | 858-551-8250 | www.weolive.com

"Like walking into the pantry in a Mediterranean village", this upscale La Jolla specialty shop has shelves stocked with "high-quality", "artisanal" olive oils , "favorite" balsamic vinegars and other gourmet accoutrements, all sold by "intelligent" salespeople who "have the answers" and are "generous with samples"; patrons can enjoy daily wine specials and plates of "local cheeses and charcuterie" on the "deck overlooking the ocean."

Windmill Farms ● *Major Market*   27 | 25 | 25 | E

Del Cerro | 6386 Del Cerro Blvd. (bet. College & Madra Aves.) | 619-287-1400 | www.windmillfarms.net

"Earth-friendly, community-friendly and surprisingly friendly to your wallet", this "amazing" Del Cerro grocer offers a "premium shopping experience" with "lots" of all-natural items, "farm-fresh" meats and produce, "brilliant" bulk foods and an "outstanding" beer selection; with an "open", "well-organized" layout and "accommodating" employees to boot, "why would you go anywhere else?"

Wine Bank ● *Wines, Beer & Liquor*   21 | 19 | 17 | E

Gaslamp Quarter | 363 Fifth Ave. (J St.) | 619-234-7487 | www.sdwinebank.com

"Serving San Diego for decades", this Gaslamp wine shop stocks a "huge selection" of worldwide vinos that includes everything from "great bargains to special bottles"; it's a "bit pricey", but weekly tastings administered by "knowledgeable" staffers are a good way to try out "rare finds."

WineStyles   *Wines, Beer & Liquor*   23 | 23 | 21 | E

Coronado | 928 Orange Ave. (bet. 9th & 10th Sts.) | 619-365-4953 | www.winestyles.net

A "fabulous wine selection" draws oenophiles to this Coronado chain link where "knowledgeable" staffers are on hand to help with selections; guests can enjoy special events and "great live music" in the tasting room or by-the-glass selections and appetizers on the outdoor patio or at the bar, making it a "fun place to go with friends after work."

Wine Time ● *Wines, Beer & Liquor*   23 | 18 | 19 | E

La Jolla | 7474 La Jolla Blvd. (bet. Marine & Pearl Sts.) | 858-551-7565

Bottles line the walls of this La Jolla wine shop, where the "nice family" that owns the place curates an "amazing" selection of "fine" vintages and offers handwritten notes on favorites; "great" deli sandwiches, "good" cheese and a solid stash of local beer seal the deal.

World Foods *Specialty Shops* | 27 | 25 | 23 | M |

City Heights | 5245 El Cajon Blvd. (bet. Dawson Ave. & 52nd St.) | 619-265-9988

Shoppers find a "world of wonders" inside this City Heights Asian market, which stocks "interesting" international items and some "unusual goodies" you "can't find anywhere" else, plus an "extensive" selection of "fresh" whole fish, which staffers will fillet and clean "five ways to Sunday"; sure, it can "sometimes be pricey", but since you can "always find something new" many still "return again and again."

Zanzibar Gourmet Market ◑ *Specialty Shops* | 24 | 22 | 20 | E |

East Village | 707 G St. (7th Ave.) | 619-230-0125 | www.zanzibarcafe.com

This "great little" East Village market attached to the cafe sib has a "delicious" array of "anything you could hope to nibble on", from pantry staples and "amazing" cheeses to sandwiches and prepared foods; "knowledgeable" staffers further help justify pricey tabs.

Zion Market ◑ *Specialty Shops* | 23 | 20 | 18 | I |

Kearny Mesa | 4611 Mercury St. (Dagget St.) | 858-268-3300 | www.zionmarket.com

"When you're missing your Asian mama's cooking" fans recommend visiting this "reasonably priced" Kearny Mesa Korean grocery where the "first-rate" selection includes "specialty foods and ingredients", ready-made items, "cheap produce" and more, plus an "unreal" butcher section; parking can be "difficult to find on the weekends", and "narrow aisles" can lead to "shopping cart fender benders", but budget-watchers say the many "deals" make it all "worth it."

SITES & ATTRACTIONS

Most Popular

The top five on this list are plotted on the map at the back of this book.

1. San Diego Zoo
2. Balboa Park
3. SeaWorld
4. San Diego Zoo Safari Park
5. Old Town Historic Park
6. PETCO Park
7. Legoland California
8. USS Midway Mus.
9. Cabrillo National Monument
10. Birch Aquarium at Scripps

TOP APPEAL

28
San Diego Zoo
San Diego Zoo Safari Park
Torrey Pines State Reserve
Balboa Park
SeaWorld

27
USS Midway Mus.
Birch Aquarium at Scripps
Reuben H. Fleet Science Ctr.
PETCO Park

26
Maritime Mus.

TOP FACILITIES

27
San Diego Zoo
SeaWorld
San Diego Zoo Safari Park
PETCO Park

26
Birch Aquarium at Scripps

Reuben H. Fleet Science Ctr.

25
San Diego Air/Space Mus.
Balboa Park
San Diego Nat. History Mus.
San Diego Mus. of Art

TOP SERVICE

26
San Diego Zoo

25
San Diego Zoo Safari Park
Birch Aquarium at Scripps
Maritime Museum
Reuben H. Fleet Science Ctr.

SeaWorld
USS Midway Museum

24
San Diego Nat. History Mus.
San Diego Hall of Champions
San Diego Mus. of Art

Excludes places with low votes

Sites & Attractions Types

Includes names, locations and Appeal ratings. These lists include low-vote places that do not qualify for tops lists.

AMUSEMENT/ THEME PARKS

Legoland CA | **Carlsbad** 25

Belmont Park | **Mission Bch** 23

AQUARIUMS

SeaWorld | **Mission Bay** 28

Birch Aquarium | **La Jolla** 27

BALLPARKS

PETCO Park | **Downtown** 27

GARDENS

Japanese Friend. Gdn. | 25
Balboa Pk

HISTORIC TOWNS

Old Town Hist. Park | **Old Town** 25

Liberty Station | **Pt Loma** 24

MUSEUMS: ART

San Diego Mus./Art | **Balboa Pk** 25

Timken Mus./Art | **Balboa Pk** 24

Mus./Contemp. Art | **multi.** 24

Mingei In'l Mus. | **Balboa Pk** 23

Mus./Photo. Arts | **Balboa Pk** 22

MUSEUMS: HALL OF FAMES

SD Hall/Champions | **Balboa Pk** 25

MUSEUMS: HISTORY

USS Midway Mus. | **Downtown** 27

Maritime Mus. | **Downtown** 26

SD Air/Space Mus. | **Balboa Pk** 26

SD Natural History Mus. | 25
Balboa Pk

SD Auto Mus. | **Balboa Pk** 25

SD Model RR Mus. | **Balboa Pk** 24

MUSEUMS: SCIENCE

Reuben Fleet Science Ctr. | 27
Balboa Pk

SD Air/Space Mus. | **Balboa Pk** 26

NATIONAL MONUMENTS

Cabrillo Nat'l Mon. | **Pt Loma** 26

PARKS

Torrey Pines Reserve | **La Jolla** 28

Balboa Park | **Balboa Pk** 28

Mission Bay Park | **Mission Bay** 26

Old Town Hist. Park | **Old Town** 25

PLANETARIUMS

Reuben Fleet Science Ctr. | 27
Balboa Pk

RELIGIOUS SITES

Mission SD/Alcala | 24
Mission Valley

ZOOS/ANIMAL PARKS

San Diego Zoo | **Balboa Pk** 28

SD Zoo Safari | **Escondido** 28

SeaWorld | **Mission Bay** 28

Sites & Attractions Locations

Includes names and Appeal ratings. These lists include low-vote places that do not qualify for tops lists.

BALBOA PARK

San Diego Zoo	28
Balboa Park	28
Reuben Fleet Science Ctr.	27
SD Air/Space Mus.	26
San Diego Mus./Art	25
SD Natural History Mus.	25
SD Hall/Champions	25
SD Auto Mus.	25
Japanese Friend. Gdn.	25
SD Model RR Mus.	24
Timken Mus./Art	24
Mingei In'l Mus.	23
Mus./Photo. Arts	22

DOWNTOWN

USS Midway Mus.	27
PETCO Park	27
Maritime Mus.	26
Mus./Contemp. Art	24

LA JOLLA

Torrey Pines Reserve	28
Birch Aquarium	27
Mus./Contemp. Art	24

MISSION BAY/ MISSION BEACH

SeaWorld	28
Mission Bay Park	26
Belmont Park	23

MISSION VALLEY

Mission SD/Alcala	24

NORTH COUNTY

SD Zoo Safari	28
Legoland CA	25

OLD TOWN

Old Town Hist. Park	25

POINT LOMA

Cabrillo Nat'l Mon.	26
Liberty Station	24

Sites & Attractions

Ratings & Symbols

Appeal, Facilities & **Service** are rated on a 30-point scale.

Cost reflects the attraction's high-season price range for one adult admission, indicated as follows:

$0 Free
‖ $10 and below
M $11 to $25

E $26 to $40
VE $41 or above

Balboa Park
28 | 25 | 23 | $0

Balboa Park | 1549 El Prado (Park Blvd.) | 619-239-0512 | www.balboapark.org

There's "so much to discover" at this "culturally rich" Downtown "treasure", hailed as one of the country's "greatest city parks", whose 1,200 "charming", largely "walkable" acres are studded with an "abundance" of "unique" attractions like the "world-class" San Diego Zoo, "don't-miss" botanical gardens, 17 "amazing" museums, including the Reuben H. Fleet Science Center and San Diego Air & Space Museum, performance venues and more; "you don't have to spend a lot" to enjoy it either, since admission to the grounds and some venues are free, plus multi-attraction discount passes are available.

Belmont Park
23 | 21 | 21 | $0

Mission Beach | 3146 Mission Blvd. (W. Mission Bay Dr.) | 858-228-9283 | www.belmontpark.com

"Riding the historic roller coaster" (circa-1925 and "made of wood so it clickity-clacks") is a "must-do" at this "funky" amusement park situated "right on the ocean" in Mission Beach, but visitors also enjoy other "wholesome fun" like arcade games, laser tag and a ropes course, plus restaurants, "touristy" shops and "sunset" walks by the water; though some say the facilities are becoming "dated", others think the "retro" appeal is part of the "quaint charm"; P.S. admission to the park is free, while ride prices vary but are "affordable."

Birch Aquarium at Scripps
27 | 26 | 25 | M

La Jolla | 2300 Expedition Way (N. Torrey Pines Rd.) | 858-534-3474 | www.aquarium.ucsd.edu

Fin fans get "up close and personal" at this "small but well-maintained" aquarium run by the Scripps Institution of Oceanography and "beautifully situated above Scripps Pier" in La Jolla, where "spectacular sea creatures" swim in a "giant", "mesmerizing" tank while "interactive" activities like a "hands-on tidal pool" provide "educational" fun for kids and "changing" exhibits "keep it interesting" for all; a "courteous, quite knowledgeable" staff adds to its appeal.

	APPEAL	FACIL.	SERVICE	COST

Cabrillo National Monument   26 | 23 | 21 | I

Point Loma | 1000 Cabrillo Memorial Dr. (south of I-8) | 619-557-5450 | www.nps.gov

Located atop a "windswept headland" where the first European expedition to the West Coast reached shore in 1542, this Point Loma national monument boasts "down-to-Mexico" views that will "take your breath away", especially "when the whales are running", making it a "must" for "nature lovers" and "history buffs" alike; in addition to the vistas, there's an "educational" visitors center, "historic" lighthouse and "amazing" tidepools to explore.

Japanese Friendship Garden   25 | 23 | 22 | I

Balboa Park | Balboa Park | 2125 Pan American Rd. E. (Park Blvd.) | 619-232-2721 | www.niwa.org

"Forget your troubles" at this "serene" tribute to Japanese sister city Yokohama in an "intimate area" of Balboa Park, where the "beautiful" garden setting, "gorgeous" blooms and koi pond transport visitors across the Pacific; it also offers instruction in everything from gardening to meditation to yoga, and there's a Tea Pavilion for refreshment; P.S. fans who find it a bit "small" are no doubt happy about an in-progress expansion that will boost its size by some nine acres.

Legoland California   25 | 25 | 24 | VE

Carlsbad | 1 Legoland Dr. (Cannon Rd.) | 760-918-5346 | www.legoland.com

"Anyone who is/was/could be a fan of Legos" will enjoy this Carlsbad theme park featuring "impressive" displays of Lego-built cities, monuments, animals and more plus "interactive" activities, "plenty" of amusement park rides and other "G-rated" attractions that will "stir the imagination" – at least if you're part of the "under-12 set" (older kids may be "bored"); admission to the on-site water park and aquarium cost extra, which no doubt irks those who already find prices "high."

Liberty Station   24 | 25 | 23 | $0

Point Loma | 2640 Historic Decatur Rd. (Roosevelt Rd.) | 619-573-9260 | libertystation.com

"Brilliantly repurposed" Spanish Colonial Revival–style buildings and "beautiful" grounds are home to "interesting" shops, restaurants, hotels, galleries, fitness classes, theater and a golf course at this residential/commercial development at Point Loma's former Naval Training Center; "lots of free" events add appeal, but some note that it can get congested on Sundays when worshipers flock to the 3,500-seat Rock Church.

Maritime Museum   26 | 25 | 25 | M

Downtown | 1492 N. Harbor Dr. (bet. Ash & Grape Sts.) | 619-234-9153 | www.sdmaritime.com

There's "lots to see" at this "well-kept" maritime museum situated "right on the bay" on Downtown's Embarcadero, where visitors can climb aboard a "wonderful collection" of "historic vessels" including the "majestic" circa-1863 *Star of India,* the *HMS Surprise* (the replica frigate featured in the film *Master and Commander*) and the USS

APPEAL | FACIL. | SERVICE | COST

Dolphin submarine; there are also permanent and visiting exhibits, special events, sails and more to educate and "entertain both young and old"; P.S. visitors can also venture to the Spanish Landing build-site of the *San Salvador,* the museum's full-sized, fully functional replica of Juan Rodriguez Cabrillo's famous ship.

Mingei International Museum   23 | 21 | 23 | I

Balboa Park | Balboa Park | 1439 El Prado (Plaza de Panama) | 619-239-0003 | www.mingei.org

There's "always something interesting" to see at this museum showcasing folk art, craft and design (its name means 'art of the people'), located in Balboa Park's House of Charm, a historic struc-ture built for the 1915 Panama-California Exposition and then re-built in 1996; the "fascinating" exhibits of textiles, jewelry, crafts and artwork from around the world are "beautifully" arranged, and "welcoming, friendly" staffers offer "well-led docent tours" to help you explore them.

Mission Bay Park   26 | 22 | 19 | $0

Mission Bay | W. Mission Bay Dr. (I-5) | 619-525-8213 | www.sandiego.gov

"A boater's dream and a lounger's paradise", this "beautiful" Mission Bay park boasts 4,235 acres and 27 miles of shoreline offering rec-reation opportunities on "both land and sea", with man-made boating bays, swimming coves, biking trails, campgrounds and picnic spots; "clean" facilities and free entry are pluses (though SeaWorld, located on the grounds, does charge) – just "arrive early to beat the crowds" that pack every "patch of grass and sand" on sunny weekends.

Mission San Diego de Alcala   24 | 23 | 21 | I

Mission Valley | 10818 Mission San Diego Rd. (Mission Gorge Rd.) | 619-283-7319 | www.missionsandiego.com

"One of the most peaceful places in San Diego" and a "must-see for history buffs", this "rustic" 18th-century church in Mission Valley is one of the "oldest missions" and "most important cul-tural sites" in California; touring the grounds – which include gardens, graveyards and ruins of the original structure – is "edu-cational" and "relaxing", though it's an active Catholic parish and thus gets "very busy" for holiday masses.

Museum of   24 | 25 | 23 | I
Contemporary Art San Diego

Downtown | 1001 Kettner Blvd. (B'way) | 619-234-1001
La Jolla | 700 Prospect St. (Silverado St.) | 858-454-3541
www.mcasd.org

Irving Gill's "fascinating architecture" is a high point at the original La Jolla location of this contemporary art museum whose collection includes more than 4,000 post-1950 works ranging from minimal-ism to Pop Art in all media; an "excellent" gift shop, "charming" cafe and "breathtaking view" afforded by its location "on the ocean" add appeal, and the entrance fee also includes admission to the mu-seum's "classy" Downtown offshoot, where docent tours often feel like "private guided visits."

APPEAL | FACIL. | SERVICE | COST

Museum of Photographic Arts

| 22 | 23 | 23 | I |

Balboa Park | Balboa Park | 1649 El Prado (Park Blvd.) | 619-238-7559 | www.mopa.org

Shutterbugs assure that "one of the world's best" photography collections – more than 7,000 photos from 850 artists including the likes of Margaret Bourke-White and Alfred Stieglitz – can be found at this stylish museum in "beautiful Balboa Park", set in a historic building that was constructed for the 1915 Panama-California Exposition (and then rebuilt after a 1978 fire); besides "changing exhibitions", it offers educational programs and film screenings and stocks "excellent books" among other items in the gift shop.

Old Town San Diego State Historic Park

| 25 | 23 | 22 | $0 |

Old Town | 4002 Wallace St. (San Diego Ave.) | 619-220-5422 | www.parks.ca.gov

"Step back in time" via this "family-friendly" state historic park where visitors can see "what life was like" during Old Town's Mexican and early American periods (1821–1872) thanks to a "well-maintained" collection of buildings (including original adobes), plazas and court-yards where staffers in traditional garb demonstrate activities such as candle making, blacksmithing and carpentry; other draws include "funky" shops, "excellent" restaurants and fiestas.

PETCO Park

| 27 | 27 | 24 | E |

Downtown | 100 Park Blvd. (bet. 7th & 10th Aves.) | 619-795-5000 | www.sandiego.padres.mlb.com

There's a "great view from any" of the 42,000 seats at this "well-designed" "sweetheart of a stadium" in a "perfect Downtown location" near the Gaslamp Quarter, where "team spirit and camaraderie" reign and you can "see the beautiful San Diego skyline" and bay; some deduct points for "difficult" parking and "quite expensive" (though "craveworthy") concessions, but to save money you can "take the trolley" and have the "helpful" ushers guide you to the Park at the Park lawn, which costs just $5 – "now if only the Padres could win a few games."

Reuben H. Fleet Science Center

| 27 | 26 | 25 | M |

Balboa Park | Balboa Park | 1875 El Prado (Park Blvd.) | 619-238-1233 | www.rhfleet.org

Let your kids "roam free and explore" at this "awesome" science museum in Balboa Park, where children – and adults – can "learn important scientific principles" via "hands-on" exhibits, "interesting, informative" displays, "amazing" planetarium shows and a "pricey" but "worthwhile" IMAX theater; it can get "a bit crowded at times", but it's "sure to inspire future scientists."

San Diego Air & Space Museum

| 26 | 25 | 24 | M |

Balboa Park | Balboa Park | 2001 Pan American Plaza (Park Blvd.) | 619-234-8291 | www.aerospacemuseum.org

Aviation "addicts" of "all ages" will enjoy this "very cool" component of Balboa Park's "museum row" housing "all sort of things related to aircraft and space travel", from dirigible artifacts to planes "from ages ago" (like a WWII Wildcat and a Nazi stealth fighter replica) to the Apollo 9 command module, plus "excellent" exhibits exploring the history of flight; add in a "friendly" staff "interested in telling stories" and enthusiasts may "never want to leave."

San Diego Automotive Museum — 25 | 24 | 22 | I

Balboa Park | Balboa Park | 2080 Pan American Plaza (El Prado) | 619-231-2886 | www.sdautomuseum.org

"One of Balboa Park's often-overlooked gems", this automotive museum boasts a permanent collection featuring "lots of vintage vehicles", like a 1932 Cadillac and 1928 Studebaker, and temporary exhibits like California Roll, which focused on style and technology that originated in the state; guests "really enjoy" talking to the volunteers, who teach "new things about old subjects" and help make it "worth walking through."

San Diego Hall of Champions — 25 | 24 | 24 | I

Balboa Park | Balboa Park | 2131 Pan American Plaza (Park Blvd.) | 619-234-2544 | www.sdhoc.com

"All the greats" of San Diego athletics are celebrated at this multi-sport museum in Balboa Park, where exhibits explore the feats of Ted Williams, Tony Gwynn, Bill Walton, Florence Chadwick and other local pro and amateur athletes; with its 68,000 sq. ft. and three levels of memorabilia, there's "nothing better" for true fans both "young and old" – except "actually playing" themselves.

San Diego Model Railroad Museum — 24 | 22 | 23 | I

Balboa Park | Balboa Park | 1649 El Prado (Park Blvd.) | 619-696-0199 | www.sdmrm.org

"Train buffs" who "just can't get enough of that lonesome whistle blowing" certainly "don't have to be railroaded" into visiting this "super-cool" museum "tucked" downstairs in a Spanish Colonial Revival–style building in Balboa Park, where a "wide variety of model train exhibits" will "entertain" kids (and grown-ups) while educating about railroad heritage and model railroading; "friendly" modelers "always willing to chat" add charm.

San Diego Museum of Art — 25 | 25 | 24 | M

Balboa Park | Balboa Park | 1450 El Prado (Pan American Rd.) | 619-232-7931 | www.sdmart.org

"You can go back time and time again" to Balboa Park's circa-1926 fine arts museum and "always see something new" thanks to its "excellent" collection of American, Asian, European (Spanish old master paintings are a specialty) and contemporary art plus temporary exhibits throughout the year; it also has an outdoor sculpture garden and offers a robust lecture series and regular cocktail parties that help make membership "worth the price."

San Diego Natural History Museum — 25 | 25 | 24 | M

Balboa Park | Balboa Park | 1788 El Prado (Park Blvd.) | 619-232-3821 | www.sdnhm.org

"Educational" and "entertaining" sums up this Balboa Park natural history museum where visitors can learn about everything from dinosaurs and the "dawn of man" to "the present" via "informative" displays, photo collections and "great traveling exhibits"; it also screens some "top-quality" films and offers lectures, family programs and more.

San Diego Zoo
28 | 27 | 26 | VE

Balboa Park | Balboa Park | 2920 Zoo Dr. (Park Blvd.) | 619-231-1515 | www.sandiegozoo.org

"World renowned and for good reason", this 100-acre zoo in Balboa Park showcases an "amazing collection" of some 4,000 creatures in "beautifully maintained", "cutting-edge" habitats, with "wonderful plant life" and a "helpful" staff throughout that help earn it Most Popular and Top Service, Appeal and Facilities honors among San Diego's attractions; it's also admired for its "state-of-the-art" breeding and conservation efforts, so while not cheap, most deem it well "worth" it – just "bring walking shoes" to tackle the "miles" of hills and paths or "hop on the double-decker bus" for an overview.

San Diego Zoo
Safari Park
28 | 27 | 25 | VE

(fka San Diego Wild Animal Park)
Escondido | 15500 San Pasqual Valley Rd. (I-78) | 760-747-8702 | www.sdzsafaripark.org

"Feel like you're on a real safari" at the San Diego Zoo's Escondido sibling, a "gigantic", 1,800-acre animal park where rhinos, elephants, "big cats" and more are cared for by "dedicated" handlers and live in "expansive" habitats that offer "so much room to roam"; it's "expensive", especially with "premium" add-ons, and a "bit of a ride" (some 40 minutes) from the city, but the likes of zip line rides, "unforgettable" night camping, "must-see" cheetah races and "successful" breeding facilities help make it "well worth it."

SeaWorld
28 | 27 | 25 | VE

Mission Bay | 500 SeaWorld Dr. (W. Mission Bay Dr.) | 800-257-4268 | www.seaworld.com

"Stay cool on a hot day" at Mission Bay's "outstanding" aquatic amusement park, where "unexpected soakings" come courtesy of "neat rides" and water shows featuring the "spectacular" Shamu and other animals; add in "educational" exhibits, aquariums filled with "colorful" creatures and staffers who are "always willing to lend a hand or answer a question", and it's worth the "costly" admission (plus there are discount combo tickets available).

Timken Museum of Art
24 | 24 | 23 | $0

Balboa Park | Balboa Park | 1500 El Prado (Park Blvd.) | 619-239-5548 | www.timkenmuseum.org

Though often overshadowed by Balboa Park's larger attractions, this "small jewel box" of a museum is "impressive in its holdings", which include European old master paintings and works by American artists plus Russian icons, bronze sculptures and 17th-century tapestries; the five-room gallery is "not intimidating or overwhelming", and best of all, "it's free."

SITES & ATTRACTIONS

	APPEAL	FACIL.	SERVICE	COST

Torrey Pines State Reserve

28 | 22 | 20 | M

La Jolla | 12600 N. Torrey Pines Rd. (I-5) | 858-755-2063 | www.torreypine.org

The "rare" Torrey Pine "flourishes" on the clifftops of this "pristine" 2,000-acre reserve in La Jolla, a "natural gem" beloved for its "unusual" rock formations, "impressive" cliffs, "scenic" beaches and "stunning" views of the "dramatic coastline"; visitors also enjoy "good outdoor exercise", hiking the eight miles of "well-maintained" trails, and on weekends, the "always helpful" staffers provide guided tours of "mother nature at her best."

USS Midway Museum

27 | 25 | 25 | M

Downtown | 910 N. Harbor Dr. (W. B'way) | 619-544-9600 | www.midway.org

"Military history buffs" and "uninitiated landlubbers" alike enjoy the "glimpse of life at sea" offered aboard this "immense" aircraft carrier docked Downtown at Navy Pier, where they can admire the many restored planes on deck, take in various exhibits and tour the "hot, close" quarters that were home to more than 200,000 sailors over the vessel's 47 years of service; "extremely knowledgeable" docents "answer any questions", and the whole experience imparts an "overwhelming sense of pride for our military."

Presented to:

By:

Date:

Occasion:

All Scripture quotations, unless otherwise indicated, are taken from *The Amplified
Bible* (AMP). *The Amplified Bible, Old Testament.* Copyright © 1965, 1987 by The
Zondervan Corporation. *The Amplified New Testament,* copyright © 1954, 1958,
1987 by The Lockman Foundation. Used by permission.

Scripture quotations marked "KJV" are taken from the *King James Version* of the Bible.

Verses marked "TLB"are taken from *The Living Bible*. Copyright © 1971.
Used by permission of Tyndale House Publishers, Inc., Wheaton, Illinois 60189.
All rights reserved.

Scripture quotations marked "NASB" are taken from the *New American Standard
Bible®*, copyright © The Lockman Foundation 1960, 1962, 1963, 1968, 1971,
1972, 1973, 1975, 1977. Used by permission.

Never Lose Heart
ISBN 1-57794-444-5
Copyright © 2001 by Joyce Meyer
Life In The Word, Inc.
P. O. Box 655
Fenton, Missouri 63026

Published by Harrison House, Inc.
P. O. Box 35035
Tulsa, Oklahoma 74153

NEVER LOSE
HEART

Encouragement for the Journey

JOYCE MEYER

Harrison House

Contents

WHEN
YOU FEEL
STRESSED

Peace comes to every situation
when we choose to listen to and obey
the Lord. We must follow Wisdom
to enjoy blessed lives.

GOD'S WORD FOR YOU

Be anxious for nothing, but in everything by prayer and supplication with thanksgiving let your requests be made known to God.

And the peace of God, which surpasses all comprehension, will guard your hearts and your minds in Christ Jesus.

PHILIPPIANS 4:6-7 NASB

o n e

WHEN YOU
FEEL STRESSED

few years ago, I went to a doctor because I was constantly sick. He told me the symptoms were the result of being under stress. I was sleeping wrong, eating improperly, and pushing myself harder and harder—all in the name of working for the Lord.

The word *stress* was originally an engineering term used to refer to the amount of force that a beam or other physical support could bear without collapsing under the strain. In our time, stress has been expanded to include mental and emotional tension.

Stress is a normal part of everyone's life. God has created us to withstand a certain amount of pressure and tension. The problem comes when we push beyond our limitations and head toward doing permanent damage to ourselves.

Peace is meant to be the normal condition for every believer in Jesus Christ. He is the Prince of Peace, and in Jesus we find our own inheritance of peace. It is a gift from the Holy Spirit, which He gives as we live in obedience to His Word.

The peace Jesus gives operates in good times or bad,
when you are abounding or being abased.
His peace operates in the middle of a storm.

GOD'S WORD FOR YOU

Do you not know that your body is the temple (the very sanctuary) of the Holy Spirit Who lives within you, Whom you have received [as a Gift] from God? You are not your own,

You were bought with a price [purchased with a preciousness and paid for, made His own]. So then, honor God and bring glory to Him in your body.

1 CORINTHIANS 6:19-20

Have you not known? Have you not heard? The everlasting God, the Lord, the Creator of the ends of the earth, does not faint or grow weary; there is no searching of His understanding.

He gives power to the faint and weary, and to him who has no might He increases strength [causing it to multiply and making it to abound].

ISAIAH 40:28-29

REFRESH THE WEARY

The first key to handling or overcoming stress is to recognize or admit we are under it. Though I was constantly having headaches, backaches, stomach-aches, neck aches, and all the other symptoms of stress, I found it very difficult to admit that I was pushing too hard physically, mentally, emotionally, and spiritually. I was doing the work I felt God wanted me to do without actually seeking Him to find out which work He wanted me to do, when He wanted me to do it, and how much of it. If we abuse ourselves, we will suffer the consequences.

Although the Lord gives power to the faint and weary, if you are worn out from continually exceeding your physical limitations, you need physical rest. The Lord may mercifully give you supernatural energy in particular instances, but you are in disobedience when you abuse your body, the temple of the Holy Spirit.

If you want God to flow and work through you, you need to take care of your body so God can use you. If you wear out your body, you don't have a spare in the drawer somewhere to pull out!

The anointing of God lifts when you operate outside of His promptings.

GOD'S WORD FOR YOU

*I, Wisdom [from God], make prudence my dwelling,
and I find out knowledge and discretion.*

PROVERBS 8:12

*The Wisdom (godly Wisdom, which is comprehensive
insight into the ways and purposes of God] of the prudent
is to understand his way. . . .*

PROVERBS 14:8

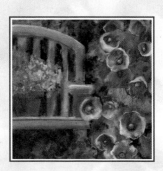

PRUDENCE

A word you don't hear very much teaching about is "prudence." In the Scriptures "prudence" or "prudent" means being good stewards of the gifts God has given us to use. Those gifts include time, energy, strength, and health as well as material possessions. They include our bodies as well as our minds and spirits.

Just as each one of us has been given a different set of gifts, each of us has been given a different ability to manage those gifts. Some of us are better able to manage ourselves than are others.

Each of us needs to know how much we are able to handle. We need to be able to recognize when we are reaching "full capacity" or "overload." Instead of pushing ourselves into overload to please others, satisfy our own desires, or reach our personal goals, we need to listen to the Lord and obey Him. We must follow Wisdom to enjoy blessed lives.

Nobody can remove all the stressors, the things causing or increasing stress, in our lives. For that reason, each of us must be *prudent* to identify and recognize the stressors that affect us most and learn how to respond to them with the right action.

God is good, and He wants you to believe
that He has a good plan for your life,
and that He is working in your situation.

GOD'S WORD FOR YOU

*If you will listen diligently to the voice of the Lord
your God, being watchful to do all His commandments
which I command you this day, the Lord your God will set
you high above all the nations of the earth.*

*And the Lord shall make you the head, and not the
tail; and you shall be above only, and you shall not be
beneath. . . .*

DEUTERONOMY 28:1, 13

*. . . now we serve not under [obedience to] the old
code of written regulations, but [under obedience to the
promptings] of the Spirit in newness [of life].*

ROMANS 7:6

ℛELIEVING STRESS

When I began to prepare this message on stress, I asked the Lord to show me how He wanted me to present the material. The answer He gave me is a message, a word, from the heart of the Father for the Body of Christ for this hour, this season.

Another important key to relieving stress is *obedience*.

We may have stress, but we will be on *top* of it, not *under* it. There is a big difference between being *under* stress and being on *top* of a situation!

All of us have situations that come our way we don't like. But, with the power of God, we can go through those circumstances stress free.

Even though, like the people in the world, we will sometimes experience stressful times, if we are obedient to God's Word and to His promptings, we can be on top of stress and not under it.

Do you believe that God is leading you into a place of victory and triumph, not into a place of defeat? Your answer as a child of God and believer in Jesus Christ would be yes! If we believers would listen to everything the Lord tells us and obey Him, we would not get into that state of defeat so often.

❧

Simply obeying the promptings of the Holy Spirit will often relieve stress quickly.

GOD'S WORD FOR YOU

Do you not know that if you continually surrender yourselves to anyone to do his will, you are the slaves of him whom you obey, whether that be to sin, which leads to death, or to obedience which leads to righteousness (right doing and right standing with God)?

ROMANS 6:16

Now therefore, if you will obey My voice in truth and keep My covenant, then you shall be My own peculiar possession and treasure from among and above all peoples; for all the earth is Mine.

EXODUS 19:5

God's Anointing Is on Obedience

God's grace and power are available for us to use. God enables us or gives us an anointing of the Holy Spirit to do what *He* tells us to do. Sometimes after He has prompted us to go another direction, we still keep pressing on with our original plan. If we are doing something He has not approved, He is under no obligation to give us the energy to do it. We are functioning in our own strength rather than under the control of the Holy Spirit. Then we get so frustrated, stressed, or burned out, we lose our self-control, simply by ignoring the promptings of the Spirit.

Many people are stressed and burned out from going their own way instead of God's way. They end up in stressful situations when they go a different direction from the one God prompted. Then they burn out in the midst of the disobedience and, struggling to finish what they started outside of God's direction, beg God to anoint them.

God is merciful, and He helps us in the midst of our mistakes. But He is not going to give us strength and energy to disobey Him continually. We can avoid many stressful situations and living "tied up in knots" simply by obeying the Holy Spirit's promptings moment by moment.

Obeying Him in the little things makes a major difference in keeping stress out of our life.

GOD'S WORD FOR YOU

Let be and be still, and know (recognize and understand) that I am God. I will be exalted among the nations! I will be exalted in the earth!

PSALM 46:10

Lean on, trust in, and be confident in the Lord with all your heart and mind and do not rely on your own insight or understanding.

In all your ways know, recognize, and acknowledge Him, and He will direct and make straight and plain your paths.

PROVERBS 3:5-6

BE STILL AND KNOW GOD

One of the main reasons so many of us are burned out and stressed out is that we don't know how to be still, to "know" God and "acknowledge" Him. When we spend time with Him, we learn to hear His voice. When we acknowledge Him, He directs our paths. We need to learn to be quiet inside and stay in that peaceful state so that we are always ready to hear the Lord's voice.

Many people today run from one thing to the next. Because their minds don't know how to be still, they don't know how to be still.

For a long time I felt I had to find something to do every evening. I had to be involved and a part of whatever was going on. I thought I couldn't afford to miss anything because I didn't want anything to go on that I didn't know about. I couldn't just sit and be still. I had to be up doing something. I was not a human being—I was a human doing.

We need to be careful to submit our ideas and plans to God, then slow down and wait. Make sure there is a sense of peace to go along with the plans and ideas. Ask the Lord for His will in your life, then be still and know that He is God.

God gives His highest and best to those whose trust is in Him. Be still and let Him show Himself strong in your life.

GOD'S WORD FOR YOU

Peace I leave with you; My [own] peace I now give and bequeath to you. Not as the world gives do I give to you. Do not let your hearts be troubled, neither let them be afraid. [Stop allowing yourselves to be agitated and disturbed; and do not permit yourselves to be fearful and intimidated and cowardly and unsettled.]

JOHN 14:27

And let the peace (soul harmony which comes) from Christ rule (act as umpire continually) in your hearts [deciding and settling with finality all questions that arise in your minds, in that peaceful state].

COLOSSIANS 3:15

Jesus, Our Prince of Peace

When we are all stressed out, we would like to eliminate the causes of the problems, but the source of stress is not really difficulties, circumstances, and situations. Stress comes from approaching problems with the world's perspective rather than faith in Jesus Christ, the Prince of Peace.

It was Jesus' blood that bought our peace, but the price we must pay for peace is a willingness to change our approach to life. We will never enjoy peace without a willingness to adjust and adapt ourselves. We must be willing to sacrifice worry and reasoning if we are to know peace. We cannot have anxiety, frustration, or rigid, legalistic attitudes and enjoy the peace of God.

Even though we will have disturbing issues to deal with, we can have Jesus' peace because He has "overcome the world" and "deprived" the world of its "power to harm" us. He left us with the power to "stop allowing" ourselves "to be agitated and disturbed"! Peace is available, but we must choose it!

The Prince of Peace, Jesus, Who lives inside those of us who have received Him, knows and will reveal to us the specific actions we need to take in every situation to lead us into peace.

It is absolutely amazing what we can accomplish in Christ if we live one day at a time in His peace.

GOD'S WORD FOR YOU

*Even when we were dead (slain) by [our own]
shortcomings and trespasses, He made us alive together in
fellowship and in union with Christ; [He gave us the very
life of Christ Himself, the same new life with which He
quickened Him, for] it is by grace (His favor and mercy
which you did not deserve) that you are saved (delivered
from judgment and made partakers of Christ's salvation).*

EPHESIANS 2:5

*But He gives us more and more grace (power of the
Holy Spirit, to meet this evil tendency and all others fully).
. . . God sets Himself against the proud . . . but gives
grace [continually] to the lowly (those who are humble
enough to receive it).*

JAMES 4:6

WORKS VERSUS GRACE

We get so frustrated because we are trying to live by *works* a life that was brought into being and designed by God to be lived by *grace*. The more we try to figure out what to do to solve our dilemma, the more confused, upset, and frustrated we become.

When you get into a frustrating situation, just stop and say, "O Lord, give me grace." Then believe that God has heard your prayer and is answering that prayer and working out that situation.

Faith is the channel through which you and I receive the grace of God. If we try to do things on our own without being open to receive the grace of God, then no matter how much faith we may have, we will still not receive what we are asking of God.

A long time ago I wrote up this statement and stuck it on my refrigerator:

Works of the flesh = Frustration.

If you can learn this principle, you will soon overcome the evil tendency to become frustrated.

We need to trust in and rely on the grace of God. He knows what we are facing in every situation of life, and He will work out things for the best if we will trust Him enough to allow Him to do so.

Remember, it is not by power or by might, but by the Spirit that we win the victory over our enemy.

GOD'S WORD FOR YOU

Now unto him that is able to do exceeding abundantly above all that we ask or think, according to the power that worketh in us.

EPHESIANS 3:20 KJV

GOD IS ABLE

This is a powerful Scripture that tells us that our God is able—able to do far above and beyond anything that you and I can ever dare to hope, ask, or even think. We need to pray, to do the asking in faith and in trust. But it is God Who does the work, not us. How does He do it? *According to* [or by] *the power* [or grace of God] *that worketh in us.* Whatever you and I receive from the Lord is directly related to the amount of grace we learn to receive.

I was putting unbelievable stress on myself trying to change. I was under tremendous condemnation because every message I heard seemed to be telling me to change, yet I couldn't change no matter how hard I tried, believed, or confessed. I was in a terrible mess because I saw all the things about me that needed to be changed, but I was powerless to bring about those changes.

The Lord has to be our Source and our Supply. He is the only One who can bring about changes in our lives. I had to learn to say, "Father, although I am not worthy of Your help, I know that the changes You want in my life are not going to work unless You add the power."

God promises to strengthen us in our weaknesses if we trust Him and turn to Him. God's grace will be sufficient in our need.

WHEN
YOU FEEL
DISCOURAGED

*Happiness and joy do not come
from the outside. They come
from within. They are a conscious
decision, a deliberate choice, one that
we make ourselves each day we live.*

GOD'S WORD FOR YOU

*[What, what would have become of me] had I not
believed that I would see the Lord's goodness in the land of
the living!*

*Wait and hope for and expect the Lord; be brave and
of good courage and let your heart be stout and enduring.
Yes, wait for and hope for and expect the Lord.*

PSALM 27:13-14

*For I know the thoughts and plans that I have for
you, says the Lord, thoughts and plans for welfare and
peace and not for evil, to give you hope in your final
outcome.*

JEREMIAH 29:11

t w a

WHEN YOU FEEL DISCOURAGED

We have all been disappointed at some time. It would be surprising if we went through the week without encountering some kind of disappointment. We are "appointed" (set in a certain direction) for something to happen a certain way, and when it doesn't happen that way, we become "dis-appointed."

Disappointment not dealt with turns into discouragement. If we stay discouraged very long, we are liable to become devastated, and devastation leaves us unable to handle anything.

Many devastated Christians are lying along the roadside of life because they have not learned how to handle disappointment. The devastation they are experiencing now most likely began with a minor disappointment that was not dealt with properly.

It is not God's will for us to live disappointed, devastated, or oppressed! When we become "disappointed," we must learn to become "re-appointed" to keep from becoming discouraged, then devastated.

When we learn to place our hope and confidence in Jesus the Rock (1 Corinthians 10:4) and resist the devil at the onset, we can live in the joy and peace of the Lord, free from discouragement.

❧

*Choose to aggressively withstand the devil so
you can live in the fullness of life God has provided
for you through His Son Jesus Christ.*

GOD'S WORD FOR YOU

. . . for God selected (deliberately chose) what in the world is foolish to put the wise to shame, and what the world calls weak to put the strong to shame.

And God also selected (deliberately chose) what in the world is lowborn and insignificant and branded and treated with contempt, even the things that are nothing, that He might depose and bring to nothing the things that are,

So that no mortal man should [have pretense for glorying and] boast in the presence of God.

1 CORINTHIANS 1:27-29

GOD CHOOSES THE UNLIKELY

When you feel discouraged, remember that God chose you for His very own purpose, however unlikely a candidate you feel. By doing so, He has placed before you a wide open door to show you His boundless grace, mercy, and power to change your life.

When God uses any one of us, though we may all feel inadequate and unworthy, we realize that our source is not in ourselves but in Him alone: "[This is] because the foolish thing [that has its source in] God is wiser than men, and the weak thing [that springs] from God is stronger than men" (1 Corinthians 1:25).

Each of us has a destiny, and there is absolutely no excuse not to fulfill it. We cannot use our weakness as an excuse because God says that His strength is made perfect in weakness (2 Corinthians 12:9). We cannot use the past as an excuse because God tells us through the apostle Paul that if any person is in Christ, he is a new creature; old things have passed away, and all things have become new (2 Corinthians 5:17).

Spend some time with yourself and take an inventory of how you feel about yourself. What is your image of yourself? Do you see yourself re-created in God's image, resurrected to a brand-new life that is just waiting for you to claim it?

Each of us can succeed at being
everything God intends us to be.

GOD'S WORD FOR YOU

. . . the Word of God . . . is effectually at work in you who believe [exercising its superhuman power in those who adhere to and trust in and rely on it].

1 THESSALONIANS 2:13

We Are a "Work in Progress"

I encourage you to say every day, *"God is working in me right now—He is changing me!"* Speak out of your mouth what the Word says, not what you feel. When we incessantly talk about how we feel, it is difficult for the Word of God to work in us effectively.

As we step out to be all we can be in Christ, we will make some mistakes—everyone does. But it takes the pressure off of us when we realize that God is expecting us to do the best we can. He is not expecting us to be perfect (totally without flaw). If we were as perfect as we try to be, we would not need a Savior. I believe God will always leave a certain number of defects in us, just so we will know how much we need Jesus every single day.

I am not a perfect preacher. There are times when I say things wrong, times when I believe I have heard from God and find out I was hearing from myself. There are many times when I fall short of perfection. I don't have perfect faith, a perfect attitude, perfect thoughts, and perfect ways.

Jesus knew that would happen to all of us. That is why He stands in the gap between God's perfection and our imperfection. He *continually* intercedes for us because we *continually* need it (Hebrews 7:25).

We do not have to believe that God accepts us only if we perform perfectly. We can believe the truth that He accepts us "in the Beloved."

GOD'S WORD FOR YOU

Fight the good fight of the faith; lay hold of the eternal life to which you were summoned and [for which] you confessed the good confession [of faith] before many witnesses.

1 TIMOTHY 6:12

BE A FIGHTER

To be aggressive is to be a fighter. Just as the apostle Paul said that he had fought the good fight of faith (2 Timothy 4:7), so he instructed his young disciple Timothy to fight the good fight of faith. In the same way, we are to fight the good fight of faith in our daily lives as we struggle against spiritual enemies in high places and in our own mind and heart.

One part of fighting the good fight of faith is being able to recognize the enemy. As long as we are passive, Satan will torment us. Nothing is going to change about our situation if all we do is just sit and wish things were different. We have to take action. Too often we don't move against the enemy when he comes against us with discouragement or fear or doubt or guilt. We just draw back into a corner somewhere and let him beat us up.

You and I are not supposed to be punching bags for the devil; instead, we are supposed to be fighters.

Now the devil wants us to fight in the natural with everybody around us. But God wants us to forget all the junk that Satan stirs up within us to get us riled up against other people. Instead, He wants us to fight against the spiritual enemies who try to war over our lives and steal our peace and joy.

Come against Satan when he is trying to get a foothold, and he will never get a stronghold.

GOD'S WORD FOR YOU

For as many as are the promises of God, they all find their Yes [answer] in Him [Christ]. For this reason we also utter the Amen (so be it) to God through Him [in His Person and by His agency] to the glory of God.

2 CORINTHIANS 1:20

CONFIDENCE IN JESUS

In several places in the Bible, for example in 1 Corinthians 10:4, Jesus is referred to as the Rock. The apostle Paul goes on to tell us in Colossians 2:7 that we are to be rooted and grounded in Him.

If we get our roots wrapped around Jesus Christ, we are in good shape. But if we get them wrapped around anything or anyone else, we are in trouble.

Nothing nor no one is going to be as solid and dependable and immovable as Jesus. That's why I don't want people to get rooted and grounded in me or my ministry. I want to point people to Jesus. I know that ultimately I will fail them in some way, just as I know they will ultimately fail me.

That's the problem with us humans; we are always liable to failure. But Jesus Christ isn't. Put your hope wholly and unchangeably in Him. Not in man, not in circumstances, not in anything or anyone else.

If you don't put your hope and faith in the Rock of your salvation, you are headed for disappointment, which leads to discouragement and devastation. We should have so much confidence in God's love for us that no matter what comes against us, we know deep inside that we are more than conquerors.

We need to come to a state of utter bankruptcy in our own ability apart from Christ. Without God, we are helpless; with Him nothing is impossible to us.

GOD'S WORD FOR YOU

. . . let us run with patient endurance and steady and active persistence the appointed course of the race that is set before us.

Looking away [from all that will distract] to Jesus, Who is the Leader and the Source of our faith [giving the first incentive for our belief] and is also its Finisher [bringing it to maturity and perfection]. He, for the joy [of obtaining the prize] that was set before Him, endured the cross, despising and ignoring the shame, and is now seated at the right hand of the throne of God.

Just think of Him Who endured from sinners such grievous opposition and bitter hostility against Himself [reckon up and consider it all in comparison with your trials], so that you may not grow weary or exhausted, losing heart and relaxing and fainting in your minds.

HEBREWS 12:1-3

KEEP ON LOOKING TO JESUS

It does not take any special talent to give up and lie down on the side of the road of life and say, "I quit." Any unbeliever can do that.

You don't have to be a Christian to be a quitter. But once you get hold of Jesus, or better yet when He gets hold of you, He begins to pump strength and energy and courage into you, and something strange and wonderful begins to happen. He won't let you quit!

I used to want to give up and quit. But now I get out of bed and start each day afresh and anew. I begin my day by praying and reading the Bible and speaking the Word, seeking after God.

The devil may be screaming in my ear, "That's not doing you one bit of good. You've been doing that for years and look what it's got you—you still have trouble."

That's when I say, "Shut up, devil! The Bible says that I am to look to Jesus and follow His example. He is my Leader, the Source and Finisher of my faith.

You and I need to make a decision today that, come what may, we are going to keep pressing on, looking to Jesus, no matter what.

GOD'S WORD FOR YOU

Do not fret or have any anxiety about anything, but in every circumstance and in everything, by prayer and petition (definite requests), with thanksgiving, continue to make your wants known to God.

And God's peace [shall be yours, that tranquil state of a soul assured of its salvation through Christ, and so fearing nothing from God and being content with its earthly lot of whatever sort that is, that peace] which transcends all understanding shall garrison and mount guard over your hearts and minds in Christ Jesus.

PHILIPPIANS 4:6-7

MEDITATE ON THE THINGS OF GOD

If you don't want to be devastated by discouragement, then don't meditate on your disappointments.

Did you know that your feelings are hooked up to your thinking? If you don't think that is true, just take about twenty minutes or so and think about nothing but your problems. I can assure you that by the end of that time your feelings and maybe even your countenance will have changed.

I got up one day thinking about a problem I had. Suddenly the Spirit of the Lord spoke to me. He said to me, "Joyce, are you going to fellowship with your problem or with Me?"

When you get disappointed, don't sit around and feel sorry for yourself. As bad as things may seem, we still have a choice. We can choose to fellowship with our problems or fellowship with God.

We can allow our thoughts to dwell on the bad things until we become totally discouraged and devastated, or we can focus our attention on all the good things that have happened to us in our life—and on all the blessings that God still has in store for us in the days ahead.

❧

Our thoughts are silent words that only we and the Lord hear, but those words affect our inner man, our health, our joy, and our attitude.

GOD'S WORD FOR YOU

Catch the foxes for us, the little foxes that are ruining the vineyards. . . .

SONG OF SOLOMON 2:15 NASB

CATCH THE FOXES

Little disappointments can create frustration, which in turn may lead to bigger problems that can produce a great deal of damage.

Besides the huge disappointments that occur when we fail to get the job promotion or house we wanted, we can become just as upset by minor annoyances. For example, suppose someone is supposed to meet you for lunch and fails to show up. Or suppose you make a special trip to the mall to buy something at a discount, but it's all sold out.

All these kinds of frustrations are actually minor, but they can add up to cause a lot of grief. That's why we have to know how to handle them and keep them in perspective. Otherwise, they can get out of hand and be blown up all out of proportion.

We have to be on our guard against the little foxes that destroy the vineyards, because all together they can do just as much damage as the serious disappointments that often accompany them.

We must learn to do as Paul did in the book of Acts when the serpent attached itself to his hand—he simply shook it off (Acts 28:1-5)! If we practice dealing quickly with disappointments as they come, they will not pile up into a mountain of devastation.

Victory is not the absence of problems;
it is the presence of God's power.

GOD'S WORD FOR YOU

The mystery of which was hidden for ages and generations [from angels and men], but is now revealed to His holy people (the saints),

To whom God was pleased to make known how great for the Gentiles are the riches of the glory of this mystery, which is Christ within and among you, the Hope of [realizing the] glory.

COLOSSIANS 1:26-27

CHRIST IN YOU, THE HOPE OF GLORY

You and I can only realize and experience the glory of God on our lives because of Christ in us. He is our hope of seeing better things.

The glory of God is His manifested excellence. As the children of God, we have a blood-bought right to experience the best God has planned for us. Satan furiously fights the plan of God in each of our lives, and his primary weapon is deception. When we are deceived, we believe something that is not true.

When we look at ourselves and our own ability, we feel defeated, but remembering that Christ lives in us is our hope of realizing the glory. It keeps us encouraged enough to press on toward better things. We limit ourselves when we look to ourselves alone and fail to see Jesus.

The Lord has destined His Church for glory. He is coming back for a glorious Church (Ephesians 5:27). God's glory can be manifested in us and on us, but only as we believe it is possible.

*God is looking for someone who will believe
and receive. He is waiting to manifest His glory
—to you and through you!*

WHEN YOU FEEL WORRIED

*God has a secret place
of abiding where worry
vanishes and peace reigns.*

GOD'S WORD FOR YOU

Humble yourselves therefore under the mighty hand of God, that he may exalt you in due time:
  Casting all your care upon him; for he careth for you.

1 PETER 5:6-7 KJV

The Spirit of the Lord God is upon me, because the Lord has anointed and qualified me. . . . To grant [consolation and joy] to those who mourn in Zion—to give them an ornament (a garland or diadem) of beauty instead of ashes ["beauty for ashes" KJV].

ISAIAH 61:1, 3

three

WHEN YOU FEEL WORRIED

od wants to take care of us, but in order to let Him, *we* must stop taking the care. Many people want God to take care of them while they are worrying or trying to figure out an answer instead of waiting for God's direction. They are actually wallowing around in their "ashes," but they still want God to give them beauty. In order for God to give us the beauty, we must give Him the "ashes."

We give Him our cares by trusting that He can and will take care of us. Hebrews 4:3 says: "For we who have believed (adhered to and trusted in and relied on God) do enter that rest. . . ."

We enter into the Lord's rest through believing. Worry is the opposite of faith. Worry steals our peace, physically wears us out, and can even make us sick. If we are worrying, we are not trusting God, and we are not entering God's rest.

What a great trade! You give God ashes, and He gives you beauty. You give Him all your worries and concerns, and He gives you protection, stability, a place of refuge and fullness of joy—the privilege of being cared for by Him.

Jesus did not worry,
and we do not have to worry either.

GOD'S WORD FOR YOU

He who dwells in the secret place of the Most High shall remain stable and fixed under the shadow of the Almighty [Whose power no foe can withstand].

PSALM 91:1

ABIDING IN PROTECTION

God has a secret place where we can dwell in peace and safety.

The secret place is the place of rest in God, a place of peace and comfort in Him. This secret place is a "spiritual place" where worry vanishes and peace reigns. It is the place of God's presence. When we spend time praying and seeking God and dwelling in His presence, we are in the secret place.

When you and I *dwell in Christ* or *dwell in the secret place*, we do not just visit there occasionally, we take up permanent residence there.

The secret place is a hiding place, a private place, or a place of refuge. It is the place we run to when we are hurting, overwhelmed, or feeling faint. It is the place we run to when we are being mistreated or persecuted, when we are in great need, or when we feel we just cannot take it anymore.

We need to be firmly planted in God. We need to know the Source of our help in every situation and in every circumstance. We need to have our own secret place of peace and security. We need to rely on God and trust Him completely.

God wants us to take refuge under the protective shadow of His wings. He wants us to run to Him!

GOD'S WORD FOR YOU

Therefore do not worry and be anxious, saying, What are we going to have to eat? or, What are we going to have to drink? or, What are we going to have to wear?

For the Gentiles (heathen) wish for and crave and diligently seek all these things, and your heavenly Father knows well that you need them all.

MATTHEW 6:31-32

Don't Be Anxious

The problem with worry is that it causes us to start saying: "What are we going to have to eat? What are we going to have to drink? What are we going to have to wear?" In other words, "What are we going to do if God doesn't come through for us?"

Instead of calming our fears and removing our worries, we begin to fret and fuss with the words of our mouth, which only makes them even more deeply ingrained.

The problem with this way of doing things is that it is the way people act who don't know they have a heavenly Father. But you and I do know we have a heavenly Father, so we need to act like it.

Jesus assures us that our heavenly Father knows all our needs before we ask Him. So why should we worry about them? Instead, we need to focus our attention on the things that are much more important—the things of God.

Seek first the Kingdom of God and His righteousness; then all these other things we need will be added to us.

53

GOD'S WORD FOR YOU

Only it must be in faith that he asks with no wavering (no hesitating, no doubting). For the one who wavers (hesitates, doubts) is like the billowing surge out at sea that is blown hither and thither and tossed by the wind.

For truly, let not such a person imagine that he will receive anything [he asks for] from the Lord.

JAMES 1:6-7

STAY IN THE POSITIVE

If we take our concerns to the Lord in prayer and then continue to worry about them, we are mixing a positive and a negative force. Prayer is a positive force, and worry is a negative force. If we add them together, we come up with zero. I don't know about you, but I don't want to have zero power, so I try not to mix prayer and worry.

God spoke to me one time and said, "Many people operate with zero power because they are always mixing the positives and the negatives. They have a positive confession for a little while, then a negative confession for a little while. They pray for a little while, then they worry for a little while. They trust for a little while, then they worry for a little while. As a result, they just go back and forth, never really making any progress."

Let's not magnify the bad—let's magnify the good! Let's make it larger by talking about it, by being positive in our thoughts, in our attitudes, in our outlook, in our words, and in our actions.

Why not make a decision to stay in the positive by trusting God and refusing to worry?

Practice being positive in each situation that arises. Even if whatever is taking place at the moment is not so good, expect God to bring good out of it.

GOD'S WORD FOR YOU

*Let the redeemed of the Lord say so, whom He has
delivered from the hand of the adversary.*

PSALM 107:2

*For [then] He will deliver you from the snare of the
fowler and from the deadly pestilence.*
*[Then] He will cover you with His pinions, and under
His wings shall you trust and find refuge; His truth and
His faithfulness are a shield and a buckler.*

PSALM 91:3-4

ℐF YOU'RE REDEEMED, SAY SO!

When you realize that the devil is trying to distract you, don't just sit around and let him beat you up with worry and negative thoughts. Open your mouth and begin to confess your authority in Christ.

Sometimes while I am preparing to speak at a church or seminar, negative thoughts will begin to bombard me. At those times I encourage myself with my own mouth and say out loud, "Everything is going to be all right."

Satan places anxious and worried thoughts in our minds, sometimes actually "bombarding" our minds with them. He hopes we will receive them and begin "saying" them out of our mouths. If we do, he then has material to actually create the circumstances in our lives he has been giving us anxious thoughts about.

Once I recognized those anxious thoughts and evil forebodings and took authority over them, God began to bring some deliverance to my life so I could start to enjoy it.

Don't be the devil's mouthpiece.

Find out what God's Word promises you and begin to declare His two-edged sword (Hebrews 4:12).

As we speak the Word out of our mouths
in faith, we wield a mighty two-edged sword
that destroys the enemy.

GOD'S WORD FOR YOU

*Beloved, we are [even here and] now God's children;
it is not yet disclosed (made clear) what we shall be
[hereafter], but we know that when He comes and is
manifested, we shall [as God's children] resemble and be
like Him, for we shall see Him just as He [really] is.*

1 JOHN 3:2

Live in the Now

In reality, the choices we make today will determine whether we will enjoy the moment or waste it by worrying. Sometimes we end up missing the moment of today because we are too concerned about tomorrow. We need to keep our mind focused on what God wants us to be doing now.

God gave me a definition of anxiety: "Anxiety is caused by trying to mentally or emotionally get into things that are not here yet (the future) or things that have already been (the past)."

One of the things that we need to understand is that God wants us to learn how to be *now* people. For example, 2 Corinthians 6:2 KJV says, "Behold, now is the day of salvation," and Hebrews 4:7 says, "Today, if you would hear His voice and when you hear it, do not harden your hearts."

We need to learn to live now. Often we spend our mental time in the past or the future. When we don't really give ourselves to what we are doing at the moment, we become prone to anxiety. If we will live in the now, we will find the Lord there with us. Regardless of what situations life brings our way, He has promised never to leave us or forsake us but to always be with us and help us (Hebrews 13:5; Matthew 28:20).

Don't waste your precious "now" worrying about yesterday or tomorrow.

GOD'S WORD FOR YOU

But be doers of the Word [obey the message], and not merely listeners to it, betraying yourselves [into deception by reasoning contrary to the Truth].

JAMES 1:22

GIVE UP EXCESSIVE REASONING

Are you always trying to figure everything out? Many of us have fallen into that ditch. Instead of casting our care upon the Lord, we go through life carrying every bit of it.

When we try to figure everything out, we are exalting our reasoning above God's thoughts. We are placing our ways higher than His ways. When God revealed to me that I had to give up excessive reasoning that was contrary to the truth, it was a real challenge. I couldn't stand it if I did not have everything figured out.

For example, God told us to do some things in our ministry several years ago that I didn't have the slightest idea how to go about doing. But God never called me to figure out exactly how to accomplish everything He asked me to do. He called me to seek *Him* rather than the answer to my problems, then obey what He told me to do.

When we worry, we lose our peace, and when we try to figure everything out, we fall into confusion. Confusion is the result of reasoning with our own understanding when we should be trusting in the Lord with all our heart to make the way for us according to His plan. When we trust that His thoughts are higher than our thoughts, we stop confusion before it starts.

God's peace is always available,
but we must choose it.

GOD'S WORD FOR YOU

So trust in the Lord (commit yourself to Him, lean on Him, hope confidently in Him) forever; for the Lord God is an everlasting Rock [the Rock of Ages].

ISAIAH 26:4

O my God, I trust, lean on, rely on, and am confident in You.

PSALM 25:2

DEVELOPING TRUST

How many times have you frustrated yourself and gotten all upset needlessly over trying situations that came your way? How many years of your life have you spent saying, "Oh, I'm believing God. I'm trusting God," when, in reality, all you were doing was worrying, talking negatively, and trying to figure out everything on your own? You may have thought you were trusting God because you were saying, "I trust God," but inside you were anxious and panicky. You were trying to learn to trust God, but you were not quite there yet.

Trust and confidence are built up over a period of time. It usually takes some time to overcome an ingrained habit of worry, anxiety, or fear. That is why it is so important to "hang in there" with God. Don't quit and give up, because you gain experience and spiritual strength every round you go through. Each time you become a little stronger than you were the last time. Sooner or later, if you don't give up, you will be more than the devil can handle.

If you are in a time of trials, use that time
to build your trust in God. Trust Him to deliver you
or bring you through successfully.

GOD'S WORD FOR YOU

Be well balanced. . . .

1 PETER 5:8

You will guard him and keep him in perfect and constant peace whose mind [both its inclination and its character] is stayed on You, because he commits himself to You, leans on You, and hopes confidently in You.

ISAIAH 26:3

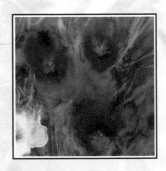

BE WELL-BALANCED

Sometimes in trying situations our anxiety gets in the way of our doing what we should. All we can do is our best, then trust God with the rest.

We function best when we have a calm, well-balanced mind. When our mind is calm, it is without fear, worry, or torment. When our mind is well-balanced, we are able to look the situation over and decide what to do or not to do about it.

Where most of us get in trouble is when we get out of balance. Either we move into a state of total passivity in which we do nothing, expecting God to do everything for us, or we become hyperactive, operating most of the time in the flesh. God wants us to be well-balanced so that we are able to face any situation of life and say, "Well, I believe I can do certain things about this situation, but no more."

Instead of getting distraught and full of fear and worry, we need to go before God and say, "Well, Lord, I'm believing You to help me in this situation, but is there something You want me to do?"

Whatever it is that God shows us to do about our problem, we need to be diligent enough to do it. Then we need to trust Him with the outcome.

Once we have done all we know to do,
we can trust God with the rest.
That is what I call faith and balance.

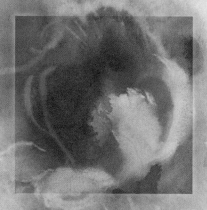

WHEN
YOU FEEL
INSECURE

*God is looking for people with
a right heart attitude toward Him,
not a perfect performance record.*

GOD'S WORD FOR YOU

May you be rooted deep in love and founded securely on love,

That you may have the power and be strong to apprehend and grasp with all the saints [God's devoted people, the experience of that love] what is the breadth and length and height and depth [of it];

[That you may really come] to know [practically, through experience for yourselves] the love of Christ, which far surpasses mere knowledge [without experience]; that you may be filled [through all your being] unto all the fullness of God [may have the richest measure of the divine Presence, and become a body wholly filled and flooded with God Himself]!

EPHESIANS 3:17-19

four

WHEN YOU FEEL INSECURE

any people have a deep feeling of insecurity about themselves because they can't accept themselves for who they are. Are you tired of playing games, wearing masks, trying to be someone other than who you are? Wouldn't you like the freedom just to be accepted as you are, without pressure to be someone you really don't know how to be?

God wants us to learn our value is not in what we do but in who we are in Him. He wants us to be willing to be who we are, weaknesses and all, because He accepts us unconditionally.

The devil's plan is to deceive us into basing our worth on our performance, then keep us focused on all our faults and shortcomings. Satan wants us to have a low opinion of ourselves so that we live ineffectively for God, being miserable and unreceptive to God's blessings because we don't think we deserve them.

It is so important to have a positive sense of self-esteem, self-value, and self-worth, to be secure in who we are in Christ, to truly like ourselves. We learn to like ourselves by learning how much God loves us. Once we become rooted and grounded in God's love, we can come to terms of peace with ourselves and stop feeling insecure.

Every one of us is imperfect,
and God loves us just the way we are.

GOD'S WORD FOR YOU

That the communication of thy faith may become effectual by the acknowledging of every good thing which is in you in Christ Jesus.

PHILEMON 1:6 KJV

For by your words you will be justified and acquitted, and by your words you will be condemned and sentenced.

MATTHEW 12:37

ELIMINATE THE NEGATIVE

If we speak badly about ourselves, we will feel condemned. Let's apply what Jesus taught about our words as the first key to overcoming insecurity *and never speak negatively about ourselves.* We must speak words that empower us—not words that weaken us. If we want to increase our self-acceptance and our opinion of ourselves, we must decide that not one more negative comment about ourselves will ever come out of our mouth.

The devil wants us to acknowledge every bad trait we see in ourselves because he doesn't want the communication of our faith to be effectual. As the accuser of the brethren (Revelation 12:9-10), he continually tries to redirect our focus from who we are in Christ back on to our shortcomings.

We need to understand who we are in Christ and see how much He has done for us through shedding His blood to make us worthy. The communication of our faith is made effectual by acknowledging every *good thing* in us *in Christ Jesus*, not by acknowledging every *wrong thing* with *us*. Acts 10:15 says: "What God has cleansed and pronounced clean, do not you defile and profane by regarding and calling common and unhallowed or unclean."

Jesus was made perfect for us. Our acceptability to God is not based on our performance, but on our faith and trust in Jesus' performance.

GOD'S WORD FOR YOU

[Righteousness, standing acceptable to God] will be granted and credited to us also who believe in (trust in, adhere to, and rely on) God, Who raised Jesus our Lord from the dead.

ROMANS 4:24

For our sake He made Christ [virtually] to be sin Who knew no sin, so that in and through Him we might become [endued with, viewed as being in, and examples of] the righteousness of God [what we ought to be, approved and acceptable and in right relationship with Him, by His goodness].

2 CORINTHIANS 5:21

Righteousness Is God's Gift

One of the first revelations God gave me out of the Word was on righteousness. By "revelation" I mean one day you suddenly understand something to the point that it becomes part of you. The knowledge isn't only in your mind—you no longer need to renew your mind to it because you don't wonder or hope it's true—you *know*.

Righteousness is God's gift to us. It is "imputed"—granted and credited—to us by virtue of our believing in what God did for us through His Son Jesus Christ. Jesus, Who knew no sin, became sin so that we might be made the righteousness of God in Jesus.

Above all else, the devil does not want us to walk in the reality that we are in right standing with God. He wants us to feel insecure, always vaguely contemplating what is wrong with us.

Jesus wants us to know that we are right with God because of what He has done for us. He wants us to live in His Kingdom and have peace and joy in the midst of every tribulation.

❦

When we keep our eyes on the true Kingdom of God—on Him, His righteousness, His peace, and His joy—the rest will be added to us in abundance.

GOD'S WORD FOR YOU

For we all often stumble and fall and offend in many things. And if anyone does not offend in speech [never says the wrong things], he is a fully developed character and a perfect man, able to control his whole body and to curb his entire nature.

JAMES 3:2

Death and life are in the power of the tongue, and they who indulge in it shall eat the fruit of it [for death or life]. [Matt. 12:37.]

PROVERBS 18:21

CELEBRATE THE POSITIVE

A key to overcoming insecurity is this: *Meditate on and speak positive things about yourself.*

Our thoughts and words about ourselves are tremendously important. In order to overcome the negative thinking and speaking that have been such a natural part of our lifestyle for so long, we must make a conscious effort to think and speak good things about ourselves to ourselves by making positive confessions.

We need to get our mouth in line with what the Word of God says about us. Positive confession of the Word of God should be an ingrained habit of every believer. If you have not yet begun to develop this important habit, start today. Begin thinking and saying good things about yourself: "I am the righteousness of God in Jesus Christ. I prosper in everything I lay my hand to. I have gifts and talents, and God is using me. I operate in the fruit of the Spirit. I walk in love. Joy flows through me."

The Bible teaches we can appropriate the blessings of God in our lives by believing and confessing the positive things God has said about us in His Word.

❧

If you will continually and purposefully speak about yourself what the Word of God says about you, you will receive positive results.

GOD'S WORD FOR YOU

He said this to indicate by what kind of death Peter would glorify God. And after this, He said to him, Follow Me!

But Peter turned and saw the disciple whom Jesus loved, following—the one who also had leaned back on His breast at the supper and had said, Lord, who is it that is going to betray You?

When Peter saw him, he said to Jesus, Lord, what about this man?

JOHN 21:19-21

Avoid Comparisons

The next important key to overcoming insecurity is simple: *Never compare yourself with anyone else because it invites condemnation.*

I really want to encourage you to stop comparing yourself with other people about how you look, what position you occupy, or how long you pray. Comparison only thwarts God's working in your life.

We also must not compare our trials and tribulations to those of other people. Some situations may seem hard to you. But you cannot look at somebody else and say, "Why is all this happening to me and everything comes up roses for you?"

Jesus revealed to Peter ahead of time some of the suffering he would go through. Peter immediately wanted to compare his suffering and his lot in life with somebody else's by saying, "What about this man?"

"Jesus said to him, If I want him to stay (survive, live) till I come, what is that to you? [What concern is it of yours?] You follow Me!" (John 21:22).

That is His answer to us also. We are not called to compare, only to comply to His will for us.

❧

God wants you to know that you are unique and that He has an individualized, specialized plan for your life.

GOD'S WORD FOR YOU

Having gifts (faculties, talents, qualities) that differ according to the grace given us, let us use them. . . .

ROMANS 12:6

I have strength for all things in Christ Who empowers me [I am ready for anything and equal to anything through Him Who infuses inner strength into me; I am self-sufficient in Christ's sufficiency].

PHILIPPIANS 4:13

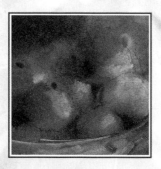

Focus on Potential, Not Limitations

In order to succeed at being yourself, build confidence, and overcome insecurity you must *focus on potential instead of limitations*. In other words, focus on your strengths instead of your weaknesses.

You and I really cannot do *anything* we want to do. We cannot do anything or everything that everyone else is doing. But we can do everything *God has called us to do*. And we can be anything *God says we can be*.

Each of us is full of gifts and talents and potentials and abilities. If we really begin to cooperate with God, we can go for the very best that God has for us. But if we get high-minded ideas and set goals that are beyond our abilities and the grace gifts on our life, we will become frustrated. We will not attain those goals, and we may even end up blaming God for our failure.

Gifts and talents are distributed by the Holy Spirit according to the grace that is on each person to handle them. If you are going to like yourself, if you are going to succeed at being yourself, you are going to have to focus on your potential—what God has created you to be—not on your limitations.

If God has called you to do something,
you will find yourself loving it despite
any adversity that may beset you.

GOD'S WORD FOR YOU

Now am I trying to win the favor of men, or of God? Do I seek to please men? If I were still seeking popularity with men, I should not be a bond servant of Christ (the Messiah).

GALATIANS 1:10

Not with eyeservice, as menpleasers; but as the servants of Christ, doing the will of God from the heart.

EPHESIANS 6:6 KJV

HAVE THE COURAGE TO BE DIFFERENT

If you are going to overcome insecurity and be the person you are called to be in Christ, *you must have the courage to be different.* To be a success at being completely and fully you, you are going to have to take a chance on not being like everyone else.

Becoming menpleasers is one of the easiest things we can do but one that can ultimately make us very unhappy. When we begin pleasing other people, we begin to hear comments that make us feel good about ourselves. That is okay as long as we do not derive our sense of worth from it. As believers, our sense of worth has to be rooted and grounded in the love of God.

We are worth something because God sent His only Son to die for us. We are worth something because God loves us, not because of what everybody else thinks about us or says about us.

As followers of Christ, we are to be led by the Spirit, not controlled by people, doing what everybody else wants us to do because we think that will gain us acceptance and approval. In the same manner, we should not try to control others, but allow them to be led by the Spirit just as we are.

Don't put God in a box. He has many ways of leading you if you will permit Him to be the Leader while you become the follower.

GOD'S WORD FOR YOU

*But as for you, the anointing (the sacred
appointment, the unction) which you received from Him
abides [permanently] in you; [so] then you have no need
that anyone should instruct you. But just as His anointing
teaches you concerning everything and is true and is no
falsehood, so you must abide in (live in, never depart
from) Him [being rooted in Him, knit to Him], just as
[His anointing] has taught you [to do].*

1 JOHN 2:27 TLB

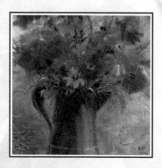

LEARN TO COPE WITH CRITICISM

If you are going to overcome insecurity, you have *to learn to cope with criticism.*

Are you a self-validating person, or do you need outside validation? Outside validation is needing somebody to tell you that you are okay. Self-validation is taking action as you are led by the Holy Ghost.

When we hear from God, we often confer too much with people. With the Holy Spirit in us, we do not need to consult with others. The writer of Proverbs says, "In the multitude of counselors there is safety" (Proverbs 11:14). The answer is to be obedient to the Spirit without refusing counsel from others who are wiser than we are.

We must learn to be secure enough to know how to cope with criticism without feeling there is something wrong with us. We must not come under bondage thinking we have to conform to other people's opinions.

Have enough confidence in who you are in Christ that you can listen to others and be open to change without feeling you have to agree with their viewpoint or meet with their approval if you don't feel their suggestion is right for you.

You may have faults, there may be things about you that need to be changed, but God is working on you the same as He is on everybody else.

GOD'S WORD FOR YOU

For we [Christians] are the true circumcision, who worship God in spirit and by the Spirit of God and exult and glory and pride ourselves in Jesus Christ, and put no confidence or dependence [on what we are] in the flesh and on outward privileges and physical advantages and external appearances.

PHILIPPIANS 3:3

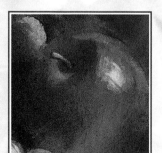

DISCOVER THE TRUE SOURCE OF CONFIDENCE

The most important key to becoming more secure is *to discover the true source of confidence*. In what do you place your confidence? That question must be settled before you can ever have God's confidence. Before your confidence can be in Him, you must remove your confidence from other things.

Is God dealing with you about where you have placed your confidence? Is it in marriage? A college degree? Your job? Your spouse? Your children?

We should not place our confidence in our education, our looks, our position, our gifts, our talents, or in other people's opinions. Our heavenly Father is saying to us, "No more; it is time to let go of all those fleshly things you have been holding so firmly for so long. It is time to put your trust and confidence in Me, and Me alone!"

You must come to the place where your confidence is not in the flesh but in Christ Jesus. Learn to trust Him: "Commit your way to the Lord [roll and repose each care of your load on Him]; trust (lean on, rely on, and be confident) also in Him and He will bring it to pass" (Psalm 37:5).

✿

Allow the Lord to shake loose from you the false sense of confidence, worth, security, and well-being you are trying so hard to derive from earthly things.

WHEN
YOU FEEL
DEPRESSED

To live as God intends for us to live,
the first thing we must do
is truly believe that it is God's will
for us to experience continual joy.

GOD'S WORD FOR YOU

I waited patiently and expectantly for the Lord; and He inclined to me and heard my cry.

He drew me up out of a horrible pit [a pit of tumult and of destruction], out of the miry clay (froth and slime), and set my feet upon a rock, steadying my steps and establishing my goings.

And He has put a new song in my mouth, a song of praise to our God. Many shall see and fear (revere and worship) and put their trust and confident reliance in the Lord. [Ps. 5:11].

PSALM 40:1-3

Be glad in the Lord and rejoice, you [uncompromisingly] righteous [you who are upright and in right standing with Him]; shout for joy, all you upright in heart!

PSALM 32:11

five

WHEN YOU FEEL DEPRESSED

eople from all walks of life have bouts with depression. There are many underlying causes for depression and a variety of treatments offered to deal with it. Some are effective, but many are not. Some help temporarily but can never permanently remove the torment of depression. The good news is that Jesus can heal depression and deliver us from it.

God has given us His joy to fight depression. If you are a believer in Jesus Christ, the joy of the Lord is inside you. Many believers know this but don't have the slightest idea how to tap into that joy or release it. We need to experience what is ours as a result of our faith in Jesus Christ. *It is God's will for us to experience joy!*

I had problems with depression myself a long time ago. But, thank God, I learned I didn't have to allow the negative feeling of depression to rule me. I learned how to release the joy of the Lord in my life!

No matter what you have gone through in life or are going through now, if you are a believer in Jesus Christ, you have His joy inside you, and you can learn how to release it to win over depression.

*The reason we can laugh and enjoy life
in spite of our current situation or circumstances
is because Jesus is our joy.*

GOD'S WORD FOR YOU

. . . but one thing I do [it is my one aspiration]; forgetting what lies behind and straining forward to what lies ahead.

PHILIPPIANS 3:13

DEAL WITH DISAPPOINTMENT

All of us must face and deal with disappointment at different times. No person alive has everything happen in life the way they want in the way they expect.

When things don't prosper or succeed according to our plan, the first emotion we feel is disappointment. This is normal. There is nothing wrong with feeling disappointed. But we must know what to do with that feeling, or it will move into something more serious.

In the world we cannot live without experiencing disappointment, but in Jesus we can always be given re-appointment!

The apostle Paul stated that one important lesson he had learned in life was to let go of what lay behind and press toward all that lay ahead!

When we get disappointed, then immediately get re-appointed, that's exactly what we're doing. We're letting go of the causes for the disappointment and pressing toward what God has for us. We get a new vision, plan, idea, a fresh outlook, a new mind-set, and we change our focus to that. *We decide to go on!*

Every day is a brand-new start! We can let go of yesterday's disappointments and give God a chance to do something wonderful for us today.

GOD'S WORD FOR YOU

But about midnight, as Paul and Silas were praying and singing hymns of praise to God. . . . Suddenly there was a great earthquake, so that the very foundations of the prison were shaken; and at once all the doors were opened and everyone's shackles were unfastened.

ACTS 16:25-26

Rejoice in the Lord always [delight, gladden yourselves in Him]; again I say, Rejoice!

PHILIPPIANS 4:4

THE POWER OF REJOICING

Throughout the Bible, God instructs His people to be filled with joy and rejoice. The apostle Paul, inspired by the Holy Spirit, instructed the Philippians twice to rejoice. Any time the Lord tells us twice to do something, we need to pay careful attention to what He is saying.

Many times people see or hear the word "rejoice" and say, "That sounds nice, but how do I do that?" They would like to rejoice but don't know how!

Paul and Silas, who had been beaten, thrown into prison, and their feet put in stocks, rejoiced by simply singing praises to God. They chose to rejoice, despite their circumstances.

The same power that opened the doors and broke the shackles off Paul and Silas and those imprisoned with them is available to people today who are imprisoned and shackled with depression.

❧

Joy can be anything from calm delight to extreme hilarity. Joy improves our countenance, our health, and the quality of our lives. It strengthens our witness to others and makes some of the less desirable circumstances in life more bearable.

GOD'S WORD FOR YOU

. . . for the joy of the Lord is your strength and stronghold.

NEHEMIAH 8:10

But none of these things move me; neither do I esteem my life dear to myself, if only I may finish my course with joy and the ministry which I have obtained from [which was entrusted to me by] the Lord Jesus, faithfully to attest to the good news (Gospel) of God's grace (His unmerited favor, spiritual blessing, and mercy).

ACTS 20:24

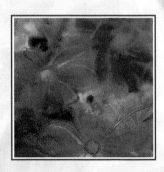

PRIME THE PUMP

When we don't feel joyful, we need to take some action to release joy before we start slipping into depression. Sometimes we must start to rejoice whether we feel like it or not. It is like priming a pump by repeatedly moving the handle up and down until the pump kicks in and the water begins to flow.

I remember my grandparents had an old-time pump. I can recall standing at the sink as a small child moving the pump handle up and down and sometimes feeling as though it would never take hold and start to supply water. It actually felt as if it was connected to nothing, and I was just pumping air.

But if I didn't give up, moving the handle up and down would soon become more difficult. That was a sign that water would start flowing shortly.

This is the way it is with joy. We have a well of water on the inside of our spirit. The pump handle to bring it up is physical exuberance—smiling, singing, laughing, and so forth. At first the physical expressions may not seem to be doing any good. And after a while it even gets harder, but if we keep it up, soon we will get a "gusher" of joy.

If joy is a fruit of the Spirit,
and the Spirit is in you, joy is in you.
What we need to do is learn how to release it.

GOD'S WORD FOR YOU

Why are you cast down, O my inner self? And why should you moan over me and be disquieted within me? Hope in God and wait expectantly for Him, for I shall yet praise Him, my Help and my God.

PSALM 42:5

WAIT EXPECTANTLY FOR GOD

Does your inner man ever feel cast down? Sometimes mine does. So did David's. When he felt that way, David put his hope in God and waited for Him, praising Him as his Help and his God.

To overcome his downcast feelings and emotions, he used songs and shouts of deliverance. That's why so many of his psalms are songs of praise to God to be sung in the midst of unsettling situations.

David knew that when he got down, his countenance went down with him. That is why he talked to himself, his soul (mind, will, and emotions), and encouraged and strengthened himself in the Lord (1 Samuel 30:6).

When we find ourselves in that same depressed state—we should wait expectantly for the Lord, praise Him Who is our Help and our God, and encourage and strengthen ourselves in Him.

We who are righteous—in right standing with God—by believing in Jesus Christ, we who take refuge and put our trust in the Lord can sing and shout for joy! The Lord makes a covering over us and defends us. He fights our battles for us when we praise Him (2 Chronicles 20:17, 20-21)!

You and I must realize and remember that depression is not part of our inheritance in Jesus Christ. It is not part of God's will for His children.

GOD'S WORD FOR YOU

*Be well balanced (temperate, sober of mind), be
vigilant and cautious at all times; for that enemy of yours,
the devil, roams around like a lion roaring [in fierce
hunger], seeking someone to seize upon and devour.*

*Withstand him; be firm in faith [against his onset—
rooted, established, strong, immovable, and determined],
knowing that the same (identical) sufferings are appointed
to your brotherhood (the whole body of Christians)
throughout the world.*

1 PETER 5:8-9

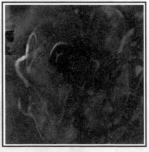

RESIST DEPRESSION IMMEDIATELY

There are many causes of depression—but only one source: Satan. He wants to keep us pressed down and feeling badly about ourselves so that we won't receive all that Jesus died to give us.

No matter what the causes of depression—physical, mental, emotional, or spiritual—as soon as we feel depression coming on, we need to resist it immediately and take whatever action the Lord leads us to take.

Don't play around with depression. As soon as we start feeling disappointed, we must say to ourselves, "I had better do something about this before it gets worse." If we don't, we will ultimately get discouraged, then depressed. Jesus gave us "the garment of praise for the spirit of heaviness" to put on (Isaiah 61:3 KJV). If we don't use what He has given us, we will sink lower and lower into the pit of depression and could end up in real trouble.

Resisting Satan at his onset will stop extended bouts of depression. We resist the devil by submitting ourselves to God and by wielding the sword of the Spirit, which is His Word (Ephesians 6:17).

❧

Anytime we feel anything that is not part of the will of God for us, that is when we need to begin to wield the sharp, two-edged sword of the Word.

GOD'S WORD FOR YOU

Therefore, [there is] now no condemnation (no adjudging guilty of wrong) for those who are in Christ Jesus, who live [and] walk not after the dictates of the flesh, but after the dictates of the Spirit. [John 3:18.]

ROMANS 8:1

No Condemnation

One of the biggest tools Satan uses to try to make us feel bad is condemnation, which certainly can be a cause of depression. According to this scripture, we who are in Christ Jesus are no longer condemned, no longer judged guilty or wrong. Yet so often we judge and condemn ourselves.

Until I learned and understood the Word of God, I lived a large part of my life feeling guilty. If someone had asked me what I felt guilty about, I could not have answered. All I knew was that there was a vague feeling of guilt that followed me around all the time.

From that experience, God gave me a real revelation about walking free from guilt and condemnation. He showed me that you and I must not only receive forgiveness from Him, we must also forgive ourselves. We must stop beating ourselves over the head for something that He has forgiven and forgotten (Jeremiah 31:34; Acts 10:15).

I believe it is nearly impossible to get depressed if the mind is kept under strict control. That is why we are told in Isaiah 26:3 that God will guard and keep us in perfect and constant peace—if we will keep our mind stayed on Him.

God has new things on the horizon of your life, but you will never see them if you live in and relive the past.

GOD'S WORD FOR YOU

*Although my father and my mother have forsaken me,
yet the Lord will take me up [adopt me as His child].*

PSALM 27:10

*See what [an incredible] quality of love the Father has
given (shown, bestowed on) us, that we should [be
permitted to] be named and called and counted the
children of God! And so we are!*

1 JOHN 3:1

GOD DOES NOT REJECT US

Rejection causes depression. To be rejected means to be thrown away as having no value or as being unwanted. We were created for acceptance, not rejection. The emotional pain of rejection is one of the deepest kinds known. Especially if the rejection comes from someone we love or expect to love us, like parents or a spouse.

If you have been depressed, it might be due to a root of rejection in your life. Overcoming rejection is certainly not easy, but we can overcome it through the love of Jesus Christ.

In Ephesians 3:18, Paul prayed for the church that they would know "the breadth and length and height and depth" of the love that God had for them and that they would experience it for themselves. He said this experience far surpasses mere knowledge.

Watch for all the ways that God shows His love for you, and it will overcome the rejection you may have experienced from other people. Every time God gives us favor, He is showing us that He loves us. There are many ways He shows His love for us all the time; we simply need to begin watching for it.

Having a deep revelation concerning God's love
for us will keep us from depression.

GOD'S WORD FOR YOU

To the praise of the glory of his grace, wherein he hath made us accepted in the beloved.

EPHESIANS 1:6 KJV

LISTEN TO WHAT GOD SAYS ABOUT YOU

God does not want us to feel frustrated and condemned. He wants us to realize that we are pleasing to Him just as we are.

The devil keeps trying to tell us what we are not, but God keeps trying to tell us what we are—His beloved children who are well-pleasing to Him.

God never reminds us of how far we have fallen. He always reminds us of how far we have risen. He reminds us of how much we have overcome, how precious we are in His sight, how much He loves us.

The devil tells us we cannot possibly be acceptable to God because we are not perfect, but God tells us that we are accepted in the Beloved because of what He has already done for us.

God wants us to know that His hand is upon us, that His angels are watching over us, that His Holy Spirit is right there in us and with us to help us in everything we do.

He wants us to know that Jesus is our Friend, and that as we walk with Him day by day, good things are going to take place in our lives.

❦

If we listen to God rather than the devil,
He will give us peace about the past,
joy for the present, and hope for the future.

WHEN YOU FEEL AFRAID

*We can live without fear
by building our faith on what
God has said in His Word.*

GOD'S WORD FOR YOU

*Fear not [there is nothing to fear], for I am with you;
do not look around you in terror and be dismayed, for I
am your God. I will strengthen and harden you to
difficulties, yes, I will help you; yes, I will hold you up
and retain you with My [victorious] right hand of rightness
and justice.*

ISAIAH 41:10

six

WHEN YOU FEEL AFRAID

ne of the benefits available to us in our spiritual inheritance as a believer in Jesus Christ is freedom from fear. But even if we are afraid, we know that we can go ahead and act on what God says, because God will be with us to protect us. He will help us, go before to fight the battle for us or deliver us, bringing us through victoriously as we obey Him.

If you feel you have missed out on some blessings in your life because of fear, you can learn how to handle or overcome fear and begin to experience the abundant life God has planned for you.

The message of "fear not, for I, the Lord, am with you" is expressed in many different ways throughout the Bible. God does not want us to fear because fear prevents us from receiving and doing all He has planned for us. He loves us and wants to bless us, and He has provided ways for us not to fear.

The only acceptable attitude (and confession) that a Christian can have toward fear is this: "It is not from God, and I will not let it control my life! I will confront fear, for it is a spirit sent out from hell to torment me."

God has a plan for your life. Receive His plan by putting your faith in Him. Make a decision today that you will no longer let a spirit of fear intimidate you and dominate your life.

Jesus is your Deliverer. As you diligently seek Him, He will deliver you from all fear.

GOD'S WORD FOR YOU

Fear not; stand still (firm, confident, undismayed) and see the salvation of the Lord which He will work for you today.

EXODUS 14:13

. . . the devil . . . was a murderer from the beginning and does not stand in the truth, because there is no truth in him. When he speaks a falsehood, he speaks what is natural to him, for he is a liar [himself] and the father of lies and of all that is false.

JOHN 8:44

FEAR IS FALSEHOOD

Jesus said that the devil is a liar and the father of all lies. The truth is not in him. He tries to use falsehood to deceive God's people into fear so they will not be bold enough to be obedient to the Lord and reap the blessings He has in store for them.

Often the fear of something is worse than the thing itself. If we will be courageous and determined to do whatever it is we fear, we will discover it is not nearly as bad as we thought it would be.

Throughout the Word of God we find the Lord saying to His people, "Fear not." I believe the reason He did that was to encourage them so they would not allow Satan to rob them of their blessing.

In the same way, because He knows we are fearful, the Lord continues to exhort and encourage us to press through what lies before us to do His will. Why? Because He knows that great blessings await us.

Fear, which is spelled f-e-a-r, stands for *false evidence appearing real*. The enemy wants to tell you that your current situation is evidence that your future will be a failure, but the Bible teaches us that no matter what our present circumstances, nothing is impossible with God (Mark 9:17-23).

Only when you know God's Word will you recognize the lies of Satan. Confess the Word of God, and it will bring you into a place of victory.

GOD'S WORD FOR YOU

For God did not give us a spirit of timidity (of cowardice, of craven and cringing and fawning fear), but [He has given us a spirit] of power and of love and of calm and well-balanced mind and discipline and self-control.

2 TIMOTHY 1:7

No Fear!

Every one of us has experienced starting to step out in faith, and even at the thought of it, fear begins to rise up in us. We need to realize that the source of fear is Satan. First John 4:18 KJV says: "There is no fear in love; but perfect love casteth out fear: because fear hath torment. He that feareth is not made perfect in love."

Satan sends fear to try to torment us into being so doubtful and miserable so that we will be prevented from doing what God wants us to do and receiving all that God has for us.

We can live without fear by building our faith on what God has said in His Word. When we open our mouth and confess what the Lord says to us and about us, God's Word will give us the power to overcome the fears that torment and prevent.

When we find ourselves trying to avoid confronting some issue in our life because of fear or dread or wondering or reasoning, we should pray and ask God to do for us what He has promised in His Word—to go before us and pave the way for us.

Ask God to strengthen you in the inner man, that His might and power may fill you, and that you may not be overcome with the temptation to give in to fear.

GOD'S WORD FOR YOU

For [the Spirit which] you have now received [is] not a spirit of slavery to put you once more in bondage to fear, but you have received the Spirit of adoption [the Spirit producing sonship] in [the bliss of] which we cry, Abba (Father)! Father!

ROMANS 8:15

I WILL NOT FEAR!

Fear robs many people of their faith.

Fear of failure, fear of man, and fear of rejection are some of the strongest fears employed by Satan to hinder us from making progress. But no matter what kind of fear the enemy sends against us, the important thing is to overcome it. When we are faced with fear, we must not give in to it. It is imperative to our victory that we determine, "I will not fear!"

The normal reaction to fear is flight. Satan wants us to run; God wants us to stand still and see His deliverance.

Because of fear, many people do not confront issues; they spend their lives running. We must learn to stand our ground and face fear, secure in the knowledge that we are more than conquerors (Romans 8:37).

Fear of failure torments multitudes. We fear what people will think of us if we fail. If we step out and fail, some people may hear about it; but they quickly forget if we forget it and go on. It is better to try something and fail than to try nothing and succeed.

Approach life with boldness. The Spirit of the Lord is in you—so make up your mind not to fear.

GOD'S WORD FOR YOU

The earnest (heartfelt, continued) prayer of a righteous man makes tremendous power available [dynamic in its working].

JAMES 5:16

PRAY ABOUT EVERYTHING AND FEAR NOTHING

Some time ago the Lord spoke these words to me: "Pray about everything and fear nothing." Over the next couple of weeks, He showed me different things about prayer versus fear. Many of them dealt with little areas in which fear would try to creep into my life and cause me problems. He showed me that in every case, no matter how great or important or how small or insignificant, the solution was to pray.

Sometimes we become afraid by staring at our circumstances. The more we focus on the problem, the more fearful we become. Instead, we are to keep our focus on God. He is able to handle anything that we may ever have to face in this life.

God has promised to strengthen us, to harden us to difficulties, to hold us up and retain us with His victorious right hand. He also commands us not to be afraid. But remember, He is not commanding us never to feel fear, but rather not to let it control us.

The Lord is saying to you and me personally, "Fear not, I will help you." But we never experience the help of God until we place everything on the line, until we are obedient enough to step out in faith.

When you feel fear, don't back down or run away.
Instead, pray and go forward even though you are afraid.

GOD'S WORD FOR YOU

If any of you is deficient in wisdom, let him ask of the giving God [Who gives] to everyone liberally and ungrudgingly, without reproaching or faultfinding, and it will be given him.

Only it must be in faith that he asks with no wavering (no hesitating, no doubting). For the one who wavers (hesitates, doubts) is like the billowing surge out at sea that is blown hither and thither and tossed by the wind.

For truly, let not such a person imagine that he will receive anything [he asks for] from the Lord.

JAMES 1:5-7

$\mathcal{F}$AITH: THE ANTIDOTE FOR FEAR

Faith is the only antidote for fear.

If you or I drank some kind of poison, we would have to swallow an antidote, or the poison would cause serious damage or even death. The same is true of the deadly toxin of fear. There must be an antidote for it, and the only antidote for fear is faith.

When fear comes knocking at our door, we must answer it with faith, because nothing else is effective against it. And prayer is the major vehicle that carries faith.

Faith must be carried to the problem and released in some way. It is possible to pray without faith (we do it all the time), but it is impossible to have real faith and *not* pray.

James tells us that when we find ourselves in need of something, we should pray and ask God for it in *simple, believing* prayer. Those two words are very important. The way we do that is by simply praying and having faith, believing that what we ask for from God we will receive in accordance with His divine will and plan.

❧

Put your faith in the Lord.
He has the power to deliver you from all fear.

GOD'S WORD FOR YOU

Now [in Haran] the Lord said to Abram, Go for yourself [for your own advantage] away from your country, from your relatives and your father's house, to the land that I will show you.

GENESIS 12:1

*D*o It Afraid!

How would you feel if God told you to leave your home, your family, and everything familiar and comfortable to you and head out to who knows where? Full of fear? That is precisely the challenge Abram faced, and it frightened him. That's why God kept saying to him again and again, "Fear not."

Elisabeth Elliot, whose husband was killed along with four other missionaries in Ecuador, tells that her life was controlled completely by fear. Every time she started to step out, fear stopped her. A friend told her something that set her free. She said, "Why don't you do it afraid?" Elisabeth Elliot and Rachel Saint, sister of one of the murdered missionaries, went on to evangelize the Indian tribes, including the people who had killed their husband and brother.

If we wait to do something until we are not afraid, we will probably accomplish very little for God, others, or even for ourselves. Both Abram and Joshua had to step out in faith and obedience to God and do what He had commanded them to do—afraid. We must do the same!

Be determined that your life is not going to be ruled by fear but by God's Word.

GOD'S WORD FOR YOU

After these things, the word of the Lord came to Abram in a vision, saying, Fear not, Abram, I am your Shield, your abundant compensation, and your reward shall be exceedingly great.

GENESIS 15:1

Courage and Obedience Produce Great Rewards

In Genesis 12:1, God gave Abram a tall order. In so many words He said, "Pack up and leave everyone you know and everything you are comfortable with and go to a place I will show you."

If Abram had bowed his knee to fear, the rest of the story would never have come to pass. He would never have experienced God as his Shield, his great compensation, and he would never have received his exceedingly great reward.

In the same way, if Joshua had not overcome his fear and been obedient to God's command to lead His people into the Promised Land, neither he nor they would ever have enjoyed all that God had planned and prepared for them.

There is power in God's Word to equip us to stop bowing our knee in fear to the devil's desires. We can do what God wants us to do, even if we have to do it afraid. We need to keep saying: "Lord, strengthen me. This is what You have told me to do, and with Your help I am going to do it, because it is Your revealed will for me. I am determined that my life is not going to be ruled by fear but by Your Word."

※

God doesn't always deliver us "from" things;
often He walks us "through" them.

GOD'S WORD FOR YOU

So we take comfort and are encouraged and confidently and boldly say, The Lord is my Helper; I will not be seized with alarm [I will not fear or dread or be terrified]. What can man do to me?

HEBREWS 13:6

Combat Fear With Prayer

Fear attacks everyone. It is Satan's way of tormenting us and preventing us from enjoying the life Jesus died to give us. If we accept the fears that Satan offers and give voice to them, we open the door for the enemy and close the door to God.

We must learn as David and the writer of Hebrews to boldly confess that God is our Helper, our Refuge, and our Stronghold.

Satan seeks to weaken us through fear, but God strengthens us as we fellowship with Him in prayer. The Bible teaches us to watch and pray: "All of you must keep awake (give strict attention, be cautious and active) and watch and pray, that you may not come into temptation. The spirit indeed is willing, but the flesh is weak" (Matthew 26:41). The major reference in this passage is to watching ourselves and the attacks that the enemy launches against our minds and our emotions. When these attacks are detected, we should pray immediately. We must remember that it is when we pray that power is released against the enemy—not when we think about praying later.

Watch and pray about everything. I believe you will find this decision to be one that will produce more joy and peace for your everyday living.

If we are ever to have real victory over the enemy,
we must resist him in prayer with faith.

THE HARRISON HOUSE VISION

Proclaiming the truth and the power
Of the Gospel of Jesus Christ
With Excellence;

Challenging Christians to
Live victoriously,
Grow spiritually,
Know God intimately.

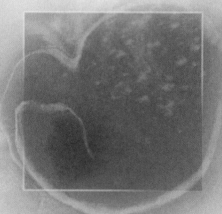

JOYCE MEYER

Joyce Meyer has been teaching the Word of God since 1976 and in full-time ministry since 1980. Joyce's Life In The Word radio broadcasts are heard across the country, and her television broadcasts are seen around the world. She travels extensively, sharing her life-changing messages in Life In The Word conferences and in local churches.

Joyce and her husband, Dave, are the parents of four children. They make their home in St. Louis, Missouri.

Additional copies of this book are available from your local bookstore.

If this book has changed your life, we would like to hear from you.

Please write us at:

🏠 Harrison House Publishers
P. O. Box 35035 • Tulsa, OK 74153
www.harrisonhouse.com

To contact the author, write:
Joyce Meyer Ministries
P. O. Box 655 • Fenton, Missouri 63026

or call: (636) 349-0303

Internet Address: www.joycemeyer.org

In Canada, write: Joyce Meyer Ministries Canada, Inc.
Lambeth Box 1300 • London, ON N6P 1T5

or call: (636) 349-0303

In Australia, write: Joyce Meyer Ministries-Australia
Locked Bag 77 • Mansfield Delivery Centre
Queensland 4122

or call: (07) 3349 1200

In England, write: Joyce Meyer Ministries
P. O. Box 1549 • Windsor • SL4 1GT
or call: 01753 831102